The Literary Genres of Edmund Burke

The Literary Genres of Edmund Burke

The Political Uses of Literary Form

FRANS DE BRUYN

CLARENDON PRESS · OXFORD
1996

Oxford University Press, Walton Street, Oxford OX2 6DP
Oxford New York
Athens Auckland Bangkok Bombay
Calcutta Cape Town Dar es Salaam Delhi
Florence Hong Kong Istanbul Karachi
Kuala Lumpur Madras Madrid Melbourne
Mexico City Nairobi Paris Singapore
Taipei Tokyo Toronto
and associated companies in
Berlin Ibadan

Oxford is a trade mark of Oxford University Press

Published in the United States
by Oxford University Press Inc., New York

© Frans De Bruyn 1996

All rights reserved. No part of this publication may be reproduced,
stored in a retrieval system, or transmitted, in any form or by any means,
without the prior permission in writing of Oxford University Press.
Within the UK, exceptions are allowed in respect of any fair dealing for the
purpose of research or private study, or criticism or review, as permitted
under the Copyright, Designs and Patents Act, 1988, or in the case of
reprographic reproduction in accordance with the terms of the licences
issued by the Copyright Licensing Agency. Enquiries concerning
reproduction outside these terms and in other countries should be
sent to the Rights Department, Oxford University Press,
at the address above.

British Library Cataloguing in Publication Data
Data available

Library of Congress Cataloging in Publication Data
De Bruyn, Frans.
The literary genres of Edmund Burke: the political uses of
literary form/Frans De Bruyn.
Includes bibliographical references and index.
1. Burke, Edmund, 1729–1797—Technique. 2. Burke, Edmund,
1729–1797—Contributions in political science. 3. Politics and
literature—Great Britain—History—18th century. 4. Political
science—Great Britain—History—18th century. 5. Literary form.
I. Title.
PR3334.B4Z63 1996 824'.6—dc20 96-24313
ISBN 0-19-812182-2

1 3 5 7 9 10 8 6 4 2

Typeset by Cambrian Typesetters, Frimley, Surrey
Printed in Great Britain on acid-free paper by
Biddles Ltd,
Guildford and Kings Lynn

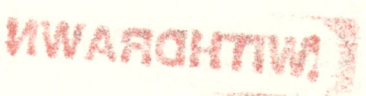

FOR
ROGER AND SHEILA
AND FOR
DAVID, JEFFREY, AND MARK

Preface

RECENT years have witnessed a welcome revival in literary studies of Edmund Burke. In part, this renewed interest in Burke as a literary figure can be explained as the product of new directions charted by literary theory. By calling into question a narrow conception of literature as 'imaginative' or 'aesthetic' writing and by proposing new relationships among texts of all kinds (as, for example, theories of discourse and intertextuality), critical theory has fostered a greater willingness to consider claims about the literary character of Burke's political writings and about their relation to a multiplicity of other discursive forms. This recontextualization has taken various directions. Some studies have placed a renewed emphasis on the rhetorical character of Burke's writings; others seek to demonstrate his participation in various 'languages' or discourses of his time, including contemporary aesthetic, economic, gender, historical, and legal discourses (among many others). In his recent book *Edmund Burke's Aesthetic Ideology* (Cambridge, 1993), Tom Furniss urges an approach that abandons an 'author-centred model of reading and textual production' altogether in favour of an analysis that treats Burke's texts as a 'weave of discourses' (p. 7). Though varied in their methodologies, these readings share an interest in focusing on the *language* (or languages) of Burke's writings and in demonstrating the ways in which that language reflects and, on occasion, comes to constitute the historical moment in which he lived.

Of the many discourses in which Burke's writings participate, one of the most important for him and his contemporaries is the discursive realm of literature. Reading Burke's œuvre as literature demands much more than simply attending to its linguistic resourcefulness, rhetorical ingenuity, and figurative manner of expression, though these are obviously important elements in any assessment of a text's literary status. Beyond these criteria are the larger constituents of a work's literary design, such as its relation to a canonical tradition of literary texts, its architectonic structure, and its generic affiliation. Burke's writings lay claim in these larger, more definitive ways to the designation of 'literature'. For him, however, this claim had a cultural and political significance very different from what writers in our own century understand as the uses and defining characteristics of literary discourse. The idiom of eighteenth-century literature—its preoccupation with genre, hierarchy, decorum, and didacticism and its sense of the literary past as a valuable, usable cultural repository—is in many respects foreign to us. This study, then, seeks to redeem Burke as a literary figure for our time by reviving a historical sense of what literary discourse meant for him and his contemporaries.

The first chapter of this book is an extensively revised and expanded version of an essay published in the *British Journal for Eighteenth-Century Studies*, 15 (1992), 35–49, entitled, ' "Wit, and Burke, and Pope": The Literary Art of Self-Defence in *An Epistle to Dr. Arbuthnot* and *A Letter to a Noble Lord*'. Chapter 4 first appeared in a collection of essays marking the bicentenary of the French Revolution: *Burke and the French Revolution: Bicentenary Studies*, ed. Steven Blakemore (Athens, Ga., 1992), 28–68. I should like to thank the Voltaire Foundation in Oxford, England, and the University of Georgia Press of Athens, Georgia, for their permission to incorporate these two publications into the present study.

Though researching and writing are often solitary undertakings, my experience with this project has proved a pleasant exception, as a far-flung community of friends, readers, and scholars generously offered their assistance. Among those who proffered their thoughtful consideration of this work in its earlier stages are my colleagues Ina Ferris, Camille La Bossière, David Staines, and Nicholas von Maltzahn. I have taken shameless advantage, moreover, of the indefatigable willingness of Roger Lund and Brean Hammond to read the latest drafts as my writing progressed. Part of this book was written while I was participating in an academic exchange between the University of Ottawa and California State University at Los Angeles. My colleagues in the English Department at CSULA were very accommodating in affording me the time to devote myself to this project. In California I owe particular thanks and fond memories to John and Donna Cleman, Steve and Rosalyn Jones, David and Helen Laird, and Tim Stowell, among many others.

I wish also to express my appreciation for the financial support of the Faculty of Arts and the School of Graduate Studies and Research at the University of Ottawa, which enabled me to pass a sabbatical leave in the winter of 1993 at the British Library in London, England. At an early stage in my work I was the fortunate recipient of a summer fellowship at the William Andrews Clark Memorial Library in Los Angeles. The unfailing courtesy and helpfulness of the staff at both libraries contributed greatly to the progress of my research. While in London I stayed at London House, a veritable home away from home for overseas scholars visiting Britain. In London I am also especially indebted to the friendship and support of Tamara Ingram and Andrew Millington.

Finally, I must acknowledge especially the many intellectual and personal debts I have incurred, not only in the writing of this book but over the years more generally. Many of these obligations will be clear from the notes and bibliography, but I should like to single out by name Ralph and Libby Cohen and Martin and Ruthe Battestin, who came into my life as teachers and mentors and have continued as valued friends. Their loyalty and generosity over the years are beyond repayment. And thanks also to Richard Gunstone for his support as this book drew near to completion.

F.D.B.

Ottawa
August 1995

Contents

Note on Citations	xii
Introduction	1
1. Alexander Pope and Burke's *A Letter to a Noble Lord*: Generic Innovation and Political Discourse	19
2. States and Estates: Burke's Georgic Arts of Political Husbandry	59
3. Gentlemen's Prospects: Viewing the World from the 'Elevation of Reason'	111
4. Theatre and Counter-Theatre in Burke's *Reflections on the Revolution in France*	165
5. Burke's *Dunciad*: The *Letters on a Regicide Peace* and Scriblerian Satire	209
A. Metamorphosis and Masquerade	209
B. Language, Genre, and Canon	250
Epilogue: The Prophetic Burke	283
Bibliography	298
Index	311

Note on Citations

AN authoritative modern edition of Edmund Burke's œuvre is being produced, at long last, under the general editorship of Paul Langford. The edition, entitled *The Writings and Speeches of Edmund Burke*, is projected at twelve volumes, but because only five volumes have been published to date, scholars currently working on Burke are faced with something of a dilemma on the question of citation. At the risk of confusing my readers, I have decided to quote, wherever possible, from the Langford edition, since most of the major texts referred to in this study have already appeared in that edition. I have otherwise relied on the eight-volume, nineteenth-century Bohn edition of the *Works*, and on James T. Boulton's edition of *A Philosophical Enquiry into the Origin of Our Ideas of the Sublime and Beautiful* (London, 1958). In my citations from Burke's letters, I have used Thomas W. Copeland's *The Correspondence of Edmund Burke*.

For ease of reference these standard editions are cited in this book as follows:

By volume and page numbers only: *The Writings and Speeches of Edmund Burke*, gen. ed. Paul Langford (Oxford, 1981–), vols. ii, v, viii and ix. Cited by permission of Oxford University Press.

Bohn: *The Works of the Right Honourable Edmund Burke*, Bohn's British Classics, 8 vols. (London, 1854–89).

Corr: *The Correspondence of Edmund Burke*, gen. ed. Thomas W. Copeland, 10 vols. (Cambridge and Chicago, 1958–78).

Introduction

> That not in Fancy's Maze he wander'd long,
> But stoop'd to Truth, and moraliz'd his song.
> Alexander Pope[1]
>
> The style of an author should be the image of his mind.
> Edward Gibbon[2]

The progress of Edmund Burke's career, in which political ambitions succeeded to, yet by no means displaced, literary aspirations, illustrates the problem that this book aims to explore, namely, the pervasively literary character of his political utterances. Burke came to London in 1750 reluctantly committed at his father's behest to the study of the law, but the allure of the capital's literary scene soon diverted him, as it had many others before, from his legal education. In his first decade of residence in London, he embarked on a number of literary projects that encompassed a wide variety of genres and subjects, including what we would today categorize as aesthetics, criticism, history, literary journalism, and political theory. Besides his well-known *Vindication of Natural Society* (1756), an ironic defence of artificial society and revealed religion, and *A Philosophical Enquiry into the Origin of Our Ideas of the Sublime and Beautiful* (1757), he launched and contributed extensively for many years to the *Annual Register,* a review of the year's events in politics, literature, arts, and society; undertook (and later abandoned) *An Essay towards an Abridgment of the English History*; sketched out *Hints for an Essay on*

---

[1] *An Epistle to Dr. Arbuthnot*, ll. 340–1 (*Twickenham Ed.*, iv. 120). Unless otherwise stated, the poetry of Alexander Pope is quoted from *The Twickenham Edition of the Poems of Alexander Pope*, ed. John Butt *et al.* (London, 1939–69); that of John Milton from *Complete Poems and Major Prose*, ed. Merritt Y. Hughes (Indianapolis, 1957); and that of James Thomson from *The Seasons*, ed. James Sambrook (Oxford, 1981), and *Liberty, The Castle of Indolence, and Other Poems*, ed. James Sambrook (Oxford, 1986).

[2] Edward Gibbon, *Memoirs of My Life*, ed. Georges A. Bonnard (London, 1966), 155.

the Drama; and contributed in some measure to *An Account of the European Settlements in America*. Then, in 1759, came a decisive break when Burke met William Gerard Hamilton, who employed Burke as his private secretary and provided him with an entrée into politics.

In some ways, however, that break was not nearly so decisive as it appears to a twentieth-century observer accustomed to regarding politics and literature as antipodean opposites. Both literary and political careers were avenues of social and economic advancement in the eighteenth century for outsiders such as Burke. Indeed, writers of Alexander Pope's generation ritually bemoaned the interpenetration of literature and politics in their time, denouncing opportunistic Whig writers and pamphleteers, who were allegedly prostituting their talents for the sake of political preferment. As an 'Irish adventurer' (the uncomplimentary characterization is Horace Walpole's), Burke was often subjected to similar criticism, yet his exertions (though they met with a different outcome) were not unlike the efforts of that other great Irish writer of the eighteenth century, Jonathan Swift, who served as Sir William Temple's secretary and bent his formidable literary talents to win ecclesiastical and political preferment, before settling down, in considerable disappointment, to his dual career as Dean of St Patrick's in Dublin and literary scourge of the age. As will become abundantly apparent in the next chapter, writers and political aspirants felt similar social and economic pressures in their attempts to preserve their independence and intellectual integrity, the former suffering 'the capricious patronage of the public' and the latter serving the bidding of their political masters and social 'betters'.[3] Individuals in both careers were keenly aware of the problems and burdens with which the existing system of patronage, deference, and clientage confronted them.[4]

Moreover, the education of the writer and the politician was in most respects identical in the eighteenth century: both careers

---

[3] See Carl B. Cone, *Burke and the Nature of Politics* (Lexington, Ken., 1957–64), i. 14.

[4] This issue is addressed by Christopher Reid in *Edmund Burke and the Practice of Political Writing* (Dublin, 1985), 73–92. My own exploration of this subject in the next chapter is indebted to his analysis.

were in the ideal deemed to be the domain of the gentleman, whose formation as a comprehensive observer of his society precluded him from undertaking professional or specialized study. The curriculum at Trinity College, Dublin, where Burke matriculated in 1744, reflected this 'liberal', as opposed to vocational, view of knowledge and was accordingly weighted heavily towards the classics, which were thought to offer the broadest overview of human nature, society, and knowledge. Though Burke studied natural and moral philosophy, among other subjects, his chief passion was for literary study, as he indicates in a letter outlining a course of reading for his childhood friend Richard Shackleton: 'For latin, I would have you read Virgils Georgics, Juvenals Satires, and a Comedy or two of Terence. For prose Salust, Cicero's Orations. ... In Greek the first six books of homer, the embassy to Achilles, and that part from the death of hector to the end of the poem. What I shew'd you of Lucian, Tabula Cebetis. and Xenophon, You should read with abundance of Care ...' (*Corr.* i. 69). Years later, when he denounced Rousseau's baneful influence on French education and mores (as a contributory cause of the French Revolution), he harked back to his early education and intellectual interests: 'We continue, as in the two last ages, to read more generally, than I believe is now done on the continent, the authors of sound antiquity' (viii. 318). Burke's remark fuses a political argument with a particular literary and cultural discourse, a fusion reflecting the conviction that the political and the literary are inseparable activities—two of the many duties or accomplishments of the gentleman.

Of even more significance to Burke's formation, judging from the evidence of his letters to Shackleton, were the extracurricular literary pursuits in which he immersed himself while at Trinity—as critic, budding poet, and founding member of a literary club. His juvenile critical opinions and poetic attempts are conventional, for the most part, but they derive from the same cultural matrix in which his later political works are cast. Thus, his lifelong interest in the culture of improvement, the subject of the second and third chapters that follow, can be traced back to his early georgic-descriptive verses in imitation of Virgil, including a topographical poem on Ballitore, the village where he received his preparatory schooling; a georgic panegyric, *To John Damer, Esq.*; and a translation of Virgil's famous lines in praise of country life in the second *Georgic*. Similarly, his commitment to the literary standard set by tragic and epic poetry, and his equally powerful fascination with the many bathetic, burlesque, and mock-heroic perversions of that standard in contemporary writing and thought (detailed in the fourth and fifth chapters of this study), are reflected in his first public production, a weekly periodical essay entitled *The Reformer* (1748). In the first number of *The Reformer*, Burke promises to wage war on dullness and bad taste, and in subsequent numbers he makes the theatre the prime object of his reforming zeal, a zeal stimulated, no doubt, by Dublin's lively theatre scene in the 1740s, in which he took a keen interest. His youthful intimacy with Alexander Pope's *Dunciad* and its cultural discourse of dullness, which he was to employ so effectively in the 1790s, is evident in his earliest productions. He even adopts the name of Pope's anti-hero in *The Dunciad*, signing one of his letters to Shackleton, 'C: Cibber Esqr Laur' (*Corr.* i. 26).

These college activities, taken for granted in the formation of the gentleman, bespeak a synergy between statesmanship and letters that was accepted without question in eighteenth-century Britain and Ireland. The rationale for this fruitful interaction is spelled out in the preamble to the constitutional laws of the undergraduate 'Club' or 'Academy of Belles Lettres' founded by Burke and three fellow-students in the spring of 1747. The preamble reads, in part,

Whatever might render us fitter, and more agreeable members of the happy community in which we live; that shou'd be the study & the practice ... of our youth, and when years draw us farther into the cares and business of life, we would be thereby enabled to go with more ease thro' the Duties of it; and more largely to contribute to the good of the publick and to the increase of our private interest. Thoughts of this nature gave birth to the Academy of Belles Lettres, a weekly club instituted for the improvement of its members in the more refin'd elegant and usefull parts of Litterature, these seeming the most likely means for attaining the great end in view[:] [t]he formation of our minds and manners for the functions of Civil Society.[5]

[5] 'The Proceedings of the Club', repr. in A. P. I. Samuels, *The Early Life, Correspondence and Writings of the Rt. Hon. Edmund Burke* (Cambridge, 1923),

The student's training in letters and the political career to which he might reasonably expect to accede both followed from the social status he enjoyed by birth. Or if he lacked the appropriate social antecedents, as in Burke's case, his literary attainments might be a step in remedying that deficiency.

Beyond the shared social and cultural experience of the writer and the political dependent, the broad perspective taken for granted in the literary enterprise of the eighteenth century further blurs the line between the two phases of Burke's career. It is important to remember that the term 'literature' represented much more for Burke and his contemporaries than it does in the present day. (The 'literary' activities of the Trinity College Club included 'speeching, reading writing and arguing, in morality, History, Criticism, Politics, and all the useful branches of Philosophy'.[6]) The modern, more narrow conception of literature was not consolidated in its present outlines until the early nineteenth century. Douglas Patey observes, 'Having once comprehended learning in general—all "things in books' clothing" in Charles Lamb's phrase—literature was redefined as "literary art," "imaginative literature," the poems, tales, and plays which paradigmatically we teach in our English classes.'[7] The proliferation of knowledge in the eighteenth century contributed to this redefinition of discourses: the criterion of *progress* was introduced to distinguish between those fields, like the modern-day sciences, in which progress could be measured and those in which progress was impossible to determine or remained a matter of debate. Burke, however, like most of his contemporaries, continued to understand 'literature' as comprehending such forms of discourse as oratory, history, philosophy, economics, and science—as comprising, in short, 'everything worthy to be read, preferably the best thoughts expressed in the

---

227. Samuels's study is the most comprehensive survey of Burke's education and early literary activities. The volume also reproduces several of Burke's | juvenile poems and all thirteen numbers of *The Reformer*. Burke's extensive literary connections in later years are chronicled in Donald Cross Bryant, *Edmund Burke and His Literary Friends* (St Louis, 1939).

[6] Samuels, *Early Life*, 228.
[7] Douglas Lane Patey, 'The Eighteenth Century Invents the Canon', *Modern Language Studies*, 18 (1988), 17–37.

best manner'.[8] Thus, despite the occasional character of many of his writings, neither he nor his audience would have perceived any radical discontinuity between the political subject-matter and the literary form of his writings. In this, as in so many other respects, Burke is a cultural conservative: his conception of the literary continues to reflect the views of the previous generation—Pope, Swift, and their contemporaries.[9]

The literary character of Burke's political discourse has not passed unnoticed in recent critical studies, but the remarkable extent to which that discourse is structured and shaped by the prevailing literary modes of the eighteenth century has not hitherto been sufficiently appreciated.[10] To put the point more accurately and more tellingly, Burke's political writings are informed throughout by the dominant literary modes of the *early* eighteenth century: the satiric and georgic-didactic genres practised in what literary critics have loosely called the 'Augustan' age. The satiric emerges in his systematic adoption, especially in his writings on the French Revolution, of the Scriblerian mode of Swift, Pope, and their associates: the literary denunciation of cultural decay and political corruption that culminates in the satiric masterpieces *Gulliver's Travels* and *The Dunciad*. The georgic-didactic, with its characteristic features of landscape views, prospect surveys, spatial imagery, and patriotic rhetoric, figures prominently in those passages where Burke pursues his 'constructive', Whig political vision, his 'civic humanist' conception (to borrow J. G. A. Pocock's formulation) of the British polity as a harmonious reconciliation of commercial and landed interests. Though these two modes predominate, they are supplemented by significant excursions into other literary forms, including the 'letter to an eminent person' form, gothic romance, tragedy, and epic.

---

[8] E. D. Hirsch, *The Aims of Interpretation* (Chicago, 1976), 140.

[9] On Burke as the last of the 'Augustan humanists', see Paul Fussell, *The Rhetorical World of Augustan Humanism: Ethics and Imagery from Swift to Burke* (Oxford, 1965).

[10] Among the most significant literary studies of Burke in recent years are James T. Boulton, *The Language of Politics in the Age of Wilkes and Burke* (London, 1963); Gerald Chapman, *Edmund Burke: The Practical Imagination* (Cambridge, Mass., 1967); and C. Reid, *Edmund Burke and the Practice of Political Writing* (Dublin, 1985).

My central argument is that Burke's persistent weaving of literary forms into his political discourse—his marriage of high literary culture and political utterance—constitutes a sophisticated imaginative enactment of his most cherished political convictions: a realization of content or ideas at the level of form. His very choice, for instance, of the literary models of the previous generation dramatizes his belief that the political and cultural enterprise of a society (the two, for him, cannot be separated) is a partnership between present and past, the living and the dead. What Burke says cannot be divorced from the way in which he says it: in fact, to his audience, familiar with the literary conventions he is drawing on, the form of his utterances is as meaningful as the content of his arguments, if not more so. So powerful is this fusion of ideas and modes of cultural expression that we may claim without exaggeration a concrete, determinate historical and political impact for Burke's acts of literary imagination.

Claims of this kind will not seem surprising or outlandish to literary critics and theorists. Recent literary theory has developed a broad range of conceptual tools enabling critics to situate a literary work in its cultural context and to assess the historical, political, and philosophical impact of a text's literary form. But the interdisciplinary character of Burke studies places a number of intellectual and institutional hurdles in the way of the critic. The problem is not only one of having to be aware of developments in academic disciplines, whether history, political theory, or philosophy, where the writer may at times feel dangerously out of his or her depth, but also that of having to address a readership of diverse intellectual interests, many of whom may be unfamilar with the discourse and assumptions of the literary critic. Thus, in the remaining pages of this Introduction I should like to draw attention briefly to some of the differences in methodological habits among scholars that have had the effect of impeding our understanding of the literary form of Burke's writings, and to offer some words of justification for my own approach to Burke through genre.

Let us consider, first, the way in which academic philosophers habitually read philosophical texts. It has often been observed that philosophers tend to regard the rhetorical, literary, or aesthetic elements of a philosophical text as accidental to its content. In part this attitude may reflect the ancient animosity between philosophy and rhetoric, in which philosophers claim a commitment to a truth that transcends historical conditions and passing modes of language and expression. In this view the philosophic past is 'a sphere of invariant meanings which are only extrinsically affected by language and historical conditions'.[11] The philosopher has traditionally subscribed to what Berel Lang punningly dismisses as a 'myth of "immaculate perception" in philosophical writing—the traditional and still common ideal of the philosopher as disembodied mind or reason in direct contact with the contents of the "real" world'.[12] The outcome, John Richetti argues, is a conception of philosophical writing as a 'consecutive conversation' or 'dialogue between the living and the dead' in which each thinker 'inherits the problems and corrects the answers of his predecessors'. But, as he further points out, this dialogue is an odd one, 'since the dead are in effect not allowed to speak their own language'.[13] Any attention to the historical character of the philosopher's writing, its rootedness in changing generic and literary conventions, is seen as irrelevant or even as an impediment to philosophical rigour. In Burke studies this methodological tendency is exemplified in the work of Frederick A. Dreyer, who argues, 'we must treat the body of Burke's writings exactly as we would interpret the statements of a formal treatise', regardless of the differing circumstances that occasioned his numerous pronouncements. 'We have no choice', Dreyer continues, 'but to assume that all of Burke's statements are equally credible or equally incredible as evidence of his theory.'[14]

Burke has never been fully accepted into the pantheon of philosophical immortals, not having escaped altogether the bonds of historical and political circumstance that tie him to his own era, but he has been embraced wholeheartedly by scholars in philosophy's sister discipline of political theory. Here we

---

[11] James Collins, *Interpreting Modern Philosophy* (Princeton, 1972), 17.
[12] Berel Lang, *The Anatomy of Philosophical Style: Literary Philosophy and the Philosophy of Literature* (Oxford, 1990), 3.
[13] John J. Richetti, *Philosophical Writing: Locke, Berkeley, Hume* (Cambridge, Mass., 1983), 9.
[14] Frederick A. Dreyer, *Burke's Politics: A Study in Whig Orthodoxy* (Waterloo, Ont., 1979), 4.

encounter a similar set of assumptions to those identified by Lang and Richetti in the history of philosophy. Specifically, political theory has preoccupied itself with the study and transmission of a tradition of classic texts, a set of 'great books' or 'master works'. A typical list or 'biblical begattery' (as Conal Condren archly designates it) of this tradition would include the names, 'Plato, Aristotle, Augustine, Aquinas, Machiavelli, Hobbes, Locke, Rousseau, Hegel, Marx, and Mill, whose major works are the sibylline books of the political theorist. Behind these stand such impressive figures as Cicero, Dante, Marsilius, More, Bodin, Hume, Bentham, Burke, Paine, and de Tocqueville.'[15] Various rationales have been offered to explain how and why these figures constitute a canon of classic political texts, including the argument Condren calls 'issue-orthodoxy', the view, namely, that the political text is defined by its focus on 'a finite range of distinct universal or "basic" issues, encapsulated by such terms as *power, justice, sovereignty, obligation, state*, or by such expressions as *the public good* or *the limits of government*'.[16] Condren's use of the term 'universal' signals that in political theory, as in philosophy more generally, the inclination has been to treat the received texts as a single field of discourse in which writers address and answer one another using a neutral political 'meta-language'. In Burke scholarship this tendency can be seen in those studies emphasizing his adherence to moral principles of natural law, which transcend particular historical, social, and political conditions: in some instances he is made to sound more like Aristotle or Aquinas than like his own contemporaries.[17]

The issues that I have briefly sketched in the previous two paragraphs will strike a familiar note to scholars of literature, who have been fighting their own battles of late over the questions of who belongs in the literary canon and by what

---

[15] Conal Condren, *The Status and Appraisal of Classic Texts: An Essay on Political Theory, Its Inheritance, and the History of Ideas* (Princeton, 1985), 58.
[16] Ibid. 44.
[17] See e.g. Francis P. Canavan, *The Political Reason of Edmund Burke* (Durham, NC, 1960); Charles Parkin, *The Moral Basis of Edmund Burke's Political Thought* (Cambridge, 1956); Peter J. Stanlis, *Edmund Burke and the Natural Law* (Ann Arbor, 1958); Leo Strauss, *Natural Right and History* (Chicago, 1953); and Burleigh T. Wilkins, *The Problem of Burke's Political Philosophy* (Oxford, 1967).

criteria. In this century Northrop Frye has perhaps come closest to articulating a totalizing theory of literature that extracts from all authors, whatever their individual characteristics, an irreducible literary discourse sounding across the centuries. In this sense Frye's theory falls in with Lang's account of the philosophical enterprise as the extraction of a 'common linguistic core' from among 'the several historically distinct languages' in which philosophers respectively wrote.[18] Recent literary theorists, however, have taken issue with essentialist claims about 'literature' and literary language, arguing, as has already been noted, that these terms have clearly meant different things to writers and readers at different times. The same point applies equally in philosophy and political theory. As Condren observes of Machiavelli, Hobbes, and Locke, none of these thinkers displays any particular self-consciousness that he is part of a tradition of political theory. Machiavelli, for example, 'claims to be original' but significantly omits any mention of a 'tradition of political reflection from which he is departing'. Condren notes, moreover, that in the case of Hobbes, 'figures quite extrinsic to the accepted tradition of political theory (such as Harvey and Galileo) are of at least as much contextual relevance to understanding his thought as are his "predecessors" within it'.[19]

What Condren has remarked about Machiavelli and Hobbes can likewise be said of Burke. His writings and speeches, as this book sets out to demonstrate, not only partake of the recognized languages of politics in his time (parliamentary discourse, legal idioms, epistolary and polemical forms of address, and so on), but range widely into other forms of contemporary discourse, including the languages of economics and agricultural improvement and the prevailing 'literary' modes of poetry, drama, and narrative. My argument will be that the formal character of Burke's written discourse profoundly affects the meaning and persuasiveness of his arguments and ideas. Rather than leaning towards what Lang calls the 'Neutralist' model of intellectual discourse, in which the form or structure of a work 'is denied any intrinsic connection to its substance', I shall argue for the

---

[18] Lang, *Anatomy of Philosophical Style*, 13.
[19] Condren, *Classical Texts*, 68–9.

necessity of reading Burke along the lines of Lang's 'Interaction' model, which asserts that 'style makes the philosopher'—and the philosophy. As Lang explains, 'the writer in this second model, in choosing a form or structure for philosophical discourse, is, *in that act*, also shaping the substance or content which the form then... will be "of". The form in other words is an ingredient of philosophical content—as the impingement of light, in the "Heisenberg Effect," influences the activity or location of the particles identified.'[20]

It is only fair to note, however, that the 'Neutralist' model has rarely been applied to Burke in all its purity. James T. Boulton, for example, in *The Language of Politics in the Age of Wilkes and Burke* (1963), argues that a close attention to literary style is indispensable to historical understanding. 'Especially', he emphasizes, 'with literature of a persuasive character, the critic is faced with the whole question of the methods of communication between men with ideas and those to whom the ideas are directed; when he examines and assesses these methods—because they involve a consideration of the intellectual, moral, cultural, and above all, emotional resources of the writer and his audience—he is dealing with evidence as important to the historian as any naked event or bare idea.'[21] Perhaps typically for the time in which it was written, Boulton's study tends to confine itself to the stylistic means at Burke's disposal—his use, in *Reflections on the Revolution in France*, of image patterns, symbolism, thematic oppositions such as 'natural order' versus 'unnatural order', and unifying devices, especially the apostrophe to Marie Antoinette. Our current inclination would be to take his analysis a step farther and probe the historical, social, and cultural significance of the conventions Burke employs. Thus, Boulton's discussion of Burke's reliance on the Swiftian satiric themes of prophecy, intoxication, and religious enthusiasm could be extended to show how Burke establishes a historical typology linking the French revolutionists with the puritan radicals of the English Revolution, a link that awakens complex ideological and political associations for him and his audience.

As a means of assessing this broader significance of Burke's

---

[20] Lang, *Anatomy of Philosophical Style*, 12, 18.
[21] Boulton, *Language of Politics*, 3.

literary practice, I propose, as I have already indicated, to view a number of his published texts against the background of the innovative generic practices that marked eighteenth-century literary culture, especially as represented by Swift and Pope. Perhaps the most compelling reason for adopting this approach is that eighteenth-century writers themselves accepted genres as a given and employed them self-consciously in the knowledge that their readers' expectations would be profoundly shaped by their generic choices. Genres were understood on all sides to reflect underlying social and psychological realities, as is immediately obvious in Alexander Pope's witty justification of decorum in *An Essay on Criticism* (1711): 'For diff'rent *Styles* with diff'rent *Subjects* sort, | As several Garbs with Country, Town, and Court.' Pope's comparison of literary styles and genres to fashions of clothing implies a link between generic and social hierarchies and underscores the extent to which neo-classical genre theory is based, in Roger Fowler's phrase, 'on fixed assumptions about psychological and social differentiation'.[22]

Eighteenth-century genre theory has long had the reputation of being, at its worst, excessively regulative and prescriptive. Regulations and prescriptions there certainly were, but generic theory and practice in the period were much more subtle, flexible, and sophisticated than the stereotyping view would allow. Critics of the time recognized the literary kinds as an interrelated hierarchy, though not necessarily an all-inclusive one, since not all possible forms were specified. Within that hierarchy, the lesser forms were understood as subsumable within the larger forms: features of pastoral, for example, could appear in comedy, and elements of georgic might be present in the epic.[23] Changes in the relations among forms occurred from time to time; for the eighteenth century the most significant change was what R. S. Crane has dubbed a 'didactic shift', in which georgic and satire rose dramatically in the hierarchy from

---

[22] Brian Lee, 'Genre', in Roger Fowler (ed.), *A Dictionary of Modern Critical Terms* (London, 1973), 82.
[23] See Ralph Cohen, 'On the Interrelations of Eighteenth-Century Literary Forms', in Phillip Harth (ed.), *New Approaches to Eighteenth-Century Literature* (New York, 1974), 35–6.

relative obscurity in the Renaissance to a position of literary dominance. Such shifts, however, do not imply that forms have some life of their own or are metaphysical essences. Forms must be understood, rather, as 'written or spoken by people . . . and addressed to people. When poets turn to one form rather than another, when critics defend one kind of hierarchy rather than another, they do so for reasons that are related to personal, public, and professional commitments.'[24]

This hierarchical, relational view of genre allowed eighteenth-century critics and writers to account for the emergence of new forms and to justify their cultural seriousness, as in Henry Fielding's famous definition of the novel in the Preface to *Joseph Andrews* as a 'comic Epic-Poem in Prose'. Equally it permitted them to explain, without any sense of strain, the literary practices of such writers as Addison, Shaftesbury, Gibbon, or Burke and to relate their intellectual productions to the prevailing literary kinds. Since the georgic, for example, demanded a mixture of instruction and pleasing embellishment from the poet, no great conceptual leap was required to recognize that a political treatise or philosophical essay could be constructed along the same lines, though with different proportions of pleasure and instruction. 'The theoretical position of interrelation of forms and mixture of parts', observes Ralph Cohen, 'leads to a view of language that combines two kinds of truth—referential and nonreferential—in the same work.'[25] Such a view of language can readily account for what we might regard as an incongruous mixture of imaginative and factual discourse in Burke's great political statements. Accordingly, eighteenth-century critical procedure significantly widens the scope of the kinds of writing that are considered to be literature.

The eighteenth-century theory of mixed kinds explains how and why Burke's political writings blend orthodox political genres, such as the formal, public letter, with structures and features from more 'imaginative' forms such as epic, tragedy, and even, in the case of his writings on India, popular gothic romance. His use of the latter genres draws on a rich critical tradition in the eighteenth century that read these forms primarily as expressions of political themes, a circumstance that

[24] Ibid. 41.   [25] Ibid. 77.

helps account for their frequent appearance in his political treatises. His *Letters on a Regicide Peace*, to name only one instance, combines significant elements of epic and mock-heroic satire with its host genre of the public letter. His use of the generic features of epic, tragedy, and georgic is also intended to appeal to the exclusive political culture of his time. The boundaries of political discourse remained circumscribed by the severely limited audience that was deemed to enjoy the rights and privileges of citizenship, an audience that was classically educated, socially élitist, and male. In 1796 Burke calculated this class of 'political citizens', or what we today call informed public opinion, at no more than 400,000 men, and of these only a much smaller number, many of them aristocrats, could aspire to public office (ix. 224). The ostensible host forms he uses throughout his career, the parliamentary speech and the personal letter, further reflect this state of affairs, for they are both modes of address adapted to the privileged, exclusive ambit of eighteenth-century politics. Thus, when Burke's writings are placed within the larger matrix of forms accepted in the period—a matrix still dominated, at least theoretically, by the traditional literary hierarchy of genres—it becomes clear how carefully and deliberately he sizes up his audience. One need only compare his *Reflections on the Revolution in France* with Thomas Paine's consciously demotic reply, *The Rights of Man*, or Mary Wollstonecraft's *A Vindication of the Rights of Men*, to recognize the validity of this point.

But in examining Burke's persistent recourse to the culturally prestigious literary forms of his age, the lengthy history of those forms also demands consideration, for a genre exists not only in synchronic relation to other genres and generic mixtures in contemporaneous use, but also in diachronic relation to its past: the history both of its use and of its various transformations. This approach foregrounds questions of historical and cultural change, questions such as what an author's selection, revision, and recombination of existing generic features reveal about the changing ways in which successive generations perceive, experience, and understand the world around them. In his anatomy of philosophical genres, for example, Berel Lang asks why the dialogue and commentary forms have fallen out of use; the answer, he suggests, is to be found in underlying institutional and conceptual factors, such as the connection between changes in the use of genres and shifts in philosophical paradigms and modes of speculation. In Burke's case, the question to be asked is not only why he imports significant features of georgic and epic into his writings, but also how his innovative reordering of these features illuminate and *embody* formally some of the core themes of his political thought. Thus, as will become apparent, his georgic mode addresses the problem of how individuals and societies experience and negotiate historical change, and highlights the advantages of 'improvement' over 'innovation' as a model for change. Similarly, the English public's gradual drift away from the 'heroic' modes Burke employs in his later writings (exemplified in Philip Francis's dismissal of Burke's famous apostrophe to Marie Antoinette in the *Reflections* as 'pure foppery') signals the dawn of a more democratic and inclusive political culture (*Corr.* vi. 86).

Burke's use of genre, it must be emphasized, is not just readerly, that is, not designed merely to provide his readers or listeners with a set of norms, conventions, or expectations to guide them in their encounters with his texts. In some instances this is indeed the case, as in his speeches detailing British malfeasance in India, which draw on the conventions of gothic fiction in an attempt to approximate people and events remote from his audience's understanding more closely to their immediate experience. But his deployment of genre is also 'writerly', both in the sense that he displays a critical self-consciousness in his choice of forms and, more importantly, in the sense that these generic choices become representationally significant. In some instances, the generic and literary conventions chosen are so deeply ingrained or taken for granted as to seem natural, 'carrying such ideological conviction, that they are invisible'.[26] More often, however, especially in the speeches and pamphlets inspired by the French Revolution, Burke's self-consciousness about genre and about writing and language generally signals a corresponding self-consciousness about political and social first principles: as is so often the case, the theorizing and innovating impulse manifests itself in times of institutional and conceptual crisis.

[26] Lang, *Anatomy of Philosophical Style*, 41.

I do not mean to suggest that Burke's polemics on the French Revolution or his famous speeches on America and India reveal him to be a poet *manqué*, churning out novels or tragic dramas or intellectual epic-poems in prose (to paraphrase Fielding) under the guise of political discourse. Though at times it may appear otherwise, Burke never loses sight of his primary purpose, which is political persuasion, and of the primary generic vehicles at his disposal, the parliamentary speech and the letter. Yet his interpolation of the features and conventions of neighbouring literary genres is far too systematic to be dismissed as only a deployment of localized rhetorical flourishes. They exist, rather, as modal elements within the dominant form, where 'form', as Cohen distinguishes it, refers to 'a combination of means to lead to a specific effect', and 'mode' identifies 'kinds of means'.[27] Thus, the letter can be a literary form in its own right or appear as a modal device in another form, serving, for example, as a narrative technique in the novel. The form/mode distinction also underscores the fact that the modal use of a genre or its features is neither continuous nor comprehensive. In other words, when Burke inserts heroic passages in his *Letters on a Regicide Peace*, he by no means reproduces the epic form in its entirety or sustains it throughout the work. He presupposes, rather, his audience's familiarity with the form as a whole and relies on that knowledge to complete or explain his use of discrete generic features. The modal use of genre functions, therefore, in a manner analogous to extended allusion, but the reference is to a family of formal features rather than a specific instance of a form.

The question of genre can be extended to the present day, as we compare our own classifications and presuppositions, which reflect our ways of seeing and knowing the world, with those of Burke and his contemporaries. One of the most interesting of these is the genre of political theory, which the academic practice of the present century has recognized *de facto* as a discrete form of discourse. John Gunnell argues, for example, that although the various individual works assigned to the canon of political theory fall under a disparate range of 'conventional categories based on their intrinsic genre and the

---

[27] Cohen 'On the Interrelations of Eighteenth-Century Literary Forms', 49.

historical context to which they belonged', they can also be approached and usefully classified in terms of the mode of intellectual inquiry we call 'political theory'. Gunnell grounds his categorization in the recognition that certain classic works 'are exemplary instances of a creative mind's encounter and engagement with the problem of political order and that, in terms of their content and the circumstances of their production, they bear certain family resemblances, and possess certain common motifs, which make it reasonable to construct a paradigm of political theory and the political theorist to which specific works conform in varying degrees'.[28] Gunnell's generic approach illuminates Burke's political discourse in several ways. As the conclusion of this study will show, it helps to account for some of the more puzzling aspects of Burke's later writings, particularly their prophetic stance and apocalyptic tone. More importantly, perhaps, Gunnell's thesis suggests a way to reconcile the two competing approaches to Burke that have dominated critical discussion in recent decades. For if, as many readers of Burke insist, his practice as a writer must be understood as a product of the historical circumstances and cultural pressures of his time, Gunnell's diachronic view of genre highlights some of the ways in which, as other readers have emphasized, Burke's œuvre also contributes to an ancient and enduring mode of inquiry that repeatedly raises the same issues—especially the problems of historical existence and the need for social and political order.

Finally, a word of justification about the texts singled out for analysis in this study. I have made no attempt to be comprehensive, having elsewhere detailed Burke's use of the conventions of gothic romance in his writings on India, and his naturalization of such aesthetic terms as 'taste' and 'sublimity' in political contexts.[29] Several of the texts examined in the following pages, especially the *Speech on Conciliation with the Colonies*,

---

[28] John G. Gunnell, *Political Theory: Tradition and Interpretation* (Cambridge, Mass., 1979), 135–6.

[29] See Frans De Bruyn, 'Edmund Burke's Gothic Romance: The Portrayal of Warren Hastings in Burke's Writings and Speeches on India', *Criticism*, 29 (1987), 415–38; and 'Edmund Burke's Natural Aristocrat: The "Man of Taste" as a Political Ideal', *Eighteenth-Century Life*, 11 (1987), 41–60.

Reflections on the Revolution in France, and *A Letter to a Noble Lord*, are among the best-known, most canonical of Burke's writings. In returning to these familiar works, among others, I am by no means suggesting that Burke's deployment of generic features and literary techniques in his other writings is somehow unworthy of notice. Nevertheless, I have been guided in my choice by the views outlined above about the interrelation of literary kinds and the mechanisms of generic innovation. Not surprisingly, those of Burke's productions where he enjoyed the greatest degree of independence as a writer and thinker exhibit in their pages the most sustained effects of his habitual interpolation of modal generic features. They are the works in which he was able to expatiate on the largest and most significant political issues of his time without being restricted unduly by specific party positions. In short, the texts that form the primary focus of this study are ones in which the fundamental premises of political conduct in eighteenth-century Britain are exposed, premises that are revealed in the cultural structures and discourses of the time, including literary forms. Those cultural and literary discourses are, of course, present throughout Burke's speeches, polemics, and correspondence, and I refer frequently in the pages that follow to his larger œuvre. By necessity, however, his letters and shorter pamphlets convey only telegraphically and intermittently the literary discourses that his larger works articulate much more comprehensively. It is to these larger texts that I turn, then, in order to demonstrate how literary form in Burke's writings embodies a political argument.

I

Alexander Pope and Burke's A Letter to a Noble Lord: *Generic Innovation and Political Discourse*

> The corruption of a Poet is the Generation of a Statesman.
> John Dryden[1]

In 1794 the Pitt administration, in a gesture strongly supported by King George III, offered Edmund Burke a sizable pension which, given his chronic financial difficulties, he accepted with gratitude. The situation was not without its ironies, as even the King noted, for in 1782 Burke had been the driving force behind the reform of the very civil list from which he was now to benefit. But that was the least of the ambiguities summoned up on this occasion. Not only did Burke lay himself open to charges, however baseless, of being a ministerial hireling, but, more broadly, his acceptance exposed a labyrinth of tensions and contradictions through which he had threaded his way from the beginning of his career, most notably, the vexed relationship of patron and client, the virtues imputed to independence and the indignities associated with dependence, the prestige of the gentleman-amateur versus the stigma of professionalism, and the disparity between hereditary privilege and hard-won personal accomplishment. Nor were these difficulties unique to Burke's experience: numerous other individuals of ability, but modest means and connections, who sought to make a place for themselves in the hierarchical order

---

[1] John Dryden, 'A Defence of an Essay of Dramatique Poesie', prefaced to *The Indian Emperour*, in *The Works of John Dryden* (Berkeley and Los Angeles, 1966), ix. 10.

of eighteenth-century Britain encountered similar obstacles in their paths. The fact that these experiences were so widely shared, combined with an ever-increasing access to the means of describing and communicating them, meant that the conditions necessary to the emergence of a new literary genre—an audience, a social rationale, and the efficient means (education and print media)—existed in a combination sufficient to call a new form into birth. Indeed, the emergence of the 'letter to an eminent person' form in the late seventeenth and eighteenth centuries presents an unusually clear-cut instance of generic change, as a new social reality calls for a mode capable of articulating and negotiating the new circumstances it has brought forth. Given the rapid emergence of this genre and its short lifespan (it died out in the early nineteenth century) and given Burke's masterly contribution to the form, the 'letter to an eminent person' makes for a useful introductory case study of the problem with which this book is chiefly concerned: the processes, mechanisms, and rationales for generic innovation.

The subject of Burke's royal pension surfaced again on 13 November of the following year during a debate in the House of Lords on the third reading of the Treasonable Practices Bill, upon which occasion the Duke of Bedford and the Earl of Lauderdale launched an attack on him, ostensibly for his recent acceptance of the pension, but more importantly for his role as the chief propagandist in the counter-revolutionary struggle against the new French regime. Their attack unexpectedly secured for them the historical fate of Alexander Pope's hapless victims in *The Dunciad*: Bedford and Lauderdale were soon to find themselves preserved for posterity like flies in amber as their attacks elicited Burke's devastating reply, *A Letter to a Noble Lord*. Burke's initial reaction to this assault upon his reputation, however, appeared in the much more private context of an unfinished letter intended to thank William Windham, a long-time political associate, for rallying to his defence as the dispute spilled over into the House of Commons. Referring to the proceedings of his political opponents, whose actions he associates with the bloodthirsty conduct of the French revolutionaries, Burke states, 'They tear our corpses from the Tombs to turn the Coffin Lead which preserves the departed into Bullets to assassinate the living' (*Corr.* viii. 339).

Readers of *A Letter to a Noble Lord* will recognize in this somewhat ghoulish conceit the germ from which one of the more memorable passages in the *Letter* was to spring: 'They have so determined a hatred to all privileged orders, that they deny even to the departed, the sad immunities of the grave. They are not wholly without an object. Their turpitude purveys to their malice; and they unplumb the dead for bullets to assassinate the living' (ix. 147–8).

This passage, which occurs near the beginning of the *Letter to a Noble Lord*, is a vividly illustrative instance of the nervous, violent rhetoric that energizes Burke's remarkable polemic, but its previous appearance in the significantly different literary context of his private correspondence poses important questions about the rhetorical and literary status of the *Letter*. Indeed, the juxtaposition of these two quotations offers a tantalizing glimpse into the literary genesis of the *Letter* and raises some important questions about motives and modes of literary production. The problem raised by a comparison of the two quotations is primarily one of intertextuality, the relations among works, rather than, as one might initially surmise, a question of the work's compositional history. Burke's remark is first recorded in a private letter intended at most for the sympathetic eyes of a few close political associates, a context very different from the formal, public letter in which it finally appears. A double transformation is at work here: first, a private communication expressing a deeply personal response is being transmuted into public polemic; and, second, a minor polemical genre, the 'letter to an eminent person', is metamorphosed into a major literary form practised by some of the most distinguished writers of the age.

Burke's *Letter to a Noble Lord* is the culmination of a long process of generic transformation and elevation. The letter's form is rooted in part in the fulsome dedications with which writers in the seventeenth and early eighteenth centuries prefaced their works, either in acknowledgment or in solicitation of the patronage they needed to support their literary careers. It also draws on a widespread rhetorical strategy in the political and journalistic discourse of the period: writers commonly framed polemical discussions of current issues or attacks on political opponents in the form of open letters addressed to the major participants, chiefly aristocratic, in the political affairs of the time. In the hands of talented writers such as Pope and Johnson, the 'letter to a noble lord' was associated, James T. Boulton observes, 'both with the defence of the writer's reputation and the denunciation of his enemies'. Whether used in a political or literary context (the two were often almost indistinguishable), the form was a vehicle primarily for 'men whose reputation derived not from hereditary rank but solely from personal talents'.[2] The generic development that culminates in Burke's *Letter* must, therefore, be understood in the particular social context that impelled writers to adopt this new mode of discourse. The underlying premiss of my argument is that changes in the relations among literary works and genres—shifts in the relative importance and popularity of certain subjects or forms, for example—reflect underlying alterations in the consciousness, the ways of seeing and understanding, of both writers and readers.[3]

The complex ways in which Burke adapts and transforms the genre of the public letter in *A Letter to a Noble Lord* may thus be examined for what they unexpectedly reveal about the contradictions he experienced in his public life. New literary kinds are seldom, if ever, created *ex nihilo*; they incorporate and recombine features of existing forms in ways that harmonize with new historical conditions and meet the changing demands of writers and audiences. Accordingly, by examining the literary models and features Burke draws on in fashioning his *Letter*, we can investigate the implications of the choices he makes as a writer. One significant parallel is suggested by the remarkable extent to which the satiric conventions and rhetorical strategies

---

[2] James T. Boulton, 'Edmund Burke's *Letter to a Noble Lord*: Apologia and Manifesto', *Burke Newsletter*, 8 (1967), 697, 695.

[3] In analysing an analogous process of generic change, Ralph Cohen argues that the elevation of the early 17th-c. broadside ballad, 'An Excellent Ballad of George Barnwell Who Was Undone by a Strumpet', into George Lillo's mid-18th-c. tragedy, *The London Merchant*, involves social and literary transformations reflecting, among other factors, a growth in commercial consciousness and a new understanding of the relations among social classes: 'The elevation of genres constitutes a process of elevating the audience's consciousness of class change.' See 'Literary History and the Ballad of George Barnwel', in Douglas Lane Patey and Timothy Keegan (eds.), *Augustan Studies: Essays in Honor of Irvin Ehrenpreis* (Newark, 1985), 19.

he uses echo those Alexander Pope employed some sixty years earlier in *An Epistle to Dr. Arbuthnot*. In Burke's case, these strategies hint at the depth of his ambivalence about his dependent social position as a client of the Rockingham Whigs, to whom he owed his seat in the House of Commons and on whose behalf he employed his pen. Like other writers in the period, he felt keenly the invidious character of the relationship between patron and client, and he was eager, as was Pope, to vindicate his political autonomy and literary independence. The term 'independence' resonates with ideological significance for both writers: hence the compelling homologies between Burke's *apologia pro vita sua* and Pope's declaration of literary independence in *An Epistle to Dr. Arbuthnot*.

In the discussion that follows, I focus primarily on Burke's use of epistolary form in *A Letter to a Noble Lord*—his choice of the public letter as the vehicle for a discourse of dissent and debate—but it is important to emphasize at the outset that the generic structure of the *Letter* is considerably more mixed than the title of the pamphlet implies. Burke introduces significant elements of georgic, Scriblerian satire, and elegy into his polemic, making it one of the most complex, structurally speaking, of all his productions. Georgic figures prominently in the solemn prospect of Windsor Castle that climaxes the *Letter*, and satire in the systematic burlesque belittlement to which Bedford is subjected. Both these modes are employed by Burke as expressions of faith in and solidarity with the past: the prospect view recalls the past by association or 'historical retrospection' and the satiric dismissal of Bedford, by its condemnation of the present, falls in with the elegist's nostalgic memory of a golden past. These additional elements of generic interpolation or transformation must, therefore, be borne in mind in the argument that follows, for they instance a complex interaction between ideology and literary form characteristic not only of Burke's writings but of eighteenth-century literature as a whole.

I

To appreciate fully Burke's (and Pope's) achievements in the 'letter to an eminent person' form, one must bear in mind its polemical, journalistic origins in the seventeenth century and its subsequent development. In the opening paragraph of Jonathan Swift's *Discourse Concerning the Mechanical Operation of the Spirit*, a pamphlet cast in the form of a letter from a projector in the Royal Society to his counterpart 'in the Academy of the Beaux Esprits in New-Holland', the correspondent recounts his difficulty in deciding upon the 'most proper Form' in which to send abroad his latest 'scientific' theory:

> To which End, I have three Days been coursing thro' *Westminster-Hall*, and *St. Paul's Church-yard*, and *Fleet-street*, to peruse *Titles*; and, I do not find any which holds so general a Vogue, as that of *A Letter to a Friend*: Nothing is more common than to meet with long Epistles address'd to Persons and Places, where, at first thinking, one would be apt to imagine it not altogether so necessary or Convenient; Such as, *a Neighbour at next Door, a mortal Enemy, a perfect Stranger*, or *a Person of Quality in the Clouds*; and these upon Subjects, in appearance, the least proper for Conveyance by the Post; as, *long Schemes in Philosophy; dark and wonderful Mysteries of State; Laborious Dissertations in Criticism and Philosophy, Advice to Parliaments*, and the like.[4]

Judging from the lengthy list of titles reading 'A Letter to . . .' in *The Eighteenth-Century Short Title Catalogue*, Swift's unnamed correspondent accurately reports the current popularity of this epistolary form, though at the same time his eager endorsement, as a thoroughgoing modern, of the latest literary fashion ironically conveys Swift's contempt for this literary innovation and its apparent rhetorical absurdity.

The correspondent aspires to the easy, conversational style of the familiar letter, in which the writer conveys the impression of negligently reporting whatever thoughts are uppermost at the time of writing, but his real purpose in putting pen to paper, which is to communicate a closely argued pseudo-scientific theory outlining the etiology of religious enthusiasm, appears irreconcilably in conflict with his choice of literary vehicle. He tacitly acknowledges as much when, after a few paragraphs of epistolary pleasantries, he abandons all pretence of addressing

---

[4] Jonathan Swift, 'A Discourse Concerning the Mechanical Operation of the Spirit', in *The Prose Works of Jonathan Swift*, ed. Herbert Davis, (Oxford, 1941–74), i. 171–2.

his antipodean correspondent: 'AND now, Sir, having dispatch'd what I had to say of Forms, or of Business, let me intreat, you will suffer me to proceed upon my Subject; and to pardon me, if I make no farther Use of the Epistolary Stile, till I come to conclude.' Compounding this confusion of literary means and ends, the author requests the recipient of his *Discourse* to '*burn this Letter*', while simultaneously acquiescing in (or at least resigning himself to) its publication. 'For, let me say what I will to the contrary, I am afraid you will publish this *Letter*, as soon as ever it comes to your Hands.'[5] With these words, the correspondent executes a manœuvre worthy of Swift himself: he ensures the publication of his *Discourse*, thus fulfilling his desire for philosophical and literary fame, yet he absolves himself of responsibility for his inflammatory pamphlet by enclosing it (rather flimsily) within the protective cover of a private and ostensibly confidential letter.

Though all writing is obviously conventional, Swift is apparently of the view that the conventions of the 'letter to an eminent person' altogether strain credulity: any sense of decorum, of the genre's grounding in social reality, he implies, is lost when a formal philosophical discourse addressed to an impersonal public is embedded in a personal, private communication. One suspects, however, that a major source of his objection is the form's popularity with his lesser colleagues in the writing trade—the swarm of moderns who threaten to overrun the realm of letters. Lacking the social standing of the gentleman-amateur, whose scholarly preserve they threaten to invade, these professional writers and scholars have adopted the epistolary mode as a way of asserting their right to address their 'betters' as equals in areas where they can claim a legitimate expertise. Though ostensibly couched in terms of flattery, epistles addressed to prominent persons often served in the period as vehicles for their authors' sly declarations of independent merit.

The worst that can be said about the purely literary quality of many of these letters is that they are as undistinguished as they are innocuous and ephemeral. Indeed, as practised by many

[5] Ibid. 172, 190.

political propagandists and journalists, the form seems plausible enough. In tracts with such titles as *A Letter to a Lord, in Answer to a Late Pamphlet, Entituled, the Causes of the Present Fears and Dangers of the Government* (1692) or *A Letter from a Member of Parliament... to a Noble Lord in his Neighbourhood, Concerning the Excise Bill* (1733), writers seek public support for their political views by addressing a peer sympathetic to their cause. In other instances, such as the pamphlet entitled, *A Letter to a Noble Negotiator Abroad, on the Present Prospect of a Speedy Peace* (1748), the writer takes issue with the views of his correspondent (usually a major participant in the events under discussion), and asserts his right to address a noble lord publicly and familiarly: 'It may possibly seem a little strange to your Excellency, to find yourself addressed in this publick Manner, but when you come to consider the Excuses I have to offer, perhaps tho' you cannot approve, you will at least forgive the Liberty that I have taken' (p. 5). Behind this author's routine verbal gesture of deference towards his addressee, which contains within it a note of self-justifying assertiveness, one detects something of the complex, changing social reality of eighteenth-century Britain—a changing scene reflected in the emergence of new forms of public discourse. The writer's mode of address recognizes the continued concentration of political power in the hands of a largely aristocratic oligarchy but affirms the increasingly influential voice of a much larger body of public opinion with its own legitimate and significant political interests.

The essential point to be borne in mind is that despite the perceived rhetorical awkwardness and implausibility of the epistolary mode of address, a point Burke freely acknowledges in his prefatory remarks to *Reflections on the Revolution in France*, the 'letter to an eminent person' flourished in the eighteenth century because it supplied an important social and political need. In the case of the *Reflections* Burke, like Swift's correspondent in *The Mechanical Operation of the Spirit*, confesses that his treatise has broken any reasonable bounds that might be said to circumscribe the letter form:

> The Author ... found that what he had undertaken not only far exceeded the measure of a letter, but that its importance required rather a more detailed consideration than at that time he had any leisure to bestow upon it. However, having thrown down his first

thoughts in the form of a letter, and indeed when he sat down to write, having intended it for a private letter, he found it difficult to change the form of address, when his sentiments had grown into a greater extent, and had received another direction. A different plan, he is sensible, might be more favourable to a commodious division and distribution of his matter. (viii. 53)

Yet, despite the difficulties Burke alludes to here, he retained the epistolary structure of his discourse when he expanded his private letter to Charles-Jean-François Depont into the published *Reflections*. Several critics have explained his rhetorical reasons for this decision.[6] Beyond any rhetorical considerations one might adduce, however, lies the fascinating problem of the forms of social and political intercourse reflected in this habitual exploitation of private correspondence as a means of addressing the public at large. Equally striking is the sudden efflorescence of this epistolary convention in the late seventeenth century and the rapid deterioration of that convention (a deterioration already evident in the acknowledged generic awkwardness of the *Reflections*) as the social reality upon which it was grounded shifts towards the end of the eighteenth century.

If the foregoing addresses the question why this polemical form, in spite of its topical ephemerality in most instances, was progressively elevated in the hierarchy of literary kinds and transformed into a genre of enduring literary interest, the puzzle remains how this Cinderella-like metamorphosis was accomplished. A comparison with other emerging forms in the period, such as the novel, is instructive: early novelists sought respectability and public acceptance for their fictions by incorporating into them features of existing genres and by claiming that their works conformed, at least in spirit, to the requirements of the heroic genres, especially the epic. The same procedures of mixing literary kinds and relating lower forms to higher ones are at work in Burke's *Letter to a Noble Lord*; thus, for example, he finds classical precedents in Horace and Juvenal for his *apologia* and includes significant elements of the georgic and the confession in the structure of his work.

---

[6] See F. P. Lock, *Burke's* Reflections on the Revolution in France (London, 1985), 114–18; and Reid, *Edmund Burke*, 8–9, 133–4.

The material basis or efficient cause for the flourishing of the letter form was the development of a reliable, convenient postal service making possible relatively rapid communication throughout the British Isles.[7] But the letter's function as a mode of political address owes more to the reality that the avenues to political power in the eighteenth century were guarded by a small number of individuals, which meant that a person such as Burke, if he wished to influence the politics of his time, had to find a way to make his opinions known to and valued by those individuals. In 1777 he revealingly stated that his 'cheif [sic] employment for many years has been that woful one, of a *flapper*', (*Corr*. iii. 389)—a self-designation placing him on a level with the servants in the court of Laputa, whose task, Gulliver reports, was to rouse the king and his courtiers from their self-absorbed inattention. Accordingly, Burke bent his formidable epistolary talents to influence, admonish, and ingratiate himself with his political friends, the Rockingham Whigs. This tactic required a careful modulation between private and public modes of address, the latter grounded in and growing out of the former, as James T. Boulton demonstrates in his analysis of a typical letter addressed to Lord Rockingham. At the outset, Boulton observes, one senses 'a speaking voice with an audience of one . . . but this gradually modulates into the orator's with an audience co-extensive at least with the whole Rockingham group ('you and your friends'). And as this more public voice takes control, so the imagery appears, carries the weight of the argument . . . and makes it memorable.'[8] In a relationship of the kind Burke enjoyed with the Rockingham Whigs, his chief political capital was his private self, for his power to shape events depended on his personal credibility with his political superiors, a credibility shaped and sustained by his talent for projecting a convincing, rational, and trustworthy persona in his private letters. Burke's voluminous private correspondence testifies to his recognition that the source of his

---

[7] Howard Anderson and Irvin Ehrenpreis, 'The Familiar Letter in the Eighteenth Century: Some Generalizations', in Anderson, Philip B. Daghlian, and Ehrenpreis (eds.), *The Familiar Letter in the Eighteenth Century* (Lawrence, Kan., 1966), 269–70.

[8] James T. Boulton, 'The Letters of Edmund Burke: "Manly Liberty|of|Speech"', in Anderson *et al*. (eds.), *The Familiar Letter*, 195.

political power lay in his private relationship with the politically powerful.

Given this intimate dynamic in eighteenth-century political relations, it is not surprising that Burke should carry over his epistolary mode of address, with its striking intermingling of public gravity and passionate private feeling, into his writings addressed to the public at large. Yet, the epistolary form does not effect this transition without undergoing a sometimes incongruous transformation or, more precisely, without coming unmoored from the social context in which the convention was originally grounded. In such works as the *Reflections on the Revolution in France*, *Letters on a Regicide Peace*, and even *A Letter to a Noble Lord* itself, the 'myth of direct communication between writer and addressee', as Christopher Reid phrases it, that reciprocity of writer and reader evident in Burke's private correspondence, has all but disappeared. The epistolary mode of address is now a largely empty formality as Burke directs his words to a numerous and anonymous public readership.

What has happened is not only that Burke increasingly found himself on the outside of the charmed circle of political leadership to which he once belonged, but also that a new, growing force on the political scene, public opinion, demanded to be consulted and informed—a pressure that in time generated more open and plausible forms of address.[9] Boswell had this larger public in mind when he commented on the usefulness of publishing parliamentary proceedings: 'the people in all parts of the kingdom have a fair, open, and exact report of the actual proceedings of their representatives and legislators, which in our constitution is highly to be valued'.[10] However narrowly this body of individuals was defined (Burke, as we have seen, estimated the informed, voting public to number no more than 400,000), it made much too large an audience to be imagined reading along over his shoulder as he penned a missive to one of his intimates. Yet he recognized the political value of mobilizing

---

[9] On the emergence of a free press in Britain and the concomitant development of public opinion as a force in political debate, see J. A. Downie, *Robert Harley and the Press: Propaganda and Public Opinion in the Age of Swift and Defoe* (Cambridge, 1979).

[10] James Boswell, *Life of Johnson*, ed. George Birkbeck Hill and L. F. Powell, (1934; repr. Oxford, 1971), i. 116.

this opinion 'without doors' (that is, public opinion outside the privileged confines of parliament), as a powerful means of influencing public policy. In the nineteenth century, the period in which British political institutions developed in the direction of mass democracy, the epistolary form of political address was to dwindle in importance as it was overtaken by other modes of mass communication, such as newspapers, which equally had their roots in eighteenth-century political discourse and practice, but which proved much more adaptable (and efficient) in addressing the ever more clamorous, numerous, and diverse public of the new century. Thus, Burke's great epistolary polemics of the 1790s stand as the triumphant realization of an unstable and ephemeral discourse: they are crowning achievements in a literary form that enjoyed its brief efflorescence in the transition from a closed, oligarchic political system to a more open and crowded political stage.

II

The rhetorical power of Burke's *Letter* in fact derives precisely from those features of the 'letter to an eminent person' that Swift derides in *The Mechanical Operation of the Spirit*. Though Burke argues that his personal grievances serve as little more than a pretext for his pamphlet—'The awful state of the time, and not myself or my own justification, is my true object in what I now write' (ix. 164)—his denunciation of the French Revolution and its 'fellow-travellers' in England is animated by his extraordinary identification of his own injured honour and reputation with the historic events unfolding on the Continent. Thus in the famous image, already quoted, of the revolutionaries' 'unplumbing' the dead in order to make bullets out of the lead of their coffins, Burke voices a thinly disguised fear of the desecration to be visited not just on his memory, but on his very corpse, should the revolution ever triumph in England. (His apprehensions even prompted him, as Captain Woodford reports, to instruct Edward Nagle that he wished to be buried 'unknown, the spot unmarked & separate from his son, wife and Brother on *account of the French Revolutionists*'.[11])

[11] Quoted in Carl B. Cone, *Burke and the Nature of Politics* (Lexington, Ken., 1964), ii. 507. Cone refers the reader to BM Add. MSS 37,843, fos. 195–6, Capt.

Burke's histrionic interpolation of himself (a carefully contrived version of that self) into his text extends, however, far beyond any association that might have come to exist in the public mind between his personality and his role as a spokesman for the antirevolutionary cause. To be sure, his authorship of *Reflections on the Revolution in France* had made him famous across Europe as the most effective of the counter-revolutionary propagandists, but a more compelling historical and literary explanation is suggested by the manner in which Burke's self-dramatization is actualized in his *Letter*. Adopting the stance of a retired and disinterested individual, whose relinquishment of personal and dynastic ambitions guarantees his independence and impartiality, Burke describes himself as besieged, pursued almost to the sacred privacy of the grave, by an importunate rabble of political opponents: 'Why will they not let me remain in obscurity and inaction? . . . They pursue, even such as me, into the obscurest retreats, and haul them before their revolutionary tribunals. Neither sex, nor age—not the sanctuary of the tomb is sacred to them.' He makes his own the cry uttered by the prophetic shade in Thomas Gray's 'Descent of Odin': 'Leave me, oh leave me to repose!' (ix. 147).

The rhetorical strategy pursued here recalls the opening lines of Pope's *Epistle to Dr. Arbuthnot*, in which the poet characterizes himself as similarly beset by an army of scribblers:

> What Walls can guard me, or what Shades can hide?
> They pierce my Thickets, thro' my Grot they glide,
> By land, by water, they renew the charge,
> They stop the Chariot, and they board the Barge.
> No place is sacred, not the Church is free,
> Ev'n *Sunday* shines no *Sabbath-day* to me.
>
> (ll. 7–12)

The parallel between the literary dunces, whose disturbance of Pope's privacy is seen to portend a widespread decay of cultural standards, and Burke's revolutionaries, who threaten with their innovations both the public institutions of Britain and the private repose of her citizens, is even more explicitly suggested in a further passage:

Woodford to Windham, 6 July 1797. See also, Bertram Sarason, 'Edmund Burke's Burial Place', *Notes and Queries*, NS 2/2 (Feb. 1955), 69–70.

The consequences [of innovation] are *before* us,—not in remote history; not in future prognostication: they are about us; they are upon us. They shake the publick security; they menace private enjoyment. They dwarf the growth of the young; they break the quiet of the old. If we travel, they stop our way. They infest us in town; they pursue us to the country. Our business is interrupted; our repose is troubled; our pleasures are saddened; our very studies are poisoned and perverted, and knowledge is rendered worse than ignorance, by the enormous evils of this dreadful innovation. (ix. 156)

Though the tone of Pope's *Epistle* is more comic than that of Burke's *Letter*, both texts convey an unsettling vision of the havoc wreaked by an unleashed, almost irresistible energy in the shape of a mob of literary and political upstarts whose disregard of existing social hierarchies and values borders on sacrilege.

A brief review of the circumstances that prompted Pope to publish *An Epistle to Dr. Arbuthnot* will make even clearer the relation between the two works. Lord Hervey, the vice-chamberlain to George II and confidant of Queen Caroline, had unwisely joined forces with Lady Mary Wortley Montagu in composing an attack on Pope in the form of satiric *Verses addressed to the Imitator of Horace* (1733). Hervey followed this with his own unaided work, *An Epistle from a Nobleman to a Doctor of Divinity* (1733), in which he dismisses Pope's poetic calling as nothing more than a mechanic's trade and obscurely hints at the poet's humble ancestry. Pope's initial reply to his enemies' '*Witty Fornication*'[12] and to Hervey's foolish verses was a lengthy prose epistle, first published by Warburton in 1751, entitled significantly 'A Letter to a Noble Lord: On Occasion of Some Libels Written and Propagated at Court, in the Year 1732–33'. 'Veined with sometimes telling irony,' remarks Maynard Mack, 'the "Letter" shows Pope seeking (without always finding) the right tone for an ordinary Englishman to take in responding to an assault from a peer of the realm.'[13] Lady Mary herself cogently summed up Pope's dilemma (and displayed the class antagonism he was faced with)

---

[12] Alexander Pope, 'A Letter to a Noble Lord. On Occasion of Some Libels Written and Propagated at Court, in the Year 1732–3', in *The Prose Works of Alexander Pope*, ii. *The Major Works, 1725–1744*, ed. Rosemary Cowler (Oxford, 1986), 447.

[13] Maynard Mack, *Alexander Pope: A Life* (New York, 1986), 608.

in a letter to her daughter written after the poet's death. In mounting their attacks on members of the aristocracy, she acidly observes, Pope and his friend Swift ungratefully turned on their benefactors, biting the hand that fed them: 'It is pleasant to consider that had it not been for the good nature of those very mortals they contemn, these two superior Beings were entitle'd by their Birth and hereditary Fortune to be only a couple of Link Boys.'[14]

In the face of such attacks, Pope turns, like other low-born individuals caught up in a conflict with their social 'betters', to the 'letter to a noble lord' as one of the few effective weapons available to him in his battle to defend his career and character:

> As I want not the humility, to think myself in every way but *one* your inferiour, it seems but reasonable that I should take the only method either of self-defence or retaliation, that is left me, against a person of your quality and power. And as by your choice of this weapon, your pen, you generously (and modestly too, no doubt) meant to put yourself upon a level with me; I will as soon believe that your Lordship would give a wound to a man unarm'd, as that you would deny me the use of it in my own defence.[15]

Pope ultimately left this reply unpublished in his lifetime. A number of practical explanations have been advanced for this prudent act of suppression—pressure from Walpole or the Queen, for instance—but Rosemary Cowler offers the additional consideration that the *Letter*, despite its 'satiric perspective', remained too 'personal' a statement, too much a betrayal of Pope's inner feelings.[16] In any event, the subject matter of the *Letter* was to undergo an extraordinary metamorphosis, a generic transformation and elevation culminating in that magnificent epistolary bill of complaint, *An Epistle to Dr. Arbuthnot*. Clothed in an elegant Horatian garb, Pope could more easily look his aristocratic enemies straight in the eye. Years later Burke was to borrow a leaf from Pope in setting himself on an equal footing with his political opponents: his own *Letter to a*

---

[14] Lady Mary Wortley Montagu, letter to Lady Bute, 23 June 1754, in *Complete Letters*, ed. Robert Halsband (Oxford, 1965–7), iii. 57.
[15] Pope, 'A Letter to a Noble Lord', in *Prose Works*, ii. 442.
[16] Rosemary Cowler, Introduction to 'A Letter to a Noble Lord', ibid. 438.

Noble Lord recapitulates, though under somewhat different circumstances, the process by which Pope had transformed a personal quarrel into an occasion of memorable literary utterance. Burke adopts a rhetorical stance in his *Letter* that parallels Pope's intermingling of personal animus and lofty disinterest in the *Epistle*. Cowler observes in Pope's case that, 'what could have been purely private (and individual) became public (and general) through the transforming art of the writer'—a remark that applies with equal justice to Burke.[17]

Pope often referred, as in the passage quoted above, to his wit and his pen as his chief weapons of self-defence. 'The life of a Wit', he states in the Preface to his *Works* of 1717, 'is a warfare upon earth'.[18] But perhaps Lord Chesterfield's characterization of wit as a form of property (in a famous speech on the Stage Licensing Bill of 1737) more acutely exposes the true value both Pope and Burke placed upon their writing: 'Wit, my Lords, is a sort of property: it is the property of those who have it, and too often the only property they have to depend on. It is indeed but a precarious dependence. Thank God! we, my Lords, have a dependence of another kind.'[19] The very term 'dependence', which in the context of his statement means the independent wealth and property of the aristocracy, also implies, in a sliding of signification, the opposite condition of subordination brought on by the pressing need to eke out a living, a circumstance that entails the sale of one's talents as a writer for a payment, a pension, or a place.

Chesterfield's ingenious characterization of the Licensing Bill and its provisions for stage censorship as 'an encroachment upon property' was intended to do little more than to score points for the opponents of the bill, yet his words give expression to revolutionary changes that were taking place during the eighteenth century in the relations between authors,

---

[17] Cowler, Introduction to 'A Letter to a Noble Lord', ibid.
[18] Pope, Preface of 1717, in *The Twickenham Edition*, i. 6.
[19] Lord Chesterfield, 'Miscellaneous Pieces, XLVI: Speech on the Licensing Bill', in *Miscellaneous Works of the Late Philip Dormer Stanhope, Earl of Chesterfield* (London, 1777), ii. 239. Reid quotes this passage as an epigraph to his chapter, 'Patronage, Deference, and the Language of Dissent', in *Edmund Burke*, in which he discusses 'other responses to patronage' (besides *A Letter to a Noble Lord*) in Burke's writings and those of his contemporaries, especially Samuel Johnson.

their works, and the means by which those works were produced. The advent of print technology had brought with it new ways of thinking about literary production—such ideas, for example, as originality and literary property. 'One of the most important of these print-created literary ideas', argues Alvin Kernan, 'has been a firm conception of the existence of the author, which print established with such substantial factuality that it has largely obliterated even the memory of an older tradition of literary anonymity extending in the European post-classical period from the oral singers of tales, through medieval manuscript culture, well into the Renaissance.' The Renaissance marked the beginning of a profound transition in the European perception and definition of authorship, though the aristocratic tradition of the poet and critic as a gentleman-amateur, for whom, in Pope's words, literature is merely 'the affair of idle men who write in their closets', survived well into the eighteenth century.[20] The custom of anonymous authorship that characterized this tradition of polite letters also continued into the period, though in the case of writers such as Swift, whose name appeared on very few of his works, anonymity was a self-conscious gesture cloaked in elaborate irony and subterfuge.

Roland Barthes and Michel Foucault, among others, have remarked on these changing conceptions of the relation between a text and its author. Foucault observes that discourses are 'objects of appropriation', though the manner of that appropriation differs from one culture or historical period to another. In those discourses containing the 'author function', particularly literary texts of the last three centuries, the form of appropriation has mirrored the forms of ownership in society at large; thus, written works have come to be regarded as the personal, private property of their authors, whose right of ownership has been enshrined in modern copyright law. Foucault's explanation for this development is that books began to be assigned to authors

---

[20] Alvin Kernan, *Printing Technology, Letters, and Samuel Johnson*, reprinted as *Samuel Johnson and the Impact of Print* (Princeton, 1987), 71; Pope, Preface of 1717, in *The Twickenham Edition*, i. 3. For a pioneering treatment of the subject of Pope and print technology, see Marshall McLuhan, 'On Pope's *Dunciad*', in Eugene McNamara (ed.), *The Interior Landscape: The Literary Criticism of Marshall McLuhan 1943–1962* (New York, 1969), 169–79.

in order to fix responsibility or blame for any transgressions—social, political, ideological—committed in the act of writing. One might also wish to point, as do Barthes and Kernan respectively, to the emergence of the 'prestige of the individual' and the dominance of print technology as factors that have fostered the modern conception of the author.[21]

In concluding his reflections on authorship, Foucault calls for a historical analysis of discourse, a methodology that emphasizes not only the formal structures and expressive value of discourses but also their 'modes of existence'—their 'modes of circulation, valorization, attribution, and appropriation'.[22] In the writings of Pope and Burke, such an analysis would seek to explain the attitudes or postures of their authorial personae towards the works into which they have been inserted. One element that both writers emphasize in their self-portraits is their independence. Pope distances himself from the sycophantic dependence of court poets such as Sporus and from the economic and intellectual servitude of the Grub Street tribe, whose writings are commissioned and controlled by persons other than themselves:

> Not Fortune's Worshipper, nor Fashion's Fool,
> Not Lucre's Madman, nor Ambition's Tool,
> Not proud, nor servile, be one Poet's praise
> That if he pleas'd, he pleas'd by manly ways;
> That Flatt'ry, e'en to Kings, he held a shame,
> And thought a Lye in Verse or Prose the same.
>
> (ll. 334–9)

Burke equally insists that his achievements and position have been attained through his own personal merits rather than the favour or bounty of others:

I possessed not one of the qualities, nor cultivated one of the arts, that recommend men to the favour and protection of the great. I was not made for a minion or a tool. As little did I follow the trade of winning the hearts, by imposing on the understandings, of the people. At every step of my progress in life . . . and at every turnpike I met, I was obliged to shew my passport, and again and again to prove my sole title to the

---

[21] Roland Barthes, 'The Death of the Author', in *Image, Music, Text*, trans. Stephen Heath (New York, 1977), 143; Kernan, *Printing*, 73–4.

[22] Michel Foucault, 'What is an Author?' in *The Foucault Reader* ed. Paul Rabinow (New York, 1984), 117.

honour of being useful to my Country, by a proof that I was not wholly unacquainted with it's laws, and the whole system of it's interests both abroad and at home. Otherwise no rank, no toleration even, for me. I had no arts, but manly arts. (ix. 160)

In this passage, as elsewhere in his *Letter*, Burke's rhetoric closely echoes Pope's—both writers asserting, for instance, that their conduct throughout their careers has been 'manly'. Their use of this word, like Johnson's definition of it in his *Dictionary* ('Not womanish'), ineluctably invokes its absent opposite: to be 'manly' means precisely *not* to be 'womanish' in the sense that the latter term evokes a condition of subordination, dependence, and oppression. But in order to enjoy true independence and self-determination, to be politically and socially enabled—to be 'manly', in short—in eighteenth-century England, one had to be a possessor of property; and in the absence of such possession both Pope and Burke found themselves relying on their wit ('a sort of property', to echo Chesterfield's phrase), in their struggles to make their way in the world. In Burke's case, the 'manly arts' by which he achieved a measure of power and influence with his political associates were the eloquent writings and speeches he composed on their behalf, texts which constituted the 'passport' or 'proof' that he was 'not wholly unacquainted' with his country's political interests. Whereas the 'virtue' or political qualification of the overwhelming majority of England's rulers was simply presumed on the basis of their ownership of property, Burke had to ground his claim to leadership in a much rockier soil, the field of his writings and speeches. Thus, like Pope, he was anxious to establish an unequivocal title to his writings by projecting his authorial self, a verbal equivalent of the lord of the manor, into his texts. The very fact that such claims ring a little hollow simply underscores the urgency of such self-definition.

One prominent element in Pope's authorial self-creation is his invention of various 'anti-selves', the contrasting portraits of Atticus, Bufo, and Sporus, against which he defines his personal and poetic values.[23] Each of the portraits enacts, in its own way, an invidious power relationship of exploitation and corrupt

---

[23] See Dustin Griffin, *Alexander Pope: The Poet in the Poems* (Princeton, 1978), 172–90.

dependence, from Atticus's circle of literary toadies and Bufo's vain and self-interested patronage to Sporus's almost literal prostitution of himself for the sake of a dubious access to the centres of political power. Burke's characterization of the Duke of Bedford in his *Letter*, though more diffusely developed than Pope's concentrated verbal portraits in the *Epistle to Dr. Arbuthnot*, performs an analogous function of defining his idealized self by a process of negation. Just as Pope's portrayal of the effeminate, androgynous Sporus emphasizes the first term of Johnson's antonymous definition of 'manly' ('not womanish'), so Burke's character of Bedford plays on the second connotation of the term ('not childish'). Pope alludes only briefly to this aspect of Sporus's unmanliness—'This painted Child of Dirt that stinks and stings'—but Burke gives it a central place in his attack on Bedford. 'I was not, like his Grace of Bedford, swaddled, and rocked, and dandled into a Legislator', he proudly declares. 'I did not come into Parliament to con my lesson' (ix. 159–60). Adopting the forbearing attitude of a tutor towards his errant charge, an unwilling schoolboy, Burke begins to correct the young man's errors: 'I have no doubt of his Grace's readiness in all the calculations of vulgar arithmetick; but I shrewdly suspect, that he is very little studied in the theory of moral proportions; and has never learned the Rule of Three in the arithmetick of policy and state' (ix. 150). One rhetorical advantage of this stance is that in taking the Duke to task for his ignorance, Burke, in his role as pedagogue, is able plausibly to introduce his own views on a wide variety of subjects and justify his conduct in the major political struggles of the time.

Though Burke, like Pope, addresses his letter to a friendly 'adversarius' (now usually identified as Lord Grenville), the customary use of the third-person mode of address with the vocative form 'your Grace' confers an ambiguous sense of audience on the *Letter*, which reads as though it were simultaneously 'spoken' to and scornfully snubbing Bedford. Indeed, readers have occasionally mistakenly assumed that the 'Noble Lord' of the letter's title is Bedford himself.[24] At times

---

[24] Burke pursues a similar strategy in his *Fourth Letter on a Regicide Peace* (actually begun before the other three *Letters* and written at about the same time as *A Letter to a Noble Lord*). The *Fourth Letter* is addressed to Lord Fitzwilliam, his

the *Letter* also reads like a debate in the House of Commons, where arguments directed at one's political opponents are ostensibly addressed to the Speaker, an impartial third party. This is the effect when Burke disputes Bedford's command of the facts regarding the statutes sponsored by the former in his administrative reforms of the early 1780s: 'Does he mean the pay-office act. I take it for granted he does not. The act to which he alludes is, I suppose, the establishment act. I greatly doubt whether his Grace has ever read the one or the other' (ix. 150–1).

This stinging remark forms part of a larger strategy by which Bedford is progressively consigned to the status of one of Pope's hapless dunces—one of the unfortunate products of the shoddy English public education system so scathingly attacked in Book IV of *The Dunciad*. In that poem Pope details the sorry progress of the nation's future leaders from Dr Busby's sadistic pedagogy at Westminster School and Bentley's pedantry as Master of Trinity College, Cambridge, to the finishing touches of dullness conferred by the customary Grand Tour. Pope's description of the 'Boy-Senator' who cowers at the appearance of Busby's ghost could easily stand as the epigraph of Burke's attack on Bedford (ll. 145–8):

> All Flesh is humbled, Westminster's bold race
> Shrink, and confess the Genius of the place:
> The pale Boy-Senator yet tingling stands,
> And holds his breeches close with both his hands.

Much of the strength of Burke's characterization of Bedford derives from the fact that the circumstances of his life so easily lent themselves to such a satiric reading. Indeed, in a striking instance of life's imitation of art, the Duke's educational career exactly recapitulated Pope's duncely paradigm. After attending Westminster School and Trinity College, Cambridge, and travelling for two years on the Continent, he took his seat in the House of Lords but confessed to Lord Holland that he 'had scarcely ever opened a book' and refrained from participating in

---

political patron, but it actually argues against a pamphlet written by Lord Auckland, who is slightly and satirically consigned, like Bedford, to a Dunciad for incompetent writers and statesmen (see Ch. 5, below).

debate for 'fear of exposing himself by speaking incorrect English'.[25] At one level, these parallels are merely an elaborate coincidence; at another level, however, they suggest how keen a social and cultural observer Pope was and how similar the underlying social and political circumstances of Burke's time were to those that prevailed in the early decades of the eighteenth century.

Perhaps the most memorable moment in Burke's portrayal of his childish and dependent anti-self is his grotesque comparison of Bedford to a sea-monster of Brobdingnagian proportions:

> The Duke of Bedford is the Leviathan among all the creatures of the Crown. He tumbles about his unwieldy bulk; he plays and frolicks in the ocean of the Royal bounty. Huge as he is, and whilst 'he lies floating many a rood,' he is still a creature. His ribs, his fins, his whalebone, his blubber, the very spiracles through which he spouts a torrent of brine against his origin, and covers me all over with the spray,—every thing of him and about him is from the Throne. Is it for *him* to question the dispensation of the Royal favour? (ix. 164)

In this passage, Burke combines the energy and verve of the earlier books of *The Dunciad*, particularly their evocation of the anarchic vitality of childhood, with the darker vision of the concluding book, in which bizarre and disturbing transformations of natural objects darkly presage cultural dissolution and the inversion of order. Thus, the tumbling, playful, frolicsome Leviathan is suddenly metamorphosed into the defeated Satan of Milton's *Paradise Lost*, supinely floating in the fiery deep (*PL* I. 196). The crucial feature of Burke's description is his emphasis on this Leviathan as a dependant, a *creature*, of the Crown. The context implicitly invoked is that of the conclusion to the book of Job, when God asserts his absolute sovereignty over even the most awesome of his creatures: 'Canst thou draw out leviathan with an hook? . . . Will he make a covenant with thee? wilt thou take him for a servant forever?' (Job 41: 1, 4). Just as Milton's 'Arch-fiend' cannot so much as stir from the burning lake except

---

[25] Henry Richard Fox, third Baron Holland, *Memoirs of the Whig Party during My Time*, 2 vols. (London, 1852–4), i. 146, 79. Holland also states, however, that once embarked upon his political career, his 'excellent disposition and strong understanding . . . enabled him to surmount an education of indulgence and neglect', 145. See also Albert H. Smyth, 'Life of Burke', in *Edmund Burke's* Letter to a Noble Lord, ed. Smyth (Boston, 1898), p. xxx.

by 'the will | And high permission of all-ruling Heaven' (*PL* I. 211–12), so also Bedford is powerless but for the god-like will and favour of the 'Royal bounty'. He is magically transported to the unnatural, monstrous, parodic world of Milton's Hell, 'Where all life dies, death lives, and Nature breeds, | Perverse, all monstrous, all prodigious things' (*PL* II. 624–5). He has become, by association, a part of the nightmare disorder conjured into existence by the French revolutionaries, a disorder vividly realized in the *Letter* through Burke's revival of a peculiarly Popeian and Swiftian satiric vision. Gerald Chapman observes, in this connection, 'Burke mastered the trick, common in Augustan satire, of transmuting historic persons into burlesque emblems of anti-culture and *lèze-intelligence* [sic], and of lodging them in a burlesque fantasy world of ugliness whose very existence pleads for its opposite.'[26] (This mock-heroic aspect of the *Letter* will be explored in greater detail in Chapter 5, in which Burke's larger debt to Scriblerian satire will be examined.)

III

Pope's readers have often noted that his portraits of his adversaries contain elements that can be referred back to Pope himself; certainly Pope's enemies recognized points of secret affinity between the poet and his literary foes (notably Addison) even if he did not. For Burke, too, his powerful, imaginative representation of his political anti-self rebounds in some ironic ways on its progenitor and can be read as a covert, unacknowledged image of the writer himself. The chief point of correspondence between the two is that both owe their positions and fortunes to the patronage of the Crown. Both are in a very real sense dependants: Burke, most immediately through his acceptance of a royal pension and more indirectly through his association with the Rockingham Whigs; and Bedford, through the Crown grants bestowed upon his ancestor by Henry VIII. This fact involves Burke in a compounding series of ironies as his argument in the *Letter to a Noble Lord* unfolds. His main

---

[26] G. Chapman, *Edmund Burke: The Practical Imagination* (Cambridge, Mass., 1967), 238.

concern is to distance himself from the Duke, who, to pursue Burke's own metaphor, has grown as grotesquely fat as a blubbery whale on the enormous bounty of the Tudor monarchy. Thus, to refute the accusation that his own acceptance of a pension is simply another, if more modest, instance of parasitism, he argues vigorously and persuasively that his subsidy is a legitimate recognition of merit and ability rather than the perpetuation of a prescriptive right, as in the case of Bedford.

But such an argument, if carried to its logical conclusion, undermines the very aristocratic system that Burke has sought to defend against the encroachments of revolutionary republicanism. Indeed, in *Reflections on the Revolution in France*, he had attacked the National Assembly for its repudiation of the fiscal obligations of the *ancien régime*, especially its royal grants and pensions (viii. 156–8). In an early review of the *Letter*, Coleridge was quick to detect this contradiction in Burke's position: 'This is not the only instance to be met with in the course of Mr. Burke's writings, in which he lays down propositions, from which his adversaries are entitled to draw strange corollaries. The egg is his: Paine and Barlow *hatch* it.'[27] Burke himself indicates that he is not unaware of the instability of his rhetoric (or indeed of the rationale for his entire political career): 'I have strained every nerve to keep the Duke of Bedford in that situation, which alone makes him my superior' (ix. 162). Burke gives no quarter to his foe, whose character and family connections he systematically demolishes in the course of his polemic. Indeed the attack on Bedford and his inherited wealth is made necessary by his desire to demonstrate that he is not simply a mouthpiece for the aristocracy: his willingness to expose the dubious historical legality of Bedford's vast estates serves as a gesture of defiant independence in a situation which his acceptance of the pension has rendered ambiguous.

Numerous readers of the *Letter* have noted how, as David Aers puts it, 'Burke's fervent self-defence actually becomes both an attack on inherited privilege and wealth, the basis of aristocracy, and a defence, even a proud celebration, of specifically bourgeois values and an ethos whose outcome is a

---

[27] Samuel Taylor Coleridge, *The Watchman*, 1 (1 Mar. 1796), in *The Collected Works of Samuel Taylor Coleridge*, ed. Kathleen Coburn (London, 1970), ii. 36.

bourgeois meritocracy rather than an aristocratic order.'[28] This outcome unexpectedly places him in an uncomfortable proximity to his most feared and hated political enemies, the French revolutionaries. That proximity stems not only from the sudden recognition of a shared ideology emerging from the slippage of Burke's rhetoric, but also from the realization that a kinship of occupation and enterprise links him and the *philosophes*, whom he holds responsible as intellectual progenitors of the Revolution:

> I am better able to enter into the character of this description of men than the noble Duke can be . . . Without any considerable pretensions to literature in myself, I have aspired to the love of letters. I have lived for a great many years in habitudes with those who professed them. I can form a tolerable estimate of what is likely to happen from a character, chiefly dependent for fame and fortune, on knowledge and talent, as well in it's morbid and perverted state, as in that which is sound and natural. Naturally men so formed and finished are the first gifts of Providence to the World. But when they have once thrown off the fear of God . . . a more dreadful calamity cannot arise out of Hell to scourge mankind. (ix. 176)

Burke is keenly aware of both the indignities and the temptations writers are subject to when they depend on their 'knowledge and talents' for their 'fame and fortune'. The *Reflections*, for example, had devoted several pages to an analysis of the alliance between the *philosophes* and the 'monied interest' in France, which had replaced the previous system of aristocratic patronage: 'What they [writers] lost in the old court protection, they endeavoured to make up by joining in a sort of incorporation of their own' (viii. 160). Deprived of a secure place in the social hierarchy, these writers sold their talents to the highest bidder, and, in consequence, 'a set of literary men [was] converted into a gang of robbers and assassins'.

Burke's observation that he has lived for many years 'in habitudes' with men of letters undoubtedly refers to his long association with Samuel Johnson and his Literary Club. The

---

[28] David Aers, 'Coleridge and the Egg that Burke Laid: Ideological Collusion and Opposition in the 1790s', *Literature and History*, 9 (1983), 152. A recent exploration of Burke's 'ambivalent' allegiance to the aristocratic order is Isaac Kramnick's *The Rage of Edmund Burke: Portrait of an Ambivalent Conservative* (New York, 1977).

reference to Johnson is apt because the latter's situation as a writer so closely mirrored Burke's own relations with his political patrons. Though Johnson achieved a large measure of independence in his professional career as a writer (and was one of the first to do so), few writers, as Alvin Kernan observes, 'worried the question of patronage so persistently as did Johnson'.[29] Like Burke, he found himself in the uncomfortable position of wishing to assert his rejection of the system of aristocratic patronage 'without repudiating the social relationship of which it was a particular instance'. To complicate his situation further, Johnson had in 1762 accepted a royal pension which he maintained was a reward for his literary achievements but which the administration at the time of the American revolution interpreted as a tacit agreement securing them his services as a government propagandist. Thus, Boswell reports, 'He complained to a Right Honourable friend ... that his pension having been given to him as a literary character, he had been applied to by administration to write political pamphlets; and he was even so much irritated, that he declared his resolution to resign his pension.'[30]

Yet, the writer who nostalgically clings to a memory of the old-fashioned reciprocity of literary patronage discovers this social vision increasingly difficult, if not impossible, to sustain. Thus, Burke found himself having to refute charges that his pension was simply payment for services rendered as a government propagandist, an accusation that placed him in a position identical to that of the literary 'cabal' in France, though on opposite sides of the political fence. In a letter to William Windham, he alludes to the insinuation of his enemies 'that what made him independent was given to him to keep him in Dependence. If I were in Parliament tomorrow which God forbid I have nothing to bind me to the ministry but gratitude. ... The Crown and Parliament expects no more service from me' (*Corr.* viii. 341). Another letter to Windham, however, written only days later, suggests a lingering sense of obligation on Burke's side. Meditating on the far-fetched possibility of enlisting to fight the French, he writes, 'However, I am willing to

---

[29] Kernan, *Print Technology*, 103.
[30] Boswell, *Life of Johnson*, ii. 317.

take my Part of it wherever you please. Tell this to Mr Pitt; and assure him, that he has not betrayd his Master by recommending his Bounty to me' (*Corr.* viii. 345). Despite his protestations to the contrary, Burke here reveals a tacit recognition that his strongly stated anti-revolutionary views have at the very least facilitated the administration's grant of his pension, even though no explicit *quid pro quo* had been exacted. His retirement from active party politics—'from the world, and from all it's affairs and all it's pleasures', as he phrases it in the *Letter* (ix. 146)— had not, in fact, meant any retreat from his vigorous anti-Jacobin crusade, which he continued to pursue in his private correspondence with members of the government and in published treatises such as the *Letters on a Regicide Peace*.

The 'author function', as it is manifested in Burke's *Letter*, plays an important role in covering over or reconciling the contradictions that his political career opened up. A brief comparison on this point with Pope's authorial self-creation in *An Epistle to Dr. Arbuthnot* is instructive because the latter's poetic career displays the same rupture between his imagined or ideal self and his actual situation. Like Burke, Pope is sensitive to the delicate problem of attacking in print a representative of an aristocratic order he otherwise endorses, as his letter to Hervey indicates: 'When I speak of *you*, my Lord, it will be with all the deference due to the inequality which Fortune has made between you and myself: but when I speak of your *writings*, my Lord, I must, I can do nothing but trifle.'[31] More importantly, Pope's stance of disinterested independence, on which he grounds his poetic virtue (in contrast with the pecuniary servitude of his professional colleagues), obscures the fact that the material basis for his independence is his success in the very literary marketplace that he now scorns as morally corrupting. In voicing his alarm at the debasing influence of hack writing, however, Pope rejects, as Brean Hammond argues, any trace of the literary work's mode of production: 'Any form of sensitivity to what the government wants, or what a patron wants, or what the reading public wants, is condemned as corruption or commercialism and it seems that only the author who is *entirely*

---

[31] Pope, 'A Letter to a Noble Lord', 442–3.

cut off from the forces that bring books into existence can be celebrated.'³²

Pope's skilful manipulation of the 'author function' in the *Epistle* is his means of concealing the tensions and ambiguities of his position, both as a writer and as a disenfranchised Catholic, and his way of appropriating his literary œuvre as his property, his aristocratic inheritance:

> But why then publish? *Granville* the polite,
> And knowing *Walsh*, would tell me I could write;
> Well-natur'd *Garth* inflam'd with early praise,
> And *Congreve* lov'd, and *Swift* endur'd my Lays;
> The Courtly *Talbot, Somers, Sheffield*, read,
> Ev'n mitred *Rochester* would nod the head,
> And *St. John's* self (great *Dryden's* friends before)
> With open arms receiv'd one poet more.
>
> (ll. 135–42)

Pope offers here his literary genealogy: he is the inheritor, the eldest son, of a courtly tradition, a 'polite', 'knowing', 'well-natur'd' aristocracy that has adopted the poet as one of its own. Towards the end of the poem, having established his aristocratic connections, Pope gives the reader a different genealogy, one that emphasizes the 'gentle Blood' from which his family has sprung. He ratifies his social and literary virtue by idealizing his own origins as the pious son of a Christian father who 'held it for a rule | It was a Sin to call our Neighbour "Fool" ' (ll. 382–3).

A certain fruitful ambiguity accrues around Pope's deployment of his facts; he stresses his filial piety (a Roman, patrician virtue) towards his mother—'Me, let the tender Office long engage | To rock the Cradle of reposing Age' (ll. 408–9)—even though she had been dead two years by the time the *Epistle* was published. His enemies, it is true, had blackened his origins as much as (if not more than) he here exaggerates them, but, if we place his strategy in a wider historical context, we come to recognize that the inscribed poet in *An Epistle to Dr. Arbuthnot*—the virtuous, self-sufficient, militantly independent poet in the poem—reflects in his 'author function . . . the juridical and

---

³² Brean Hammond, *Pope* (Brighton, 1986), 93.

institutional system that encompasses, determines, and articulates the universe of discourses'.[33] Pope's autobiographical self-realization serves as a manifesto of his right to his enjoyment of his literary 'property' and as his qualification to 'speak' his satiric discourse.

Burke similarly enlists his private self to stabilize his sometimes boldly outspoken public discourse. Having attacked Bedford's origins, a move that implicitly undermines the principles of prescriptive right and aristocratic privilege, he is now anxious to reaffirm the existing order and the genetic argument used to justify it. One of the chief means by which he accomplishes this is through a rhetorical transformation of himself into an aristocratic co-equal with Bedford and Lauderdale. In the opening pages of the *Letter*, he adopts a juridical metaphor, insisting on his right to have his conduct judged by a jury of his equals: 'I claim, not the letter, but the spirit of the old English law, that is, to be tried by my peers. I decline his Grace's jurisdiction as a judge. I challenge the Duke of Bedford as a juror to pass upon the value of my services' (ix. 149). Burke's pun on the word 'peers' and his exclusion of the Duke from the jury that is to judge the merits of his case complicate the relations of class and standing between him and Bedford, ironies reinforced by the subsequent strokes of his self-portrait. The most poignant and personal element in this portrait is his grief-stricken account of his only son's premature death, shattering the dynastic ambitions he had fondly pursued on the latter's behalf. The imagery with which he describes this cataclysm is revealing: 'The storm has gone over me; and I lie like one of those old oaks which the late hurricane has scattered about me. I am stripped of all my honours; I am torn up by the roots, and lie prostrate on the earth!' (ix. 171). The image of the oak, as all readers of Burke are aware, is his favourite metaphor for the stability and continuity of the aristocratic order, a circumstance that makes his application of it to his own situation doubly significant. Perhaps the most celebrated instance of this motif is the passage in a letter from Burke to the Duke of Richmond in which he contrasts his humble origins with the Duke's exalted family connections:

---

[33] Foucault, 'What is an Author?', 113.

> You people of great families and hereditary trusts and fortunes are not like such as I am, who whatever we may be by the Rapidity of our growth and of the fruit we bear, flatter ourselves that while we creep on the Ground we belly into melons that are exquisite for size and flavour, yet still we are but annual plants that perish with our season and leave no sort of traces behind us. You, if you are what you ought to be, are the great Oaks that shade a country and perpetuate your benefits from Generation to Generation. (*Corr.* ii. 377)

In this letter, written in 1772, Burke is content to characterize himself as an 'annual' growth that, although sheltered by the perpetual oak, perishes with the onset of winter, but in *A Letter to a Noble Lord* he explicitly identifies himself with the mighty tree itself, albeit a blasted and uprooted one. The illusion of continuity that the long-lived oak conveys has been shattered by the winds of revolutionary change just at the time when Burke was about to plant his own family tree alongside his country's more luxuriant growths. As an organic metaphor for the aristocracy's self-perpetuating ideology, therefore, the oak proves to be a prophetically unstable vehicle.

The public and the private are both implicated in Burke's image of the uprooted oak, as they are throughout the *Letter*. Indeed, he recognizes from the beginning that Bedford's and Lauderdale's personal attacks on him are motivated 'from zeal to the cause' rather than from any deep-seated personal animus. It is simply that Burke, like Pope before him, has become so prominently identified with a particular cultural and political stance (in this instance, the counter-revolutionary cause), that even in the twilight of his approaching death he remains a force to be feared. 'Why will they not let me remain in obscurity and inaction? . . . Must I be annihilated, lest, like old *John Zisca's*, my skin might be made into a drum, to animate Europe to eternal battle, against a tyranny that threatens to overwhelm all Europe, and all the human race?' (ix. 147). Nowhere are these public and private selves more thoroughly merged than in Burke's elegaic tribute to his son, who was to have justified through his exertions the confidence that the Crown had placed in Burke's family with its conferral of a royal pension:

> Had it pleased God to continue to me the hopes of succession, I should have been, according to my mediocrity, and the mediocrity of the age I live in, a sort of founder of a family; I should have left a son, who, in all

the points in which personal merit can be viewed . . . would not have shewn himself inferior to the Duke of Bedford, or to any of those whom he traces in his line. His Grace very soon would have wanted all plausibility in his attack upon that provision which belonged more to mine than to me. He would soon have supplied every deficiency, and symmetrized every disproportion. It would not have been for that successor to resort to any stagnant wasting reservoir of merit in me, or in any ancestry. (ix. 170)

In adapting the strategy of genetic self-justification to his own situation, Burke offers the reader an inverted, prospective genealogy—one that looks forward to the family name he had hoped to establish. The very phrase, 'symmetrized every disproportion', suggests by metonymy the architectural confirmation (a Palladian mansion, perhaps) that would have accompanied his family's new-found status. But though his obsession with his family line apes the attitudes of the aristocracy, his determination to establish it on the basis of 'personal merit' argues an endorsement of a new attitude of professionalism characteristic of self-made men of letters (like Burke himself) in an age of print technology. He longed in vain to pass on a landed inheritance to his son, yet the only title he might have been able to bequeath was a seat in the House of Commons rather than the Lords, the pocket borough of Malton controlled by Lord Fitzwilliam. Even the avenues through which political merit could establish itself remained ironically in the gift of the Duke of Bedford's peers.

The uncomfortable intensity of Burke's grief, together with the sometimes baroque language in which it is expressed, points to what remains for many readers the central critical crux of the 'letter to a noble lord' form—the undeniable fact that the source of its energy lies so near the surface in the author's outraged sense of personal grievance. Rosemary Cowler singles out this same problem in Pope's initial reply to Lord Hervey, which suffers, in her view, from a lack of distance and control. As an example she cites the following passage in Pope's 'Letter', arguing that the simile of animal sacrifice invoked there by the poet 'become[s] Hervey's, with Pope losing control of it as he elicits distress from the reader rather than scorn'. Pope writes,

I know your Genius and hers so perfectly *tally*, that you cannot but join in admiring each other, and by consequence in the contempt of all such as myself. You have both, in my regard, been like... *Two Princes*, and I like a *poor Animal* sacrificed between them to cement a lasting League: I hope I have not bled in vain; but that such an amity may endure forever!

This uncertainty and vulnerability of tone vanish, according to Cowler, in the *Epistle to Dr. Arbuthnot* where, secure behind his satiric mask, Pope sets 'his sights more coldly on his prey'.[34] Her view falls in with Maynard Mack's influential reading of Pope as a poet whose satire succeeds by transcending its historical moment—finding, in Hervey's case, 'what would be found representatively offensive about such a figure, always, everywhere, and by all'.[35] But in tracing the social and historical relationships that propelled the rapid development of the 'letter to a noble lord' form, one is driven to the opposite conclusion. What makes Burke's or Pope's *apologia pro vita sua* so compelling is precisely its rootedness in the life and circumstances of its author and its frank espousal of the cult of authorship—the writer as a celebrity and personality.

IV

Paul Fussell has noted the powerfully elegaic mood of the *Letter to a Noble Lord*, a mood in which the public and private modes of Burke's epistle are reconciled or find their common expression. The elegy, argues Fussell, is a significant and characteristic literary mode for the conservative, whose motive is 'moral and social action, the maintenance of continuity and coherence, the vivification of the present by a linkage to the temporal chain of being that is the past'.[36] That sense of mourning for a passing cultural order in the *Letter* (and Burke's larger sense of society as a contract among the dead, the living, and those yet to be born) become associated with his own private grief:

I live in an inverted order. They who ought to have succeeded me are gone before me. They who should have been to me as posterity are in the place of ancestors. I owe to the dearest relation (which must ever

---

[34] Cowler, *Prose Works*, 438, 446.
[35] Mack, *Alexander Pope*, 610.
[36] Fussell, *Rhetorical World of Augustan Humanism*, 283.

subsist in memory) that act of piety, which he would have performed to me; I owe it to him to shew that he was not descended, as the Duke of Bedford would have it, from an unworthy parent. (ix. 171).

This passage spells out Burke's motive for his initial recourse to the 'letter to a noble lord' form and explains his transformation of the genre through his inclusion of other literary modes and forms that equally serve as powerful reminders of the past. These include, as has previously been observed, the georgic, with its illustrious classical pedigree, and satire, which, as Fussell reminds us, blends naturally with 'elegiac action, for all satire assumes some identifiable paradigm of virtue which folly has willingly let die'.[37]

The pervasive elegiac and nostalgic stance of the *Letter* cannot be sustained, however, without a certain literary sleight of hand on Burke's part. Like his early eighteenth-century literary predecessors, he is a socially unlikely heir of the classical tradition to which he lays claim. His very recourse to the modern 'letter to an eminent person' form underscores, as I have already argued, the instability of his position. This circumstance explains Burke's commitment to an intertextual understanding of literary forms, in which new or ephemeral genres are legitimized by their appropriation of features belonging to older, more prestigious kinds. Indeed, from the moment of the letter's conception, Burke sought a classical sanction for his literary and social presumption, as his correspondence with Windham indicates: 'I had made some progress in a Letter to Lord Grenville, who behaved handsomely in the House of Lords; in that I took some Notice (as much as he deserved) of the Duke of Bedford. As to him I may say—Tecum est mihi Sermo Rubelli!' (*Corr.* viii. 342).

Burke's Latin tag—'It is to you, Rubellius ... that I speak'— directs the reader to Juvenal's eighth *Satire* (l. 39), which opens with the pointed (and pertinent) question, 'Stemmata quid faciunt?':

What avail your pedigrees? What boots it, Ponticus, to be valued for one's ancient blood, and to display the painted visages of one's forefathers? ... Though you deck your hall from end to end with ancient waxen images, Virtue is the one and only true nobility. ... For

[37] Ibid. 283.

who can be called 'noble' who is unworthy of his race, and distinguished in nothing but his famous name?[38]

Burke's own position mirrors exactly that of Juvenal's low-born Roman speaker, who 'pleads the cause of the unlettered noble', but perhaps even more important than the striking parallel is the legitimacy this official, classical precedent confers upon his ambivalent protest. The classical tradition accommodates Burke's dissatisfaction and permits him, paradoxically, to register his social discontent in the guise of a *defence* of the existing order. Significantly, however, he suppresses any explicit reference to the Juvenalian precedent in the published version of *A Letter to a Noble Lord*. As with Pope and Swift in their deployment of the mock-heroic mode, the cultural and literary norm from which Burke launches his attack is present only by implication; the overwhelming experience for the reader is in fact that of a writer on the offensive, marshalling forces withering and corrosive in their effects. If this is 'elegiac action' or a rhetoric of nostalgia, it is emphatically a militant rather than a quiescent nostalgia.

That militancy manifests itself, first of all, in Burke's bold identification of himself and his private fate with the historical destiny of Britain. Thus, the tone of elegiac action, the curious perspective generated in the *Letter* of an epoch and its heroic representative witnessing their own passing and burial, is heightened by a resonance of parallel historical action: the revolutionaries here turn the very bricks and mortar of the aristocratic establishment against itself, just as previously the coffins of the dead, the departed partners in the social contract, have been desecrated to furnish lead for revolutionary bullets. These grim images derive from the polemical literature of the English Revolution. In his *Elegy upon the most Incomparable King Charls the First*, Bishop Henry King had castigated the insurrectionary forces in precisely the same terms:

> ... neither Tomb nor Temple could escape,
> Nor Dead nor Living, your Licentious Rape.
> Statues and Grave-stones o'r men buried
> Rob'd of their Brass, the Coffins of their Led.
> (ll. 169–72)

[38] Juvenal, *Satire VIII*, in *Juvenal and Persius* (Loeb Classical Library), trans. G. G. Ramsay (Cambridge, Mass., 1979), 158–61.

Taking a leaf from Swift, Burke exploits a historical typology in which the events of the Civil War (and, elsewhere in the *Letter*, those of the Reformation under Henry VIII) are allegorized as precursory types of the French Revolution. More daringly and melodramatically, he aligns his personal lot with the history of his country by insisting on a parallel between the acts of desecration charged to the Puritans in the 1640s and the attempts of Bedford and Lauderdale to blacken his reputation and profane his memory. In both cases coffins of the dead (or near-dead) are 'unplumbed' (the Miltonic pun on the Latin etymology of the word is well chosen) to harass the living—and Burke, with one foot in the grave, aligns himself by turns with both the living and the dead. Having identified himself so closely with the fate of his country, past and present, he 'vindicates the English past', as one reader of the *Letter* puts it, by 'vindicating himself'.[39] The line between public and private, which the 'letter to a noble lord' form so ambivalently straddles, is all but erased.

The crowning instance of militant nostalgia in the *Letter* is Burke's concluding verbal portrait of the late Lord Keppel. His rhetorical strategy in invoking the memory of Keppel falls in with Pope's aristocratic genealogy in *An Epistle to Dr. Arbuthnot*, linking the poet with the previous generation of great men renowned for their taste and judgement. Burke's recollection of Keppel emphasizes the filial, familial bond between them, a bond that he makes bold to extend to his son Richard, whose passing had blasted his dynastic hopes. He underscores their intimate connection, moreover, by his calculatedly off-hand mention of a portrait of Keppel in his possession, a picture executed by their mutual friend Joshua Reynolds: '[Lord Keppel] was much in my heart, and I believe I was in his to the very last beat. It was after his trial at Portsmouth that he gave me this picture. With what zeal and anxious affection I attended him through his agony of glory, what part my son in the early flush and enthusiasm of his virtue, and the pious passion with which he attached himself to all my connections, with what prodigality we both squandered ourselves in courting almost every sort of enmity for his sake' (ix.

---

[39] Stephen H. Browne, *Edmund Burke and the Discourse of Virtue* (Tuscaloosa, Ala., 1993), 110.

181). The trial to which Burke refers was a court martial of Keppel, then an admiral, for his alleged incompetence during an engagement with the French fleet off the Isle of Ushant on 24–7 July 1778. Suspecting government treachery, the Rockingham Whigs, with whom Keppel was associated, rallied to the admiral's side, and Burke was designated to help compose the address with which the Admiral introduced his successful court defence. In gratitude for Burke's active support, Keppel presented him with a portrait of himself, one of five executed by Sir Joshua Reynolds.

Burke's invocation of Keppel's memory met with the sharp disapproval of several readers, including Horace Walpole. Though Walpole was full of admiration for the intellectual powers displayed in the *Letter*, he felt that Burke had gone altogether too far with his panegyric on Keppel and dismissed the entire passage as '*déplacé*' and 'preposterous'.[40] Yet, despite this sneer at Burke's apparent lapse of taste, the decision to close the *Letter* with an appeal to Keppel is well calculated, for it crystallizes the central issues addressed in the *Letter*, especially the ironies arising from Burke's ambiguous political and social position. It would appear that Bedford, who is Keppel's nephew, has much the stronger, because hereditary claim upon the honours and accomplishments of his uncle. But Burke strips Bedford of his dynastic pretensions by asserting a connection even stronger than that of kinship. The men who came to Keppel's aid when he was threatened with court martial, disgrace, and perhaps even death were his friends in the Rockingham party, not the members of the family into which his sister had married. On the contrary, many of the Bedford clan's political connections were in varying degrees arrayed in opposition against him. Not only had the Bedford party been largely absorbed into Lord North's administration, under whose aegis the court martial of Keppel went forward, but the First Lord of the Admiralty, Lord Sandwich, an old rival of Keppel's (who, according to the Duke of Richmond, was not to be trusted 'for a piece of ropeyarn'), had himself been a close associate of

---

[40] Horace Walpole, *The Correspondence of Horace Walpole*, ed. W. S. Lewis *et al.* (New Haven, 1937–83), xxxiv. 215.

the fourth Duke of Bedford before the latter's death in 1771.[41]

Burke thus invites his readers to infer that he deserves recognition over Bedford as Keppel's true heir and descendent—by spiritual if not physical propinquity. Bedford is merely a relation by blood; Burke, by ability and service—'otherwise', as he had declared earlier in the *Letter*, 'no rank . . . for me' (viii. 160). Moreover, his connection with Keppel, as with the rest of the Rockingham Whigs, is based on principle: he moves away from the prevailing eighteenth-century view that 'connections' meant ties by marriage, consanguinity, or patronage in favour of the view that connections had to be sustained by a shared political creed and programme of action. From this point of view the Bedfords were hardly a connection at all. They had defected to the government side of the House in 1768, and their loyalties had splintered after the death of the fourth Duke whereas the Rockingham Whigs had remained resolutely in opposition. One branch of the party followed Earl Gower, and another group associated with Lord Sandwich, while the Duke's widow, the Dowager Duchess of Bedford, retained substantial control of her husband's electoral interest and pursued her own course. So much, Burke implies, for the fidelity and principles of the Bedfords, who appear motivated solely by the bad old pursuits of place and profit. In speaking out against those principles that had animated his uncle, the current Duke of Bedford has acted not as the scion of a great family but as the spokesman for a 'vile faction'—the 'faction of the homicides' (ix. 185–6). Under these circumstances Burke asserts the priority of his claim to Keppel's legacy and of his right to hang Keppel's likeness in his own family gallery.

Whatever personal satisfaction Burke's appropriation of the Bedford family portrait gallery may have afforded him, his tribute to Keppel also resonates with ideological significance. He commemorates Keppel in a grand, epic manner reminiscent

---

[41] Letter from the Duke of Richmond to Admiral Keppel, 19 Nov. 1776, quoted in Thomas Keppel, *The Life of Augustus Viscount Keppel* (London, 1842), ii. 4. On the Bedford party and its role in the parliamentary politics of the 1770s and 1780s, see I.R. Christie, *The End of North's Ministry: 1780–82* (London, 1958), 203–9 *et passim*; and H. Butterfield, *George III, Lord North, and the People: 1779–80* (1949; repr. New York, 1968), 117–38 *et passim*.

of Reynolds: 'Though it was never shewn in insult to any human being, Lord Keppel was something high. It was a wild stock of pride, on which the tenderest of all hearts had grafted the milder virtues. He valued ancient nobility; and he was not disinclined to augment it with new honours' (ix. 182). The character and role Burke assigns to Keppel echo repeated idealizations of the gentleman in the literature and portraiture of the eighteenth century, including Burke's own composite portrait of the natural aristocrat in *An Appeal from the New to the Old Whigs* (Bohn, iii. 85–6). John Barrell has noted, in reference to James Thomson's *The Seasons*, how such descriptions function as

> the nearest imaginable equivalent, in verse, of the style of heroic, of 'historic' portraiture we associate particularly with Sir Joshua Reynolds. The distinction between one gentleman and another, is, as often in Reynolds's work, less remarkable than what they are represented as having in common—the same blend of the great but few virtues and attributes necessary to the patriot: a piercing intelligence, a patriotic ardour, and a disinterested spirit. That uniformity is imagined as justified in portrait painting by the exemplary functions of the art: the ideal of Reynolds is that portraiture increases in importance as a genre the more nearly it approaches history painting—the more, that is, that it discovers a universal nobility of feature, of character, of virtue in its subjects, and the less therefore that it represents them as particular men.[42]

The attributes of Reynolds's heroic style highlighted by Barrell are precisely those Burke stresses in his account of Keppel, which glosses over the particulars of the man's career—his naval service, for instance—and types him instead as the epitome of the gentleman and paints in rich colours his ancient, noble ancestry. 'His goodness of heart, his reason, his taste, his publick duty, his principles, his prejudices' (ix. 182)—these are the broad strokes (though never instanced or specified) that make up Burke's character of Keppel.

Burke in fact senses no need to furnish details, to particularize his portrait with the evidence of Keppel's actions or decisions. Keppel's character is simply to be presumed from his family connections and social position: 'He considered [nobility] as a

---

[42] John Barrell, *English Literature in History 1730–80: An Equal, Wide Survey* (London, 1983), 69–70.

sort of cure for selfishness and a narrow mind; conceiving that a man born in an elevated place, in himself was nothing, but every thing in what went before, and what was to come after him' (ix. 183). Keppel the man is assimilated to his social role of gentleman, which, in turn, is grounded in the ideals of 'civic humanism', the view that possession of landed property confers upon the individual the necessary wealth, leisure, and independence to become rational, pursue virtue, and exercise the responsibilities of citizenship. In the lengthy preamble to Keppel's defence at his trial in Portsmouth, which was written by Burke, the same gentlemanly qualities of comprehensiveness and disinterestedness are emphasized. Keppel maintains that his 'forty years' endeavours' had not been 'marked by the possession of any one favour from the Crown', nor had he 'intrigued, or solicited the command' but rather received it 'entirely unsought'. Moreover, in exercising his command he had acted on 'principles of large discretion . . . [and] foresight'.[43] A comparison of the revised version of the trial, from which these citations are taken, with an earlier, verbatim version reveals that the extensive characterization of Keppel as a disinterested officer and gentleman was largely an addition to the initially published transcript.[44] Clearly, Burke regarded this vindication of Keppel as a gentleman as central to his refutation of the charges of misconduct and neglect of duty. The subject of the gentleman and the pivotal role he plays in Burke's conception of the polity will be the subject of the two chapters that follow; for the present, it suffices to recognize how thoroughly idealized and emblematic a figure Burke constructs out of the actual Lord Keppel.

---

[43] *The Proceedings at Large of the Court-Martial, on the Trial of the Honourable Augustus Keppel . . . on Thursday, January 7th, 1779 . . . Taken in Short Hand, by W. Blanchard, for the Admiral, and Published by his Permission* (London, 1779), 123–4.
[44] See *An Authentic and Impartial Copy of the Trial of the Hon. Augustus Keppel . . . Taken in Short Hand, by a Person who attended during the whole Trial. And Printed by the Desire of a Society of Gentlemen* (Portsmouth, 1779). The various printed versions of the trial and Burke's contributions to each are detailed in William B. Todd, *A Bibliography of Edmund Burke* (London, 1964), 92–7. For a discussion of Burke's role in the trial, see Michel Fuchs, 'Edmund Burke et Augustus Keppel', *Études Anglaises*, 18 (1965), 18–26. See also Burke, *Correspondence*, iv. 30–1, 35–8, 42–4.

Burke's character of Keppel allows him to conclude the *Letter* on a suitably deferential note, without actually conceding, however, the ambiguities he has been negotiating throughout his polemic. For if, on the one hand, Keppel is Bedford's uncle and the very personification of Old Whig aristocratic virtues, 'who was himself given to England, along with the blessings of the British and Dutch revolutions' (ix. 186), he is also, as one astute reader of the *Letter* notes, 'a figure created in Burke's own likeness'.[45] Like Pope in *An Epistle to Dr. Arbuthnot*, Burke has moved well beyond the rhetorical appropriation of an illustrious ancestry to an assertion of himself as the actual, rather than presumptive, embodiment of the values that men of Keppel's class are meant to represent. Just as Pope proudly maintains the disinterested independence that ought to define the situation of his ignobly noble foes, so too Burke, throughout his long political career, has enacted, as if by proxy, the role of the gentleman that an accident of birth had assigned to others. That role, as will become apparent, is inscribed in the life of the country gentleman he purchased for himself and in the comprehensiveness with which he grasped and was able to articulate the complexity of his country's political relations.

Pope ends his verse epistle by retreating demurely into the domestic sphere, though the effect of his poem has been to render problematic the distinction between his domestic and his public selves. Burke too concludes by demarcating the boundary between his personal quarrel with Bedford and the public, political differences that divide them: 'He never shall, with the smallest colour of reason, accuse me of being the author of a peace with Regicide. But that is high matter; and ought not to be mixed with any thing of so little moment, as what may belong to me, or even to the Duke of Bedford' (ix. 187). Yet this seemingly innocuous conclusion conceals perhaps the most savage irony of all, for the burden of Burke's argument has been diametrically opposite to what he so self-deprecatingly concedes in his closing sentence. What once belonged to Bedford now belongs to Burke, and what belongs to Burke has been vindicated as rightfully his and, indeed, as belonging also to the nation.

---

[45] Browne, *Edmund Burke*, 115.

2
States and Estates: Burke's Georgic Arts of Political Husbandry

> The happy rustic turns the fruitful soil,
> And hence proceeds the year's revolving toil;
> On this his country for support depends,
> On this his cattle, family, and friends.
> . . . .
> By arts like these divine Etruria grows,
> From such foundations mighty Rome arose.
> Virgil, *Georgics*, 2, trans. Edmund Burke[1]
>
> But these are not the honours of the dome
> Where Burke resides and strangers find a home
> . . . .
> Like Virgil, prince of Latin poets, he,
> Lover of rural life and poesy,
> Improves with skilful industry the soil,
> Cheers the poor peasant, and rewards his toil.
> from Mary Leadbeater, 'Beaconsfield'[2]

'You will observe,' writes Burke in *Reflections on the Revolution in France*, 'that from Magna Charta to the Declaration of Right, it has been the uniform policy of our constitution to claim and assert our liberties, as an *entailed inheritance* derived to us from our forefathers, and to be transmitted to our posterity; as an estate specially belonging to the people of this kingdom' (viii. 83). This statement, which introduces a celebrated passage

---

[1] Published in *Poems on Several Occasions* (Dublin, 1748). Repr. in James Prior, *Life of the Right Honourable Edmund Burke*, 3rd edn. (London, 1839), 14–16; and excerpted in A. P. I. Samuels, *The Early Life, Correspondence and Writings of the Rt. Hon. Edmund Burke* (Cambridge, 1923), 92–3.
[2] Quoted in Peter Burke, *The Public and Domestic Life of the Right Honourable Edmund Burke*, 2nd edn. (London, 1854), 125.

eulogizing the British constitution, establishes what he calls a 'philosophic analogy' between his country's constitutional principles and its system of land tenure and ownership. British society, he asserts, is like a landed estate, and the citizens of the commonwealth are like landowners and tenants in the English countryside, whose relation to their land and their posterity should ideally be one of aristocratic stewardship: 'one of the first and most leading principles on which the commonwealth and the laws are consecrated, is lest the temporary possessors and life-renters in it, unmindful of what they have received from their ancestors, or of what is due to their posterity, should act as if they were the entire masters; that they should not think it amongst their rights to cut off the entail, or commit waste upon the inheritance, by destroying at their pleasure the whole original fabric of their society; hazarding to leave to those who come after them, a ruin instead of a habitation' (viii. 145).

Burke's characterization of the British constitution as an 'entailed inheritance' is significant, for it signals just how concretely his analogy is grounded in the economic and social practices of his time. The practice of entailing an estate not only ensured that the eldest male heir would inherit the family fortune but also guaranteed that the current holder of the property was restricted from doing what he liked with it: the possessor was, in Burke's phrase, merely a 'life-renter'. When the heir came of age, father and son could agree to dispose of land, but the social pressure to preserve the family property was enormous. In G. E. Mingay's words, 'Both father and son felt the obligation to maintain the family inheritance and carry it forward to future generations, and they understood that the status of the family depended on it.'[3] From these legal arrangements it was easy to argue by analogy for a special relationship between Britain's great landed families and the country's constitutional and historical continuity, as Burke does in a oft-cited letter to the Duke of Richmond:

---

[3] G. E. Mingay, *English Landed Society in the Eighteenth Century* (London, 1963), 34. For a discussion of the legal expedients of 'entail' and 'strict settlement', see Lawrence Stone and Jeanne C. Fawtier Stone, *An Open Élite? England 1540–1880* (Oxford, 1984), 72–82.

The immediate power of a D. of Richmond or a Marquis of R[ockingha]m is not so much of moment but if their conduct and example hands down their principles to their successors; then their houses become the publick repositories and offices of Record for the constitution, Not like the Tower or Rolls Chappel where it is searched for and sometimes in Vain, in rotten parchments under dripping and perishing Walls; but in full vigour and acting with vital Energy and power in the Characters of the leading men and natural interests of the Country. (*Corr.* ii. 377, dated post 15 November 1772)

Burke's analogy, like Jesus' parable of the talents, also encourages a sense of responsibility in the landholder, prompting him to leave to his successor an estate of greater value than he had inherited. All these concerns—of stewardship, inheritance, and continuity—coalesce, as will become apparent, in the eighteenth-century's allegiance to the discourse of improvement.

The link in this passage between patrimony and patriotism, estate and country, is a literary and political commonplace that hardly originates with Burke—far from it—but in this instance the source or inspiration of the illustration is to be found as much in his practical pursuits as in his literary and political interests. Early in his political career Burke had himself become the possessor of a not inconsiderable estate, and, as his own correspondence and contemporary observers equally testify, he took a keen interest in its operation. Thus, a passing remark in a letter to his boyhood friend Richard Shackleton announcing his purchase of 'Gregories', an imposing Palladian house and grounds situated near Beaconsfield, adumbrates a complex of themes, a web of social practices and literary discourses, that had preoccupied him from his student days at Trinity College, Dublin, and came to inform the political writings of his maturity:

I have made a push with all I could collect of my own, and the aid of my friends to cast a little root in this Country. I have purchased an house, with an Estate of about 600 acres of Land in Buckinghamshire 24 Miles from London; where I now am; It is a place exceedingly pleasant; and I propose, God willing, to become a farmer in good earnest. You who are classical will not be displeased to hear, that it was formerly the Seat of Waller the Poet, whose house, or part of it, makes at present the Farmhouse within an hundred yards of me. (*Corr.* i. 351)

Burke proposes, first of all, 'to cast a little root in this Country'—to establish, that is, a landed inheritance—though whether he is ambitious to strike roots that will eventually produce an aristocratic oak (in emulation of his great Whig patrons) or grow only 'annual plants that perish with our Season', he diplomatically omits to say (*Corr.* ii. 377). He vows, moreover, 'to become a farmer in good earnest'. This was no idle pledge, as Arthur Young, the great eighteenth-century proponent of agricultural improvement, attested. Young reported enthusiastically on Burke's agricultural experiments (including such projects as deep ploughing, drainage, crop rotation, and livestock feeding) and remarked approvingly, 'His country is much indebted to him for giving so laudable an attention to the improvement of her husbandry.'[4] Finally, in Burke's mention of Edmund Waller as a former proprietor of his lands, he invokes aristocratic, classical, and literary associations to define the context within which his rural activities are to be understood and interpreted.[5] In 1784 when Shackleton's daughter Mary visited Burke at Beaconsfield, she composed verses in praise of her host which touch elegantly on all these themes of rural praise:

> Lo! there the mansion stands in princely pride;
> The beauteous wings extend on either side:
> Unsocial pomp flies from the cheerful gate,
> Where hospitality delights to wait.
> . . . .
> For here of old, yon waving woods among,
> With Waller's strains the joyful valleys rung.[6]

Entailed inheritance, estate improvement, classical ideals of rural life—in drawing together these topics of eighteenth-century cultural discourse, Burke appears to be charting well-trodden, thoroughly cultivated ground. Thus, when he argues,

---

[4] Arthur Young, *The Farmer's Tour through the East of England* (London, 1771), iv. 84.

[5] For accounts of Burke's self-fashioning as a landed gentleman and gentleman farmer, see Carl B. Cone, *Burke and the Nature of Politics* (Lexington, Ken., 1957), i. 123–43; and Cone, 'Edmund Burke, the Farmer', *Agricultural History*, 19 (1945), 65–9. For Burke's early interest in the literature of rural praise, see Samuels, *The Early Life of Burke, passim.*

[6] Mary [Shackleton] Leadbeater, *The Leadbeater Papers* (London, 1862), i. 136.

in elaborating on his characterization of the British polity as an inherited estate, 'the people of England well know, that the idea of inheritance furnishes a sure principle of conservation, and a sure principle of transmission; without at all excluding a principle of improvement' (viii. 83–4), the terms of his argument—conservation balanced against improvement— appear altogether unexceptionable in their harmony and consistency. But a closer examination of his language in its late eighteenth-century context reveals unexpected stresses, unstable and contradictory meanings. One need only juxtapose William Cowper's disapproval of his countrymen's blind worship of improvement with Burke's characteristically affirmative use of the term to recognize that his account of the British constitution is far from unproblematic:

> Mansions once
> Knew their own masters; and laborious hinds
> Who had surviv'd the father, serv'd the son.
> Now the legitimate and rightful lord
> Is but a transient guest, newly arriv'd,
> And soon to be supplanted. He that saw
> His patrimonial timber cast its leaf,
> Sells the last scantling, and transfers the price
> To some shrewd sharper, ere it buds again.
>
> . . . .
> Improvement too, the idol of the age,
> Is fed with many a victim. Lo, he comes!
> Th' omnipotent magician, Brown, appears!
> Down falls the venerable pile, th' abode
> Of our forefathers—a grave whisker'd race,
> But tasteless. Springs a palace in its stead.[7]
>   (*The Task*, III. 746–69)

Cowper's view of the ancestral estate suggests that principles of 'inheritance' and 'conservation' are wildly incompatible with the mania for improvement which swept the British countryside in the period. In Cowper's eyes improvement is a destructive, corrosive force that obliterates rather than preserves the past.

It is important to recognize, at the outset, that the word

---

[7] William Cowper, *The Task*, in *The Poetical Works of William Cowper*, ed. Humphrey Summer Milford, 4th edn. (London, 1934), 180.

'improvement' had a semantic resonance and complexity for the eighteenth century that it no longer carries today. Its meaning was a ground of contestation. Thus, when Burke adopts 'improvement' as a key term in his political discourse, a wealth of associations, some of them unwelcome and unintended, crowd in upon his argument. An example of this is William Marshall's usage in describing the primitive farming practices of Devonshire farmers, which included, to his amazement, the biblical spectacle of winnowing grain with the wind: 'Their KNOWLEDGE is of course confined; and the SPIRIT OF IMPROVEMENT deeply buried under an accumulation of custom and prejudice.'[8] Clearly, Burke would not have welcomed this opposition between 'improvement' and 'custom' or 'prejudice', but Marshall's usage serves as a warning that an argument by analogy can lead to unintended conclusions.

One might be accused of taxing Burke unfairly with these complex meanings, particularly when he uses a word only in passing or in a local rhetorical context. But the concept of improvement and the larger analogy of the estate within which it is lodged clearly hold a special significance for Burke, beyond the numerous other analogies and illustrations that flowed from his pen. One means of verifying this claim is to observe the transformative power of this recurrent metaphor in Burke's prose, its capacity to transcend its immediate rhetorical context, becoming in the process a formal principle in the text, like the organizing pull of a magnet on a sheet of iron filings. At the level of content, improvement functions as a powerful political principle in Burke's writings, but its full articulation leads to a realization of the content of his idea at the level of form. This process of exfoliation of content into form is described by Fredric Jameson: 'here form is regarded not as the initial pattern or mold, as that from which we start, but rather as that with which we end up, as but the final articulation of the deeper logic of the content itself'.[9]

---

[8] William Marshall, *The Rural Economy of the West of England* (London, 1796), i. 106, 184.

[9] Fredric Jameson, *Marxism and Form: Twentieth-Century Dialectical Theories of Literature* (Princeton, 1971), 328–9.

All this sounds rather abstract and demands further elaboration. The features of Burke's political discourse I propose to explore in this chapter must be situated, first of all, within the larger social and economic discourse of improvement prevalent in eighteenth-century English society. One soon discovers, however, that this optimistic language of practical affairs in turn draws many of its themes and rhetorical conventions from the ancient literary tradition of the pastoral and the georgic. This continuing reliance on traditional literary forms and modes of thought by authors of technical treatises on economics or agriculture has been observed by Richard Feingold, who argues,

> It is precisely because the countryside and the farm, actual and literary, have served for over two thousand years as moral ideas, imaginative touchstones for the criticism of social and political life, that the pastoral and the georgic could become so crucially important to men, poets and projectors and political economists, who sought for an understanding of their burgeoning England. If the pastoral and the georgic are forms of social and political understanding, then it should not be surprising that their attitudinal and expressive habits can be seen, in their strengths and weaknesses, in the imaginative and critical thought of political economists and agrarian capitalists as well as of poets.[10]

The ideology of improvement and imperial expansion demanded the muse and found its voice in a poetry of praise whose formal roots can be traced back to Virgil's *Georgics*. A similar relationship of content to form is to be found, as will become apparent, in Burke's political writings. His 'philosophic analogy' of the estate and its improvement manifests itself in his works not only as a political doctrine but also as a distinctive georgic mode of writing that becomes a recurrent and familiar feature of his prose.

---

[10] Richard Feingold, *Nature and Society: Later Eighteenth-Century Uses of the Pastoral and Georgic* (New Brunswick, NJ, 1978), 2–3. For further discussions of the georgic tradition in British literature, see John Chalker, *The English Georgic: A Study in the Development of a Form* (Baltimore, 1969); Ralph Cohen, 'Innovation and Variation: Literary Change and Georgic Poetry', in Ralph Cohen and Murray Kreiger, *Literature and History: Papers Read at a Clark Library Seminar, March 3, 1973* (Los Angeles, 1974), 3–42; and Dwight L. Durling, *Georgic Tradition in English Poetry* (New York, 1934; repr. Port Washington, NY, 1964); Anthony Low, *The Georgic Revolution* (Princeton, 1985).

Of course, eighteenth-century literature also records a very different response to historical and literary change in the period, as the great satires of Pope and Swift eloquently testify. And their literary example, too, casts a long shadow over Burke's writings, which can often be as savagely satirical as celebratory in tone. This scathing, 'Scriblerian' mode, especially apparent in such late works as *Letters on a Regicide Peace*, will be the subject of the final chapter in this book, but it is well to remind ourselves that satire and georgic are two sides of the same literary coin, both performing similar normative functions in the period, as Ian Watt has observed: 'The supreme values of the landed interest and of Augustan literature were alike . . . in their rural nature, and in their emphasis on preservation and constructive improvement rather than on radical change.'[11] (Watt's generalization about eighteenth-century literature could equally stand as the epigraph to Burke's political œuvre.)

Yet satire and georgic perform their normative function in different ways, the former condemning deviations from social norms and the latter often veiling over manifestations of radical social change with a nostalgic gauze of classical and rural ideals. Of these two strategies, the confrontational, critical stance of eighteenth-century satire has clearly struck twentieth-century readers as more authentic than the celebratory manner of the period's georgics, which have occasionally been dismissed as little more than propaganda. The initial task, then, must be to reclaim a historical understanding of the georgic and its erstwhile popularity: to recover some sense of the ways in which the georgic mode, 'in its blend of formal conservatism with an enthusiasm for those happenings we have come to recognize as revolutionary in industry, agriculture, society, and politics', offered Burke and his contemporaries an indispensable language to articulate their experience of political and social change.[12] At the same time, the historical perspective of two intervening centuries compels us to recognize the many questions that the georgic leaves unobserved, unspoken, unanswered; thus, our examination of Burke's 'georgic' vision must seek to elucidate

---

[11] Ian Watt, 'Two Historical Aspects of the Augustan Tradition', in R. F. Brissenden (ed.), *Studies in the Eighteenth Century* (Toronto, 1968), 84.

[12] Feingold, *Nature and Society*, 8.

not only his explicit language of celebration and affirmation but also the contradictions, gaps, and silences of his georgic discourse.

I

Before elaborating on Burke's georgic mode and his special uses of the term 'improvement', it will be useful to describe at some length the broader meaning of that term for eighteenth-century British writers. The word often appears in the period in tandem with its evil twin 'innovation'. The two terms subsist in a binary opposition, defining each other primarily by mutual exclusion. The shared semantic element in the two words is the idea of change, but they connote radically opposing processes of change. Whereas 'improvement' suggests amelioration, advancing or raising what exists to a better quality or condition (*OED*), 'innovation' implies radical alteration, the introduction of novelties and new forms, often by violent means. The opposition between the two was well established; in his *English Improver, or a New Survey of Husbandry*, published in 1649, Walter Blith urges his readers not to dismiss his agricultural experiments as destructive innovations: '*let me beg away thy Prejudice, take heed of Calumniation; Say not such Improvements are Innovations before thou have proved them, as the Author hath by irrefragable Demonstration, and infallible Experience*'.[13] Until very recently, as the *OED* testifies, 'innovation' was a word invariably used in a negative sense; Dryden's usage in *Absalom and Achitophel* is paradigmatic: 'All other Errors but disturb a State; | But Innovation is the Blow of Fate' (799–800).

Of the two terms, 'improvement' has undergone a more complex development, accumulating layers of meaning rich in figurative application. Etymologically it traces back to the Old French *en preu*, meaning 'into profit', and its initial usage centres on the notion of turning something (money or land) to profitable use. The word became increasingly associated with profit-making agricultural activities, such as the enclosing of

---

[13] Walter Blith, 'The Epistle to the Ingenious Reader', *The English Improver, or a New Survey of Husbandry* (London, 1649), n.p.

common or waste land, but, as Raymond Williams notes in *Keywords*, a significant mutation in meaning occurred when it acquired the wider sense of 'making something better', refining oneself (or one's surroundings) morally, aesthetically, or intellectually. This shift is signalled in Isaac Watts's well-known children's hymn, 'How doth the little busy Bee | Improve each shining Hour!' At best, the newer meaning of 'improvement' coexisted uneasily with the older sense: Williams points to the example of Jane Austen, who displays in her novels an awareness of 'the sometimes contradictory senses of improvement, where economic operations for profit might not lead to, or might hinder, social and moral refinement'.[14] These contradictions constitute what might be called an ideological fault line: the connotative shift in the word's meaning tends to assimilate a purely economic activity to social and ethical concerns, progressively blurring and concealing the essential distinction between the two.[15]

The semantic instability surrounding the word 'improvement' is recapitulated in the larger context of the eighteenth-century discourse of improvement. The title of one of the period's innumerable manuals of agricultural improvement, an anthology of essays edited by Alexander Hunter, aptly illustrates this ambiguity. Hunter entitles his collection, *Georgical Essays: in which The Food of Plants is particularly considered, Several new Composts recommended, and Other important Articles of Husbandry explained, Upon the Principles of Vegetation*, and includes on his title-page the aptly chosen epigraph, 'Search profitable knowledge'. On the one hand the reader is offered a practical, technical body of knowledge intended to increase the fertility and profitability of lands and crops. On the other hand the pursuit of a more scientific, systematic knowledge of agriculture is extolled as an end in itself, tending to the

---

[14] Raymond Williams, *Keywords: A Vocabulary of Culture and Society* (London, 1976), 132–3.

[15] See Andrew McRae, 'Husbandry Manuals and the Language of Agrarian Improvement', in Michael Leslie and Timothy Raylor (eds.), *Culture and Cultivation in Early Modern England: Writing and the Land* (Leicester, 1992), 35–62. McRae observes, 'The term ['improvement'] draws together legal, moral and economic implications in order to justify radical processes of change in the English countryside' (p. 35).

intellectual and moral improvement of the individual: 'Wherever we cast our eyes a field of contemplation opens to our view. The animal, vegetable, and mineral worlds teem with matter for the exercise of our minds'. But perhaps the most striking feature of Hunter's title is its avowal of a classical paternity: Virgil is named as a philosophical and poetical forebear of the agricultural revolution. Such claims, as A. J. Sambrook notes, were almost obligatory for writers of treatises on agricultural improvement, however widely their actual advice diverged from any classical ideal: 'those scores of eighteenth century manuals which taught the squire how to treble his rentals by engrossing, short leases, inclosure of commons and the application of newly discovered or rediscovered agricultural techniques almost invariably invoked the classical agricultural philosophy and quoted Virgil's *Georgics*'.[16]

In its purely practical sense, the term 'improvement' was commonly applied to three distinct, but interrelated, kinds of economic activity. First, it referred to the introduction of new techniques for improving soils, breeding livestock, increasing stock yields, and reclaiming waste lands. The greatly increased provision of animal fodder made possible the breeding of far larger numbers of livestock, which in turn augmented the supply of manure for fertilizing. This virtuous cycle greatly increased the quality and output of the food supply. Applying these new methods required economies of scale, often achieved through land enclosures, and large investments of capital, available only to larger and wealthier landowners. As a result, smaller landholders, tenants, and labourers sometimes endured material hardship or were driven off the land to join the swelling ranks of city dwellers. Second, improvements in infrastructure, chiefly roads and canals, accompanied the revolution in agriculture and were, as Arthur Young recognized, intimately bound up with the changes taking place in the countryside:

The cultivation of the earth cannot be carried near to perfection without [an] ease of moving the product of it.... When... the bounty was given, which proved such a noble encouragement, and the

---

[16] Alexander Hunter, *Georgical Essays* (London, 1770–2), ii. 9; A. J. Sambrook, 'The English Lord and the Happy Husbandman', *Studies in Voltaire and the Eighteenth Century*, 57 (1967), 1360.

improvements which an increase of riches spread over the country, co-operated in rendering an ease of conveyance every where an universal necessary of life, rivers were daily made navigable, and all the roads of the kingdom wonderfully improved.[17]

These improved communications were financed in part by the landowners themselves, whose increased wealth from rents paid on their estates was invested in transportation schemes, industries, mines, and urban development. Thus, the mania for improvement embraced the nascent industrial revolution, endorsing change of a significantly different character from that taking place on the farm. Finally, and somewhat contradictorily, 'improvement' designated not only activities of investment and production but also a peculiarly eighteenth-century mode of conspicuous consumption: expensive aesthetic improvements in houses, gardens, and estates, which absorbed much of the landowners' increasing wealth. The alteration, especially, of landscapes—the *furor hortensis* of Capability Brown and Humphry Repton—could be highly destructive, with the occasional relocation of entire villages and the rerouting of roads to accommodate the landscaper's grandiose designs. Though contemporary observers, including Pope, Cowper, and Richard Payne Knight, often noted in scathing terms the deleterious effects of such improvements, they rarely challenged improvement as a principle, seeking only to correct abuses and excesses.

Taken together, these sorts of innovations in practice and technology, introduced from the sixteenth to the eighteenth centuries, have come to be called the agricultural revolution. Modern historical research has demonstrated how complex and protracted a process this revolution actually was. Eric Kerridge argues that most of the improvements upon which the eighteenth century so prided itself had in fact been introduced in the previous two centuries, with the latter period simply consolidating what had been pioneered earlier. Similarly, J. D. Chambers

---

[17] Arthur Young, *Political Essays Concerning the Present State of the British Empire* (London, 1772), 155. For a discussion of the importance of improvements in transport to the marketing of agricultural products, with the increasing growth of the population and its concentration in urban areas, see Richard Perren, 'Markets and Marketing', in *The Agrarian History of England and Wales*, vi. 1750–1850, ed. G. E. Mingay (Cambridge, 1989), 190–274.

and G. E. Mingay point out that, 'those celebrated eighteenth-century pioneers, Tull, Townshend, and Coke of Norfolk, were more the popularizers of the new methods of intensive cultivation than the originators of them'. The word 'improvement' itself, as Andrew McRae shows, was coming into steadily increasing use during the sixteenth and seventeenth centuries.[18] The important points to be borne in mind in the present discussion, however, are the extent to which such eighteenth-century figures as Tull and Townshend were seen by their contemporaries as pioneers and the enthusiasm with which the word 'improvement' was adopted as the mantra of emerging agrarian capitalism. The period's claim to the title of 'age of improvement' is less exclusive than it liked to think, but the wide currency of the perception, amounting to an ideological belief, that improvement was a defining characteristic of the age and the influence of that self-perception upon thinkers such as Burke are the primary concerns of this chapter.

That poetic observers, in their praise of rural improvement, should revive the language and conventions of the ancient georgic, the classical praise of rural life, seems hardly surprising. In *The Progress of Agriculture; or, The Rural Survey* (1804) Thomas Batchelor hails, in celebrative, Virgilian strain, the burgeoning prosperity of English rural life as the basis for the country's imperial and commercial strength:

> And thus, around my natal soil I see
> The bless'd effects of peaceful industry.
> And thine, fair Freedom! thine the gen'rous hand
> That guards, improves, and dignifies the land:
> If thou but smile, fair Ceres' jocund train

---

[18] Eric Kerridge, *The Agricultural Revolution* (London, 1967); J. D. Chambers and G. E. Mingay, *The Agricultural Revolution: 1750–1880* (London, 1966), 59–60 *et passim*; McRae, 'Husbandry Manuals', 35–7. Among the many historical studies of the agricultural revolution, see *The Agrarian History of England and Wales*, v(2). *1640–1750: Agrarian Change*, ed. Joan Thirsk (esp. ch. 19, 'Agricultural Innovations and their Diffusion', 533–89); and vi. *1750–1850*, ed. Mingay (esp. ch. 1, 'The Changing Rural Landscape, 1750–1850', 7–83, and ch. 4, 'Farming Techniques', 275–383) (Cambridge, 1985–9); and E. L. Jones, 'Agriculture and Economic Growth in England, 1660–1750: Agricultural Change', *Journal of Economic History*, 25 (1965), 1–18. For an introductory overview, with a useful bibliography, see J. V. Beckett, *The Agricultural Revolution* (Oxford, 1990).

> Spread, o'er the trembling swamp, th' unfertile plain;
> Or spend on wilds, or frowning heaths, the day,
> While seasons rise, and gradual roll away.
> At length subdu'd and tam'd th' obdurate soil,
> Abundant harvests crown their various toil.
>
> . . . .
>
> And Commerce proudly bids her gay canals
> Pierce through the hills and shine along the dales;
> While o'er her streams the waving pennant's fly,
> And wealthy cities meet th' astonish'd eye.[19]

The Virgilian themes of the virtues and civilizing influence of work, the tranquillity and ease of country life, and the harmony that can subsist between art (industry, improvement) and nature are predictably present in Batchelor's verses. Burke himself, as a student at Trinity College, Dublin, had paid tribute to the prevailing poetic fashion with his creditable translation of the famous panegyric to country life in Virgil's second *Georgic* (from which the first epigraph to this chapter is taken).[20]

Richard Feingold demonstrates, however, that these georgic themes and habits of expression also recur persistently, unlikely though it may at first seem, in the writings of journalists, economists, and political theorists of the day. As a case in point he cites a striking passage from a chapter in Adam Smith's *Wealth of Nations* entitled, 'Of the Natural Progress of Opulence':

Upon equal, or nearly equal profits, most men will chuse to employ their capitals rather in the improvement and cultivation of land, than either in manufactures or in foreign trade. The man who employs his

---

[19] Thomas Batchelor, 'The Progress of Agriculture; or, the Rural Survey', in *Village Scenes, The Progress of Agriculture, and Other Poems* (London, 1804), 75–6. Batchelor's poem echoes the rhetoric of numerous other 18th-c. formal georgics, among them John Philips' *Cyder* (1708); Robert Dodsley's 'Agriculture' (in *Public Virtue* (1753)); John Dyer's *The Fleece* (1757); and James Grainger's *The Sugar-Cane* (1764). For a brief consideration of several of these figures, see O. H. K. Spate, 'The Muse of Mecantilism: Jago, Grainger, and Dyer', in Brissenden (ed.), *Studies in the Eighteenth Century*, 119–31.

[20] For studies of the historical impact of the agricultural revolution on British literature, see (besides Richard Feingold, Anthony Low, and the collection of essays edited by Michael Leslie and Timothy Raylor), Kenneth MacLean, *Agrarian Age: A Background for Wordsworth* (New Haven, 1950); and Raymond Williams, *The Country and the City* (New York, 1973).

capital in land, has it more under his view and command, and his fortune is much less liable to accidents than that of the trader.... The capital of the landlord, on the contrary, which is fixed in the improvement of his land, seems to be as well secured as the nature of human affairs can admit of. The beauty of the country besides, the pleasures of a country life, the tranquillity of mind which it promises, and wherever the injustice of human laws does not disturb it, the independency which it really affords, have charms that more or less attract every body; and as to cultivate the ground was the original destination of man, so in every stage of his existence he seems to retain a predilection for this primitive employment.[21]

Smith is arguing for the value of manufacturing and its potential to coexist harmoniously with agriculture, but in praising the values of capital investment and hard work, he falls naturally into the language of rural praise; the poetic voice of James Thomson echoes in his prose:

> The happiest he! who far from public Rage,
> Deep in the Vale, with a *choice Few* retir'd,
> Drinks the pure Pleasures of the RURAL LIFE.
> . . . .
> This is the Life which those who fret in Guilt,
> And guilty Cities, never knew; the Life,
> Led by primeval Ages, uncorrupt,
> When Angels dwelt, and GOD himself, with Man![22]
> (*Autumn*, ll. 1236–8, 1348–51)

Feingold suggests that for eighteenth-century writers, including economists such as Adam Smith, the Virgilian conception of civilization, with its values of tranquillity, independence, frugality, and virtuous work, offered a moral yardstick against

---

[21] Adam Smith, *An Inquiry into the Nature and Causes of the Wealth of Nations*, ed. R. H. Campbell and A. S. Skinner (Oxford, 1976), i. 377–8. See also Feingold, *Nature and Society*, 27–8. Arthur Young's essay 'On the Pleasures of Agriculture' furnishes an equally striking example of the 18th-c. economist's capacity to combine hardheaded financial advice with a poetic, Virgilian perspective on the value and virtue of agricultural pursuits. Thus, Young catalogues, in rapturous terms, the delights of rural life, such as 'that season of joy when crouded barns prove insufficient for the increase which art and industry command. When the orchard's loaded branches bid streams nectareous warm the peasant's heart: and the rifled sweets of incense-breathing spring flow from the labours of the industrious bee' (*Annals of Agriculture*, ii [1784], 477).

[22] James Thomson, *The Seasons*, ed. James Sambrook (Oxford, 1981), 196, 200.

which to measure the enduring value of the changes their own society was experiencing. In his own words, 'What seems clear is that some version of pastoral or georgic was invoked regularly as a perspective on the nation's vigor, and then as a means of defining . . . an appropriate judgment of the character of human social experience in a heady new climate of change felt as progress. Smith, arguing here on behalf of manufacturing, insists that it be recognized as a cause of improvement, a positive achievement of civilization, even as he recognizes the valid resources the gentler countryside possesses for judging that active and risky enterprise.'[23] To debate at this point the applicability of Feingold's thesis to Burke's own use of the georgic in his political writings would be to anticipate our argument; we might reasonably expect to find that this intermingling of literary and intellectual discourses functions very differently in a political treatise than in a work on economics. The formation of such generic mixtures, however, is a familiar feature of eighteenth-century literature, and readers accustomed to the complex allusiveness of a mixed form such as the mock-epic would recognize similar cultural impulses shaping the prose of Smith or Burke.

II

One of the most characteristic features of the eighteenth-century georgic (and the one that falls in most closely with the language and ideology of improvement) is the visual survey of a landscape or prospect view. Burke is an extensive borrower of this familiar poetic feature, which finds perhaps its most classic expression in Alexander Pope's lush picture of the English countryside in *Windsor-Forest*:

> Here in full Light the russet Plains extend;
> There wrapt in Clouds the blueish Hills ascend:
> Ev'n the wild Heath displays her Purple Dies,
> And 'midst the Desert fruitful Fields arise,
> That crown'd with tufted Trees and springing Corn,
> Like verdant Isles the sable Waste adorn.
> Let *India* boast her Plants, nor envy we

[23] Feingold, *Nature and Society*, 30.

> The weeping Amber or the balmy Tree,
> While by our Oaks the precious Loads are born,
> And Realms commanded which those Trees adorn.
> . . . .
> Here *Ceres'* Gifts in waving Prospect stand,
> And nodding tempt the joyful Reaper's Hand,
> Rich Industry sits smiling on the Plains,
> And Peace and Plenty tell, a STUART reigns.
> (ll. 23–42)

The poet moves from an idealized description of an actual landscape (almost an image of the Golden Age) to various topics of reflection prompted by the scene: prosperity, patriotism, imperial trade, and political power. The prospect before him exemplifies the Virgilian ideal of nature improved by art, but the improving art that transforms this landscape is, as the visual imagery and the careful syntactic qualifications imply, very much an eighteenth-century conception of art, thoroughly grounded in the period's epistemological bias towards observation, experience, and experiment.

Another of Pope's prospect views, the concluding lines of *An Epistle to Burlington*, testifies even more eloquently to the shaping power of improvement:

> You too proceed! make falling Arts your care,
> Erect new wonders, and the old repair
> . . . .
> Bid Harbors open, public Ways extend,
> Bid Temples, worthier of the God, ascend;
> Bid the broad Arch the dang'rous Flood contain,
> The Mole projected break the roaring Main;
> Back to his bounds their subject Sea command,
> And roll obedient Rivers thro' the Land;
> These Honours, Peace to happy Britain brings,
> These are Imperial Works, and worthy Kings.
> (ll. 191–2, 197–204)

The landscape view here is more obviously a composite of many views than the prospect of Windsor Forest, a circumstance that discloses its status as a *paysage moralisé* (or equally a *paysage politisé*). In both passages Pope grapples with important ethical and political questions: the nature of the good polity, the proper channelling of human energy and ingenuity, and the rationale for empire. The improvement of houses, estates, and public works is central to Pope's vision: improvement becomes a justification for imperial expansion and the exploitation of nature.

In *Reflections on the Revolution in France* Burke adapts the poetic practice of the prospect view to his own polemical purposes when he comes to review the economic state of France at the time of the Revolution. Arguing that the country enjoys considerable wealth and prosperity, despite its political defects, he launches into an extensive survey of the French landscape:

> Indeed, when I consider the face of the kingdom of France; the multitude and opulence of her cities; the useful magnificence of her spacious high roads and bridges; the opportunity of her artificial canals and navigations opening the conveniences of maritime communication through a solid continent of so immense an extent; when I turn my eyes to the stupendous works of her ports and harbours, and to her whole naval apparatus, whether for war or trade; when I bring before my view the number of her fortifications, constructed with so bold and masterly a skill, and made and maintained at so prodigious a charge, presenting an armed front and impenetrable barrier to her enemies upon every side; when I recollect how very small a part of that extensive region is without cultivation, and to what complete perfection the culture of many of the best productions of the earth have been brought in France; when I reflect on the excellence of her manufactures and fabrics, second to none but ours, and in some particulars not second; when I contemplate the grand foundations of charity, public and private; when I survey the state of all the arts that beautify and polish life; when I reckon the men she has bred for extending her fame in war, her able statesmen, the multitude of her profound lawyers and theologians, her philosophers, her critics, her historians and antiquaries, her poets, and her orators sacred and profane, I behold in all this something which awes and commands the imagination, which checks the mind on the brink of precipitate and indiscriminate censure, and which demands, that we should very seriously examine, what and how great are the latent vices that could authorize us at once to level so spacious a fabric with the ground. (viii. 179–80)

This vast periodic sentence employs all the perceptual techniques and language of the prospect view, including the characteristic shift, about halfway through the passage, from a physical survey to an imaginative one—in this instance, a mental inventory of France's cultural monuments and achievements. The rhetorical strategy of the passage, with its reiterated dependent clauses impelling the reader forward to a seemingly inevitable conclusion, reproduces the structure of Pope's prospect view in *Windsor-Forest*, where the poet's series of visual observations ends in the confident political affirmation, 'And Peace and Plenty tell, a STUART reigns'. In Burke's case the political moral to be deduced from his survey of France is that no system of government fostering the kind of prosperity and cultural wealth displayed by the kingdom of France can be beyond redemption: 'I do not recognize, in this view of things, the despotism of Turkey' (viii. 180). To paraphrase Pope, his argument is, in effect, 'And Peace and Plenty tell, a BOURBON reigns'.

In offering this prospect view as the centrepiece of his argument about the degree of corruption and oppression that can be said to exist in France, Burke shrewdly adapts the form of his analysis to support his contention. This point becomes clearer when the composition of his landscape portrait is considered. Unlike the poetic views of the period, Burke's affords no actual geographical vantage point: it is in fact a conjectural topography inspired, as his supporting evidence suggests, by published economic analyses of France (especially those of Necker and Calonne, erstwhile ministers of Louis XVI) rather than his own personal survey. Indeed, the eyewitness accounts of others, such as Arthur Young's *Travels* [in France], *During the Years 1787, 1788, and 1789*, often contradict Burke in many particulars. Thus, upon viewing the opulent theatre at Nantes, Young exclaims,

Mon Dieu . . . do all the wastes, the deserts, the heath, ling, furz, broom, and bog, that I have passed for 300 miles lead to this spectacle? What a miracle, that all this splendour and wealth of the cities in France should be so unconnected with the country! There are no gentle transitions from ease to comfort, from comfort to wealth: you pass at once from beggary to profusion.[24]

---

[24] Arthur Young, *Travels, During the Years 1787, 1788, and 1789. Undertaken more particularly with a View of ascertaining the Cultivation, Wealth, Resources, and National Prosperity, of the Kingdom of France* (Bury St Edmunds, 1792), 89. The quotation is from the entry for 21 Sept. 1788.

The striking contrast between these two landscapes—the one an uncultivated waste and the other a scene of improvement and industry—draws attention to the manner in which Burke deliberately politicizes his perception of landscape: the organizing principle of his scene is not the human eye but a political argument.

The presentation of the French landscape as prosperous and productive is crucial to Burke's argument because, as an eighteenth-century Whig, he holds to the view that political despotism is inimical to commercial and cultural greatness. This, certainly, is Young's refrain in his *Travels*, where he emphasizes repeatedly that the economic and material backwardness he has witnessed in France is owing to that country's defective government. Enlightened government and prosperity, in this view, are linked to the widespread ownership of property: people who own and improve property will defend their liberties in order to protect what they own. Thus, by projecting France as a vision of opulence, Burke invites his readers to conclude that the political institutions of the *ancien régime* were more progressive than the French revolutionaries have cared to admit: 'I must think such a government well deserved to have its excellencies heightened; its faults corrected; and its capacities improved into a British constitution' (viii. 180). His calculated use of the word 'improved' in this context signals its transformation from an economic or aesthetic term into a crucial political concept—essentially a Burkean doctrine of political change.

The same transformation can be observed in another well-known passage that makes use of the analogy of improvement, Burke's representation of the French polity as a decayed, neglected edifice: 'Your constitution, it is true, whilst you were out of possession, suffered waste and dilapidation; but you possessed in some parts the walls, and in all the foundations of a noble and venerable castle. You might have repaired those walls; you might have built on those old foundations' (viii. 85). This image alludes to the practice of altering and rebuilding ancient country houses in order to bring them up to the latest aesthetic fashion. In political terms it argues against discontinuity, seeking to channel the forces of historical change by preserving as much of existing forms as possible.

Burke's adaptation of the georgic mode to the purposes of his political discourse plays out at the level of form the process of change-within-continuity that he advocates politically. Just as the original contours of the country house (to revert for a moment to this favourite analogy) remain visible despite successive renovations, so too Burke's adaptations of the classical georgic retain formal and thematic links with their generic original. Both these transformations—of architectural and literary form—involve a dialectical interplay of form and content to which Burke is always keenly alive. Writing in 1780 on the subject of constitutional change, he signals his explicit awareness of this dialectical process:

> But the Bane of the Whiggs has been the admission among them of the Corps of Schemers; who, in reality, and at bottom, mean little more than to indulge themselves with Speculations; but who do us infinite Mischief, by persuading many sober and well meaning people that we have designs inconsistent with the Constitution left us by our forefathers. You know how many are startled with the Idea of innovation. Would to God it were in our power to keep things *where they are*, in point of *form*; provided we were able to improve them in point of *Substance*. The *Machine itself* is well enough to answer any good purpose, provided the *materials* were sound. (*Corr.* iv. 295).

This revealing passage acknowledges the inevitability of change but seeks to contain it by grafting, as much as possible, the new onto the old: 'the useful parts of an old establishment are kept, and what is superadded is to be fitted to what is retained' (viii. 216). New wine is to be poured into old bottles.

But at what point, Burke appears to ask, does a change in 'substance' lead to a complete transformation of the form as well? It seems impossible to make substantial alterations in existing political establishments without also inducing a metamorphosis in their outward shape. In the present context the same question may be asked about Burke's commitment to an ideology of improvement, for the changes that were being introduced into the English countryside in the name of improvement were to be as revolutionary in their scope as the political upheavals in France after 1789. Contemporary writers and observers (Goldsmith, Cowper, and Crabbe, among others) drew attention to the widespread dislocation that accompanied changes in agricultural practice. Twentieth-century historical research has shown that the caricature—exemplified by Goldsmith's *The Deserted Village*—of a peasantry torn from the land as a consequence of land enclosures and forced to emigrate or move to noisome industrial centres is a gross oversimplification of an enormously complex historical process which often produced unexpected gains and losses. But change there was, of incalculable effect. Even as Burke celebrated improvement as a means of change that preserved the best, the old walls and foundations, of the inherited order, the pressure of improvement was inexorably transforming the economic, social, and, ultimately, political structure of rural Britain.[25] The ever-pragmatic Arthur Young noted this process with approval: 'Landlords, by giving up ancient customs in the leases by which they let their farms, and falling by degrees into a system of improvement, by aiding their tenants, have done great things towards advancing of husbandry.'[26] His observation implies, contrary to Burke, that 'ancient customs' do not survive the winds of improvement, any more than natural landscapes survived the assiduous attentions of a Capability Brown. The tensions inherent in the discourse of improvement, its uneasy marriage of georgic forms and bucolic themes with the enthusiastic rhetoric of commercial progress, surface in Burke's prose as well: the reconciliation of form and substance, which he regards as a political necessity of the first importance, will not easily be effected.

III

One of the means by which Burke seeks to stabilize his discourse of improvement is to insist on a sharp distinction between improvement and innovation and to define these as two mutually exclusive processes of change. This opposition reflects

---

[25] The conventional historical view, expressed by Karl Marx, was that 'the intermittent but constantly renewed expropriation and expulsion of the agricultural population supplied the urban industries ... with a mass of proletarians' (*Capital: A Critique of Political Economy* trans. Ben Fowkes (Harmondsworth, 1990), i. 908; see esp. chs. 27–30). This thesis, restated by J. L. and Barbara Hammond in *The Village Labourer, 1760–1832* (London, 1911), was challenged in the 1950s by J. D. Chambers ('Enclosure and Labour Supply in the Industrial Revolution', *Economic History Review*, 2nd ser., 5 (1953), 319–43) and has been subject to further revision since. The complexity of the historical debate notwithstanding, there can be no doubt of the vast scale, impact, and consequences of agrarian change in the 18th and 19th centuries.   [26] *Political Essays*, 155.

the received linguistic usage of the period; even Charles James Fox, with whom Burke broke politically in 1791, accepted without question that 'improvements were not to be confounded with innovations; the meaning of which was always odious, and conveyed an idea of alterations for the worse'. The two terms could be applied arbitrarily (and often were) in order to fix the permissible limits of political debate. Both Burke and Fox could agree, for instance, that to innovate meant to tear down pre-existing institutions and replace them with new, untried forms and relations. The crucial problem, therefore, was to determine what kinds of reforms or changes were improvements and what were innovations—where, in short, to draw the line. On this question Burke and Fox differed markedly.

To the radical William Godwin the entire debate about improvement and innovation as opposed modes of change was a sterile one which promoted a false distinction between the two terms in order to forestall significant reform altogether. Burke's advocacy of improvement over innovation, in his view, was nothing more than a smokescreen for political reaction and stasis. Godwin's response was to cut through this obfuscatory debate by conflating the two terms and by placing Burke squarely on the side opposed to any change whatsoever. 'Incessant change, everlasting innovation', he argues, 'seem to be dictated by the true interests of mankind. But government is the perpetual enemy of change.' Then, in an unmistakable reference to Burke, he defines this 'enemy of change' in terms that deliberately echo the *Reflections:* 'They [governments] prompt us to seek the public welfare, not in alteration and improvement, but in a timid reverence for the decisions of our ancestors.'[27] By his conscious and seemingly unprecedented reversal of meaning in his use of the word 'innovation' (foreshadowing its positive modern connotation of advantageous new procedures or inventions) and his rejection of the long-standing antonymy between innovation and improvement, Godwin reappropriates the discourse of improvement for the radical enlightenment and seeks to reimbue it with a spirit of progress and optimism.

[27] William Godwin, *Enquiry Concerning Political Justice and Its Influence on Morals and Happiness*, ed. F. E. L. Priestley (Toronto, 1946), i. 245.

In writing the words quoted above Godwin may very well have had in mind the passage in *Reflections* cited in the opening paragraphs of this chapter. The passage in question characterizes the British constitution as an 'entailed inheritance', but with an entail that does not exclude 'a principle of improvement'. Contrasting this view of constitutional change with the more radical theories of Dr Richard Price and the Revolution Society, Burke asserts in the same paragraph, 'A spirit of innovation is generally the result of a selfish temper and confined views. People will not look forward to posterity, who never look backward to their ancestors' (viii. 83). Here, as elsewhere in his writings, Burke assumes an *ad hominem* tone when he introduces the subject of innovation: innovators are persons of 'selfish temper and confined views'. This personal note is symptomatic of the predominantly satiric and ironic vein of his rhetorical assaults upon the proponents of revolutionary innovation. If the discourse of improvement is georgic, celebratory in tone (Conor Cruise O'Brien calls this Burkean style his 'Whig manner: rational, perspicacious, business-like'), its obverse is, in O'Brien's phrase, 'a peculiar kind of furious irony', irony with an unmistakably Irish pedigree.[28] Thus, when Burke casts his eye over contemporary, revolutionary France, immediately following his prospect survey of the kingdom under Louis XVI, he exclaims, 'From its general aspect one would conclude that it had been for some time past under the special direction of the learned academicians of Laputa and Balnibarbi' (viii. 182). He is referring, of course, to the kingdom of philosophers and mathematicians described in Book III of *Gulliver's Travels*, a nation ruled by abstract reasoners rather than practical politicians. His condemnation of the forces of innovation takes its satiric cue from his fellow Irishman, Jonathan Swift, that great master of the Scriblerian mode. In the writings of Swift and the other great Tory satirists of the age of Walpole he finds a ready-made discourse of political and cultural criticism that proves endlessly adaptable to the circumstances of the 1790s.

A full examination of Burke's use of the Scriblerian satirical mode must be deferred to the concluding chapter of this study,

---

[28] Conor Cruise O'Brien, Introduction to Edmund Burke, *Reflections on the Revolution in France* (Harmondsworth, 1969), 42–3.

but one thread of that satiric language, its suspicion of innovators and projectors, finds its way (albeit by a process of negation) into his discourse of improvement. Having invoked a comparison between the fomentors of revolution in France and the 'learned academicians of Laputa and Balnibarbi', Burke proceeds to tease out the implications of his parallel:

> the leaders of the legislative clubs and coffee-houses are intoxicated with admiration at their own wisdom and ability. They speak with the most sovereign contempt of the rest of the world. They tell the people, to comfort them in the rags with which they have cloathed them, that they are a nation of philosophers; and, sometimes, by all the arts of quackish parade, by shew, tumult, and bustle, sometimes by the alarms of plots and invasions, they attempt to drown the cries of indigence, and to divert the eyes of the observer from the ruin and wretchedness of the state. (viii. 182–3)

It is not difficult to detect in the self-admiration and arrogance of these Parisians the outlines of Swift's self-absorbed Laputan courtiers, who treat Gulliver with 'some Degree of Contempt' and remain perpetually 'abstracted and involved in Speculation'. The consequences of their speculations are precisely the 'ruin and wretchedness' Burke associates with revolutionary France: 'the Houses [of Balnibarbi were] very strangely built, and most of them out of Repair. The People in the Streets walked fast, looked wild, their Eyes fixed, and were generally in Rags. . . . I never knew a Soil so unhappily cultivated, Houses so ill contrived and so ruinous, or a People whose Countenances and Habit expressed so much Misery and Want.'[29] So much, as Burke indicates in an identifying footnote, 'for the idea of countries governed by philosophers'.

Burke's recourse to a Swiftian satirical language in describing his opposition to innovation—particularly, in this context, his revival of the elaborate Scriblerian satire of abuses in modern learning—suggests that he shares with Swift a number of fundamental assumptions about the limits of knowledge, the nature of politics, and the scope of political action. For Burke, the 'science of constructing a commonwealth, or renovating it, or reforming it, is, like every other experimental science, not to be taught *à priori*'. On the contrary, it requires 'a deep

---

[29] Jonathan Swift, *Gulliver's Travels*, in Swift, *The Prose Works*, xi. 173–5.

knowledge of human nature and human necessities'. Such knowledge is to be obtained not through theoretical speculation, but rather through practical experience of human behaviour, needs, and desires. 'What is the use', he asks, 'of discussing a man's abstract right to food or to medicine? The question is upon the method of procuring and administering them. In that deliberation I shall always advise to call in the aid of the farmer and the physician, rather than the professor of metaphysics' (viii. 111). Burke's profound sense of the limits of useful political action—preferably no more than 'a direct application of a remedy to the grievance complained of'—echoes the King of Brobdingnag in *Gulliver's Travels*:

> He confined the Knowledge of governing within very *narrow Bounds;* to common Sense and Reason, to Justice and Lenity, to the Speedy Determination of Civil and criminal Causes. . . . And, he gave it for his Opinion; that whoever could make two Ears of Corn, or two Blades of Grass to grow upon a Spot of Ground where only one grew before; would deserve better of Mankind, and do more essential Service to his Country, than the whole Race of Politicians put together.[30]

Making two blades of corn grow where only one grew before— a programme of agricultural improvement, in short—is the king's ideal of constructive political action. His illustration of political utility might have been drawn from one of the period's innumerable manuals of agricultural improvement, and it directly anticipates Burke's preference for the advice of the farmer over the metaphysician in arriving at solutions to political problems. The king's famous comment was widely approved by agricultural writers, who frequently quoted it in their pamphlets. James Anderson, for instance, cites the king's words as the title-page epigraph to his *Essays Relating to Agriculture and Rural Affairs*, and Arthur Young echoes them in one of his many encomia on the British gentleman-farmer: 'Eighteen quarters of wheat raised on one acre of land! What a signal for emulation, and carrying the power of culture to the highest pitch!'[31]

---

[30] Swift, *The Prose Works*, xi. 135–6.
[31] James Anderson, *Essays Relating to Agriculture and Rural Affairs*, iii. (Edinburgh, 1796). Arthur Young, *Political Essays*, 157. See also Walter Harte, *Essays on Husbandry* (London, 1764), ii. 16.

The French authorities, meanwhile, conduct themselves like Swift's projectors in the Grand Academy of Lagado, carving up France into geometrical squares for administrative purposes:

> The French builders, clearing away as mere rubbish whatever they found, and, like their ornamental gardeners, forming every thing into an exact level, propose to rest the whole local and general legislature on three bases of three different kinds; one geometrical, one arithmetical, and the third financial. . . . For the accomplishment of the first of these purposes they divide the area of their country into eighty-three pieces, regularly square, of eighteen leagues by eighteen . . . called *Departments*. These they portion, proceeding by square measurement, into seventeen hundred and twenty districts called *Communes*. These again they subdivide, still proceeding by square measurement, into smaller districts called *Cantons*, making in all 6,400. (viii. 220–1)

The French builders proceed like their gardeners, who favour geometrical regularity and symmetry in their landscape designs over the unforced naturalness and irregularity of the English garden. In drawing this comparison Burke merely reiterates a commonplace of eighteenth-century landscape theory. 'Consult the Genius of the Place in all', advises Pope, the advocate of 'good sense' in English estate improvement: 'Without it, proud Versailles! thy glory falls' (*Epistle to Burlington*, ll. 57, 71).

The association of French absolutism with rigid French landscaping tastes, epitomized by Versailles, and British liberty with the relative informality of the English garden is updated by Burke to include a new species of French tyranny. If anything, the French revolutionaries have improved on the regularity and symmetry of their inherited design: 'In the groves of *their* academy, at the end of every visto, you see nothing but the gallows' (viii. 128). Burke's analogy revealingly discloses both the character of the improver and the limits of his activities. Not only must the improver beware of violating the topography and situation of the land, imposing an artificial terrain or theoretical scheme, but he must, in order to avoid this trap, be a man of taste, with the proper education and due sensitivity to the character of the place to be improved. The improver should, in a word, be a gentleman: Burke's ideology of improvement is designed in part to redefine and thereby to perpetuate the role of the gentleman and the aristocrat as a leader of his society.

The French revolutionaries, by contrast, have ignored, in their imposition of an artificial administrative grid, the human topography or social ecology of France. Burke drives this point home with sarcastic verve: 'No man ever was attached by a sense of pride, partiality, or real affection, to a description of square measurement. He will never glory in belonging to the Checquer, N° 71, or to any other badge-ticket' (viii. 244). Like Swift, he satirizes the projecting spirit by a mock-obsessive attention to arithmetical detail, beginning with the passage quoted in the previous paragraph and carrying on through a lengthy analysis of the cumbersome new electoral system proposed for the country (see viii. 221–9). The cumulative effect, as in the first of Swift's *Drapier's Letters*, is a kind of statistical *reductio ad absurdum*: the new constitutional proposals are swept away by an onrushing tide of numbers. Having conducted his unwitting reader through pages of detailed analysis, Burke remarks with an air of innocence, 'I am afraid I have gone too far into their way of considering the formation of a constitution. They have much, but bad, metaphysics; much, but bad, geometry; much, but false, proportionate arithmetic' (viii. 229). The entire scheme, 'this new pavement of square within square', is a 'semiorganization made on the system of Empedocles and Buffon' (viii. 221).

Burke's account of these French constitutional experts and their plans calls to mind the account Lord Munodi gives Gulliver of the projectors in Lagado, who busily promote 'Schemes of putting all Arts, Sciences, Languages, and Meckanicks upon a new Foot'. By contrast with his countrymen, Munodi professes himself 'content to go on in the old Forms; to live in the Houses his Ancestors had built, and act as they did in every Part of Life without Innovation'. For adhering stubbornly to old and tried ways, Munodi and several like-minded gentlemen have been accused of opposing 'the general Improvement of their Country'.[32] Swift's portrait of Munodi anticipates Burke's conception of the public-spirited gentleman, whose activities, both practical and political, sustain the inherited order and promote the general prosperity of his country. Burke's allusion to Gulliver's account of Laputa and Balnibarbi, therefore, is twofold, for enclosed in the satirical denunciation

---

[32] Swift, *Gulliver's Travels*, in *Prose Works*, xi. 176–7.

of the abuse of reason and its dire consequences is a bucolic portrayal of human civilization in rural harmony. The dominant satiric mode of the Munodi episode enfolds an exquisite georgic vision, enacting formally the dialectical interplay of innovation and improvement that we have been tracing in Burke's writings. Within the devastated countryside that is the legacy of Laputan policy, Gulliver is struck by the contrasting appearance of Munodi's estate: 'we came into a most beautiful Country; Farmers Houses at small Distances, neatly built, the Fields enclosed, containing Vineyards, Corngrounds and Meadows. Neither do I remember to have seen a more delightful Prospect.' This 'prospect' (the term carries both aesthetic and economic connotations) bears all the hallmarks of an improved countryside, with enclosed fields and neatly renovated cottages. The general air of improvement is underscored by the tasteful appearance of Munodi's house and gardens: 'the House . . . was indeed a noble Structure, built according to the best Rules of ancient Architecture. The Fountains, Gardens, Walks, Avenues, and Groves were all disposed with exact Judgment and Taste.'[33]

Swift is perhaps his own best commentator on the political import of this bucolic scene. In the paragraph concluding the last of his *Drapier's Letters*, he writes,

> The cultivating and Improvement of Land, is certainly a Subject worthy of the highest Enquiry in any Country. . . . [F]ew *Politicians*, with all their Schemes, are half so useful Members of a Commonwealth, as an *honest Farmer*; who, by skilfully draining, fencing, manuring and planting, hath increased the intrinsick Value of a Piece of Land; and thereby done a *perpetual Service* to his Country; which it is a great Controversy, whether any of the *former* ever did, since the Creation of the World; but no Controversy at all, that Ninety-nine in a Hundred, have done Abundance of Mischief.[34]

The rhetoric of improvement appears to be deployed here in all its colours: Arthur Young himself could willingly have subscribed to these sentiments. But the acerbic tone of Swift's final words hints at an element missing from his georgic discourse: the celebratory tone of the enthusiast, the optimistic fascination

---

[33] Ibid., 175–6.
[34] 'An Humble Address to Both Houses of Parliament', *The Drapier's Letters*, ibid. x. 140–1.

with progress and commercial energy. He grants that the farmer's activities of 'draining, fencing, manuring, and planting' are invaluable to civilization, but he refuses to recognize that experiments, like those of the Royal Society, can contribute to the practical knowledge and prosperity of the farmer. On the contrary, a good portion of his satire on the Academy of Projectors in Lagado is devoted to an ironic dismissal of 'new Rules and Methods of Agriculture and Building, and new Instruments and Tools for all Trades and Manufactures'.

Swift's conception of improvement is a severely circumscribed one. In his aesthetic improvements Munodi adheres to the 'best Rules of ancient Architecture', an adherence which implies that he defines 'improvement' in terms of a return to the practice of classical times rather than the promotion of new discoveries. This restrictive conception of improvement represents a radical conservatism that borders on immobilism: an opposition to change or progress of any kind. Burke's conservatism is more flexible; he displays a subtler awareness than does Swift of the processes of history, and as a practical politician he is alive to the inevitable breezes of change. 'We must all obey the great law of change', he writes in his *Letter to Sir Hercules Langrishe* (1792), a pamphlet advocating the enfranchisement of Irish Roman Catholics. 'All we can do ... is to provide that the change shall proceed by insensible degrees' (ix. 634). Consonant with this awareness, Burke recognizes a much looser, more shifting boundary between improvement and innovation than Swift's rigid demarcation. Depending on the circumstances, the line of intellectual and political orthodoxy might ease or tighten.

This fluid process can be seen at work in Burke's stigmatization of Empedocles and Buffon as archetypes of the dogmatic, innovative thinker. Empedocles, the Greek philosopher who posited that all matter is composed of the four elements of earth, air, fire, and water, might readily be seen as the epitome of the mad, speculative philosopher, but Buffon presents a more complex, ambiguous case. It may be that Burke regarded the French naturalist's taxonomic approach to his subject as unduly mechanistic and artificial (Buffon's subordination of orders, genera, and species being analogous to the new French political arrangement of *départements*, *communes*, and *cantons*), or perhaps he shared the theological misgivings that had been voiced about Buffon's conception of geological history. Still, the high value Buffon placed on experience and observation in his studies ought to have recommended him to Burke.

The example of Buffon indicates how the discourse of improvement becomes progressively more circumscribed in Burke's writings of the 1790s: his defensive rhetoric represents an ideological circling of the wagons harking back to the literary posture of Pope and Swift in the early eighteenth century. A writer whose work and methods Burke might otherwise have approved is here consigned to an intellectual Dunciad that grows increasingly crowded as the decade unfolds. Burke's summary dismissal of Buffon is symptomatic of the increasing strain placed on his artificial, yet indispensable, distinction between improvement and innovation. The contradictory character of his discourse reaches a climax in his last, feverish polemics, the *Letters on a Regicide Peace* and *A Letter to a Noble Lord*, where the ideological faultlines of his thought run close to the surface. Yet, from this confusion emerges a realignment, a new synthesis, of forms and ideas that adumbrates a powerful new political discourse for the nineteenth century.

IV

The central text witnessing to this transformation is Burke's celebrated peroration on Windsor Castle in *A Letter to a Noble Lord*, a passage that triumphantly proclaims the continuity of form, both literary and political, even as it concedes the reality of underlying radical change:

> But as to *our* country and *our* race, as long as the well compacted structure of our church and state, the sanctuary, the holy of holies of that ancient law, defended by reverence, defended by power, a fortress at once and a temple, shall stand inviolate on the brow of the British Sion—as long as the British Monarchy, not more limited than fenced by the orders of the State, shall, like the proud Keep of Windsor, rising in the majesty of proportion, and girt with the double belt of it's kindred and coeval towers, as long as this awful structure shall oversee and guard the subjected land—so long the mounds and dykes of the low, fat, Bedford level will have nothing to fear from all the pickaxes of all the levellers of France. As long as our Sovereign Lord the King, and his faithful subjects, the Lords and Commons of this realm—the triple

cord, which no man can break ... [a]s long as these endure, so long the Duke of Bedford is safe: and we are all safe together—the high from the blights of envy and the spoliations of rapacity; the low from the iron hand of oppression and the insolent spurn of contempt. Amen! and so be it: and so it will be,

> Dum domus Aeneae Capitoli immobile saxum
> Accolet; imperiumque pater Romanus habebit.
>
> (ix. 172–3)

This solemn paean, which Burke is said to have regarded as the most successful of all his performances, enacts a dazzling series of ideological remappings, at the literary, historical, political, social, and economic levels, which collectively articulate for the coming generation a conservative countervision to the French Revolution.

To begin at the literary, or more particularly, the generic level, this passage stands as the culmination of a long chain of poetic allusion to Windsor Castle and its environs in the seventeenth and eighteenth centuries, beginning with John Denham's *Coopers Hill* and carried forward in Otway's *Windsor Castle*, Pope's *Windsor-Forest*, and even Gray's *Ode on a Distant Prospect of Eton College*. As in the previously examined landscape survey of France in the *Reflections*, the prospect Burke describes here is a composite view. The celebrated landscape of the Thames river valley, dominated by William the Conqueror's imposing Norman fortress, is conflated with the explicitly georgic prospect of the 'fat Bedford level', a huge tract of reclaimed, improved fen land in East Anglia, whose protective system of dykes and drainage canals counteract the destructive effects of flood and tide. Given the considerable distance that actually separates these places, the link between them must be supplied by the mind's eye, which is prompted, through a succession of literary and historical allusions, to a political perception of the scene. Once again, a political argument, rather than the human eye, grounds the construction of landscape.

This politicization of vision can be traced back ultimately to Virgil's *Georgics*, but more immediately to *Coopers Hill*. Denham's poem is framed by two views that parallel the double scene set forth by Burke: first, near the beginning of his poem, Denham reflects at length on Windsor Castle and its environs;

then, in his concluding lines he portrays the devastating power of the river Thames in flood and its destructive effects upon the surrounding agricultural landscape.

> When a calm River rais'd with sudden rains,
> Or Snows dissolv'd, o'reflows th' adjoyning Plains,
> The Husbandmen with high-rais'd banks secure
> Their greedy hopes, and this he can endure.
> But if with Bays and Dams they strive to force
> His channel to a new, or narrow course;
> No longer then within his banks he dwells,
> First to a Torrent, then a Deluge swells:
> Stronger, and fiercer by restraint he roars,
> And knows no bound, but makes his power his shores.[35]
>
> (ll. 349–58)

The image of an overflowing river is a traditional literary portent of civil disorder, but in Denham's poem it acquires, as will become apparent, a specific political and constitutional focus. In an earlier version of *Coopers Hill* (1642), this passage had underscored the need for moderation on both sides in England's political struggles, as the original ending of the poem emphasizes:

> Therefore their boundlesse power let Princes draw
> Within the Channell, and the shores of Law,
> And may that Law, which teaches Kings to sway
> Their Scepters, teach their Subjects to obey.
>
> (ll. 351–4)

But the final version of the poem, completed after the civil war in 1655, concludes with the image of an irresistible deluge, an emblem of inundating political chaos.

The rhetoric of Burke's passage follows the pattern of the earlier version of *Coopers Hill*. The flood threatened by the 'pickaxes of all the levellers of France' has not as yet overwhelmed the 'mounds and dykes of the low, fat, Bedford level' because the land continues to enjoy the protection of the 'proud Keep of Windsor'. Like Denham in his 1642 version,

---

[35] John Denham, *Coopers Hill*, in Brendan O Hehir, *Expans'd Hieroglyphicks: A Critical Edition of Sir John Denham's* Coopers Hill (Berkeley and Los Angeles, 1969), 161–2. I quote from the final, 1655 edn. of the poem.

Burke projects a landscape that demands to be 'read' in the optative mood: he expresses the hope that British political institutions will withstand the impending revolutionary storm. His pun on 'level' and 'levellers' makes explicit the historical parallel he sees between the English civil war, with its irruption of popular violence culminating in the death of Charles I, and the revolution in France, where ancient institutions and their restraining influence have similarly been swept away. Implicit in the prospect views offered by both writers, however, are the traces of a third level of literary expression and historical reality, Virgil's *Georgics*, written during the protracted struggle that was to bring Octavian, later Augustus Caesar, to power.

The image of the overflowing river in Denham and Burke recalls two passages in Book 1 of the *Georgics*. The first is a description of fertile fields overwhelmed by storm and flood:

> Oft, too, comes rushing from the sky a vast column of waters, the clouds mustering from the length and breadth of heaven, and making their dark storms into one great murky tempest; down crashes the whole dome of the firmament, washing away before the mighty rain-deluge all those smiling crops, all for which the ox toiled so hard. The dykes are filled, the deep streams swell with a roar, and the sea glows again through every panting inlet. (1. 322–7)[36]

The second passage, which appears toward the end of the first *Georgic*, adds a political dimension to this conventional description of uncontrolled nature. The context is Virgil's account of the omens and natural prodigies that presaged the assassination of Julius Caesar: 'With the sweep of its frenzied torrent it bears down whole forests, that king of rivers, Eridanus, hurling before it, far as the plain extends, stall and cattle alike' (1. 481–3).[37] At the time he wrote these lines, the outcome of the civil disorder that followed Caesar's death was still in doubt, hence the prayer for peace and for Octavian's success that concludes the first *Georgic*. Like Denham and Burke, Virgil seeks to avert the omen of disaster by setting its consequences boldly before the reader's eye and by prognosticating an alternative outcome of unity, peace, and plenty—a

---

[36] Virgil, *Georgics* 1, in *The Works of Virgil Translated into English Prose*, trans. John Conington (London, 1890), 44.   [37] Ibid. 49.

future to be achieved by trading swords for ploughshares and spears for pruning hooks.

Fredric Jameson has suggested that the relation between the 'emergent, strong form' of a genre (such as Virgil's *Georgics*) and the genre's subsequent historical manifestations is to be understood as one of 'formal *sedimentation*'. The initial form embodies a more or less explicit ideological 'message' that remains sedimented in the form when it is revived and 'refashioned' in a different social and cultural context: 'The ideology of the form itself, thus sedimented, persists ... as a generic message which coexists—either as a contradiction or, on the other hand, as a mediatory or harmonizing mechanism—with elements from later stages.'[38] For seventeenth- and eighteenth-century writers the generic message of the *Georgics* was in many respects a harmonizing one because the historical forces they detected at work in their own time so closely paralleled the conditions of Virgil's Rome: 'civil war, land expropriation, new capital formation, and the prospect of a period of national unity and peaceful prosperity somewhere just ahead'.[39]

Yet the analogy between England and Augustan Rome was also a troubling one for observers in the eighteenth century, since the *pax Romana* was bought at the price of Rome's republican liberties and institutions.[40] Thus, the triumphant poetic account of the all-conquering Caesar that concludes Book 4 of the *Georgics* inevitably aroused deep ambivalence in Virgil's eighteenth-century readers: 'Such was the song I was making; a song of the husbandry of fields and cattle, and of trees; while Caesar, the great, is flashing war's thunderbolt over the depths of Euphrates, and dispensing among willing nations a conqueror's law, and setting his foot on the road to the sky' (4. 559–62).[41] Eighteenth-century writers shied away from this convergence of the georgic and the heroic: though the parallel between Rome's imperial triumph and Britain's own nascent

---

[38] Fredric Jameson, *The Political Unconscious: Narrative as a Socially Symbolic Act* (Ithaca, NY, 1981), 140–1.   [39] Low, *Georgic Revolution*, 124.
[40] For a discussion of the problematic nature of the Augustan legacy for 18th-c. Britain, see Watt, 'Two Historical Aspects of the Augustan Tradition', in Brissenden (ed.), *Studies in the Eighteenth Century*, and Howard D. Weinbrot, *Augustus Caesar in 'Augustan' England: The Decline of a Classical Norm* (Princeton, 1978).
[41] Virgil, *Georgics*, 107.

imperial ambitions was inviting, their inevitable awareness of the historical sequel, in which Rome slid from agrarian self-sufficiency and republican virtue into political instability, social decadence and luxury, and economic dependence on slavery, undercuts Virgil's prophetic optimism with an ominous historical prospect.[42]

The heroic perspective of imperial peace, permanence, and prosperity in Virgil's *Georgics*—in Jameson's terms, the form's persistent 'ideological message'—is contradicted, therefore, by the ironic recognition of subsequent practitioners of the genre that the georgic spirit and the civilization it promises are a precarious cultural vision, to be fought for and defended with vigilance. Even Burke, in his heroic prospect of Windsor Castle, implicitly acknowledges the transitoriness of the scene he describes, for the lines he cites from *The Aeneid* as the concluding flourish of his powerful tribute to political permanence—'so long as the house of Aeneas shall dwell on the Capitol's moveless rock, and a Roman father shall be the world's lord'—refer to a long-vanished historical reality. The modern georgic mode thus records a significant conceptual change from its classical forebear, a change that is noted, as Ralph Cohen points out, 'by the fact that poetic features which were recessive or backgrounded or even nonexistent in the previous type are now dominant or foregrounded'.[43]

Cohen observes in particular that Virgil's account in Book 1 of the destructive effects of uncontrolled nature is accorded a new prominence by his modern imitators, who transform this Virgilian allusion into an extended political argument. This reordering of formal features reflects a new political consciousness in seventeenth-century England. Denham's description of the raging Thames in *Coopers Hill* furnishes a case in point; the passage is clearly intended to be read as an allusion to a specific constitutional issue and not only as a conventional topos of civil disorder. The river has come to symbolize royal power, which is legitimately channelled by customs and laws, such as Magna

---

[42] A case in point is James Thomson, whose georgic optimism in *The Seasons* is tempered in his later poem *Liberty* by an awareness of the deleterious effects to which commercial and imperial success can lead.

[43] Cohen, 'Innovation and Variation', 10.

Carta, but which will turn into a raging, destructive torrent if aggressive attempts are made to dam and alter its course, that is, if royal power is forcibly subjected to popular will. Denham's political dialectic is a binary model of *concordia discors* or political harmony between the royal prerogative on the one hand and the subjects' liberty on the other. Such a balance was achieved with the signing of Magna Carta,

> wherein the Crown
> All marks of Arbitrary power lays down:
> Tyrant and slave, those names of hate and fear,
> The happier stile of King and Subject bear.
> (ll. 329–32)

But this reconciliation of opposing interests was, as Denham concedes, rarely achieved in English history: both sovereign and subject have habitually encroached upon each other's sphere, and 'one excesse | Made both, by striving to be greater, lesse'. In the most recent conflict the consequence of popular attempts to force the royal prerogative into a narrower channel has been the unrestrained deluge that concludes the 1655 version of *Coopers Hill*.

Denham's hierarchical, binary interpretation of the flooded-river image does not, however, pass uncontested by his contemporaries. As early as 1642, at about the time that he was composing the first drafts of his poem, the analogy of the overflowing river was appropriated to illustrate a different conception of constitutional balance. In *His Majesty's Answer to the Nineteenth Propositions of Both Houses of Parliament* (18 June 1642), written by two of Charles I's advisers, the English government is defined not as a hierarchical system of descending authority meeting ascending privileges, but as a tripartite sharing of political power:

There being three kinds of government among men, absolute monarchy, aristocracy and democracy, and all these having their particular conveniences and inconveniences, the experience and wisdom of your ancestors hath so moulded this out of a mixture of these acts as to give to this kingdom (as far as humane prudence can contrive) the conveniences of all three, without the inconveniences of any one, as long as the balance hangs even between the three estates, and they run jointly on in their proper channel (begetting verdure and fertility in the meadows on both sides) and the overflowing of either on either side raise no deluge or inundation.[44]

In his wide-ranging study of European political discourse, *The Machiavellian Moment*, J. G. A. Pocock identifies this document as a genuine case of paradigmatic historical change: it introduced a new way of articulating and perceiving political relationships, a formulation so clearly answering a pressing historical need that it quickly became received constitutional wisdom, to be reaffirmed and reiterated endlessly in the ensuing century and a half.

To argue for a balance of three estates (implying proportionate equality) as indispensable to political stability, rather than the descending hierarchy of kingship, is, as Pocock demonstrates, to introduce the language of classical republicanism into a polity that had previously defined itself solely in terms of patriarchy and monarchy. Each element in this new balance of interests contributes to the whole its characteristic virtue, while checking the vices to which the other partners are subject (such as monarchy's tendency towards tyranny and democracy's drift towards demagoguery and mob rule). Moreover, following on the premisses of this new language, the balance of the system becomes a bulwark against the vagaries of fortune, symbolized by the river in its uncontrollable periods of flood. Pocock explains how this novel constitutional theory transforms the meaning, if not the form, of inherited georgic imagery:

> The government of England ... without ceasing to manifest the element of monarchy, is being presented as a classical republic; and we catch a glimpse of Machiavelli's imagery of fortune. The three elements [of mixed government] constitute a river, that ancient symbol of time: while it runs in its proper channel, bringing richness and fertility, the themes of order and descending grace are still being invoked; but once we hear that the balance is necessary to prevent 'deluge and inundation,' the river has become that of fortune, against which princes and republics erect dykes by the aid of virtue.[45]

---

[44] Quoted in J. G. A. Pocock, *The Machiavellian Moment: Florentine Political Thought and the Atlantic Republican Tradition* (Princeton, 1975), 362. For the full text, see 'The king's answer to the Nineteen Propositions', in J. P. Kenyon (ed.), *The Stuart Constitution, 1603–88* (Cambridge, 1966), 21.

[45] Pocock, *Machiavellian Moment*, 363.

Burke's prospect view of Windsor Castle effects the same symbolic metamorphosis, in this instance reinterpreting the feudal political order represented by the Norman fortress. First, as Paul Fussell shows, Burke's emphasis on the castle's 'kindred and coeval towers' transforms a feudal instrument of royal pre-eminence into an image of mixed government—a physical embodiment of the constitutional settlement of 1689. Just as the castle is both delimited and defended by its twin towers, so too the Crown is both circumscribed and supported by the lords and commons. Second, the language of fortune, that image of civil chaos against which a balance of power is the chief defence, re-emerges (somewhat disguised) in Burke's vision of a flood of French 'levellers', who aspire to demolish with their pickaxes the protective dykes and mounds of the agricultural landscape. The flood that threatens the counterpoise and harmony of the land is no longer the pent-up torrent of royal rage but the democratic current of revolutionary mob rule. Further echoes of the age-old conception of the goddess Fortune, who personifies the insecurities inherent in any struggle for political power and stability, can be heard in Burke's characterization of these latter-day levellers as creatures dominated by caprice, irrationality, and passion—consumed by 'the blights of envy ... [and] the spoliations of rapacity'. At this point the language of the georgic and that of Scriblerian satire coalesce in a characteristically Burkean, but also a representatively eighteenth-century literary expression of political virtue beset by the vagaries of corruption and fortune.

Burke performs a masterful verbal sleight of hand in purifying Windsor Castle of its historical associations with royal coercion and transforming it into a benign symbol of constitutional government. Indeed, he appears to have accomplished nothing less than the desire he had expressed in 1780 of promoting substantial political change while retaining the outward appearance of continuity with the past. None the less, there is a point beyond which substantial alterations in political institutions and social relations either precipitate changes in external forms (or in the perception of those forms), or render them altogether meaningless. Social, intellectual, economic, and technological innovations such as the Reformation or the invention of the printing press can so alter circumstances as to make the continuity of institutions and customs largely a matter of appearances. The notable element in Burke's analysis of political and social change is his identification of innovation as the wild card in the game. Machiavelli had been much concerned about the destabilizing effects of political innovation (understood in the narrow sense of the overthrow or replacement of a previous ruler or form of government), which exposed the state to uncertainty or 'fortune', but Burke's attention is focused on a much broader and more unpredictable process of change.

Indeed, 'innovation', as understood in its broad, eighteenth-century sense, largely replaced 'fortune' in the political vocabulary of the period as a key term to explain destructive social and political change. This shift is also reflected in the use of georgic imagery, as Burke makes clear by his association of French 'levellers', whom he later explicitly identifies as innovators and projectors, with the effects of raging floods. Equally telling is the link he establishes between improvement and the fruitful control of flood waters, bringing 'verdure and fertility' to the land, instead of devastation. The agent of that control is the constitutional government represented by Windsor Castle, but that agency is further personified in the person of King George III, characterized in Burke's own words as a 'benevolent Prince' who promotes 'the commerce, manufactures and agriculture of his kingdom; in which his Majesty shews an eminent example, who even in his amusements is a patriot, and in hours of leisure an improver of his native soil' (ix. 167). With these words the political and cultural remapping of Windsor is complete. The castle and its environs have become a country estate, and the king is affectionately regarded as the lord of the manor. The contrasting image of kingship, from which George III has so gloriously deviated, is that of Henry VIII, 'a *levelling* tyrant, who oppressed all descriptions of his people, but who fell with particular fury on every thing that was *great and noble*' (ix. 167). Henry VIII was not only a feudal despot but also, as the term 'levelling' implies, a dangerous constitutional innovator, whose baneful influence survives in the current Duke of Bedford, an undeserving beneficiary of Henry's confiscatory depredations.

In characterizing the king as a country gentleman, Burke literalizes his conception of Britain, in its political arrangements, as a great landed estate. Burke's view of his sovereign was widely shared by his contemporaries, who referred to their king with polite amusement as 'Farmer George'. In the Preface to Nathaniel Kent's *Some Particulars of the King's Farm, at Windsor*, William Fermor remarks, 'his Majesty is not only a great Encourager of Agriculture, but a considerable practical Farmer himself.—It has at all times been a profession much honoured and encouraged by the wisest Monarchs in all countries.'[46] In the 1790s the king established two model farms at Windsor, a 1,000-acre 'Norfolk' farm and a 400-acre 'Flemish' farm, where he conducted experiments with the use of oxen as draft animals. He was also instrumental in introducing the notable wool-producing merino sheep into England and in 1792 presented Arthur Young with a merino ram named 'Don'. The king's gift prompted Young to write, 'How many millions of men are there that would smile, if I were to mention the sovereign of a great empire giving a ram to a farmer.'[47]

Young's comment illustrates perfectly the perceptual shift underlying the georgic discourse Burke has inherited. In contrast with the warlike figure of Octavian, who conquers the world by force of arms, and his modern antitype Henry VIII, George is a pacific king, who has become the 'sovereign of a great empire' by encouraging agriculture, trade, and commerce. This opposition traces back to *Coopers Hill*, in which the destructive effects of Henry VIII's religious and political innovations ('may no such storme | Fall on our times', writes Denham) are contrasted with the beneficent influence of the river Thames, which the poet presents as a natural emblem of good kingship. The Thames is a natural improver of the native soil: it fertilizes the land along its banks through annual inundations, and it provides an avenue of trade and commerce with the rest of the world. 'In this flooding', remarks Brendan O Hehir, 'the Thames is moderate and predictable; it never by angry, unruly, or unexpected inundations destroys the wealth it has fostered: it is not a king of the type of Henry VIII. . . . In [its commercial] activity likewise the Thames is compared to a "wise king," and again, though

---

[46] Nathaniel Kent, *Some Particulars of the King's Farm, at Windsor, in 1798* (Oxford, n.d.), pp. iii–iv.
[47] Arthur Young, *Annals of Agriculture*, xvii. (1792), 529.

without emphasis in the poem, its activity is contrary to the disruptive activity of Henry VIII.'[48] The model of kingship idealized in the river and in the person of George III is one of commercial rather than martial greatness: empires are now to be won through trade and improvement instead of military prowess.

In his *Essays on Husbandry* (1764), Walter Harte links this shift in georgic language to changes in the perception of economic and political relationships:

> People are naturally increased by industry in husbandry; and the self-same industry falls by degrees into trade and commerce. Whatever else enriches a state, is not a constant feeding stream,
>
> > (Tho' deep, yet clear, tho' gentle, yet not dull,
> > Strong without rage, without o'erflowing full;)
>
> but a momentary impetuous torrent, more destructive than fruitful.—It was a received opinion amongst the antients, that a large, busy, well-peopled village, situated in a country thoroughly cultivated, was a more magnificent sight than the palaces of noblemen and princes, in the midst of neglected lands.[49]

A nation's wealth, Harte argues, is the product of its people's 'industry': any other means of enriching the state, such as conquest or plunder, is 'but a momentary impetuous torrent, more destructive than fruitful'.

Significantly, in defining the 'constant feeding stream' of industry, Harte cites the most famous lines Denham ever wrote, two couplets that were to become the poetic touchstone of eighteenth-century social and aesthetic ideals:

> > O could I flow like thee, and make thy stream
> > My great example, as it is my theme!
> > Though deep, yet clear, though gentle, yet not dull,
> > Strong without rage, without ore-flowing full.[50]
> >   (ll. 189–92)

These lines project an image of harmonious power, a balance implying a tolerance of variety within a framework of order and

---

[48] O Hehir, *Expans'd Hieroglyphicks*, 196.
[49] Harte, *Essays on Husbandry*, i. 10–11.
[50] Denham, *Coopers Hill*, in O Hehir, *Expans'd Hieroglyphicks*, 151.

a reconciliation of contrasting and opposing forces. This balance is the ideological justification of the change that improvement brings. In employing the river image to define his use of the heroic couplet, the emerging dominant verse form of the period, Denham implicitly links literary form and ideological concerns: the harmony of balance, whether political or literary, is reified as a natural and enduring phenomenon—as natural as the river Thames, whose stream brings agricultural and commercial prosperity.

Harte's concluding observation that a prosperous village presents a more magnificent prospect than the palace of a nobleman serves as a gloss on eighteenth-century Britain's idealization of its monarch as a farmer rather than a warrior. This transformation in the public perception of the king is symptomatic of a much broader redefinition, traced by Anthony Low, of what may be said to constitute 'virtuous and public-spirited behavior . . . from the martial ideal that is proper to feudalism to the georgic ideal that is proper to a newly centralized and peaceful nation-state'.[51] As is so often the case, a change in historical reality preceded a change in perceptions and definitions. By the late Middle Ages, the military functions of the gentry were already on the decline, with 'scutage' or a payment of money substituting for a knight's personal military service, and the gentry's agricultural activities were increasing in importance.[52]

But the chorus of praise for the pursuits of the gentleman farmer certainly reaches a crescendo in the eighteenth century, as such writers as Harte, Kames, Kent, Marshall, and Young extol the ideal of the gentleman and aristocrat as improver over the martial aristocratic ideal represented by a Marlborough. In this vein, Young offers words of praise for Burke's great Whig patron, Lord Rockingham, whose 'husbandry . . . is much more worthy of attention than that of any palace'. What singles out Rockingham for Young's attention is his leadership in encouraging the cultivation of turnips as animal fodder: 'Much more genuine fame ought to attend such an action, than the gaining a

---

[51] Low, *Georgic Revolution*, 123.
[52] G. E. Mingay, *The Gentry: The Rise and Fall of a Ruling Class* (London, 1976), 18–25.

score of battles: The senseless rabble may praise the military hero; it belongs to *the few* to venerate the spirited cultivator.'[53] Indeed, the lowly turnip brought lasting fame to another prominent Whig, Charles, Viscount Townshend, who was dubbed 'Turnip Townshend' for his efforts in popularizing its cultivation. Townshend was immortalized in Pope's poetry, alongside such figures as Bathurst and Burlington, as the ideal improving aristocrat: 'Who then shall grace, or who improve the Soil? | Who plants like BATHURST, or who builds like BOYLE.'[54] Anecdotal or literary accounts like these, it should be said, are often subjective and misleading. The fact that writers felt the need to shout these effusions of praise and encouragement from the sidelines implies, according to G. E. Mingay, that the great landowners were themselves more concerned with rents and estate administration than with experimentation in husbandry techniques, leaving the work of discovery to country gentlemen, owner-occupiers, and major tenants.[55] None the less, the literary articulation of this ideal points to a cultural need whose urgency can perhaps be measured by the extent to which the ideal contradicts the historical facts.

Lord Kames, himself an improver and man of letters, participates in this process of ideological redefinition and

---

[53] Arthur Young, *A Six Months Tour through the North of England* (London, 1770), i. 307, 316–17.

[54] *Epistle to Burlington*, ll. 177–8. Pope refers to Townshend in his *Horatian Imitations* (*Epistle* II. ii. 270–3). Young comments in *Annals of Agriculture*, v (1786), 'the name of this Lord Townshend is repeated with an increase of applause and eulogy for his agriculture, by writers; and relished by whole nations of readers who scarcely know an iota of his political life. . . . [T]he memory of this lord, though a man of great abilities, will in a few ages be lost as a minister and a statesman, and preserved only as a farmer. What is this but the triumph of good sense and of that gradual refinement of the human mind which the universal culture of experimental philosophy has effected? The period will perhaps arrive when this spirit will be matured, and politicians and military heroes registered in colours which have not yet been assigned them.' (In G. E. Mingay (ed.), *The Agricultural Revolution: Changes in Agriculture 1650–1880* (London, 1977), 104–5.

[55] *English Landed Society*, 163–88. Not the least of the problems confronting the agricultural historian is that of definitions. The aristocracy, gentry, and yeomanry were all landowners, but they differed greatly in the degrees of wealth, privilege, and social and political influence they enjoyed. The term 'gentleman' is an equally vexed one, referring at different times and in different ways to all or parts of the above groups. Some of these problems of definition will be addressed in the next chapter.

shrewdly places it in a historical perspective: 'In former times, hunting was the only business of a gentleman. The practice of blood made him rough and hard-hearted. . . . How delightful the change, from the hunter to the farmer, from the destroyer of animals to the feeder of men!'[56] Kames's new gentleman, as Feingold points out, has successfully negotiated the self-transformation into a shrewd man of practical affairs, thus ensuring his survival and continuing influence in a modern economic order. And, as ideological justification for this metamorphosis, the entrepreneurial activities of the modern gentleman continue to be presented in the moral and literary language of the georgic. Thus, in introducing a lengthy Virgilian passage on the physical, intellectual, and moral benefits of the agricultural life, Kames casts a quick eye over the balance sheet: 'In the view of profit, agriculture is fit for every man. But my present view is to recommend it, as of all occupations the most proper for gentlemen in a private station.'[57] No clash is perceived between the values of capitalism and the georgic traditions of the countryside.

V

Yet this process of ideological redefinition does not unfold altogether seamlessly. Burke, for his part, looks upon the Duke of Bedford as a class traitor, a dangerous innovator who has embraced, without forethought, a revolution that proclaims as its ultimate aim the eradication of the very social class to which Bedford himself belongs. As he did previously in the *Reflections*, Burke translates this political apostasy into georgic terms by imagining the Duke's estates as a laboratory for a squadron of mad French political projectors:

His Grace's landed possessions are irresistibly inviting to an *agrarian* experiment. They are a downright insult upon the Rights of Man. . . . There is scope for seven philosophers to proceed in their analytical experiments, upon Harington's seven different forms of republicks, in

---

[56] Henry Home, Lord Kames, *The Gentleman Farmer. Being an Attempt to Improve Agriculture, by Subjecting It to the Test of Rational Principles* (Edinburgh, 1776), p. xviii.   [57] Ibid. p. xv.

the acres of this one Duke. Hitherto they have been wholly unproductive to speculation; fitted for nothing but to fatten bullocks, and to produce grain for beer, still more to stupify the dull English understanding. . . . What a pity it is, that the progress of experimental philosophy should be checked by his Grace's monopoly! (ix. 177–8)

Burke imagines, in a rhetorical *tour de force* reminiscent of Swift's most inventive satirical catalogues, the innumerable 'constitutions ready made, ticketed, sorted, and numbered', that might be tried out on the Duke's lands. He singles out James Harrington, the author of *The Commonwealth of Oceana* (1656), as the inspiration for the French innovators, thus underscoring the typological link he previously established between the English and French revolutions. He proffers, in short, a revised version of Swift's tale of Count Munodi, reminding his readers of his earlier account in the *Reflections*: 'Their geographers, and geometricians, have been some time out of practice. It is some time since they have divided their own country into squares. . . . They want new lands for new trials' (ix. 178).

Like the projectors in Lagado, who propose new methods in architecture as well as in agriculture, the French innovators also cast their envious eyes on Bedford's architectural treasures:

They have calculated what quantity of matter convertible into nitre is to be found in Bedford House, in Woburn Abbey, and in what his Grace and his trustees have still suffered to stand of that foolish royalist Inigo Jones, in Covent Garden. . . . Their Academy del *Cimento* (per antiphrasin) with Morveau and Hassenfrats at it's head, have computed that the brave Sans-culottes may make war on all the aristocracy of Europe for a twelvemonth, out of the rubbish of the Duke of Bedford's buildings. (ix. 178)

Here Burke makes reference, as he indicates in a footnote, to the discovery of French chemists that mortar can be converted into saltpetre or potassium nitrate, an essential component of gunpowder: 'There is nothing, on which the leaders of the Republick, one and indivisible, value themselves, more than on the chymical operations . . . by which they reduce the magnificent ancient country seats of the nobility, decorated with the *feudal* titles of Duke, Marquis, or Earl, into magazines of what they call *revolutionary* gunpowder' (ix. 179). In contrast with Burke's conversion of Windsor Castle into a country house and a symbol of mixed government, a demonic metamorphosis is underway in France, where 'strong *chateaus*' and '*feudal* fortresses' (ix. 179) have been reduced to ruins in order to furnish the revolution with ammunition. Windsor Castle itself, Burke's touchstone of political and economic improvement, ironically offers the potential to be a magazine of explosive innovation, rather than the bulwark of a fertile estate.

Burke's contrast between improvement and innovation, between constructive and destructive change, could hardly be dramatized more graphically. Yet, in order to expose the incongruity of Bedford's armchair support for a cause that threatens his class interests, Burke is compelled to suppress some glaring contradictions in his own analysis of revolutionary innovation. Thus, he presents the Duke on his estates as a bluff country squire whose main preoccupation is 'to fatten bullocks, and to produce grain for beer'; his acreage has hitherto 'been wholly unproductive to speculation' (ix. 177). Yet Bedford's reputation with his contemporaries is very much at odds with Burke's account of him. In fact, he was a celebrated proponent of agricultural improvement, rather than the inert, somnolent squire suggested in Burke's description. As such, he can be characterized, contrary to his opponent's view, as a speculator— in both the economic and intellectual senses of that term. 'The splendid exertions', writes Thomas Batchelor, 'of the late Duke of Bedford display a scientific character, which has few equals in the history of agriculture.'[58] Like King George III at Windsor, of whose improving activities Burke writes so approvingly, Bedford ran a model farm at Woburn; moreover, he was nominated to the original Board of Agriculture in 1793 and became the first president of the Smithfield Club. Burke finds it necessary, however, to discount Bedford's contributions to agricultural improvement, lest an acknowledgment of his improving zeal be misconstrued as an endorsement of his innovatory political views.

Burke's dilemma is that while he is anxious to endorse an ideology of economic improvement, he is unwilling to concede the need for political change that improvement brings in its

---

[58] Thomas Batchelor, *General View of the Agriculture of the County of Bedford* (London, 1808), 32.

wake—he is unwilling, in short, to recognize that the beneficial improvement he endorses has set in motion a process of change and dislocation revolutionary in its scope. Or rather, if we are to do justice to the complexity of his vision, we must recognize that at various junctures he does see both sides of the picture. He acknowledges on one level the destructive potential of unregulated capital—'We dread the operation of money', he exclaims in a speech against Warren Hastings (Bohn, vii. 449)—but perceives on another level its indispensability in a modern economy.[59] This ideological uncertainty is mirrored in Thomas Batchelor's *The Progress of Agriculture*, which celebrates rural progress in general and Bedford's contributions in particular. Batchelor's verses fall in with the georgic mode of Denham and Pope, imitating their use of the prospect survey and presenting the theme of improvement in terms of the classic contrast between controlled and uncontrolled river waters. But a note of uncertainty creeps into an otherwise conventionally laudatory poem: the voice of the peasant is heard lamenting the destructive effects of agricultural change.

> Fled is your long-accumulating store,
> Your houses, meadows, fields are theirs no more
> . . . .
> Monopoly has rear'd her gorgon head,
> To strike the source of rural comforts dead.
> . . . .
> Why shall the slender comforts of the poor,
> In futile pomp, augment the rich man's store?
> Why must the low, laborious, starveling band
> For ever curse *Improvement's* ruthless hand?[60]

Significantly, Batchelor uses the terms 'improvement' and 'innovation' interchangeably in his poem, referring in these

---

[59] On this point, see David Bromwich, *Politics by Other Means: Higher Education and Group Thinking* (New Haven, 1992), 55–6: 'For the market is just where the spirit of reckless innovation begins. It is an institution that cannot affect to speak sincerely for public virtue or the common good or any of the more local values that conservatives evoke to shore up against the tidal weight of modernity. The market has been the single most volatile and relentless force for modernization in our time.' These effects, Bromwich maintains, are a source of great embarrassment to present-day American conservatives who accept uncritically the workings of the capitalist market, but the same dilemma, I would argue, already confronts Burke in the late 18th-c.   [60] Batchelor, *The Progress of Agriculture*, 89, 92.

same lines to 'Innovation's fatal hand'. He recognizes that the distinction Burke is fond of drawing between beneficial and harmful change is in many respects an artificial one, and he seeks to redefine the problem of change in political and social terms.

Thus, as he airs the peasant's complaint, Batchelor is quick to qualify his criticism: 'I ask not Science to withdraw her hand, | Nor hoary Custom still to rule the land.'[61] He is no agricultural Luddite: new methods and new technologies are not harmful in themselves. But he objects that the privileged few have manipulated the process of change to their own advantage, accumulating ever greater wealth and power at the expense of the rural masses. Land enclosures, for example, have eroded the ancient rights on which the slender livelihood of the rural poor depended. Sounding a personal note, Batchelor laments that '*inclosure's* fatal page' compelled his own son to seek his fortune in the army, resulting in his death in the Napoleonic wars. Though his analysis is often confused, he senses a connection between the anti-revolutionary struggle of Britain against France and the entrenchment of a new order of privilege in Britain's improved countryside. Batchelor's response to the change he sees around him is an uneasy, contradictory mixture of old and new: he advocates the political leadership of 'progressive' aristocrats such as Bedford who pursue the cause of 'liberty and equal laws':

> Is there a name superior to the rest,
> Whom Agriculture's laurel wreaths invest . . .
> 'Tis thine, O *Bedford*! thine which shall extend,
> As far as peace and freedom own a friend![62]

Virgil's happy husbandman reappears in Batchelor's poem as one of Bedford's tenants, who 'breathes, when slaves and bigot minds defame, | A grateful sigh to gen'rous *Russel's* name'.[63] Ironically, the very person whom Burke excoriates as an unwitting abetter of revolutionary innovation is presented here as a model of the modern improving gentleman, whose vocation is the arts of peace rather than of war.

Batchelor's poem, with its hesitations and contradictions,

---

[61] Ibid. 90.   [62] Ibid. 98.   [63] Ibid. 78.

signals the attenuation of the georgic form, and its eventual demise as a new consciousness of the forces that are shaping nineteenth-century Britain demands new forms for its articulation. Pope's 'unbounded *Thames*' in *Windsor-Forest*, which 'flow[s] for all Mankind', has become Blake's 'charter'd Thames',[64] a river that no longer distributes freely its natural riches but is artificially confined by commercial greed. Yet, if the georgic disappears from view as a literary form, it lives a curious afterlife in political and economic discourse, which now increasingly distinguishes itself from the previously more undifferentiated discourse of humane letters. The thematic concerns of the georgic, in short, now fall within the purview of new, specialized academic disciplines, such as economics and agricultural science. In this chapter we have been tracing in Burke's political writings a single strand of this process of differentiation. But Burke is a transitional figure, whose works never lose the traces of the older, more inclusive conception of humane letters; and in one of his most overtly technical tracts, *Thoughts and Details on Scarcity*, we can see the final working-out of the dialectic of form and content that dominates his discourse of improvement.

In this economic pamphlet, Burke argues that neither the prices of agricultural products nor the cost of labour should be controlled by government: both must be left to the marketplace— to the 'laws of commerce, which are the laws of nature, and consequently the laws of God' (ix. 137). He maintains that the interests of farmers and labourers are identical, for the latter must be happy and well fed if they are to work efficiently for their employers. This fortunate congruity of interests operates only because, as C. B. Macpherson points out, Burke insists upon regarding the 'wage relation [as] part of a natural chain of subordination'; the farmer and the labourer are bound, in Macpherson's reading of Burke, by obligations that are a 'curious blend of free contract and customary status'.[65]

Though Burke's subject-matter is the laws of economics, he sees no incongruity in turning back to the georgic writers of

---

[64] 'London', in *Songs of Experience* (1794). See *William Blake's Writings*, ed. G. E. Bentley, Jr. (Oxford, 1978), i. 191.
[65] C. B. Macpherson, *Burke* (Oxford, 1980), 59–60.

ancient Rome for confirmation of his theory of labour and social relations:

> [O]f all the instruments of his [the farmer's] trade, the labour of man (what the ancient writers have called the *instrumentum vocale*) is that on which he is most to rely for the repayment of his capital. The other two, the *semivocale* in the ancient classification, that is, the working stock of cattle, and the *instrumentum mutum*, such as carts, ploughs, spades, and so forth, though not all inconsiderable in themselves, are very much inferiour in utility or in expence; and without a given portion of the first, are nothing at all. For in all things whatever, the mind is the most valuable and the most important; and in this scale the whole of agriculture is in a natural and just order; the beast is as an informing principle to the plough and cart; the labourer is as reason to the beast; and the farmer is as a thinking and presiding principle to the labourer. An attempt to break this chain of subordination in any part is equally absurd. (ix. 125)

He refers here to Varro's classification of the instruments of labour in *De Res Rusticae* (1. 17), which in turn draws on Aristotle's *Politics*. Though written in prose, Varro's treatise is very much a part of the georgic tradition that Burke has been drawing on in forming his ideology of improvement. Jacques Heurgon points out that the utility and practical bias of Varro's project, 'ne s'opposaient pas ... au désir de faire œuvre littéraire'.[66] Indeed, in both subject-matter (the breeding of large animals and beekeeping) and spirit and ideology, his book is widely regarded as an important source for Virgil, who began writing his *Georgics* at about the time Varro's work appeared.

The central theme that links Varro, Virgil, and Burke is the necessity of work: how is labour to be organized so as to be of the greatest benefit, morally and materially, to all? Burke's response to this question blends, typically, the old and the new, for he recognizes, as Macpherson has argued, that the new economics of farming will succeed only if certain features of the traditional social order are perpetuated, in particular the natural subordination of ranks. In Macpherson's words, 'the traditional order which he cherished was not simply any hierarchical order but a capitalist one'.[67] Nowhere is this blending of tradition and

---

[66] Jacques Heurgon, Introduction to Varro, *Économie Rural* [*Res Rusticae*] (Paris, 1978), i. p. xlv. [67] Macpherson, *Burke*, 61.

change more forcefully articulated than in the *Reflections*, when Burke argues that the accumulation of capital requires the preservation of a hierarchical social order:

To be enabled to acquire, the people, without being servile, must be tractable and obedient. The magistrate must have his reverence, the laws their authority. The body of the people must not find the principles of natural subordination by art rooted out of their minds. They must respect that property of which they cannot partake. They must labour to obtain what by labour can be obtained; and when they find, as they commonly do, the success disproportioned to the endeavour, they must be taught their consolation in the final proportions of eternal justice. Of this consolation, whoever deprives them, deadens their industry, and strikes at the root of all acquisition as of all conservation. (viii. 290).

The Whig economic order of eighteenth-century Britain, with its espousal of the ideology of improvement, had successfully adapted itself to the country's traditional political and social structures. The French Revolution, in contrast, by calling status and subordination into question, threatened the very conditions of economic improvement that the Whigs had so conspicuously exploited.

It is in this context that one begins to appreciate fully Burke's literary accomplishment in appropriating the formal literary tradition of the georgic to articulate his political and economic vision of improvement. The form of his argument has been fully adapted to its content, an accomplishment that realizes at the literary level the ideal of political change he had expressed in his letter of 1780. In large measure this was the political direction that Victorian England was to take. And yet, as the rapid demise of the georgic in the early nineteenth century (both as a poetic genre and a mode of discourse) suggests, the response to change, however measured and restrained, produces unintended and far-reaching consequences. Not least of these is the ironic outcome that Burke was among the very last writers to use the cultural discourse of the georgic in all its literary and political complexity.

3
Gentlemen's Prospects: Viewing the World from the 'Elevation of Reason'

Perhaps the most salient formal|contribution of seventeenth- and eighteenth-century poets to the georgic tradition they inherited from their classical forebears and revived in their topographical poems is, as we have observed, the prospect survey. James Thomson's *The Seasons*, one of the most ambitious and extended adaptations of georgic form in the eighteenth century, is punctuated by such passages of visual assessment, moments when the narrator stands back and takes a broad view, an 'equal wide Survey', as he phrases it in *Summer*, vouchsafing him (and the reader) a glimpse of the order that underlies the welter of detail crowding the poem:

> Here let us sweep
> The boundless Landskip: now the raptur'd Eye,
> Exulting swift, to huge AUGUSTA send,
> Now to the *Sister-Hills* that skirt her Plain,
> To lofty *Harrow* now, and now to where
> Majestic *Windsor* lifts his Princely Brow.
>
> . . . .
>
> HEAVENS! what a goodly Prospect spreads around,
> Of Hills, and Dales, and Woods, and Lawns, and Spires,
> And glittering Towns, and gilded Streams, till all
> The stretching Landskip into Smoke decays!
> Happy BRITANNIA![1]

This spatial view, extending outwards from the viewer's immediate surroundings to infinity, embraces in its accumulating sweep an aristocratic political ideal. The elevation of the

---

[1] James Thomson, *Summer*, in *The Seasons*, ll. 1617, 1408–13, 1438–42; pp. 133, 124–5.

viewer's vantage point and its location on the aristocratic estate signal the ideal of embracing the nation in all its multifarious aspects and of identifying the national interest with those of the gentleman.[2] The vantage point of the viewer permits an extension in time as well as in space: the historical and political associations aroused by the surrounding estate carry the mind's eye into the past and the future, as though events in time were laid out spatially before the surveyor.

From first to last Edmund Burke's speeches and writings employ the same organizational strategy. In one of his most effective and earliest deployments of the prospect survey, the *Speech on Moving His Resolutions for Conciliation with the Colonies* (1774), he indicates his rhetorical intentions unmistakably:

Mr. Speaker, I cannot prevail on myself to hurry over this great consideration [of our profitable economic connections with America]. It is good for us to be here. We stand where we have an immense view of what is, and what is past. Clouds, indeed, and darkness rest upon the future. Let us, however, before we descend from this noble eminence, reflect that this growth of our national prosperity has happened within the short period of the life of man. (Bohn, i. 459)

What follows this introduction is a comprehensive political, historical, economic, and sociological survey of America breathtaking in its authority, scope, and sympathy. Burke's entire programme for dealing with the recalcitrant colonists, including the six resolutions he is proposing in his speech, follows logically from the evidence that his 'wide survey' lays open to the view of his parliamentary colleagues. The prospect of America forms, therefore, the structural core of his speech, around which the rest of his discourse coalesces. It convinces because of its apparent comprehensiveness and objectivity.

Or does it? However eloquent and masterful, Burke's *Speech on Conciliation* did not succeed in deflecting the British administration from its ultimately disastrous course in its confrontation with America. Such an outcome hardly comes as a surprise to anyone acquainted with the dynamics of eighteenth-century (or, for that matter, twentieth-century) parliamentary politics. Whatever its immediate political impact, however, the

---

[2] See Ralph Cohen, *The Unfolding of* The Seasons (Baltimore, 1970), 100.

Speech remains noteworthy for its heroic attempt to enact a lofty eighteenth-century political and cultural ideal: the model role of the gentleman, whose birth, education, and property ensure his competence and disinterest in the exercise of national leadership.

I use the term 'heroic' advisedly, because the ideal of the gentleman, for reasons to be explored in detail below, was increasingly called into question, made subject to revision, and laid open to attack in the course of the eighteenth century. In this connection, Burke's formal inclusion of the 'gentleman's prospect' in each of his most memorable speeches and political polemics represents a subtle and sophisticated response to the problem of the gentleman, whose role mutated in the course of the eighteenth century from an attenuated version of the renaissance courtier (in the mould of Castiglione's courtly ideal) to exemplar of civic virtue. Some aspects of this transformation have already been touched in the previous chapter; in the pages that follow I wish, first of all, to outline the eighteenth-century definition of the ideal gentleman, particularly as reflected in the 'prospect' literature of the period; then, to consider some of the practical problems and contradictions this conception occasioned; and, finally, to assess, at both the literary and political levels, Burke's contribution to this debate.

Before turning to the eighteenth-century ideal of the gentleman, however, it will be useful to say a few words by way of definition and to review what modern historians have concluded to be the social reality underlying the ideal. Such terms as 'aristocracy', 'gentleman', and 'gentry' are notoriously slippery and difficult to define. The term 'aristocracy', for example, originally denoted a form of government—rule by the best—and only much later came to mean the men and women, usually of hereditary nobility, who were deemed to make up the ruling group. Thus, excellence became confused with social standing, making possible a new and hostile coinage—'aristocrat'—by the time of the French revolution.[3] Some sense of the ambiguity and contested meaning that surrounded these terms in the late eighteenth century can be gained from a letter Burke wrote to

---

[3] Jonathan Powis, *Aristocracy* (Oxford, 1984), 6–7. See also J. V. Beckett, *The Aristocracy in England: 1660–1914* (Oxford, 1986).

Lord Fitzwilliam on 21 November 1791, in which he notes that the real object of the French Revolution is not to destroy absolute monarchy, but 'totally to root out that thing called an *Aristocrate* or Nobleman and Gentleman, (*Corr.* 6. 451). Burke's subsequent discussion of a *'natural* aristocracy' in *An Appeal from the New to the Old Whigs*, to which we will turn below, marks an attempt to return to the original conception of the term. Further confusion is occasioned by the fact that 'aristocracy' and 'nobility' are not altogether interchangeable terms; not all peers were wealthy or extensive landowners, landownership being the accepted economic criterion of aristocracy, nor were all the great landowners of England members of the nobility.[4]

At the next level of the social hierarchy, the gentry, definitions are even more problematic. Put simply, a gentleman was a person of independent means who lived on an unearned income derived preferably, but by no means exclusively, from land and who did not pursue any occupation or profession for gain. But the question of the level of income necessary to maintain this status has been widely debated. The poorer members of the gentry may well have enjoyed smaller incomes than the country's more prosperous farmers, but a well-to-do farmer such as Jane Austen's Robert Martin (in her novel *Emma*, which anatomizes the minute social gradations of the English countryside) was none the less not quite a gentleman. Some historians, such as J. H. Tawney, have included professionals (physicians, lawyers), prominent merchants, and comfortable farmers in the gentry, arguing that what marked these groups as socially cohesive was their social intermingling and their similarity in education and attitudes, rather than their possession of land.[5] However desirable a concrete, objective definition might be, it is clear that, as with so many social phenomena, perceptions have played a large role in defining the gentleman. A sceptical observer might well ask what it was about a certain kind of

---

[4] J. H. Porter, 'The Development of Rural Society', in *The Agrarian History of England and Wales*, gen. ed. Joan Thirsk (Cambridge, 1967–). vi. 836–8.

[5] R. H. Tawney, 'The Rise of the Gentry', *Economic History Review*, 1st ser. 11 (1941), 1–38. For a more detailed examination of the gentry in British history, see G. E. Mingay, *English Landed Society in the Eighteenth Century* (London, 1963), and his later study, *The Gentry: The Rise and Fall of a Ruling Class* (London, 1976).

income, education, and leisure that magically transformed an ordinary individual into that ineffable creature. To answer this question we must get at the rationale that lay behind the list of qualifications by which an individual was deemed to be a gentleman. One valuable means of ascertaining that rationale, which grows out of the ways in which persons perceive and come to understand the world around them, is to examine literary accounts: in this instance the inherent subjectivity of the literary text can be an evidential strength, rather than a limitation. Accordingly, to shed further light on these questions, I should like to turn to the prospect survey, one of the most characteristic literary manifestations of gentlemanly discourse in the eighteenth century.

I

The gentleman's superior qualifications for national leadership, criteria that Burke defends as 'a class of legitimate presumptions', are reflected in his special ability to embrace as a unified whole the multifarious elements that make up a wide prospect; thus, when such a scene is set forth (as in *The Seasons*), it is almost invariably attributed to the gentleman's gaze. One of those gazers in Thomson's poem is George Bubb Dodington, to whom *Summer* is dedicated. His entitlement to the role of gentleman-observer is vindicated in a complimentary Horatian epistle, 'The Happy Man' addressed to him in 1729. In that poem Thomson lauds Dodington, not only as a man of wealth, but as a gentleman whose comprehensive intellect, superadded to his material fortune, has brought him happiness. Fortune has furnished him a mind,

> Where *Judgment* sits clear-sighted, and surveys
> The Chain of *Reason* with unerring Gaze;
> Where *Fancy* lives, and to the brightening Eyes
> Bids fairer Scenes, and bolder Figures rise;
> Where *social Love* exerts her soft Command
> And plays the *Passions* with a tender Hand,
> Whence every *Virtue* flows, in rival Strife,
> And all the *moral Harmony* of Life.[6]

---

[6] James Thomson, *Liberty, The Castle of Indolence, and Other Poems*, ed. J. Sambrook (Oxford, 1986), 285.

The perspective of the gentleman-observer is founded on sense experience, especially visual experience, which Lockian empiricism posits as the basis of all knowledge. But what the gentleman sees is crucially supplemented, as Thomson emphasizes in his compliment to Dodington, by the mental operations of judgement, which connect the raw data of experience and abstract the underlying order: the 'chain of reason' and 'the moral harmony of life'.

It would seem that an intelligent observer of any social class ought to be capable of the intellectual accomplishment that Thomson here ascribes to Dodington, but, as John Barrell shows in *English Literature in History: 1730–80*, the consensus of opinion in the period held that any attempt to see society whole or to grasp the wider world coherently could only be undertaken by an individual whose outlook was not clouded by self-interest, political bias, or professional partiality. Where was such a paragon to be found? Not, apparently, among persons of determinate occupations—artisans, tradespeople, merchants, professionals—for their knowledge was considered too specialized and too directed towards specific ends to enable them to see comprehensively or to look beyond their private goals to larger public interests. However praiseworthy such men (let alone women) might be—however honest, frugal, prudent, and industrious—their private virtues could not be turned to public account because their professional bias prevented them from taking more than a partial view of their society or adjudicating its interests. The only person of whom it could be said that private and public virtue coincided was the comprehensive observer, the gentleman.[7] This individual, fortunately free from professional and occupational responsibilities, enjoyed the precious advantages of time and leisure, two necessary (if not sufficient) prerequisites for wisdom. In *Reflections on the Revolution in France* Burke quotes Ecclesiasticus 38: 25–34 in support of this proposition: 'The wisdom of a learned man cometh by opportunity of leisure: and he that hath little business shall become wise. How can he get wisdom that holdeth the

---

[7] John Barrell, *English Literature in History: An Equal, Wide Survey* (London, 1983), 33.

plough, and that glorieth in the goad, that driveth oxen, and is occupied in their labours, and whose talk is of bullocks? . . . They shall not be sought for in publick counsel, nor sit high in the congregation . . .' (see viii. 101).

Burke's citation of Ecclesiasticus appears as a footnote to his unfavourable analysis of the composition of the Estates General of France, particularly the membership qualifications of the representatives for the third estate. His analysis emphasizes that the prime requisite in a legislator must be a disinterested and inclusive understanding: 'when men are too much confined to professional and faculty habits . . . they are rather disabled than qualified for whatever depends on the knowledge of mankind, on experience in mixed affairs, on a comprehensive connected view of the various complicated external and internal interests which go to the formation of that multifarious thing called a state' (viii. 95). This declaration, with its insistence that the statesman be capable of taking 'a comprehensive, connected view' of things, defines the wise legislator in terms that recall Thomson's prospect observer. Like Thomson, Burke relies on visual and spatial metaphors to define the gentleman's unique capacity for reconciling the conflicting interests of society, and he shares the poet's recognition of the mysterious complexity and concatenation of the objects under the gentleman's scrutiny.

Burke supports his argument by surveying the occupational make-up of the French legislature. The preponderance of the membership of the third estate, he notes with dismay, are lawyers, and, withal, 'the inferior, unlearned, mechanical, merely instrumental members of the profession', rather than the flower of the fraternity, its 'distinguished magistrates', 'leading advocates', and 'renowned professors' (viii. 93). The consequences flowing from this fact are as inevitable as night follows day: 'Who could conceive, that men who are habitually meddling, daring, subtle, active, of litigious dispositions and unquiet minds, would easily fall back into their old condition of obscure contention, and laborious, low, unprofitable chicane? Who could doubt but that, at any expence to the state, of which they understood nothing, they must pursue their private interests, which they understood but too well?' (viii. 94). Pursuing their private interests at the expense of the French polity, they will inevitably produce a '*litigious constitution*' for their country, one that will procure them a perpetual and lucrative role in the future functioning of the state.

Burke is scarcely more optimistic about the other two professional groups dominating the legislature, physicians and 'dealers in stocks and funds'. 'The sides of sick beds', he notes sarcastically, 'are not the academies for forming statesmen and legislators' (viii. 94); and as for investors, the source of their interest in the state, money and credit, is so portable and evanescent as to provide no foundation whatsoever for stable and consistent political views. The instability and abstractness of paper credit was a source of deep anxiety in the eighteenth century, an anxiety epigrammatically voiced by Pope in *An Epistle to Bathurst*: 'Blest paper-credit! last and best supply! | That lends Corruption lighter wings to fly!' (ll. 69–70). The circulation of money and credit was thought not only to corrupt public authority by facilitating relationships of patronage and dependence, but also, at the most fundamental level, to undermine the very basis for civic personality or citizenship. An individual involved in trade was deemed to be so focused on concrete particulars—the value of commodities, for instance—that he or she was unable to generalize about the good of the whole, that is, exercise political and philosophical rationality. Burke was well aware of the volatility, passion, and irrationality of the individual whose life and sense of self were grounded in the symbolic property of coin and credit; in a well-known comparison of the 'noble ancient landed interest' with the 'new monied interest', he remarks, 'The monied interest is in its nature more ready for any adventure; and its possessors more disposed to new enterprizes of any kind. Being of a recent acquisition, it falls in more naturally with any novelties' (viii. 159).

By contrast, the crucial enabling condition of the gentleman's disinterested stance in the political affairs of his society was his possession of property. Because landed property was immovable, its owners were presumed to take a permanent interest in the affairs and political health of their country. The hereditary ownership of property, it was thought, not only furnished gentlemen with the necessary leisure to become wise, but also motivated them to provide for the happiness of their countrymen, whose labours were the source of their prosperity. G. E.

Mingay sums up the centrality of landownership in the economic, political, and social structure of eighteenth-century Britain:

> Landed property was the foundation of eighteenth-century society. The soil itself yielded the nation its sustenance and most of its raw materials, and provided the population with its most extensive means of employment; and the owners of the soil derived from its consequence and wealth the right to govern. Land was not of course the only important type of property but it was supreme: more tangible than the Funds, more stable than merchants' stock-in-trade, and more certainly valuable than industrialists' machines and implements . . . Moreover, the wealth, power and social influence produced by ownership of land enabled the landowning classes to control all local government beyond the bounds of the larger towns and to secure a dominating representation in Parliament itself. Above all, land was immovable and indestructible; and the very permanence of land gave stability to the society that was based upon it.[8]

The landowner's permanent stake in his country thus provided both the incentive and the means for his disinterest, his taking an enlarged view of the public interest. Barrell goes so far as to suggest that, 'The fixed nature of landed property made it arguably analogous to that viewpoint, beyond space and time, from which God surveyed his creation—an analogy that . . . had long been a crucial element in the claim for the disinterestedness of the man of landed property.'[9]

A number of writers in the eighteenth century set out composite portraits of the 'Compleat English Gentleman' (to borrow a phrase from Defoe). One of the most imposing of these portraits is Burke's account of the natural aristocrat in *An Appeal from the New to the Old Whigs,* a description unrolled for the reader in a magisterial periodic sentence:

> To be bred in a place of estimation; to see nothing low and sordid from one's infancy; to be taught to respect one's self; to be habituated to the censorial inspection of the public eye; to look early to public opinion; to stand upon such elevated ground as to be enabled to take a large view of the wide-spread and infinitely diversified combinations of men

---

[8] Mingay, *English Landed Society,* 3. See also L. Stone and J. C. F. Stone, *An Open Élite? England 1540–1880* (Oxford, 1984), 11–16.
[9] Barrell, *English Literature in History,* 72.

and affairs in a large society; to have leisure to read, to reflect, to converse; to be enabled to draw the court and attention of the wise and learned, wherever they are to be found;—to be habituated in armies to command and to obey; to be taught to despise danger in the pursuit of honour and duty; to be formed to the greatest degree of vigilance, foresight, and circumspection, in a state of things in which no fault is committed with impunity, and the slightest mistakes draw on the most ruinous consequences—to be led to a guarded and regulated conduct, from a sense that you are considered as an instructor of your fellow-citizens in their highest concerns, and that you act as a reconciler between God and man—to be employed as an administrator of law and justice, and to be thereby amongst the first benefactors to mankind—to be a professor of high science, or of liberal and ingenuous art—to be amongst rich traders, who from their success are presumed to have sharp and vigorous understandings, and to possess the virtues of diligence, order, constancy, and regularity, and to have cultivated an habitual regard to commutative justice—these are the circumstances of men, that form what I should call a *natural* aristocracy, without which there is no nation. (Bohn, iii. 86)

In the context of the present discussion, the detail in this portrait that most immediately attracts attention is, perhaps, the 'elevated ground' from which the gentleman can absorb a 'large view' of the 'infinitely diversified combinations' of individuals and forces at work in his society. He enjoys the leisure to reflect broadly on issues confronting the nation and the social position to command the views and expertise of a wide cross-section of his countrymen. Burke's gentleman is a generalist, rather than a specialist. Emancipated from a determinate intellectual or professional point of view, he feels free to draw without prejudice upon all interests and perspectives. Thus, he places himself 'amongst rich traders' without becoming one of them, and he attracts 'the court and attention of the wise and learned' without shackling his mind to one or another intellectual system (one recalls here Burke's professed aversion to abstract theory) or burying himself in an avalanche of technical detail. He is, in short, 'a professor of high science, or of liberal and ingenuous art'.

Burke's epithets here—'liberal and ingenuous'—are carefully chosen: the latter term, for instance, as both Johnson's *Dictionary* and the *OED* remind us, referred in the eighteenth century to activities 'Befitting a free-born person, or one of honourable station'. Burke's usage of 'ingenuous' in this sense seems more than a little tautologous, but his addition of the attribute 'liberal' clarifies his meaning considerably, for, as the *OED* explains, 'liberal' was originally 'the distinctive epithet of those "arts" or "sciences" . . . that were considered "worthy of a free man"; opposed to *servile* or *mechanical*'. More broadly, the term denotes pursuits directed to 'general intellectual enlargement and refinement', rather than 'narrowly restricted to the requirements of technical or professional training'. (Significantly, the *OED* offers citations from Burke's *Abridgment of English History* to illustrate its definitions of both these words.)

One consequence of pursuing 'mechanical' as opposed to 'liberal' arts is that such pursuits, focused as they necessarily are upon concrete objects, offer the individual no occasion to generalize from particulars or assess the formal relations among ideas. Burke's natural aristocrat, by contrast, has the time and means to reflect, a word that echoes the terminology of Locke, who defines reflection as that faculty of the mind which transforms concrete sense experience into complex, abstract ideas. This superior capability for reasoning was often adduced as an argument for the legitimacy of the eighteenth-century hierarchy of political authority. Thus, for example, when Burke, in his *Letter to Sir Hercules Langrishe*, describes the Irish response to religious repression, he acknowledges that the people can readily sense oppression and misconduct, but he insists that they cannot be relied upon to find appropriate remedies for such abuses. The 'sober, rational, and substantial' part of the Irish nation must be separated from the masses, who are unable to go beyond identifying '*practical* oppression'. They must never be 'called into council' to deliberate about '*the real cause,* or *the appropriate remedy*' for their grievances, 'because their reason is weak; because when once roused, their passions are ungoverned; because they want information; because the smallness of the property which individually they possess renders them less attentive to the consequence of the measures they adopt in affairs of moment' (ix. 621). The irrationality and ungovernable passion of the common people, as described here, make up an anti-political portrait that negates at every point Burke's portrayal of the natural aristocrat's cool rationality. And that rationality and breadth of perspective are here, once again, explicitly predicated upon the individual's possession of extensive property.

When combined in a single individual, the traits of rationality or judgement, controlled emotional response, and property ownership formed what the eighteenth century commonly referred to as the 'man of taste'. For Burke, as a number of recent commentators have argued, taste or aesthetic judgement is central to his conception of political leadership.[10] He repeatedly invokes taste as an indispensable moral touchstone, a test of the individual's fitness for the exercise of political power. An explanation for this sweeping conception is not far to seek. In the 'Introduction on Taste' prefaced to the second edition of *A Philosophical Enquiry into the Origin of Our Ideas of the Sublime and Beautiful,* Burke emphasizes that judgement must accompany sensibility in any true act of aesthetic perception: 'But as many of the works of imagination are not confined to the representation of sensible objects, nor to efforts upon the passions, but extend themselves to the manners, the characters, the actions, and designs of men, their relations, their virtues and vices, they come within the province of the judgment, which is improved by attention and by the habit of reasoning.'[11] The man of taste possesses, in Burke's phrase, 'rectitude of judgment', the word 'rectitude' connoting not only correctness but also moral integrity. The statesman and the connoisseur are thus almost identical in character, each endowed with sensibility and sound judgement, a union of qualities that Burke came to regard as the very embodiment of the gentleman. The same bias of mind that fits one to judge of a work of art—or, indeed, of a landscape prospect—is also requisite to the exercise of civil leadership.

This gentlemanly ideal of political disinterestedness can be

---

[10] See Neal Wood, 'The Aesthetic Dimension of Burke's Political Thought', *Journal of British Studies*, 4 (1964), 41–64; R. T. Allen, 'The State and Civil Society as Objects of Aesthetic Appreciation', *British Journal of Aesthetics*, 16 (1976), 237–42; Ronald Paulson, *Representations of Revolution (1789–1820)* (New Haven, 1983), 57–73; Frans De Bruyn, 'Edmund Burke's Natural Aristocrat: The "Man of Taste" as a Political Ideal', *Eighteenth-Century Life*, 11 (1987), 41–60; and Christopher Reid, *Edmund Burke and the Practice of Political Writing* (Dublin, 1985), 34–50.

[11] Edmund Burke, *A Philosophical Enquiry*, ed. J. Boulton (London, 1958), 22–3.

seen as a precursor of or precondition for the emerging doctrine of aesthetic disinterestedness. Both forms of disinterest are predicated on the possession of property, which Burke persistently defines in aesthetic and moral, as well as economic and legal, terms. In this light, his dictum, 'the place of every man determines his duty' acquires a new meaning: the 'place' that determines the gentleman's virtues and responsibilities is not only his social station and moral situation, but also his physical place, his estate. It is this conception of the estate that Burke has in mind when he compliments the Duke of Dorset on the tastefulness of his country house, emphasizing in particular the historical prospect that the estate embodies:

as for the place, I who am something of a lover of all antiquities must be a very great admirer, of Knowle. I think it the most interesting thing in England. It is pleasant to have preserved in one place the succession of the several Tastes of Ages; a pleasant habitation for the time, a grand repository of whatever has been pleasant at all times. This is not the sort of Place which every Banker, contractor, or Nabob can create at his pleasure. (*Corr.* vi. 394–5).

This 'goodly prospect', Burke claims, cannot be bought with money; the taste that it represents is the product of many generations, nurtured by the security and continuity of property. In mentioning the 'Nabob' as one of the hopeless aspirants to 'Taste' and 'Place', he alludes to his fear that vulgar fortune-hunters, newly returned from India, will use their ill-gotten wealth to buy their way into the ruling circles of Britain and make their narrow self-interest the guiding light of national policy. They are guided, not by comprehensive views, but only by the dazzling glare of their money, obscuring their view of any other object.

As if all these qualities do not already form a sufficiently exalted portrait of the ideal gentleman, Burke adds a sacerdotal dimension to his role: the gentleman acts 'as a reconciler between God and man'. This would seem to be a bold claim, especially in a Protestant society accustomed to the doctrine that Christ is the only true mediator between the human and the divine. Perhaps, in ascribing this God-like function to the gentleman, Burke falls in with the excessively fulsome rhetoric of other writers of his time, especially those, such as Thomson, who attribute the generalized catalogue of virtues Burke has enumerated to actual flesh-and-blood individuals. To survey 'The Chain of *Reason* with unerring Gaze', as Thomson claims of Bubb Dodington, is to exercise divine power, to see the world as only God can see it. One is driven to protest, as Barrell remarks of Richard Steele's portrait of the 'Fine Gentleman' in *The Guardian*, 34 (20 April 1713), that 'this creature is more easily described than discovered'.[12]

II

Steele acknowledges that his 'Fine Gentleman' is indeed a *rara avis*—'A finished Gentleman is perhaps the most uncommon of all the great Characters in Life'—but Burke is considerably less qualified in his definition. Whereas Steele makes it clear that his is an idealized and imagined portrait of the gentleman, Burke asserts that his delineation of the natural aristocrat 'is formed out of a class of legitimate presumptions, which, taken as generalities, must be admitted for actual truths' (Bohn, iii. 85–6). He concedes that his description, in all its details, was to be regarded as a composite 'taken as generalities', with no single individual ever combining in his person all the characteristics enumerated—though Burke's heartfelt eulogy for Lord Keppel in the concluding pages of *A Letter to a Noble Lord* would suggest otherwise. The crucial point, however, is that Burke wants to insist on the actual truth, the concrete attainability, of the circumstance he sets forth: 'Men, qualified in the manner I have just described, form in nature, as she operates in the common modification of society, the leading, guiding, and governing part' (Bohn, iii. 86).

None the less, as his use of the word 'presumptions' implies, Burke's certainty of the existence of a natural aristocracy in all the perfection he attributes to it is less than absolute. A hint of empirical uncertainty, of mere probability or supposition, creeps in under the shadow of the phrase 'legitimate presumptions'. That element of doubt is present in many eighteenth-century accounts of the gentleman, including Defoe's *The Compleat English Gentleman*, in which Defoe berates his titled and genteel

---

[12] Barrell, *English Literature in History*, 37.

countrymen for living down to their literary stereotypes: the boorish, fox-hunting, claret-swilling squire and the affected, modish fop—two sides, in his view, of the same brass coin of ignorance. Though Burke is unwilling to state the case in anything like the blunt, satirical terms Defoe employs, his many polemics, letters, and speeches, especially his extensive prospect surveys, can be convincingly read as attempts to enact or appropriate, on behalf of his often heedless social 'betters', the political roles their birth and rank have called upon them to play.

A related problem posed by the ideal of the gentleman is that the outlines of the ideal were all too often applied in a debased manner, as in Thomson's dedication of his *Poem Sacred to the Memory of Sir Isaac Newton* to Sir Robert Walpole:

> Tho', by the wise Choice of the best of *Kings*. [sic] You are engag'd in the highest and most active Scenes of Life, balancing the Power of *Europe*, watching over our common Welfare, informing the whole Body of Society and Commerce, and even like Heaven dispensing Happiness to the Discontented and Ungrateful; tho' thus gloriously employ'd, yet are You not less attentive, in the Hour of Leisure, to the Variety, Beauty, and Magnificence of Nature, nor less delighted, and astonish'd at the Discoveries of the incomparable *Newton*. The same comprehensive Genius which Way soever it looks must have a steady, clear, and unbounded Prospect.[13]

As a professional politician, Burke had a great deal more respect for Walpole's political acumen than did most of the significant writers of Walpole's own day. But even if one places the most favourable construction on the great prime minister's life and actions, he remains a figure of far lesser stature than the model of perfection Thomson limns in his dedication.

The problematic status of the gentleman, however, goes well beyond the perceived failure of individuals to measure up to their job description. The very possibility of sustaining a comprehensive, disinterested view, as the gentleman is called upon to do, becomes increasingly problematic in an age of rapid change and steadily increasing complexity. Many of these anxieties are reflected in Thomson's *The Seasons*, which, despite its deployment of comprehensive prospect views and its

---

[13] Thomson, *Liberty . . . and Other Poems*, 6.

extravagant praise for aristocratic friends, unfolds a vision of a society that is not exempted from critical scrutiny. If, as Ralph Cohen is surely right to observe, the flattery Thomson lavishes on his little pantheon of gentlemen must strike the modern reader as reprehensible, it is tempered by and ultimately subsumed in the poem's larger perspective, which recognizes that even the greatest human knowledge is inevitably limited and that only God can see the whole. The world of Thomson's poem is fragmentary, imperfect, and discordant, a world in which glimpses of a larger harmony are but adumbrations of an all-embracing divine order, which must, even from the most comprehensive earthly prospect, be taken on faith. Only the 'second birth | Of heaven and earth' will unveil the universal prospect as God sees it:

> The great eternal *Scheme*
> Involving All, and in a *perfect Whole*
> Uniting, as the Prospect wider spreads,
> To Reason's Eye refin'd clears up apace.
> . . . .
> And what your bounded View, which only saw
> A little Part, deem'd *Evil* is no more:
> The Storms of WINTRY TIME will quickly pass,
> And one unbounded SPRING encircle All.
> (*Winter*, ll. 1046–9, 1066–9)

To assert otherwise, of course, would be to risk the imputation of impiety or even atheism.

But if the gentleman's share in the common frailties and limitations of humanity necessarily circumscribes his perspective, he nevertheless occupies a privileged position in the providential order, as the designation Burke confers upon him of 'reconciler between God and man' implies. Placed at the pinnacle of the visible scale of being, the gentleman can see further than others and enjoys at least a share in the divine vision of the harmonious whole. Thus, for example, from his vantage point of retirement at Hagley Park, Lord Lyttelton is able to grasp the 'happy world' in the prospect that surrounds him:

> We feel the present DEITY, and taste
> The Joy of GOD to see a happy World!
> These are the Sacred Feelings of thy Heart,

Thy Heart inform'd by Reason's purer Ray,
O LYTTELTON, the Friend!
(*Spring*, ll. 902–6)

This happy reconciliation of divine and human perspectives (which calls to mind Pope's rationalist arguments in *An Essay on Man*) resolves one problem only to involve Thomson in another set of difficulties. The harmony of the gentleman's perspective in *The Seasons* is bought, Barrell argues, at the expense of comprehensiveness. He achieves his harmonious view of the world, first of all, by withdrawing from it: only the gentleman's retired country estate affords the prospect views Thomson describes in his poems, not the city with all its bustle and squalor. Seen from a distance, the noisome smoke of the town blends aesthetically into the far horizon of the prospect: 'The stretching Landskip into Smoke decays!' (*Summer*, 1441). Reduced to a smudge, the town can be assimilated into the design of the prospect.

The reader, then, is left to puzzle with a number of unresolved questions and paradoxes. In the first instance, as Barrell succinctly observes, 'if the "comprehensive view" is attained only by an act of retirement, it is by an act which seems to acknowledge that view to be partial. It is because the town, buried in smoke and divided by interest, inhibits a clear and disinterested vision of the world, that we must retire to the country to see clearly.'[14] Purchased at this rate, however, disinterest becomes indistinguishable from detachment and disengagement, as interests and pursuits vital to the nation recede from view to the point of invisibility and are moved, as it were, quite out of the picture. Moreover, if the world really is, as it appears to the eye of the retired gentleman, a 'goodly Prospect' with 'Perfection fram'd',[15] then there remains, logically speaking, nothing to spur him to action, no corruption, abuses, or urgent national priorities upon which to exercise his impartial public virtue and comprehensive knowledge.

The logical embarrassment of Thomson's position is not a problem that particularly detains Burke, for his paradigm of the natural aristocrat demands the gentleman's full engagement in

---

[14] Barrell, *English Literature in History*, 60–1.
[15] Thomson, *Summer*, l. 1438; *Spring*, l. 857.

society as a regulator of its 'infinitely diversified combinations of men and affairs'; nor does he regard such engagement as compromising the gentleman's capacity for impartiality and disinterest. Thomson's association with the Country party and its opposition to Walpole (despite the flattering dedication cited above) undoubtedly contributed to his view that a comprehensive and unbiased perspective could be maintained only by persons distanced from the hurly-burly of politics and commerce. Pocock comments on the dilemma the Country attitude posed for its adherents: 'corruption could be avoided only by those willing both to enjoy no source of income but their estates, and to eschew either the possession or the pursuit of executive power . . . and it was to be the recurrent problem of all Country parties that they could not take office without falsifying their own ostensible values'.[16] In his self-fashioning as a literary voice of absolute independence, 'To VIRTUE ONLY and HER FRIENDS, A FRIEND' (*Imitations of Horace, Satire* II. i. 121), Alexander Pope represents an uncompromising literary expression of this view. In fact, Pope stakes out an extreme position on this issue, arguing that any trace of indebtedness, whether to party, publisher, or patron, fatally undermines a writer's moral integrity. Burke, as will become apparent, also grapples with the problem of maintaining an impartial and comprehensive view of things, while also advocating particular political positions, but as a committed Whig, he rejects the premiss that engagement in political struggle necessarily entails an abandonment of the larger perspective that defines the ideal gentleman. In short, he would be the first to repudiate his friend Oliver Goldsmith's famous characterization of him as one, 'Who, born for the universe, narrowed his mind, | And to party gave up what was meant for mankind.'[17]

At a deeper level of engagement, the contradictions that surface in Thomson's poem point to significant economic and social changes taking place in the eighteenth century. The traditional, inherited view of society and the gentleman's role in

---

[16] J. G. A. Pocock, *The Machiavellian Moment* (Princeton, 1975), 409.

[17] Oliver Goldsmith, 'Retaliation,' in *The Poems of Thomas Gray, William Collins, Oliver Goldsmith*, ed. Roger Lonsdale (London, 1969), 749, ll. 31–2.

it had been of a congeries of warring and conflicting interests requiring the disinterested intervention of the gentleman to regulate competing claims. In the eighteenth century, however, these competing interests were increasingly seen in a more positive light: individuals pursuing their private economic ends, for example, were recognized as unwitting contributors to the public good. This new conception of national cohesion posed two acute problems for the gentleman: his adjudicative role seemed to become more and more irrelevant in a self-regulating economic and political system, and the increasing complexity of the system itself, with its proliferation of occupations and growing division of labour, rendered less and less plausible the ideal that the gentleman could comprehend the whole. Moreover, the ownership of property itself—the ostensible basis for the gentleman's civic pre-eminence—was becoming identified as a political and economic interest of its own, one increasingly bound up, through mortgages and marital alliances, with the instability of commerce and credit. The ownership of land apparently no longer guaranteed continuity and breadth of political vision.

The proliferation of knowledge in the eighteenth century posed another challenge to the ideal of the omnicompetent gentleman. Samuel Johnson was one of the first to understand clearly that the explosion of knowledge fostered by the spread of the printed word had made it difficult for anyone to master a single discipline (let alone all branches of knowledge) without systematic, professional application. Knowledge had become so vast that the task of study, like economic and industrial processes, had to be subdivided. The age of the specialist had dawned, and the goal of achieving general understanding had henceforth to be shared by many. This new reality put the gentleman at a double disadvantage, for not only was the ideal of comprehensive understanding a receding mirage, but also the attainment of knowledge had become a laborious commitment that transformed the attitude of disinterest from a virtue into a liability. Specialized professions and occupations were no longer to be derided as demeaning, fragmentizing pursuits, yet this shift of perspective rendered even more acute the problem (or the very possibility) of locating a lasting perspective from which a sense of the whole could be grasped. In *An Essay on the History of Civil Society*, Adam Ferguson points to the evils of specialization as a factor in the decline of ancient Athens:

> Under the *distinction* of callings, by which the members of polished society are separated from each other, every individual is supposed to possess his species of talent, or his peculiar skill, in which the others are confessedly ignorant; and society is made to consist of parts, of which none is animated with the spirit that ought to prevail in the conduct of nations.... It happened, accordingly, that the business of state, as well as of war, came to be worse administered at Athens, when these, as well as other applications, became the object of separate professions; and the history of this people abundantly shewed, that men cease to be citizens, even to be good poets and orators, in proportion as they came to be distinguished by the profession of these, and other separate crafts.[18]

Knowledge is no longer to be understood by the metaphor of the landscape, which the observer, from a vantage-point *outside* the panorama, can grasp in its entirety, but rather by that of the maze—the landscape seen now from the inside, where each observer takes a different path and attains a different and inevitably partial prospect.

Barrell's analysis, which we have been retracing over the last few pages, provides an explanatory framework for assessing Burke's reliance on the prospect survey in his political writings and his complex understanding of the gentleman's political role, but the brief summary just outlined should not be taken to suggest that the ideal of the gentleman and the possibility of comprehensive understanding he represents was suddenly perceived to be untenable. On the contrary, in an age when gentlemen as a social class still retained effective political and social power (despite growing awareness of the complexity of the social order and the legitimacy of other classes and interests), writers such as Thomson, Pope, and Burke, among others, remained committed to finding modes of representation that reaffirmed the gentleman's intellectual and political authority. Thus, for instance, Thomson chronicles the career of Peter the Great, who abandons the distanced prospect by immersing himself in it:

---

[18] Adam Ferguson, *An Essay on the History of Civil Society* (1767; repr. Philadelphia, 1819), 392–3.

> [Peter] in every Port,
> His Scepter laid aside, with glorious Hand
> Unweary'd plying the mechanic Tool,
> Gather'd the Seeds of Trade, of useful Arts,
> Of Civil Wisdom, and of Martial Skill.
> (*Winter*, ll. 967–71)

Peter's interventionist conduct proves exceptional, however, for it is dictated by his inheritance of a 'neglected empire' immersed in 'Gothic darkness'. His circumstances, therefore, do not offer a likely model for the statesmen and leaders of 'politer' nations. Nevertheless, if, as Barrell puts it, 'the possibility of a comprehensive, authoritative, and optimistic understanding of a society, now perceived as infinitely complex, is to be preserved', Peter's mythical career—shaped, like that of Shakespeare's Prince Hal, by his temporary descent into the lives of the commonalty—furnishes a useful, even necessary, fiction for the eighteenth century.[19]

One other possible solution to the epistemological problem of comprehensive knowledge posed by Thomson's poem demands our attention because it points a way (one that Burke himself will begin to explore) out of the cultural impasses examined above. Ralph Cohen argues that the most truly comprehensive, disinterested perspective in *The Seasons* is not enjoyed by Lyttelton or any other gentleman, but remains, rather, the privilege of the poem's 'speaker-commentator' or narrator, 'the man of many muses or roles'. It is the speaker, in Cohen's view, who most convincingly expounds an overarching vision of 'blending, harmony, peace, commerce and patriotism', and who, by virtue of his 'class anonymity', is able to comprehend all strata of British society: 'Socially, the speaker observes the rural workers, the squires and the lords of the manor; moving freely among the different groups, he himself becomes a model of mobility from one class to another. The observer of the poor reapers is also the friend of Lyttelton, so that he is both a defender of class distinctions and a successful social climber'.[20] 'Defender of class distinctions' and 'social climber'—both these designations can, with fair accuracy, be applied to Burke, who,

---

[19] Barrell, *English Literature in History*, 71.
[20] Cohen, *Unfolding of* The Seasons, 95.

like Thomson, is anxious to vindicate the authority of the gentleman, without debarring himself and men like him from a share in that authority and, by extension, in the privileged view of the whole ascribed to the gentleman. Burke's writings, as we shall see, participate in the growing ambition of eighteenth-century authorship (expressed perhaps most clearly and overtly in the poetry of Pope), to claim access for the professional writer to the gentleman's preserve—to inherit the gentleman's licence, in Pope's words, to 'Expatiate free o'er all this scene of Man' (*Essay on Man*, I. 5).

III

The foregoing discussion of Thomson's use of the prospect survey demonstrates how a literary feature or procedure can embody cultural perceptions, and it furnishes a context that makes intelligible Burke's repeated deployment of the same literary feature in his political writings. As will soon become apparent, however, Burke's reliance on an inherited literary procedure by no means entails the conclusion that his political motives coincide at every juncture with those expressed in his literary models. Though many correspondences with Pope and Thomson will emerge in the analysis that follows, it is important to remember that the significance of a writer's reliance on a given literary pattern lies as much in carefully observed differences between an adaptation and its models as in the more obvious parallels.

This fact becomes clear upon closer inspection of a characteristically Thomsonian passage in Burke's *Speech on Conciliation with the Colonies*. As a preparative for his detailed analysis of the American character and temper, Burke offers a bird's-eye view of that character in action as he surveys the whale-fishery of New England:

Whilst we follow them among the tumbling mountains of ice, and behold them penetrating into the deepest frozen recesses of Hudson's Bay and Davis's Straits, whilst we are looking for them beneath the arctic circle, we hear that they have pierced into the opposite region of polar cold, that they are at the antipodes, and engaged under the frozen serpent of the south. Falkland Island, which seemed too remote and romantic an object for the grasp of national ambition, is but a stage and resting-place in the progress of their victorious industry. Nor is the equinoctial heat more discouraging to them, than the accumulated winter of both the poles. We know that whilst some of them draw the line and strike the harpoon on the coast of Africa, others run the longitude, and pursue their gigantic game along the coast of Brazil. No sea but what is vexed by their fisheries. No climate that is not witness to their toils. Neither the perseverance of Holland, nor the activity of France, nor the dexterous and firm sagacity of English enterprise, ever carried this most perilous mode of hard industry to the extent to which it has been pushed by this recent people; a people who are still, as it were, but in the gristle, and not yet hardened into the bone of manhood. When I contemplate these things; when I know that the colonies in general owe little or nothing to any care of ours, and that they are not squeezed into this happy form by the constraints of watchful and suspicious government, but that, through a wise and salutary neglect, a generous nature has been suffered to take her own way to perfection; when I reflect upon these effects, when I see how profitable they have been to us, I feel all the pride of power sink, and all presumption in the wisdom of human contrivances melt and die away within me. My rigour relents. I pardon something to the spirit of liberty. (Bohn, i. 462)

In referring to this oratorical set-piece as a 'Thomsonian' passage, I do not mean to suggest that Burke is imitating any particular portion of the poet's verse, but rather that his rhetorical procedure mirrors Thomson's in several significant ways. The first of these is Burke's reproduction of the sublime mode characteristic of Thomson's most memorable poetic displays. Burke in fact conflates the two extremes that mark the boundaries of Thomson's imaginative flights in *The Seasons*: the poem's bold ventures into the 'torrid' and the 'frigid' zones. One of the most memorable episodes in Thomson's exploration of the polar regions in *Winter* is his account of Sir Hugh Willoughby's fatal voyage of 1553–4 in search of the north-east passage:

>   Such was the BRITON's Fate,
> As with *first* Prow, (what have not BRITONS dar'd!)
> He for the Passage sought. . . .
>
> . . . .
>
> In these fell Regions, in *Arzina* caught,
> And to the stony Deep his idle Ship
> Immediate seal'd, he with his hapless Crew,

> Each full-exerted at his several Task,
> Froze into statues; to the Cordage glued
> The Sailor, and the Pilot to the Helm.
> (*Winter*, ll. 925–7; 930–5)

The sombre, even tragic, tone of Thomson's description contrasts sharply with the triumphal strain of Burke's progress, but the heroic scale is the same—the might and audacity of human endeavour measured against the grandest possible geographic scale, from 'equinoctial heat' to 'accumulated winter'. And both writers are quick to draw historical and political lessons from their heroic views, Thomson offering his customary patriotic salute to British intrepidity ('what have not BRITONS dar'd!') and Burke educing, as will become apparent, an altogether more profound political moral.

The heroic context that both invoke is literary as well as natural. In Thomson's case the tableau of the frozen pilot and sailor is, of course, entirely fictional and brings to mind the fate of Palinurus in Virgil's *Aeneid*, whereas Burke, moving in the opposite direction, marvels, with his reference to the 'remote and romantick' Falklands, how much stranger indeed is antipodean fact than the most extravagant fictions of heroic romance. By placing the Americans in this explicitly heroic context (deriving ultimately from Milton and Virgil), Burke seeks to impress upon his auditors the incalculable value of the object that they stand in danger of squandering through neglect and ignorance. America is no longer an exotic curiosity, serving merely 'to amuse . . . with stories of savage men, and uncouth manners' (Bohn, i. 460), but rather the cornerstone of an empire that potentially rivals the grandeur of imperial Rome—if only his countrymen have the imagination to see the rich jewel that lies within their grasp. The sympathetic enlargement of that imagination is, therefore, Burke's chief aim in deploying his poetic view: parliament and the nation must be made to see, to feel, their interest in an object apparently 'so remote from our eye, and so little connected with our immediate feelings' (ii. 178).[21]

---

[21] *Observations on a Late State of the Nation*; see G. W. Chapman, *Edmund Burke: The Practical Imagination* (Cambridge, Mass., 1967), 20–2.

Burke also supports his argument with cold, hard evidence. His speech begins, in fact, with an impressive recital of statistics demonstrating the exponential increase in the value of British trade with America over the previous seven decades, but the gentleman-statesman cannot hope to win his audience over solely in this manner. Many years later, in the *Letters on a Regicide Peace*, he was to explain why he always felt obliged to supplement, or more accurately to supplant, empirical evidence with the poetic views that appear in most of his speeches:

In truth, the tribe of vulgar politicians are the lowest of our species. There is no trade so vile and mechanical as government in their hands. Virtue is not their habit. They are out of themselves in any course of conduct recommended only by conscience and glory. A large, liberal and prospective view of the interests of States passes with them for romance; and the principles that recommend it for the wanderings of a disordered imagination.... Littleness in object and in means, to them appears soundness and sobriety. They think there is nothing worth pursuit, but that which they can handle; which they can measure with a two-foot rule; which they can tell upon ten fingers. (ix. 267)

Burke here employs the word 'politician' as a term of the vilest opprobrium, a usage that continues to strike a responsive chord in the late twentieth century, though the term's primary meaning today is that of a person experienced in the art or science of government. But the politician, in Burke's sense, lacks the visionary power of the poet (and orator): this passage voices once again, as Ferguson does in his account of ancient Athens, the bias against persons of determinate professions, those who pursue only 'that which they can handle; which they can measure with a two-foot rule', as opposed to the gentleman possessed with a 'large, liberal and prospective view of the interests of States'. The former include the 'sophisters, oeconomists, and calculators' whose time, as Burke laments in his *Reflections*, has succeeded to the age of chivalry (viii. 127).

Statistics and measurements are often symptoms for Burke (as for Swift before him) of the theorist and rationalist, of those who presume to deduce a political course of action from abstract principles, instead of from tried experience. Government should be, above all, 'a practical thing, made for the happiness of mankind, and not to furnish out a spectacle of uniformity, to gratify the schemes of visionary politicians' (Bohn, ii. 29).[22] In the *Reflections*, not surprisingly, he lumps 'politicians' together with 'the whole clan of the enlightened' (viii. 138)—the Rousseaus and Voltaires, latter-day projectors who claim a rational understanding of the mainsprings of human nature. Thus, to return to the *Speech on Conciliation*, his inclusion of the 'prospective view' of American economic activity (as represented by their whaling industry) immediately after his review of the relevant facts and figures signals to his audience that he is no mere politician. On the contrary, his assurance in handling the view of America in his speech constitutes an unspoken claim to the title of gentleman, whatever his real ancestry.

The responses of those who heard Burke's speech appeared to acknowledge the substance of this claim. His brother, Richard, reported in a letter to Richard Champion the impressions he gleaned from members in the lobby of the House of Commons: 'I found, that in the clear opinion of his hearers, there was more knowledge of the Subject, a greater compass of understanding, far more political wisdom, a clearer insight into the nature of Government in general, and such an intire intimacy with our own Government and Constitution in particular, that surpassed very far any thing they had ever expected to hear from any man' (*Corr.* iii. 139–40). Richard's assessment enumerates in a single sentence the impressive list of gentlemanly intellectual qualifications that Burke, many years later, laid out more fully in his 'character' of the natural aristocrat. The reactions of his aristocratic patrons, especially the Duke of Richmond, were perhaps even more revealing, not least because these men were the genuine article: aristocrats by birth and title. Richmond positively glowed with admiration in a letter written to Burke upon his perusal of the published *Speech*:

> It is so calm, so quiet, so reasonable, so just[,] so proper, that one cannot refuse conviction to every Part. At other Times, wit, or strong Pictures, or violent Declamations may be proper. There may be a season for Poetry. But in the present awfull moment, the grave sober language of Truth and cool Reason is much better timed. And You appear in this speech, not that lively astonishing orator that some other

---

[22] *Letter to the Sheriffs of Bristol.*

of Your works shew you to be, but the most wise, dispassionate, and calm Statesman. (*Corr.* iii. 171)

Richmond confers upon his correspondent the supreme accolade of 'Statesman', but the details of his praise appear in some respects to gainsay the analysis we have been pursuing. Burke is praised for restraining his muse, for avoiding 'wit, or strong Pictures, or violent Declamations'—in short, for eschewing all the ornaments of poetry. Conor Cruise O'Brien remarks wryly that in Richmond's assessment, 'one can see the sort of thing the Rockinghams liked to hear from Burke, and the sort of thing that made them nervous'.[23]

What made them nervous, of course, was the Burke one encounters in his apostrophe to Marie Antoinette in the *Reflections*, the notorious Burke of the famed purple passages, in full rhetorical flight. Yet, with the possible exception of *Letters on a Regicide Peace* (and even there), this violent rhetorical mode is one that he deploys sparingly in his writings. Richmond is in fact using the word 'poetry' in a narrow sense here, referring only to elevated, impassioned diction—the kind of poetry that might be associated with Burke as the period's leading theorist of the sublime. In his speech on America, however, his use of poetic forms and features remains squarely in the Augustan tradition of public, didactic discourse exemplified by Pope and Thomson, rather than the private, self-absorbed mode of later eighteenth-century poets like Collins and Gray. The ideal he aspires to is the rational poetic discourse of Pope's *Essay on Man*, which opens as a dialogue between two disinterested, landed gentlemen who beat 'this ample field' of intellectual inquiry for philosophical game (I. 9). The metaphor of shooting is well chosen, for just as the pursuit of game was restricted to those enjoying a considerable annual income from land, so too, by implication, the most comprehensive of rational discourses, such as that exemplified by *An Essay on Man*, can only be a dialogue among gentlemen.

The comparison with *An Essay on Man* is apt in a number of ways, for Pope's poem also aspires to comprehensiveness of view: 'Let us . . . | Expatiate free o'er all this scene of Man; | A

[23] Conor Cruise O'Brien, *The Great Melody: A Thematic Biography and Commented Anthology of Edmund Burke* (Chicago, 1992), 152.

mighty maze! but not without a plan' (I. 3–6). By choosing Lord Bolingbroke as his interlocutor, Pope signals his own membership in the select company of gentlemen and confers upon his poem the highest possible social endorsement. Burke (also, like Pope, an outsider) is similarly anxious to secure for himself and his *Speech on Conciliation* the supreme political and cultural accolade reserved for the comprehensive viewer. Richmond accords him the title of statesman with little apparent reserve, emphasizing the gentlemanly wisdom, reason, and dispassionateness of his oration, but Burke does not wait upon the predictably partisan commendation of a member of his own party. Following Pope's lead in *An Essay on Man,* he inscribes the mode of gentlemanly dialogue into the very structure of his speech. This he does by making the fullest possible use of the 'prospect survey' technique and by assigning his view to a noble lord of another party, within whose lifetime America has become the notable prospect outlined in his speech.

Thus, Burke imagines a guardian angel in the year 1704 conducting Lord Bathurst, Pope's lifelong Tory friend, to a high eminence, from which he is shown, like Adam in the concluding books of *Paradise Lost,* a future prospect of his country:

Suppose, Sir, that the angel of this auspicious youth ... should have drawn up the curtain, and unfolded the rising glories of his country, and whilst he was gazing with admiration on the then commercial grandeur of England, the genius should point out to him a little speck, scarce visible in the mass of the national interest, a small seminal principle, rather than a formed body, and should tell him—'Young man, there is America—which at this day serves for little more than to amuse you with stories of savage men, and uncouth manners; yet shall, before you taste of death, show itself equal to the whole of that commerce which now attracts the envy of the world. ...' Fortunate man, he has lived to see it! Fortunate indeed, if he lives to see nothing that shall vary the prospect, and cloud the setting of his day!

(Bohn, i. 460)

Trade statistics hardly seem promising material for treatment in the heroic mode, yet Burke manages to bring his dry subject to life—to animate the historical reality behind his statistical tables—and to underscore the objectivity of his view by attributing it to a man whose heroic gaze is guided by nothing less than divine authority. Within Bathurst's lifetime the value of

Britain's trade with America alone has come to rival the sum total of her commerce at the time of his birth.

Burke's choice of Bathurst as his exemplar of the gentlemanly gaze is a clever stroke in a number of respects. Bathurst's political career, from the time he was elected a Tory MP for Cirencester in 1705 to his death in the months following Burke's speech in 1775, conveniently spanned the period in which America came of age. Moreover, his association with the Tories, rather than Burke's Whig associates, guarantees the comprehensiveness and impartiality of the vision ascribed to him by placing it beyond narrow party interests. Finally, Bathurst's name had already been mythologized in Pope's poetry as the literary type of the public-spirited gentleman: 'Who then shall grace, or who improve the Soil? | Who plants like BATHURST, or who builds like BOYLE' (*Ep. to Burl.*, ll. 177–8). Not for the first time Burke borrows elements from the discourse of the Opposition writers of Walpole's day, a circumstance underscoring the broad cultural consensus represented by the ideal of the gentleman-observer.

The angel who directs Bathurst's attention to the 'little speck' that is America recalls the role of the stern archangel Michael in Book XI of *Paradise Lost*, when he escorts Adam to high ground in order to unfold before him in God-like perspective the future of mankind:

> So both ascend
> In the Visions of God: It was a Hill
> Of Paradise the highest, from whose top
> The Hemisphere of Earth in clearest Ken
> Stretcht out to the amplest reach of prospect lay.
> (*PL* XI 376–80)

The significance for Burke of this Miltonic allusion can best be grasped by recalling a later, more explicit reference to these same verses—a passage in which Burke casts Montesquieu, the great French enlightenment thinker he so greatly admired, in the role of Adam:

Think of a genius not born in every country, or every time; a man gifted by nature with a penetrating, aquiline eye; with a judgment prepared with the most extensive erudition. . . . Think of a man, like the universal patriarch in Milton, (who had drawn up before him in his prophetic vision the whole series of the generations which were to issue from his loins,) a man capable of placing in review, after having brought together from the east, the west, the north, and the south, from the coarseness of the rudest barbarism to the most refined and subtle civilization, all the schemes of government which had ever prevailed amongst mankind. (Bohn iii. 113)

Like Adam, Montesquieu is credited with almost superhuman powers of perception, an 'aquiline eye' and a keenness of judgement that enable him to penetrate not only to the remotest corners of the known world, but also through the mists of time to the furthest reaches of human history.

Montesquieu represents the high-water mark in Burke's idealization of the comprehensive, disinterested gentleman. The extravagance of his claims for the French thinker exposes, ultimately, the unsustainability of the ideal, a point I shall return to below. Burke tacitly acknowledges as much when he praises Montesquieu as, 'a genius not born in every country, or every time' and describes his work as encyclopedic in scope: 'weighing, measuring, collating, and comparing [all forms of government], joining fact with theory, and calling into council, upon all this infinite assemblage of things, all the speculations which have fatigued the understandings of profound reasoners in all times!' (Bohn iii. 113). A similar irony can be observed in Milton's account of Adam's comprehensive perspective on human history, which he obtains only through divine grace, as '*Michael* from *Adam's* eyes the Film remov'd | Which that false Fruit that promis'd clearer sight | Had bred' (*PL* XI. 411–13). Like Thomson's observer in *Summer*, who sees harmoniously because the tumult of urban life has been reduced to an infinitesimal speck, Adam sees clearly only because he has been temporarily relieved of the intellectual and perceptual disabilities occasioned by his fall into sin.

IV

The Miltonic strand in the genealogy of the prospect view merits further consideration because it brings together three of the most potent cultural reference-points by which eighteenth-century literary discourse defined itself. The first of these strands is biblical: readers of Milton have pointed variously to Moses on

Mount Pisgah (Deut. 34: 1–4) or to the prophets Ezekiel and Daniel (Ezek. 40: 1–2; Dan. 10: 13), as sacred precedents for the poet's concluding prospect view. The question of the precise scriptural source need not detain us. What is important to note, chiefly, is the weight of biblical authority that underwrites the comprehensiveness of the viewer and the extent to which 'viewing' is redefined as prophetic 'vision'. This weight of biblical precedent is supplemented by the prestige of classical epic, in which prophecies and prospects also compose an important element. Thus, Adam's vision of humanity's future also calls to mind such epic precedent as the prophetic vision Aeneas receives of Rome's future greatness during his descent to the underworld in the *Aeneid*, Book 6.

This prophetic dimension will resurface in an unexpected guise in Burke's late writings on the French Revolution, where it manifests itself as jeremiad and lamentation. Equally, his account of the natural aristocrat in *An Appeal from the New to the Old Whigs* as 'a reconciler between God and man' acknowledges the divine sanction or vision with which the viewer's function is invested. The prophetic element in the prospect view is closely related to its temporal dimension: just as the prospect view encourages what Samuel Johnson called 'historical retrospection', so too it projects history into the future, laying out prospects in the sense of anticipation or looking forward. '*Prophesie*', as the New England Puritan Nicholas Noyes observes, is simply '*Historie antedated*; and *Historie* is *Post-dated Prophesie*'.[24] In Burke the prophetic gesture is a thoroughly secularized one. Though he is often credited with almost supernatural foresight, especially as regards the course of the French Revolution, that prescience can be explained, as Conor Cruise O'Brien argues, by his, 'penetrating powers of observation, judicious inference from what was observed, and thorough analysis of what was discerned by observation and inference'—in short, by his exercise of the rational qualifications of the comprehensive viewer.[25]

The link between the biblical and epic contexts in the

---

[24] Nicholas Noyes, *New-Englands Duty* (Boston, 1698), 43, quoted in Sacvan Bercovitch, *The American Jeremiad* (Madison, 1978), 15.
[25] O'Brien, *Great Melody*, 403.

Miltonic prospect view comes by way of the georgic. Milton does not spring immediately to mind as a poet in the georgic mode, yet, as Anthony Low maintains, the georgic ideal is central to his second great heroic poem, *Paradise Regained*. Adam's ascent of the mountain of vision in *Paradise Lost* looks ahead to the events of the later poem, which takes as its subject Satan's triple temptation of Christ in the wilderness (Luke 4: 1–13; Matt. 4: 1–11). Thus, the height to which Michael conducts Adam prefigures, as Milton makes clear, the 'exceeding high mountain' from which Satan tempts Jesus with 'all the kingdoms of the world, and the glory of them':

> Not higher that Hill nor wider looking round,
> Whereon for different cause the Tempter set
> Our second *Adam* in the Wilderness,
> To show him all Earth's Kingdoms and thir Glory.
>   (*PL* XI. 381–4)

Milton's choice of georgic as the dominant mode of *Paradise Regained* can be understood, Low argues, as a formal reply to his earlier epic: '*Paradise Regained* depicts the moment when, for the first time in history, georgic takes on a new and more hopeful significance, as the georgic spirit is given the power to bring Eden back within human reach. Under Michael's tutelage, Adam foresaw the happy transformation of the curse of labor; the georgic agent of that transformation is the hero of *Paradise Regained*.'[26] Milton's poem elevates the georgic and its theme of virtuous labour to a heroic pitch, foreshadowing the shift in generic hierarchies that would come to characterize eighteenth-century poetry.

One of Milton's most striking excursions into georgic in *Paradise Regained* occurs when Satan takes Jesus to the mountain top. Before Satan diverts Jesus' attention to scenes of wealth, power, and dominion, the poet describes the actual prospect laid out before them, a scene of georgic, rather than imperial and martial splendour:

> It was a Mountain at whose verdant feet
> A spacious plain outstretcht in circuit wide
> Lay pleasant; from his side two rivers flow'd,

---

[26] A. Low, *The Georgic Revolution* (Princeton, 1985), 322.

> Th'one winding, th'other straight, and left between
> Fair Champaign with less rivers intervein'd
> Then meeting join'd thir tribute to the Sea:
> Fertile of corn the glebe, of oil and wine;
> With herds the pastures throng'd, with flocks the hills;
> Huge Cities and high tow'r'd, that well might seem
> The seats of mightiest Monarchs; and so large
> The Prospect was, that here and there was room
> For barren desert fountainless and dry.
> (PR III. 253–64)

In this scene georgic shades into pastoral: the effects of sin and the necessity of labour that form a central preoccupation of the realistic georgic are here largely absent. Instead of labour's curse—the bread earned by the sweat of one's brow—the scene shows labour's fruits in a manner reminiscent of the periodic inventories of the world's fertile agricultural landscapes that punctuate Virgil's *Georgics*. But into this idyllic scene Satan introduces what Low characterizes as, 'the epic temptation at its purest and broadest': Jesus is offered military power sufficient to subdue the enemies of Israel and restore her to Davidic glory.[27] Jesus replies that when the time for action comes he will not need Satan's 'politic maxims, or that cumbersome | Luggage of war there shown me, argument | Of human weakness rather than of strength' (PR III. 400–2). This renunciation of martial heroism and imperial ambition, a central Miltonic theme, is counterbalanced by a new, georgic heroic ideal, that of labouring in the Father's vineyard, building a new Eden through arduous and unostentatious effort.

The troubled question of imperial ambition and its effects on the body politic is never far from the surface in Virgil's *Georgics*. Not surprisingly, Milton's application of this characteristic Virgilian theme is radical and critical, but he is by no means the only writer of the Restoration and eighteenth century to give voice to the georgic's oppositional potential. Burke's speeches on America are a case in point, but before returning to them it will be useful to cite, by way of comparison, his speeches on India, which constitute his most searching indictment of Britain's imperialist ambitions. The imaginative core of that

---

[27] Ibid. 345.

critique is the visual prospect of the Indian subcontinent he periodically strives to set before his listeners and readers. Thus, in his *Speech on the Nabob of Arcot's Debts*, he describes to the Commons the consequences of English extortionate greed in the Carnatic, a district of southern India. According to Burke, in their attempts to extend the influence of the Nabob of Arcot, who owed huge debts to the East India Company, English officials succeeded in provoking the wrath of Haidar Ali, the ruler of Mysore, who swept in like a 'black cloud' that

> poured down the whole of its contents upon the plains of the Carnatic.—Then ensued a scene of woe, the like of which no eye had seen, no heart conceived, and which no tongue can adequately tell. All the horrors of war before known or heard of, were mercy to that new havoc. A storm of universal fire blasted every field, consumed every house, destroyed every temple.' (v. 519)

In order to bring home to his audience the scale of the destruction wrought by corrupt British officialdom, whom he holds fully responsible for the desolation of the Carnatic, Burke lays out a prospect view familiar to his listeners:

> The Carnatic is a country not much inferior in extent to England. Figure to yourself, Mr. Speaker, the land in whose representative chair you sit; figure to yourself the form and fashion of your sweet and cheerful country from Thames to Trent, north and south, and from the Irish to the German sea east and west, emptied and embowelled (May God avert the omen of our crimes!) by so accomplished a desolation. Extend your imagination a little further, and then suppose your ministers taking a survey of this scene of waste and desolation; what would be your thoughts if you should be informed, that they were computing how much had been the amount of the excises, how much the customs, how much the land and malt tax, in order that they should charge . . . for public service, upon the relicks of the satiated vengeance of relentless enemies, the whole of what England had yielded in the most exuberant seasons of peace and abundance?
>
> (v. 520–1).

Besides approximating, by analogy, the exotic, strange, and unfamiliar to scenes that lie within the imaginative grasp of his auditors, Burke here presses home the dichotomy between the gentleman of comprehensive view (of whom, he suggests, the Speaker of the House is a leading example) and the money-grubbing professional who has no further view of his role as governor of India than his personal emolument. Once again, the extensive grasp of the liberal imagination is contrasted with greedy calculations and narrow figures. This antithesis is like that figured forth by Milton in Book III of *Paradise Regained*; Burke distinguishes between the prelapsarian, pastoral landscape of England and a postlapsarian landscape disfigured by the consequences of a headlong, heedless pursuit of wealth, power, and glory—the selfsame objects with which Satan tempts Jesus.

In stark contrast with the narrow self-interest shown by officials of the East India Company, the indigenous rulers of the Carnatic have acted in the georgic spirit of comprehensiveness and benevolence that ought to mark the British gentleman. Burke points to the extensive network of irrigation works, built and maintained at great expense, that previously supported the flourishing agriculture and trade of the country. But such public works, he notes sarcastically, 'are not the enterprizes of your power, nor in a style of magnificence suited to the taste of your minister'. Unglamorous as they are, however, these undertakings are the true marks of imperial splendour and gentlemanly disinterest: 'These are the monuments of real kings, who were the fathers of their people; testators to a prosperity which they embraced as their own. These are the grand sepulchres built by ambition; but by the ambition of an unsatiable benevolence, which ... had strained ... to extend the dominion of their bounty beyond the limits of nature, and to perpetuate themselves through generations of generations, the guardians, the protectors, the nourishers of mankind' (v. 522). Burke exalts his conception of the gentleman into a touchstone for evaluating the conduct of British officialdom charged with overseeing her colonies. This is evident not only in the new model of virtuous, heroic behaviour underwritten by the georgic spirit, substituting the gentleman farmer for the knight and warrior, but also in the breadth of outlook demanded of those who superintend a complex, multifarious empire. On both scores Hastings and his subordinates in the East India Company have proved abject failures.

The georgic spirit of labouring and building, of promoting prosperity and livelihood, has thus become for Burke the moral yardstick by which Britain's imperial ambitions are to be measured. And by that measure, as he notes in his *Speech on*

Fox's India Bill, the British have fallen woefully short of the standard set by previous, supposedly barbaric, invaders of India, including the 'Arabs, Tartars, and Persians':

> With us no pride erects stately monuments which repair the mischiefs which pride had produced, and which adorn a country, out of its own spoils. England has erected no churches, no hospitals, no palaces, no schools; England has built no bridges, made no high roads, cut no navigations, dug out no reservoirs. Every other conqueror of every other description has left some monument, either of state or beneficence, behind him. Were we to be driven out of India this day, nothing would remain, to tell that it had been possessed, during the inglorious period of our dominion, by any thing better than the ouran-outang or the tiger. (v. 402)

This passage closely echoes the sentiments expressed in Pope's *Epistle to Burlington*, his georgic celebration of public works and improvements as the only true monuments of imperial greatness: 'These Honours, Peace to happy Britain brings, | These are Imperial Works, and worthy Kings' (ll. 203-4).[28] In the post-colonial context of the late twentieth century, which repudiates the very notion that one people can impartially exercise political and economic dominion over another, the moral criterion of imperial rule invoked by Burke and Pope will strike many readers as little more than an elaborate rationalization of a history of exploitation. Yet, the passage of time and changing political standards must not be permitted to obscure the legacy of Burke's involvement in Indian affairs, which stands, in P. J. Marshall's words, as 'a towering landmark in the debate about imperial responsibility in any context' (v. 2).[29] The Burke who railed against 'geographical morality'—one set of rules for Europe and another for Africa and Asia—and who defined his constituency in Indian matters as 'a set of people, who have none of your Lillies and Roses in their faces; but who

---

[28] For a fuller citation and discussion of these lines, see Ch. 3. The heroic dimension of the 'Imperial Works' described by Pope is underscored by his echo in this couplet of Dryden's translation of *Aeneid*, 6. 1177: 'These are Imperial Arts, and worthy thee.' (*Works of John Dryden*, ed. E. Niles Hooker and H. T. Swedenberg (Berkeley and Los Angeles, 1956–), v. 566.

[29] Marshall's comment appears in his Introduction to vol. v. of the new Oxford ed. of Burke's writings and speeches.

are the images of the great Pattern as well as you and I' does not stand in need of as much correction from later generations as they might imagine (*Corr.* v. 255).

A similar strategy lies behind the prospect of America in Burke's *Speech on Conciliation*. His prospect survey seeks to liberate the imaginations of his countrymen, to make them recognize that Britain's true imperial interests extend far beyond the mother country's rights of taxation or her assertion of parliamentary power over the colonies. 'Do you imagine then,' he asks, 'that it is the land tax act which raises your revenue? that it is the annual vote in the committee of supply which gives you your army? . . . No! surely, no! It is the love of the people; it is their attachment to their government, from the sense of the deep stake they have in such a glorious institution.' To the 'profane herd of . . . vulgar and mechanical politicians, who . . . far from being qualified to be directors of the great movement of empire, are not fit to turn a wheel in the machine', this liberal conception of political allegiance 'will sound wild and chimerical'. But to the gentleman of comprehensive view, 'to men truly initiated and rightly taught, these ruling and master principles . . . are in truth every thing, and all in all. Magnanimity in politics is not seldom the truest wisdom; and a great empire and little minds go ill together' (Bohn, i. 509).

Again and again, when Burke seeks to take the true measure of a political policy or a society's institutions, he tests them against the standard set by the georgic vision of human purpose and felicity. This is true not only of his writings on America and India, but also of his searching assessments of revolutionary France. Besides the prospect survey of France in the *Reflections* (cited in the previous chapter), which underwrites Burke's conviction that the French *ancien régime* was fundamentally benevolent, the third of his *Letters on a Regicide Peace* deploys perhaps the most elaborate view of all, a prospect intended to expose what he believes to be the hollowness and pusillanimity of Britain's policy of negotiation with the French Directory in 1795. Posing the question, 'For whose use, entertainment, or instruction, are all those over-strained and over-laboured proceedings in Council, in Negotiation, and in Speeches in Parliament, intended?', Burke surveys the nations of Europe in search of an answer:

The King of Prussia has hypothecated in trust to the Regicides his rich and fertile territories on the Rhine, as a pledge of his zeal and affection to the cause of liberty and equality. He has seen them robbed with unbounded liberty, and with the most levelling equality. The woods are wasted; the country is ravaged; property is confiscated; and the people are put to bear a double yoke, in the exactions of a tyrannical Government and in the contributions of an hostile irruption. Is it to satisfy the Court of Berlin, that the Court of London is to give the same sort of pledge of it's sincerity and good faith to the French Directory? . . . Is it [the Pope], who, from the miracles of his beneficent industry, has done a work which defied the power of the Roman Emperors, though with an enthralled world to labour for them; is it him, who has drained and cultivated the *Pontine Marshes*, that we are to satisfy of our cordial spirit of conciliation, with those who, in their equity, are restoring Holland again to the Seas, whose maxims poison more than the exhalations of the most deadly fens, and who turn all the fertilities of Nature and of Art into an howling desert?[30] (ix. 319, 322–3)

At every turn in his lengthy survey Burke measures the destructiveness of French policy in terms of its effects upon agriculture and land—the cornerstone of any nation's economy and the necessary foundation of its culture, in all senses of that term. One recalls his mention of the 'low, fat Bedford level' in the prospect view of Windsor Castle that climaxes *A Letter to a Noble Lord*: the placid productivity of the Duke of Bedford's acres is the pledge of the intrinsic wisdom of British institutions and policies. By contrast, the French are allowing a similar rich tract of reclaimed land in Holland to revert to the sea, turning into a watery desert 'all the fertilities of Nature and of Art'.

V

Burke plausibly claims his survey of Europe to be comprehensive—'Having run round the whole circle of the European system wherever it acts' (ix. 326)—but he is rather more hard-pressed to present it as altogether disinterested. On the subject of France, Burke was, in fact, highly partisan: his survey forms part

---

[30] The full survey of Europe, 'from the east to the west, from the north to the south', occupies 8 pages in the Oxford edn: ix. 319–26.

of an argument that advocates an uncompromising response to revolutionary France. The very vehemence with which he argues his case in *Letters on a Regicide Peace* is symptomatic of Britain's failure to achieve a national consensus on the question of how to deal with the revolutionary republic. Under these circumstances, when not only policies, but also fundamental constitutional and political principles were being hotly contested, the stance of disinterestedness and comprehensiveness increasingly bore the appearance of a polite fiction, at best, or an ideological subterfuge, at worst.

The implausibility of reconciling the polemical vehemence of the *Regicide Peace* pamphlets with a posture of gentlemanly impartiality highlights the sorts of contradictions we have already noted in the eighteenth-century conception of the comprehensive gentleman. In the concluding pages of this chapter I should like to suggest some of the ways in which Burke seeks to anticipate and obviate these contradictions and to consider briefly the increasingly obvious breakdown of the ideal of comprehensiveness by the dawn of the nineteenth century.

Burke's reconciliation of some of the logical incongruities in which the ideal of the gentleman has involved him invites a reconsideration of some of the political doctrines that posterity has identified as most characteristically his, namely, his defence of political parties and his views on parliamentary representation. On the latter point Burke is famous for arguing that members of parliament are elected not to serve the narrow interests of their constituents, but to exercise their best judgement in the service of the nation as a whole. In a pre-election address to his constituents in Bristol (in 1780), he declares, 'Let me say with plainness . . . that if by a fair, by an indulgent, by a gentlemanly behaviour to our representatives, we do not give confidence to their minds, and a liberal scope to their understandings; if we do not permit our members to act upon a *very* enlarged view of things; we shall at length infallibly degrade our national representation into a confused and scuffling bustle of local agency' (Bohn, ii. 130).[31] This statement

---

[31] *Speech at the Guildhall, in Bristol, Previous to the Late Election in That City, upon Certain Points Relative to His Parliamentary Conduct* (1780).

enjoins judgement, liberality, and a *very* enlarged view of things' upon the people's representatives, but it equally insists on some of the same 'gentlemanly' behaviour in the electors themselves, who, if they lack individually the capacity to see beyond the narrow interests of Bristol, ought to recognize that it is in their interest to be represented by a member who knows how best to pursue the well-being of his constituents in a national and international context of competing claims and overriding exigencies. None the less, how this alchemical transformation is to be effected—how the electors, from their local, parochial perspective, can be expected to endorse a representative of enlarged, national, disinterested views—is a question that, for the moment, remains a mystery. The reality of the problem, however, is underscored by the sequel to Burke's speech from the hustings: realizing from his canvass of the voters that he stood little chance of retaining his seat, he withdrew his candidacy on the day of the poll and was returned to the House instead as the member for the pocket borough of Malton.

Yet if popular representation provides an uncertain mechanism for ensuring that disinterested voices will be heard in the political councils of the nation, the alternative is that the court will enjoy a 'monopoly of mental power' along with the many other powers it possesses: 'When the popular member is narrowed in his ideas, and rendered timid in his proceedings, the service of the crown will be the sole nursery of statesmen' (Bohn, ii. 130). Burke is reminding his audience of the bitter constitutional debate that had framed the tumultuous political struggles of the previous two decades, especially the Wilkite disturbances and the American Revolution. In the view of his political associates, the Rockingham Whigs, the court under George III had set out to undermine the role of parliament and, through the mechanism of a 'double cabinet' and the court's powers of influence and patronage, to direct the parliamentary administration, which for the previous two generations had been firmly under the control of the Whig aristocracy. This subterfuge, Burke charges, was justified on the pretext that only the court and the Crown possessed a sufficient capacity for public-spiritedness to counteract the centrifugal forces of faction, self-interest, and corruption—an argument closely resembling Lord

Bolingbroke's doctrine of the 'Patriot King'. As a political descendent of Walpole, Burke has little use for such a position:

> To recommend this system to the people, a perspective view of the Court gorgeously painted, and finely illuminated from within, was exhibited to the gaping multitude. Party was to be totally done away, with all its evil works. Corruption was to be cast down from Court, as *Atè* was from Heaven. Power was thenceforward to be the chosen residence of public spirit; and no one was to be supposed under any sinister influence, except those who had the misfortune to be in disgrace at Court, which was to stand in lieu of all vices and all corruptions. A scheme of perfection to be realized in a Monarchy far beyond the visionary Republick of Plato. . . . And it was constantly in the mouths of all the runners of the Court, that nothing could preserve the balance of the constitution from being overturned by the rabble, or by a faction of the nobility, but to free the Sovereign effectually from that Ministerial tyranny under which the Royal dignity had been oppressed in the person of his Majesty's grandfather. (ii. 265–6)

In this view the only place in the kingdom sufficiently elevated to command a comprehensive prospect and far enough removed from the clash of opposing interests is the throne itself. Only the king can be a gentleman.

Ironically, the very arguments that Bolingbroke and the Country party had used to denounce the Walpole ministry as a sink of corruption, self-interest, and degeneracy are trained by Burke upon what appears to him as a latter-day incarnation of the very scheme that Bolingbroke had devised to restore public virtue in his time. In Burke's view, however, there is no 'Patriot King', but only a Court cabal, a 'Faction which presumptuously choose to call themselves [the King's] *friends*' (ii. 291). His response is to revert to the traditions that in his belief had guided the Whigs at the time of the Glorious Revolution: 'The Whigs of those days believed that the only proper method of rising into power was through hard essays of practised friendship and experimented fidelity. At that time it was not imagined, that patriotism was a bloody idol, which required the sacrifice of children and parents, or dearest connexions in private life, and of all the virtues that rise from those relations . . . or that disinterestedness was clearly manifested at the expence of other people's fortunes' (ii. 317). This glowing account of the early Whigs serves to introduce Burke's celebrated definition of political party, which rejects the almost unanimous view of his day that parties are at best a necessary and regrettable evil:[32] 'Party is a body of men united, for promoting by their joint endeavours the national interest, upon some particular principle in which they are all agreed' (ii. 317).

In the context of the present discussion, what is notable about Burke's definition of party is the extent to which it is couched in the very terms normally reserved to characterize the gentleman or, in Bolingbroke's case, the patriot king. Party exists to promote the 'national interest', not self-interest; it is grounded in a disinterestedness that regards politics as the very antithesis of a 'zero sum' game in which one person's gain is 'manifested at the expence of other peoples misfortunes'. Burke characterizes the party relationship as arising naturally out of the connections of family and friendship: 'Commonwealths are made of families, free commonwealths of parties also; and we may as well affirm, that our natural regards and ties of blood tend inevitably to make men bad citizens, as that the bonds of our party weaken those by which we are held to our country' (ii. 315). On the contrary, the obligations of friendship teach the individual to regard 'somebody besides himself' and, in the conduct of public business, to 'consult some other interest than his own' (ii. 316).

The family ties upon which party is founded are assimilated to the connections and private conduct of the gentleman: 'It is therefore our business carefully to cultivate in our minds, to rear to the most perfect vigour and maturity, every sort of generous and honest feeling that belongs to our nature. To bring the

---

[32] Whether or not Burke had in mind anything like the modern conception of a regular party system is a point that historians have hotly debated, though his 19th-c. readers clearly thought so. At the very least, however, Burke's defence of party as a legitimate, positive force, rather than a necessary evil, proved indisputably to be an idea with a future. As Paul Langford observes in his Introduction to vol. ii of Burke's writings and speeches (Oxford, 1981), 'In retrospect it is obvious enough that the concept of political party, and basically in terms of Burke's view of it as a legitimate element within the State, with a proper role to play in the business of stable and orderly government, was not merely a likely development in the modern evolution of the British constitution, but an almost inevitable one. In short, Burke was rowing with the tide' (p. 12). For an extensive theoretical analysis of Burke's conception of party, see Harvey C. Mansfield, Jr., *Statesmanship and Party Government: A Study of Burke and Bolingbroke* (Chicago, 1965).

dispositions that are lovely in private life into the service and conduct of the commonwealth; so to be patriots, as not to forget we are gentlemen' (ii. 320). Indeed, Burke has in mind a very particular sort of family connection, as he makes clear in his *Letter to the Sheriffs of Bristol*:

> I may be called in reproach a *party man*; but I am little affected with such aspersions. In the way which they call party, I worship the constitution of your fathers; and I shall never blush for my political company. . . . If I have wandered out of the paths of rectitude into those of interested faction, it was in company with the Saviles, the Dowdeswells, the Wentworths, the Bentincks; with the Lenoxes, the Manchesters, the Keppels, the Saunderses; with the temperate, permanent, hereditary virtue of the whole House of Cavendish. . . . These, and many more like these, grafting public principles on private honour, have redeemed the present age, and would have adorned the most splendid period in your history. (Bohn, ii. 37–8)

Burke's conception of party as a body of gentlemen acting in concert can be seen as his response to the problematic status of the ideal of the gentleman. He recognizes that no living individual can embody the sum of virtues that comprise the 'Finished Gentleman', for, as he notes in the *Thoughts on the Present Discontents*, 'we are born only to be men', not 'angels' (ii. 320). Moreover, a 'patriot king' or a statesman such as Mr Pitt, however great his abilities, wields a power that is 'in a great deal personal, and therefore transient' (ii. 264), rather than institutional and enduring. But the deficiency of individual human weakness can be supplied when persons band together, pooling their experience, capacities, and judgements, like the 'Whig connexions' under George I and George II: '[Their power] was rooted in the country. For, with a good deal less of popularity, they possessed a far more natural and fixed influence.' That influence grew out of their possession of vast property, their long experience in government, their 'ties of blood, of alliance, of friendship' and the multifarious connections arising from their pre-eminent social, economic, and political situation (ii. 264). Whatever their shortcomings, Burke argues, the Whigs can legitimately claim to represent a broader and more comprehensive cross-section of the views and interests of the British people than can any other political grouping in the country; as a party, in short, they possess in greater measure the attributes of the impartial gentleman than any one among them does as an individual.[33]

This defence of the Whigs as a party of national scope and interest by no means went uncontested: Catharine Macaulay, for example, attacked the *Thoughts on the Present Discontents* as a flimsy cover for the 'manœuvres of Aristocratic faction and party, founded on and supported by the corrupt principle of self-interest'.[34] In her view 'party' remained the dirty word that eighteenth-century usage had overwhelmingly made of it. It is in this context of almost universal opprobrium that Burke's positive view of party as promoting the public weal shows its force and originality. Not only does it bring realistically within human grasp that otherwise unrealizable model, the natural aristocrat, but also it reconciles the gap between the gentleman's private and public selves that the ideal of disinterestedness had inevitably created. For if such writers as Thomson and Pope—and other adherents of the Country ideology—had set an unattainably high standard by insisting that disinterest and a harmonious grasp of the whole could be purchased only at the impossible rate of a rigid independence and retirement from the unseemly jostling for advantage in city and court, Burke holds out the possibility that interest and disinterest, the public and the private, can be reconciled. Such a reconciliation had been effected in the time of the Roman republic: 'It was their wish, to see public and private virtues, not dissonant and jarring, and mutually destructive, but harmoniously combined, growing out of one another in a noble and orderly gradation, reciprocally supporting and supported' (ii. 316).

The musical analogy Burke employs here is a venerable trope in western political discourse, dating back to classical times. Cicero, for whom Burke had great esteem, makes use of it, as does Pope in the third book of *An Essay on Man*: ' 'Till jarring int'rests of themselves create | Th'according music of a well-mix'd State' (ll. 293–4). But Pope, like Thomson's observer in

---

[33] On this point, see Frank O'Gorman, *Edmund Burke: His Political Philosophy* (London, 1973), 38–40. O'Gorman comments on the passage cited here, 'Party for Burke was a means of placing at the disposal of the state these attributes of the aristocracy' (39).

[34] Catharine Macaulay, *Observations on a Pamphlet, Entitled, Thoughts on the Cause of the Present Discontents* (London, 1770), 6.

The Seasons, achieves this harmonious perspective only from the lofty cosmic vantage of his philosophical poem: the same scene, reported from close up in his satires, sounds infinitely more discordant, like a babel of voices rather than a choir. It was Burke's genius to urge a practical solution to this classic conundrum of eighteenth-century thought, not with a blind faith that individuals pursuing their private ends would unwittingly contribute to the public weal, but with a practical mechanism that would permit the negotiation and reconciliation of opposing interests.

The rationale for Burke's views on parliamentary representation, especially his doctrine of virtual representation, is also to be sought in his characterization of the comprehensive and disinterested gentleman, for without the conception of national trusteeship implicit in the figure of the gentleman, any notion of virtual representation would verge on a cynical subterfuge. Burke defines virtual representation in *A Letter to Sir Hercules Langrishe* as 'that in which there is a communion of interests, and a sympathy in feelings and desires between those who act in the name of any description of people, and the people in whose name they act, though the trustees are not actually chosen by them' (ix. 629). In an age of instant opinion polls, this theory of representation sounds implausible, nor did it adequately describe, even in its original context, the existing system of representation or Burke's actions as a representative. One could argue that his opposition in the 1770s to a coercive policy against the Americans, a position diametrically counter to the current of public opinion at the time, stretched any notion of virtual representation to the breaking point.[35] Yet Burke wore his unpopular views on the American revolution like a badge of honour, declaring unrepentantly to his constituents at Bristol, 'I conformed to the instructions of truth and nature, and maintained your interest, against your opinions, with a constancy that became me' (Bohn, ii. 138). Such a view, if it is to avoid blurring into a rationale for oppression, must be grounded in an external standard of 'truth' and 'nature', a standard accessible to the gentleman of comprehensive views, who is answerable,

---

[35] See O'Gorman, *Edmund Burke*, 54–6. See also Chapman, *Edmund Burke*, 136–42.

ultimately, to divine providence for the exercise of his judgement and discretion. The representative must not sacrifice 'his unbiassed opinion, his mature judgment, his enlightened conscience' to his constituents: 'These he does not derive from your pleasure ... [but] are a trust from Providence, for the abuse of which he is deeply answerable. Your representative owes you, not his industry only, but his judgment; and he betrays, instead of serving you, if he sacrifices it to your opinion' (Bohn, i. 446–7).

The atmosphere of these remarks has proved too rarified for posterity, as, indeed, it was for Burke's own constituents, who rejected him in favour of a more complaisant representative. But just when one fears losing Burke in the clouds, his views take on a more practical, pragmatic cast. If his argument for gentlemanly disinterest and independence is deployed, on the one hand, against a shortsighted populace, it is also asserted, on the other, against the constricting patronage of his aristocratic masters. In both instances Burke makes his mastery of the prospect survey, the discourse of rationality and comprehensiveness, the grounds for an insistent claim to independence. In his 'Speech at the Conclusion of the Poll' thanking the voters of Bristol for his election to the House of Commons in 1774, Burke reminds his audience (a scant four months before his famous *Speech on Conciliation with the Colonies*) that his responsibilities as a member extend to the farthest reaches of the British empire: 'We are members for that great nation, which however is itself but part of a great *empire*, extended by our virtue and our fortune to the farthest limits of the east and of the west. All these widespread interests must be considered; must be compared; must be reconciled if possible' (Bohn, i. 448). This declaration prefigures that great attempt at reconciliation in his *Speech* of the following March, in which the prospect survey we have examined above serves to justify at large his decision to disregard the wishes of his constituents. After 1780, however, when Burke no longer had to answer to a body of independent voters, the pressure to compromise his stance of gentlemanly independence came chiefly from above, from his aristocratic patrons. With them he used his formidable command of political issues—demonstrated, again, by his ease in calling up prospect views on any subject imaginable—to argue for his own, informed perspective on political events. In 1777, as has already been noted, he remarked ruefully on this often thankless role, characterizing his 'cheif employment' as 'that woful one, of a *flapper*'. Like the servants Gulliver observes at the court of Laputa, Burke must continually remind his superiors of their larger connections and responsibilities, their duties as gentlemen (*Corr.* iii. 389).

This circumstance exposes, finally, the great irony implicit in Burke's command of the prospect survey, for it marks him, rather than his Whig patrons, as the real gentleman or omnicompetent surveyor. The 'class of legitimate presumptions' he attributes to the natural aristocrat in *An Appeal from the New to the Old Whigs* has proved to be more presumable than actual, not least because society has grown too complex for any generalist, however gifted, to encompass it. Burke has, in effect, shouldered the role that the 'natural aristocrat' is called upon to play, and he succeeds to the extent that he does only because he has devoted his entire life to the part. In the process he emerges, ironically enough, as an early exemplar of a new breed, the professional politician. That professionalism can be concealed, however, perhaps even from Burke himself, by its subordination to the direction of the Rockingham party, which now embodies corporately the gentlemanly attributes of disinterest and comprehensiveness. And beneath the cloak of that same party, Burke can shelter his social, political, and intellectual aspirations to the status of gentleman. His conception of party is flexible enough to permit such men of ability as himself to rise in the service of their country without threatening the ideal of the natural aristocrat. Yet his enactment of the attributes of the gentleman (without, in the strictest sense, being one) was not, as we have seen in his *Letter to a Noble Lord*, without its evident tensions. In the *Letter* he grapples with the problem of reconciling the actual ability of individuals such as himself with the presumptive virtue of the natural aristocrat, and he does so by assimilating his own virtues to those of the gentleman, demonstrating, through his repeated use of the prospect survey, his acquaintance with the 'whole system' of his country's 'interests both abroad and at home' (ix. 160). Significantly, as his association with the Rockingham Whigs weakened in the 1780s and 1790s, he channelled his energies into political causes (India, Ireland, and

France) that brought his powers of comprehensive observation into ever greater prominence. More and more, in the latter half of his career, he sought to embody a political ideal that the hereditary political leadership of his country was, to his mind, increasingly abandoning.

VI

We have been tracing, in this and the previous chapter, the interrelated ideals of the gentleman as improver and as a man of comprehensive, disinterested view, ideals firmly rooted in his ownership of landed property, which guaranteed his commitment to the general good rather than to any partial interest. The literary discourse of the georgic proved a logical and resonant choice for the expression of these ideals in all their cultural, historical, and political complexity. If this hypothesis about the connection between literary and cultural discourses is correct, it would be reasonable to assume that as the conception of the gentleman was transformed in the nineteenth century, a corresponding reordering took place in the literary discourses used to express that altered conception. And that is indeed what happened. Ina Ferris summarizes the ways in which the Victorians redefined the figure of the gentleman in an industrial age:

Like their eighteenth-century predecessors, the Victorians privileged an ethical model of the gentleman, but theirs tended to generalize private rather than public virtues. In the complicated political and economic matrix of an industrial society, the whole question of public virtue (knowledge of the general good) had become much more problematic, and Victorian definitions generally displaced the issue by valorizing what could be called relational virtues. The Victorian gentleman, that is, was modest, true, simple, pure, kindly, and upright in his dealings with others. His social authority depended on the moral notion of personal conduct, rather than on the civic notion of independence that had sustained earlier models.[36]

The stress on conduct in the Victorian view of gentlemanliness represents a broadening of the ideal, making it available to the

---

[36] Ina Ferris, 'Thackeray and the Ideology of the Gentleman', in John J. Richetti (ed.), *The Columbia History of the British Novel* (New York, 1994), 408.

middle classes of society, who could more easily infiltrate the ranks of the gentleman by adopting certain modes of conduct than by the acquisition of landed estates. This more flexible notion of the gentleman resolves the sense of anxiety and embarrassment that accompanied Burke in his relations with his Whig patrons: the ambiguities that rendered his status as a gentleman uncertain disappear as the numbers of the politically enfranchised expand and the idea of the gentleman loses its élite, civic humanist character. Symptomatic of this change is the fact that the literary treatment of the gentleman in the nineteenth century shifts from the exclusive, classically based form of the georgic to the more broadly based and popular form of the novel. As a form expressing middle-class aspirations, the novel supplants the georgic, which loses the literary dominance it had enjoyed for more than a century.

All this takes us beyond the scope of the present study, but it is worth pausing, in conclusion, to consider an early manifestation of this reordering of literary hierarchies in the 1790s. Whatever Burke's own insecurities about his place in the natural aristocratic order that he had exerted so much energy to define and defend, he identified sufficiently with its assumptions to heap scorn on such a figure as Richard Price when that dissenting divine presumed to adopt the gentlemanly rhetoric of the prospect view: 'Then viewing, from the Pisgah of his pulpit, the free, moral, happy, flourishing, and glorious state of France, as in a bird-eye landscape of a promised land he breaks out into ... rapture' (viii. 115). The Miltonic vantage point permitted Adam and Jesus in *Paradise Lost* and *Paradise Regained* is sarcastically denied to Milton's spiritual descendent, who is derided as a footling, latter-day Moses. To Burke, Price is one of those men 'confined to professional and faculty habits' (viii. 95) who are unqualified to sit in the councils of the nation. This exclusion of Price had a subtle logic all its own, as Robin Gilmour explains: '[Eighteenth-century Britain] conferred gentility on the army officer; on the clergyman of the established church, but not the Dissenter; on the London physician, but not the surgeon or attorney; on the man of "liberal education", but only if he had received that education at Oxford or Cambridge, from which Dissenters were excluded.' This seemingly arbitrary set of distinctions was in fact designed to ensure 'the prestige of those occupations which reinforced the stability of a social hierarchy based on the ownership of land'.[37]

Burke's ridicule of Price, however, attracted the indignant attention of Mary Wollstonecraft, who greatly admired the radical dissenter. She castigated Burke for his *ad hominem* attack on Price—'In reprobating Dr. Price's opinions you might have spared the man'—but her most telling defence was to adopt for herself the stance of gentlemanly and Miltonic disinterestedness that Burke sought to deny Price, let alone a woman such as Wollstonecraft. In a gesture of potentially revolutionary import (since she was neither a man nor a possessor of property), she incorporated the rhetoric of the prospect survey into her own writings, as in the following passage from her *Vindication of the Rights of Woman*:

'Let me now as from an eminence survey the world stripped of all its false delusive charms. The clear atmosphere enables me to see each object in its true point of view, while my heart is still. I am calm as the prospect in a morning when the mists, slowly dispersing, silently unveil the beauties of nature, refreshed by rest'.[38]

Calmly observing objects in their 'true point of view', Wollstonecraft appropriates for herself the qualities of disinterest, independence, rationality, and comprehensiveness that Burke and earlier practitioners of the prospect survey claimed exclusively for the gentleman. In so doing she redefines class and gender relations in late eighteenth-century Britain, and in her text she enacts this political and cultural reordering at both the formal and the discursive levels.

In her earlier pamphlet, *A Vindication of the Rights of Men*, Wollstonecraft had attacked at its very roots Burke's conviction that political competence could only be grounded in landed property. The very condition that ostensibly guaranteed the gentleman's disinterest—his hereditary possession of property—presented, in fact, an insurmountable impediment to his acquisition of civic virtue: 'How can [the gentleman] discover

---

[37] Robin Gilmour, *The Idea of the Gentleman in the Victorian Novel* (London, 1981), 7.
[38] Mary Wollstonecraft, *Vindication of the Rights of Woman*, in Janet Todd and Marylin Butler (eds.), *The Works of Mary Wollstonecraft* (London, 1989), v. 179. Further references are noted in the text (*VW*).

that he is a man, when all his wants are instantly supplied, and invention is never sharpened by necessity? Will he labour, for every thing valuable must be the fruit of laborious exertions, to attain knowledge and virtue . . . when the flattering attention of sycophants is a more luscious cordial?'[39] Only the middle classes, precisely because they lack property and are therefore forced to live by their wits, will exert themselves sufficiently to acquire the rationality and independence requisite to political leadership: 'Abilities and virtues are absolutely necessary to raise men from the middle rank of life into notice; and the natural consequence is notorious, the middle rank contains most virtues and abilities. Men have thus, in one station, at least an opportunity of exerting themselves with dignity' (VW 126).

Moreover, the very feature of middle-class education that, in Burke's view, disables the individual from acquiring civic personality—its emphasis on specialized and professional training—is seen by Wollstonecraft as underwriting the necessary material and intellectual independence of the active citizen. In preparing himself for a profession, a middle-class man keeps 'his eye steadily fixed on some future advantage (and the mind gains great strength by having all its efforts directed to one point). . . . The human character has ever been formed by the employments the individual, or class, pursues; and if the faculties are not sharpened by necessity, they must remain obtuse' (VW 129, 120). She turns Burke's argument back upon him by observing that gentlemen and monarchs are equally confined by 'professional and faculty habits': the atmosphere of deference, luxury, and undeserved adulation in which they habitually move has corrupted them and fatally undermined their abilities. If, therefore, 'the character of every man is . . . formed by his profession', it follows that society must be 'very careful not to establish bodies of men who must necessarily be made foolish or vicious by the very constitution of their profession' (VW 87).

Yet, society compounds its error by according women the same puerile, fawning attention that it lavishes upon its governors. Wollstonecraft tartly observes, 'A king is always a king—and a woman always a woman: his authority and her sex,

---

[39] Mary Wollstonecraft, *Vindication of the Rights of Men*, in *Works*, v. 42. Further references are noted in the text (VM).

ever stand between them and rational converse' (*VW* 125). So long as men continue to pay women unearned 'regal homage' (*VW* 90), women will feel no incentive to pursue rationality and virtue, a disabling state of affairs compounded by the subordinate position in which women are kept, which debars them from the exercise of judgement and responsibility. In this respect they are like soldiers, trained to obey without question: 'Every corps [of soldiers] is a chain of despots, who, submitting and tyrannizing without exercising their reason, become dead weights of vice and folly on the community' (*VW* 86). That degeneracy is grounded not in sex but in the habits of intellectual and psychological submissiveness that 'effeminize' many of the men, as well as women, in her class-ridden society, including Edmund Burke, whom she tellingly characterizes as a 'slave of impulse' and an author of 'sprightly sallies' and 'sentimental exclamations' (*VM* 26, 8).

In contrast, Wollstonecraft is anxious to assume the mantle of 'manly' virtue, though, as Mary Poovey shrewdly observes, her 'noisy bravado' in *The Rights of Men* conceals an insecurity 'about how to present the outrage she felt and how to give her largely subjective responses authority'.[40] One of the most telling strategies she adopts is to appropriate for herself the forms of 'manly' discourse that Burke, by advocating attitudes of 'generous loyalty to rank and sex ... proud submission ... [and] subordination of the heart', has implicitly relinquished. Thus, she counters his use of the prospect survey in the *Reflections* with her own extended view—a view for which she claims an even greater comprehensiveness than Burke can muster. She scathingly demystifies the gentleman's claim to comprehensiveness and disinterest (and, hence, to political leadership) by exposing the inadequacy of his retired vantage point:

I know, indeed, that there is often something disgusting in the distresses of poverty, at which the imagination revolts, and starts back to exercise itself in the more attractive Arcadia of fiction. The rich man builds a house, art and taste give it the highest finish. His gardens are

---

[40] Mary Poovey, *The Proper Lady and the Woman Writer: Ideology as Style in the Works of Mary Wollstonecraft, Mary Shelley, and Jane Austen* (Chicago, 1984), 58.

planted, and the trees grow to recreate the fancy of the planter. ...
Every thing on the estate is cherished but man. ... But if, instead of
sweeping pleasure-grounds, obelisks, temples, and elegant cottages, as
objects for the eye, the heart was allowed to beat true to nature, decent
farms would be scattered over the estate, and plenty smile
around. (*VM* 56).

In this view the possession of property and the retired leisure it
permits impedes, rather than promotes, political virtue: the rich
man's eye is blind to all but a factitious reality.

The passage just quoted appears immediately after
Wollstonecraft's citation of Burke's blunt concluding remarks in
the *Reflections* about the necessity for subordination and
inequality of property: 'The body of the people must not find
the principles of natural subordination by art rooted out of their
minds. They must respect that property of which they cannot
partake. They must labour to obtain what by labour can be
obtained; and when they find, as they commonly do, the success
disproportioned to the endeavour, they must be taught their
consolation in the final proportions of eternal justice' (viii. 290).
Her response is to offer the reader her own prospect view, a view
grounded on the premiss that a society which encourages
equality, industry, and rationality in all its citizens, male and
female, rich and poor, can indeed enjoy the blessings of
material, intellectual, and emotional sufficiency for all: 'What
salutary dews might not be shed to refresh this thirsty land, if
men were more *enlightened*! Smiles and premiums might
encourage cleanliness, industry, and emulation—A garden more
inviting than Eden would then meet the eye, and springs of joy
murmur on every side' (*VM* 56).

Wollstonecraft ratifies her claim to superior rationality by
setting out what she regards as a more comprehensive view than
Burke's, one that refutes his view at every point. Interestingly,
she accepts the same fundamental Whig premiss as her
opponent—that political despotism is inimical to commercial
greatness—but she arrives at a contrary view of both Britain and
France because her position as gazer (less limited by property
and social class) enables her to see further and more clearly:

Returning once from a despotic country to a part of England well
cultivated, but not very picturesque—with what delight did I not
observe the poor man's garden!—The homely palings and twining

woodbine, with all the rustic contrivances of simple, unlettered taste, was a sight which relieved the eye that had wandered indignant from the stately palace to the pestiferous hovel, and turned from the awful contrast into itself to mourn the fate of man, and curse the arts of civilization!

Why cannot large estates be divided into small farms? these dwellings would indeed grace our land. Why are huge forests still allowed to stretch out with idle pomp and all the indolence of Eastern grandeur? Why does the brown waste meet the traveller's view, when men want work? ... Domination blasts all these prospects; virtue can only flourish amongst equals. ... In this great city, that proudly rears its head, and boasts of its population and commerce, how much misery lurks in pestilential quarters! ... Where is the eye that marks these evils? ... If society was regulated on a more enlarged plan ... if, turning his eyes from the ideal regions of taste and elegance, [man] laboured to give the earth he inhabited all the beauty it is capable of receiving ... he who ... wishes to convince or persuade society that this is true happiness and dignity is not ... a short-sighted philosopher.

(VM 147–50)

Wollstonecraft may indeed have been an inexperienced writer when she wrote this passage, but, as is clear from her conscious adoption of the rhetorical and generic features Burke uses in the *Reflections*, she understands perfectly well their political and ideological significance. She turns Burke's own weapons against him, claiming the georgic virtues for the modest farmer and rural labourer, rather than the opulent gentleman. This is not to overlook what these two combatants have in common, nor to ignore the limitations of her perspective. Thus, while she demands a space for political action on the part of middle-class and female Britons, her discourse does not extend to the liberation of those she calls the 'vulgar'—the vast majority of her countrymen, whose cause was to be championed by other, more radical voices. What she shares with Burke, however, is a perspective sharpened by her position as outsider: like the narrator-observer in Thomson's *Seasons*, both Wollstonecraft and Burke have appropriated for themselves, chameleon-like, the authority of the disinterested gentleman.

4
Theatre and Counter-Theatre in Burke's Reflections on the Revolution in France

'I shall not live to behold the unravelling of the intricate plot, which saddens and perplexes the awful drama of Providence, now acting on the moral theatre of the world,' wrote Edmund Burke in the opening paragraphs of the *Letters on a Regicide Peace*, his last great polemic on the French Revolution (ix. 188). The metaphor invoked here of revolution as grand, tragic theatre must be one of the most sustained leitmotivs running through the outpouring of letters, pamphlets, speeches, and treatises that the events in France provoked from Burke's prolific pen. In his earliest recorded comment on the Revolution, he wrote to Lord Charlemont on 9 August 1789 of his 'astonishment at the wonderful Spectacle which is exhibited in a Neighbouring and rival Country—what Spectators, and what actors' (*Corr.* vi. 10). The perception that all the political world's a stage is certainly not new with Burke, nor is it a point of novelty to observe, as Thomas Paine had been quick to note in 1791, that the theatrical metaphor is central to Burke's histrionic interpretation of revolutionary events. James T. Boulton voices the consensus of interpretative opinion with his argument that the theatrical references in *Reflections on the Revolution in France* are intended 'to arouse the emotional fervour normally associated with serious drama and to suggest that the proper state of mind for observers of the French Revolution is that appropriate to watching a tragedy'.[1]

---

[1] James T. Boulton, *The Language of Politics in the Age of Wilkes and Burke* (London, 1963), 144.

Boulton's thesis is unexceptionable as far as it goes, but its perspective by no means exhausts the extraordinary range and complexity of Burke's theatrical allusions in his writings on the French Revolution. Taking Boulton's statement as his jumping-off point, Peter H. Melvin argues that Burke is not only advancing his own conception of the political uses of drama but also drawing attention, with characteristic insight, to the Jacobins' revolutionary political artistry, particularly their radical, totalizing conception of revolution as theatre: 'The whole of revolutionary society was to become a vast theatre; everyone was to become an actor, a dissembler, except the Jacobins themselves.'[2] As Burke himself states in the *Regicide Peace* tracts, 'All sorts of shews and exhibitions calculated to inflame and vitiate the imagination, and pervert the moral sense, have been contrived' (ix. 242).

The purpose of these public spectacles, which, Burke charged, included public rituals of denunciation—sons calling for the execution of their parents and parents denouncing their children as 'royalists' or 'constitutionalists' (ix. 242)—was to purify and revolutionize French society through the coercive power of terror and mutual suspicion. Whatever their inward beliefs, citizens would be driven to enact a show of revolutionary zeal: 'Anxiety which provoked mere conformity would finally produce febrile activity on behalf of the Revolution.'[3] Equally importantly, the theatrical rituals of the *ancien régime*, those public spectacles designed to enforce symbolically the authority of the existing order, were being replaced systematically by new ceremonies and observances. Thus, for a time the pomp of the Roman Catholic Church gave way to the rationalistic Cult of the Supreme Being; in Burke's horrified words, 'they institute impious, blasphemous, indecent theatric rites, in honour of their vitiated, perverted reason, and erect altars to the personification of their own corrupted and bloody Republick' (ix. 241).

Reflections on the Revolution in France was written in the opening months of the Revolution, long before the concerted theatricality of the revolutionary government became apparent. One might wish to credit Burke with a proleptic insight into the

---

[2] Peter H. Melvin, 'Burke on Theatricality and Revolution', *Journal of the History of Ideas*, 36 (1975), 451.   [3] Ibid.

development of revolutionary ideology and behaviour—by no means a frivolous or fanciful hypothesis.[4] But, another explanation can be offered for the pervasive presence of the theatrical metaphor in the *Reflections*, which is present not simply as an extended allusion embedded in the text but as an integral, architectonic element in its design. The event that occasioned the *Reflections*, Dr Richard Price's sermon at the Old Jewry commemorating the Glorious Revolution, furnishes a decisive clue. Burke's reading of Price's published sermon, *A Discourse on the Love of Our Country*, together with its appended congratulatory correspondence between the Revolution Society and the French National Assembly, alerted him suddenly to the danger the principles promulgated by the French Revolution posed to the domestic politics and social equilibrium of England. This primary concern, the risk of the revolutionary infection spreading from France to England (to borrow a favourite Burkean image), decisively influenced the shape of his argument in the *Reflections*, which, though ostensibly addressed to a French correspondent, is directed in the first instance to an English readership.

Thus, with his primary audience in mind, he is careful to address his readers in the sometimes arcane forms of eighteenth-century British political discourse. In particular, he draws attention to what might be called a 'discourse of the crowd', employing emerging forms of mass political protest in late eighteenth-century England as a fundamental structural element in his treatise. Burke dwells at length on what E. P. Thompson has aptly labelled the 'counter-theatre' of the crowd, which countered with its own symbolism the studied theatrical style of official authority, with its coronations, levees, and Lord

---

[4] In his biography of Burke, Conor Cruise O'Brien describes the tendency of undergraduate readers to jump to the conclusion 'that the direst events of the Revolution—the September Massacres, the Terror, the executions of the King and Queen—had already taken place when the *Reflections* was written'. All of these events, together with the eventual military despotism of Napoleon (which Burke also foresaw), lay well in the future in 1790, when his analysis was published. O'Brien argues, 'Burke's astonishing capacity to see into the ways in which events were moving derived, not from any mystical intuition, but from penetrating powers of observation, judicious inference from what was observed, and thorough analysis of what was discerned by observation and inference' (*The Great Melody* (Chicago, 1992), 403).

Mayor's days, and which opposed its own calendar of political observances to the official calendar of political celebrations and commemorations in Hanoverian England.[5] The central dramatic plot of the *Reflections*, the October 1789 march upon Versailles, which forms the emotional climax of Burke's treatise, cannot be understood fully unless it is read in the context of the ritualized language of late eighteenth-century English insurrectionary behaviour. He assimilates the novel and the unknown (the dizzying spectacle in France) to the known and familiar (civil affrays such as the Wilkite disturbances and the Gordon riots), and invokes potent English political myths dating from the Civil War and the Glorious Revolution in a violent struggle to establish the interpretative boundaries that will govern the English response to events in France. Burke finds himself locked in a conflict with the Revolution's well-wishers, both moderates and radicals, for interpretative authority: whose reading of the Revolution and whose appropriation of the symbols and rituals of English political discourse are to prevail?

In giving such vivid life to the dramatic counter-theatre of the Revolution, Burke also poses some interesting questions about the official or culturally sanctioned theatre of his time, which finds itself under challenge by new modes of literary consciousness and expression. In the *Reflections* a contestation of literary genres is especially apparent, as heroic tragedy finds itself being written out of the generic hierarchy. In response Burke inserts an episode of tragic sensibility into his discourse (the assualt upon the royal family), and he adds, by way of commentary on his unusual narrative procedure, a lengthy critical passage defending the authenticity of traditional tragedy and the emotional responses aroused by it. All this is in vehement rejoinder to what he regards as spurious, upstart attempts to refigure the Revolution as a lyric, comic celebration in which a new, demotic cast of protagonists treads the stage. If hierarchy could be challenged in one quarter, it could be questioned in others as well, including the hierarchical conception of literary form. The eighteenth-century model of literary genres as an interrelated

---

[5] E. P. Thompson, 'Patrician Society, Plebeian Culture', *Journal of Social History*, 7 (1974), 382–405. See also Ronald Paulson, *Popular and Polite Art in the Age of Hogarth and Fielding* (Notre Dame, Ind., 1979), 26–30.

system had proved flexible in accommodating new forms such as the novel, but it also made possible new ways of thinking about the relations among forms and modes of expression. Such a re-evaluation might lead to the questioning of the very premisses of hierarchy upon which the prevailing theory of genres rested. The *Reflections* witnesses to and protests the rapid process of literary innovation underway at the turn of the nineteenth century: it fuses literary and cultural criticism with political polemic in a memorable synthesis.

I

The most celebrated of the many responses to Burke's *Reflections* is Thomas Paine's *Rights of Man* (1791). That Paine's reply deserves its high reputation is evident in the incisiveness with which he defines the clash of interpretative discourses in the debate that the *Reflections* has triggered: 'I cannot consider Mr Burke's book in scarcely any other light than a dramatic performance; and he must, I think, have considered it in the same light himself, by the poetical liberties he has taken of omitting some facts, distorting others, and making the whole machinery bend to produce a stage effect. Of this kind is his account of the expedition to Versailles. . . . It suits his purpose to exhibit the consequences without their causes. It is one of the arts of the drama to do so.' To Burke's tragic scenes he seeks to counterpose truth: fact opposes fiction in this passage, and life confronts art.[6]

In a fundamental sense, Paine sees no interpretative clash at all between his and Burke's accounts of the Revolution, but only the opposition of reality to quixotic delusion. 'Mr Burke should recollect that he is writing History, and not *Plays*; and that his readers will expect truth, and not the spouting rant of high-toned exclamation.' Paine does not pause to reflect that historiography is as much a narrative or dramatic art as the writing of plays, an insight that Burke instinctively grasped. By assigning appropriate 'facts' and 'causes' to explain the 'consequences' that Burke dwells upon, Paine ineluctably commits

---

[6] Thomas Paine, *Rights of Man*, ed. Henry Collins (Harmondsworth, 1969), 81–2.

himself to his own narrative or version of events. He cannot do otherwise, for the effort to understand discrete historical events inevitably involves him in the articulation of a plot or story. Defending his sequence of explanation as more accurate and comprehensive than Burke's, Paine argues, 'If the crimes of men were exhibited with their sufferings, stage effect would sometimes be lost, and the audience would be inclined to approve where it was intended they should commiserate.'[7] True enough, one is inclined to respond, but then the audience would be viewing a different play, as Paine intends they should.

The dramatic scenes Burke places at the centre of his *Reflections* exploit a powerful double perspective, offering two simultaneous versions of the march on the king and queen at Versailles. One of these is the familiar tragic plot: the violent assault upon Marie Antoinette, followed by the *Via Dolorosa* of the royal family's forced return to Paris—Burke's 'Jacobean tragedy', as Ronald Paulson terms it.[8] The other is the same sequence of events with the revolutionary crowd placed in the foreground, not unlike, in a sense, the foregrounding of Satan in the opening books of *Paradise Lost*. Though he views the crowd close up, Burke is observing its behaviour disapprovingly from above, very much in the manner that Alexander Pope surveys the antics of the dunces in his *Dunciad*. Pope's poem invokes a generic hierarchy in which serious, elevated discourse is assimilated to the genres of tragedy and epic and is contrasted with the inferior, impure discourse of the dunces, which is grotesque, burlesque, and bathetic. Pope and Burke are caught up in an elaborate rhetoric of exclusion, associating their cultural and political enemies with the grotesque, low elements of the street and carnival—an outdoor, urban culture, both repellent and fascinating, that was progressively repudiated and displaced in the eighteenth century by the more 'rational' and respectable pleasures of the coffee house, salon, and spa. At the same time, the visionary force that fires them both and energizes their writing draws its power, paradoxically, from precisely those

---

[7] Paine, *The Rights of Man*, 72, 82.
[8] Ronald Paulson, *Representations of Revolution (1789–1820)* (New Haven, 1983), 76.

subterraneous elements their impassioned discourse seeks to exorcize and exclude. As Peter Stallybrass and Allon White note with reference to Pope, 'whilst Augustan poetry witnesses an unprecedented labour of transduction in which it battled against the Smithfield Muse to cleanse the cultural sphere of impure and messy semiotic matter, it also fed voraciously and incessantly from that very material'.[9]

The emotional intensity and texture of authenticity that Burke communicates in his descriptions of crucial, dramatic revolutionary events—despite his having been witness to none of them—originate in his experience of the Wilkite disturbances and the Gordon Riots in London, the latter disorders a scant ten years in the past at the time of the French Revolution. Burke recalls Lord George Gordon in the *Reflections*, drawing an explicit parallel between the English 'mob . . . which pulled down all our prisons' and the Parisians who stormed the Bastille in July, 1789 (viii. 135). His parliamentary speeches of the early 1790s attest repeatedly to his conviction that significant correlations existed between the two events. During the Gordon Riots of 1780, he experienced at first hand the fury of the mob, whipped up into an anti-Catholic frenzy; as an outspoken supporter of the Catholic Relief Act (1778), he had become a direct target of the rioters. Though soldiers were dispatched to protect his London house, from which books and pictures had been prudently removed, Burke himself refused to be intimidated by the crowd and went out deliberately 'in the street amidst this wild assembly into whose hands I deliverd myself informing them who I was' (*Corr.* iv. 246).

A report of the parliamentary debates following the riots (19 or 20 June 1780) records briefly Burke's impressions of what he had seen:

He went into a full account of the late riots; expatiated on the inhumanity of the mob; said that Mr. Langdale, with twelve children, had suffered to the amount of 50,000l. . . . The inhumanity of fanatics,

---

[9] Peter Stallybrass and Allon White, *The Politics and Poetics of Transgression* (London, 1986), 108. On the carnivalesque and the interrelation of high and low culture, see Mikhail Bakhtin, *Rabelais and His World*, trans. Helene Iswolsky (Cambridge, Mass., 1968); and Terry Castle, *Masquerade and Civilization: The Carnivalesque in Eighteenth-Century English Culture and Fiction* (London, 1986).

he said, was such, that after the destruction of the school near the city, a petition had been presented, desiring that the poor man, who owned it, might not have a lease of the land again to build another. . . . [H]e quoted, in a facetious manner, the names of several women—not being able to read and write themselves, these monsters were desirous of preventing others from receiving education. . . . Mr. Burke stated, in a very long speech, the means taken to bring about all the mischief; he said it had happened by the zeal of wicked and abandoned men, who had gone about industriously misleading poor, ignorant, and deluded people.[10]

Though this account offers little more than the barest summary of Burke's speech, it highlights a number of elements that were to figure prominently in his subsequent descriptions of the Parisian mob. His appeal to the emotions of his auditors through affecting personal anecdotes, his exaggerated characterization of the rioters as base, inhumane, 'wicked and abandoned' fanatics and monsters, his singling out of the women participants as latter-day furies, and his recognition of a symbolic selectiveness in the crowd's choice of victims—all these elements in his analysis of the Gordon Riots recur conspicuously in the famous narrative of the march on Versailles.

In that account, the Parisians invading the palace are transformed into a 'band of cruel ruffians and assassins, reeking with . . . blood', and they leave in their destructive wake a scene 'swimming in blood, polluted by massacre, and strewed with scattered limbs and mutilated carcases'. Burke's narrative continues,

Two . . . of the gentlemen of birth and family who composed the king's body guard . . . with all the parade of an execution of justice, were cruelly and publicly dragged to the block, and beheaded in the great court of the palace. Their heads were stuck upon spears, and led the procession; whilst the royal captives who followed in the train were slowly moved along, amidst the horrid yells, and shrilling screams, and frantic dances, and infamous contumelies, and all the unutterable abominations of the furies of hell, in the abused shape of the vilest of women. (viii. 121–2)

---

[10] Edmund Burke, *The Speeches of the Right Honourable Edmund Burke, in the House of Commons, and in Westminster-Hall* (London, 1816), ii. 178–9.

Even a cursory comparison with contemporary accounts reveals how Burke has embellished and heightened the facts; what he hoped, however, was to furnish an account that would ring imaginatively true for his audience.[11] This he accomplishes by attributing to the Parisian throng precisely those characteristics that distinguished, at least in the estimation of the English élite, the behaviour of London crowds. Standing at one remove from the French Revolution, Burke offers his readers an English fiction because English political realities are his primary concern.

II

To understand fully the discourse of the crowd that informs Burke's crowded, bloody scene, one must revive imaginatively a sense of the ceremonial and theatrical splendour with which official authority clothed itself in the period—the rituals and symbolism of the courts, the Church, and the Crown. The example of Tyburn, the awful rites of public execution, conveniently illustrates both the pageantry with which government and law exercised their power and the means by which the crowd subversively undercut such awe-inspiring spectacles. In his *Enquiry into the Causes of the Late Increase of Robbers* (1751), Henry Fielding draws attention to the self-conscious theatricality of the rites by which justice was enforced: executions, he suggests, should be performed like a well-written tragedy, in which a 'Murder behind the Scenes, if the Poet knows how to manage it, will affect the Audience with greater Terror than if it was acted before their Eyes'.[12] Fielding does not

---

[11] Cf. the account of the attack upon Versailles in *Memoirs of Madame de La Tour du Pin*, trans. Felice Harcourt (1969; London, 1985), 125–37. For a discussion of the social composition of the crowds participating in the Gordon Riots, see George Rudé, *The Crowd in History: A Study of Popular Disturbances in France and England 1730–1848* (1964; London, 1981), 60–1. See also, Dorothy Marshall, *Dr. Johnson's London* (New York, 1968), 236–8.

[12] Henry Fielding, *An Enquiry into the Causes of the Late Increase of Robbers* (London, 1751), 123. Douglas Hay's 'Property, Authority, and the Criminal Law', in Hay et al., *Albion's Fatal Tree: Crime and Society in Eighteenth-Century England* (New York, 1975), 26–31, details the elaborate spectacle and ritual that surrounded the administration of justice in eighteenth-century England. Another essay in the same volume, Peter Linebaugh's 'The Tyburn Riot against the Surgeons', 65–9, describes the theatrical and counter-theatrical spectacle of public hangings in the period.

argue that executions be carried out in private but instead inveighs against the prevailing carnival atmosphere on hanging days, which often transformed malefactors into anti-heroes or even martyrs to the rigours of justice. Accordingly, he insists that an atmosphere of dramatic solemnity must be maintained— if necessary, by artifice: 'The Execution should be in the highest degree solemn. It is not the Essence of the Thing itself, but the Dress and Apparatus of it, which make an Impression on the Mind, especially on the Minds of the Multitude to whom Beauty in Rags is never a desirable, nor Deformity in Embroidery a disagreeable Object'. As a successful dramatist, Fielding might be expected to display a keen awareness of the administration of justice as a dramatic enactment, but his analysis is none the less striking in its emphasis on the external trappings of spectacle as crucial elements in the maintenance of order and authority. Burke is of the same mind, arguing that the fomenters of the Gordon Riots should be punished with the greatest possible dramatic solemnity: '*six*, at the very utmost . . . ought to be brought out and put to death, on one and the same day, in six different places, and in the most solemn manner that can be devised' (Bohn, v. 516).[13]

The symbolism of this official theatre was not lost on the crowd, which often staged its own plebian counter-theatre or crowd rituals parodically mimicking the actions of its 'betters'. Thus, as John Brewer reports,

> on April Fool's day 1771, effigies of the Princess Dowager, Lord Bute, the Speaker of the House of Commons and the two Fox brothers were placed in two carts preceded by a hearse, and taken through the streets of London to the properly constituted execution place of all traitors, Tower Hill, where they were decapitated by a chimney-sweep who also doubled as the officiating minister; they were then ceremoniously burnt. . . . Here was ritual retribution on a parallel with that actually exacted during the Revolution in France.[14]

---

[13] Fielding, *Enquiry*, 124; Burke, 'Some Thoughts on the Approaching Executions'.

[14] John Brewer, *Party Ideology and Popular Politics at the Accession of George III* (Cambridge, 1976), 184. The incident was reported in *Gentleman's Magazine* (1771) 188, and in *Middlesex Journal* (2 April 1771). George Rudé discusses this and similar incidents in *Wilkes and Liberty: A Social Study* (1962; repr. London, 1983), 164 *et passim*.

The crowd's actions mimic the solemnities of a public execution: 'the ritual of authority became the rites of the mob'. This deliberate act of mimesis—the appropriation of the trappings of authority by a subordinate group to enact *their* conception of justice—disturbed and obsessed the authorities, as is evident in the singlemindedness with which they hunted down the standards, trophies, and symbols of the crowd during popular protests. The reason for this preoccupation with symbolic trappings is not difficult to fathom. Brewer cites the astute observation of Adam Ferguson in his *Essay on the History of Civil Society* that any civil order organized on the basis of hierarchy and subordination depends heavily on public ritual to mark subtle gradations of status and power:

> The object of every rank is precedency, and every order may display its advantages to their full extent. The sovereign himself owes great part of his authority to the sounding titles and dazzling equipage which he exhibits in public. The subordinate ranks lay claim to importance by a like exhibition, and for that purpose carry in every instant the ensigns of their birth, or the ornaments of their fortune. What else could mark out to the individual the relation in which he stands to his fellow subjects, or distinguish the numberless ranks that fill up the interval between the state of the sovereign and that of the peasant? Or what else could, in states of a great extent, preserve any appearance of order, among members disunited by ambition and interest, and destined to form a community, without the sense of any common concern?[15]

Without the official theatre of state—coronations, state openings of parliament, court levees, Lord Mayor's Days—individuals would lack a collective focus, a point of cynosure, upon which to fix a sense of community and common enterprise. With the advent of an increasingly rootless, atomized, capitalist social order, 'disunited by ambition and interest', these rites of state seem to Burke more crucial than ever; at the very time that subordination comes increasingly under pressure, its indispensability as an instrument of social control becomes more and more apparent. 'The magistrate must have his reverence, the laws their authority,' he argues. 'The body of the people must not find the principles of natural subordination by art rooted

---

[15] Adam Ferguson, *Essay on the History of Civil Society* (1767); repr. Philadelphia, 1819), 126. See also Brewer, *Party Ideology*, 183–4.

out of their minds. They must respect that property of which they cannot partake' (viii. 290). The keen consciousness of rank and forms of deference in the period ensured that parodies of official theatre from below were often viewed with alarm rather than amusement. It was one thing to adopt a parodic discourse from above, as Pope does in his mock-heroic poems, but quite another to do so from the déclassé perspective of the dunces.

A similar obsession with counter-theatrical symbolism can be detected in Burke's description of the Parisian crowd at Versailles. He dwells on the throng's trophies, the two 'heads . . . stuck upon spears' leading the procession, which bring to mind the grisly and monitory spectacle of the traitors' heads customarily left grinning and festering on Temple Bar. The marchers on Versailles perform a consummate act of counter-theatre, 'all the *parade* of an execution of justice' (emphasis mine), which is all the more terrifying to Burke because it has begun to literalize what had previously been a purely symbolic discourse (as in the mock executions described above by Brewer). Though often destructive in their effects, the English rituals of political protest—'effigy burning; the hanging of a boot from a gallows; the illumination of windows (or the breaking of those without illumination); the untiling of a house'—tended to channel promiscuous violence, directing it at specific targets.[16] With the French revolutionaries these rituals have taken a demonic turn, escalating crowd violence to a new level of ferocity and apparent indiscriminateness.

Burke strains for a comparison sufficiently sensational to convey his sense of the monstrous indignity visited upon the royal family as they were triumphantly escorted back to Paris on 6 October 1789: 'It was . . . a spectacle more resembling a procession of American savages, entering into Onondaga, after some of their murders called victories, and leading into hovels hung round with scalps, their captives, overpowered with the scoffs and buffets of women as ferocious as themselves, much more than it resembled the triumphal pomp of a civilized martial nation' (viii. 117). The contrast between theatre and counter-theatre is made explicit here: the 'triumphal pomp of a

---

[16] Thompson, 'Patrician and Plebeian', 400. See also Rudé *Crowd in History*, 62.

civilized martial nation' (a phrase of exquisite, if unintentional, irony) is set against the savage spectacle of the Parisian mob, whose symbols are no longer a boot or an effigy but the bloody scalps of their victims. Burke seeks to counter the obvious symbolic force of the triumphal return to Paris by transmuting the context or discursive field within which its symbolism can become intelligible. Like Swift, who subverts Puritan claims to divine afflatus by explaining the 'operation of the spirit' in the mechanical terms of pseudo-scientific discourse, conflating inspiration and libido, he undercuts the corporate and political legitimacy of the Parisian crowd's actions by reducing them to a context of anarchic savagery—that of a pre-social, Hobbesian state of nature. The protests of the crowd are thus drained of any political significance and can be read only as acts of blind, irrational violence. Burke vehemently denies any coherence or intelligibility to the crowd's counter-theatrical discourse, even as he affirms the official theatre of France's 'triumphal pomp', its coercive military might.[17]

III

The ritual of official theatre in eighteenth-century Britain was closely tied up with calendrical observances—anniversaries of important historical events—whose commemoration had great

---

[17] In his essay, 'The French Revolution and the Condition of England: Crowds and Power in the Early Victorian Novel', in Ceri Crossley and Ian Small (eds.), *The French Revolution and British Culture*, (Oxford, 1989), 123–40, David Lodge demonstrates how the memories and myths of crowd behaviour in the French Revolution informed the representation of crowds and violence in the fictions of several generations of Victorian novelists. He argues that these novelists—Dickens, Gaskell, Disraeli, and Kingsley, among others—responded not only to actual history, but also to 'a highly imaginative, quasi-fictional interpretation of that history' (127). Lodge acknowledges Burke's role in contributing to this 'quasi-fictional interpretation', but he underestimates the extent of Burke's influence by mistakenly assuming that his depiction of the revolutionary crowd is confined to the pages of the *Reflections* and that these remarks are merely 'asides in an argument that is essentially abstract—constitutional, moral, philosophical' (p. 133). As will become apparent when we return to this subject in connection with the *Letters on a Regicide Peace* (Ch. 5), Burke's repelled fascination with the power of the crowd in the French Revolution surfaces again and again in his writings of the 1790s. I suspect he played a larger role than Lodge estimates in shaping these Victorian attitudes and modes of representation.

symbolic and ideological significance. In the urbanized and increasingly politicized atmosphere of Georgian England, the time-honoured dates of the agricultural year (May Day, Plough Monday, Twelfth Night, etc.) were displaced by celebrations of the nation's political landmarks: the reigning monarch's birthday; the birthday and accession of Charles II, marking the Restoration (29 May); the date of the Hanoverian succession (1 August); the birthday of William III and the occasion of his landing at Torbay, celebrated as the anniversary of the Glorious Revolution (4 November); and Guy Fawkes' Day (5 November). These holidays together constituted a Hanoverian political calendar designed, as John Brewer remarks, 'to inculcate loyal values in the populace, and to emphasize and encourage the growth of a national political consensus'.[18] On a number of occasions, however, particularly in the first half of the century, the calendar became a focus for ideological conflict, with Whigs and Tories, Hanoverians and Jacobites celebrating rival Hanoverian and Stuart anniversaries with processions, effigy-burnings, oaths, toasts, and commemorative sermons. Thus, for example, Jacobite attempts to burn William III in effigy on 4 November 1715 were broken up by Whig supporters, who in turn organized pope-burning processions and anniversary celebrations of their own as demonstrations of loyalty to George I.[19]

By mid-century, with the question of the royal succession no longer in dispute, the dates of the political calendar were celebrated in a spirit of general unanimity. But with the emergence of this public consensus, the calendar and its rituals of observance, like other symbols of official authority, became in their turn the targets of parody and mock-imitation. The radical movement that coalesced around John Wilkes in the 1760s created, according to Brewer, a counter-calendar of celebrations parodying the established cycle of anniversaries. 'Wilkes's birthday, the anniversary of the St. George's Fields Massacre, the numerous Middlesex elections, the release of

---

[18] John Brewer, 'Commercialization and Politics', in Neil McKendrick, John Brewer, and J. H. Plumb, *The Birth of a Consumer Society: The Commercialization of Eighteenth-Century England* (London, 1982), 247.

[19] Nicholas Rogers, 'Popular Protest in Early Hanoverian London', *Past and Present*, 79 (May 1978), 77–9.

Wilkes from the King's Bench, each of these occasions was feted not merely as a celebration but as a means of impinging upon the popular political conscience in a way that the government had employed for over a generation.'[20]

The demonstrations that marked these counter-celebrations were generally orchestrated by that most characteristic eighteenth-century institution, the club. The proliferation of local clubs, lodges, and societies in the period served a wide variety of purposes: economic, social, political, literary, and intellectual. Through their pooling of financial, intellectual, and organizational resources, these voluntary associations conferred a degree of independence upon their members from traditional economic and political relationships of clientage and aristocratic patronage. Radical leaders such as Wilkes found in the clubs a ready source of financial and political support which they shrewdly exploited. Unlike the loyalist societies or 'mug-house' clubs of the early Hanoverian years, which were organized by the Whig gentry to inculcate loyalty to the new regime, the later associations provided an organizational foundation for independent political thought and initiative.

The symbolism and discursive activity organized around the political calendar and the clubs forms a salient, though often overlooked, constituent of the historical context within which the *Reflections* was conceived. In reviving this feature of the political culture in which Burke and the *Reflections* were immersed, I do not mean to provide a kind of scenic historic landscape or backdrop against which his work can picturesquely be situated. The aim, rather, is to 'historicize' Burke's treatise: to remind ourselves, as Michael McKeon observes of literary texts in general, that the text 'partakes of historical process: that it is a strenuous and exacting labor of discourse that seems thereby to detach itself from its historical medium, but that bears within its own composition the distinguishing marks of its continuity with the world it has ostensibly left behind'.[21] The *Reflections* has been spectacularly successful in rising above the intellectual

---

[20] McKendrick, Brewer, and Plumb, *Consumer Society*, 248. See also Brewer, *Party Ideology*, 178–9; and Rudé, *Wilkes and Liberty*.

[21] Michael McKeon, 'Historicizing *Absalom and Achitophel*', in Felicity Nussbaum and Laura Brown (eds.), *The New Eighteenth Century: Theory, Politics, English Literature* (New York, 1987), 37.

fray, as indicated by its status as a classic of political philosophy and of modern conservatism, but when it is resituated in the historical discourse of its time, its tone of magisterial authority gives way to one of strenuous striving and debate—a debate immersed in the contemporary, historically specific discourse symbolized by the Hanoverian calendar.

The opening pages of the *Reflections* establish the ground on which this initial battle in the propaganda war over the French Revolution is to be fought. The event Burke identifies as having occasioned his treatise, the annual meeting of the Revolution Society on 4 November 1789, does not, on the face of it, appear to pose much of a threat: 'I find, upon enquiry, that on the anniversary of the Revolution in 1688, a club of dissenters, but of what denomination I know not, have long had the custom of hearing a sermon in one of their churches; and that afterwards they spent the day cheerfully, as other clubs do, at the tavern' (viii. 56). Burke admits that there is, on the surface, 'nothing' here to which he can reasonably 'take exception'; he even acknowledges that he has 'the honour to belong to more clubs than one, in which the constitution of this kingdom and the principles of the glorious Revolution, are held in high reverence' (viii. 56, 54). But having implicitly recognized the important role of clubs like the Revolution Society as voices and moulders of public opinion, he proceeds to repudiate and exclude what he implicitly affirms. He sets out not only to dispel any impression that the Revolution Society acts 'in some sort of corporate capacity, acknowledged by the laws of this kingdom, and authorized to speak the sense of some part of it' (viii. 57), but also to deny its legitimacy as a political voice in any capacity whatsoever, public or private.

In his vehement exclusion of the Revolution Society and its activities from the realm of legitimate political discourse, Burke betrays a profound anxiety over the power of counter-theatrical symbolism. He reiterated this anxiety on numerous occasions, including in a speech to the House of Commons on 6 May 1791, in which he links clubs and their subversive activities, anniversaries, and the spectre of civil disorder:

> Were there not clubs in every quarter, who met and voted resolutions of an alarming tendency? ... Did they not preach in their pulpits

doctrines that were dangerous, and celebrate at their anniversary meetings, proceedings incompatible with the spirit of the British constitution? ... He recurred to the events of the year 1780, and mentioned the dreadful consequences of the riots occasioned by Lord George Gordon. Had he at that time cautioned the House to beware of the Protestant Association, and other caballing meetings, he supposed his cautions would have been treated in the same way as those he offered now.[22]

His great fear is that the Hanoverian political calendar is about to be appropriated, or even displaced, by a revolutionary ideology with its own commemorative festivals, as he notes with dismay in *Thoughts on French Affairs* (1791):

The appointment of festive anniversaries has ever in the sense of mankind been held the best method of keeping alive the spirit of any institution. We have one settled in London; and at the last of them, that of the 14th of July, the strong discountenance of Government, the unfavourable time of the year, and the then uncertainty of the disposition of foreign Powers, did not hinder the meeting of at least nine hundred people, with good coats on their backs, who could afford to pay half a guinea a head to shew their zeal for the new principles. (viii. 379–80)

Not only Bastille Day, but also the 5 and 6 October, commemorating the exultant return of the people of Paris with their king and queen, might well become a 'festive anniversary' in a revolutionary calendar: hence, Burke's eagerness to characterize the events of those two days as a 'horrid, atrocious, and afflicting spectacle' (viii. 117) rather than a triumphal progress. But try as he might to exclude this popular discourse and dismiss its proponents as outside the limits of rationality and respectability, he is none the less forced to acknowledge amongst this 'rabble' the presence of many individuals with a considerable stake in their country—'with good coats on their backs' and guineas in their pockets.

Burke also fears a revival of the ideological conflict that the dates of the political calendar had occasioned in the early Hanoverian period. Dr Price's commemorative sermon sets forth a revisionist picture of the Glorious Revolution which threatens, in Burke's view, to make 4 November a celebration of

---

[22] Burke, *Speeches*, iv. 20–2.

political ideals that are potentially revolutionary in scope. The question at issue is what kind of narrative will be fashioned out of the facts of history; in a nation deeply imbued with the habit of defining itself in terms of its past, what version of that past, what memory, is to prevail? 'In history a great volume is unrolled for our instruction', affirms Burke, but its value depends much on *how* it is told, as he immediately warns: 'It may, in the perversion, serve for a magazine, furnishing offensive and defensive weapons for parties in church and state, and supplying the means of keeping alive, or reviving dissensions and animosities, and adding fuel to civil fury' (viii. 189). This danger is evident in the revolutionary typology Price has created by juxtaposing three historical dates: the execution of Charles I, the Glorious Revolution, and the recent events in France— 'confounding all the three together' (viii. 66), as Burke puts it. First, he accuses Price and his followers of turning the annual celebration of the Glorious Revolution into a subversive affirmation of radical democratic principles (thereby resituating the 4 November as a ground of partisan conflict, which it had so frequently been earlier in the century, rather than as the confirmation of political consensus that it subsequently became). Second, he suspects them of transforming the anniversary of Charles's execution, 30 January, from a day of solemn commemoration into one of unseemly celebration. Finally, to complete their revised political calendar, they include Bastille Day as a holiday appropriate to be observed by freedom-loving Englishmen.

In a speech before the House of Commons on 11 May 1792, Burke offers his scenario of the consequences that will follow from such observances; dissenters and radicals, he predicts, 'met to commemorate the 14th of July, shall seize the Tower of London and the magazines it contains, murder the governor, and the Mayor of London, seize upon the king's person, drive out the House of Lords, occupy your gallery, and thence, as from an high tribunal, dictate to you'.[23] Here the counter-theatre of the crowd, the mock-ceremonial of the street, ceases to be a symbolic gesture and threatens suddenly to become a genuine social explosion; the dream-like visions of Pope's

---

[23] Burke, *Speeches*, iv. 64.

Dunciad, in which the carnivalesque, populist entertainments of the Smithfield muses invade the precincts of Westminster, threaten to become a demonic, nightmarish reality. This has already happened in France, where the National Assembly has dwindled into 'a profane burlesque' performing a 'farce of deliberation':

> They act like the comedians of a fair before a riotous audience; they act amidst the tumultuous cries of a mixed mob of ferocious men, and of women lost to shame, who, according to their insolent fancies, direct, control, applaud, explode them; and sometimes mix and take their seats amongst them; domineering over them with a strange mixture of servile petulance and proud presumptuous authority. (viii. 119)

The symbolic inversion alluded to in this passage—the *mundus inversus* or 'world upside-down' topos in which traditional hierarchies of parent and child, husband and wife, master and servant are overturned—has burst its symbolic bounds and, in the process of literalization, has been transformed into a revolutionary action.

A central question in modern studies of the counter-theatrical and the carnivalesque has been whether such parodic behaviour represents a genuine mode of subversion or serves simply as a social 'safety valve', perhaps even as a reinforcement of the existing order.[24] If Burke seemed inclined to something like the latter view in his assessments of the Gordon Riots, he swings decisively to the former in his appraisal of the events of 1789. The example of France has charged the symbolic, wish-fulfilling fantasies of counter-theatre with prophetic energy: 'The most wonderful things are brought about in many instances by means the most absurd and ridiculous ... and apparently, by the most contemptible instruments' (viii. 60). Accordingly, popular demonstrations can no longer be regarded as harmless releases of energy but must be repressed as subversive enactments of radical change.

IV

To speak of inversion or a 'world upside-down' motif is to adopt the point of view of the dominant strata of society, who

---

[24] On this point see, e.g. F. Jameson, *The Political Unconscious* (Ithaca, NY, 1981), 84.

naturally view alternative forms of expression as culturally worthless and politically illegitimate. Thus, from Burke's perspective, the 'famous sermon of the Old Jewry' can be nothing else than a farcical dramatic performance—a farrago of 'Plots, massacres [and], assassinations' to satisfy a depraved, bloodthirsty audience: 'A cheap, bloodless reformation, a guiltless liberty, appear flat and vapid to their taste. There must be a great change of scene; there must be a magnificent stage effect; there must be a grand spectacle to rouze the imagination, grown torpid with the lazy enjoyment of sixty years security.... The Preacher found them all in the French revolution' (viii. 115). Burke sounds a familiar Scriblerian note, linking political upheaval with decadence in cultural standards—a decline symbolized by the the bathetic taste of Dr Price's audience for cheap sensation and 'grand spectacle'. Here, as with Pope's powerful prophecy of universal darkness in *The Dunciad*, something of a conscious act of imagination is required to shake oneself free of Burke's compelling vision and to view circumstances for a moment from the dunces' perspective. Yet, that perspective is involuntarily inscribed in Burke's text, and the same events that he by turns regards as farcical or tragic assume the shape of apocalyptic comedy when they are seen through the eyes of his political opponents. The opposition between these two literary paradigms, played out in the pages of the *Reflections*, constitutes the structural core of the work: the familiar political and cultural symbolism of theatre and counter-theatre supply not only the content but also the fundamental form of Burke's polemic.

The elements that compose both these dramas, comic and tragic, are borrowings, as Ronald Paulson notes, from the Swiftian metaphors of radical dissent in *A Tale of a Tub*, a text inspired or, perhaps more accurately, haunted by the memory of the English Civil War:

> Burke's argument is determined less by logic than by a Swiftean chain of association that links Richard Price's Revolutionary Society speech (which set him off) with the dissenters, their incendiary sermons, illumination and zeal, divine afflatus, the regicide Reverend Hugh Peters, memories of the Civil War, and the "leading in triumph" of King Charles I. The last becomes the type of (or analogue for) the conveyance of Louis XVI to Paris by the crowd, with (to complete the

parallel with Charles I) the element of predictability or prophecy in the inevitable execution that lies ahead.[25]

The comic version of these events is revealed in a lengthy passage from Price's sermon which Burke cites to illustrate his contention that the preacher's discourse amounts to nothing more than melodramatic farce, the comedy 'of a fair before a riotous audience'. He singles out the peroration of Price's sermon, in which the latter alludes to the *Nunc dimittis* of Simeon and applies it to the French Revolution: ' "I could almost say, *Lord, now lettest thou thy servant depart in peace, for mine eyes have seen thy salvation.* . . . I have lived to see *Thirty Millions of People*, indignant and resolute, spurning at slavery, and demanding liberty with an irresistible voice. *Their King led in triumph, and an arbitrary monarch surrendering himself to his subjects*" ' (viii. 115–16). The events of the Revolution and particularly of 5–6 October 1789 strike Dr Price as a divine, apocalyptic comedy, which draws its archetypal shape and inspiration, as the allusion to Simeon suggests, from the story of the birth of Christ, who has come to earth to overthrow tyranny and redeem human society. The irreconcilability of the two men's political visions is dramatized in the clash of their discourse: the same events that Burke denounces as 'Theban and Thracian Orgies' are, he exclaims in horror, compared by Price 'with the entrance into the world of the Prince of Peace . . . announced by the voice of angels to the quiet innocence of shepherds' (viii. 122–3).

Burke unwittingly underscores the apocalyptic appeal of Price's discourse by describing the preacher, in what is clearly intended to be a derisive comparison with the towering biblical figure of Moses, as 'viewing, from the Pisgah of his pulpit, the free, moral, happy, flourishing, and glorious state of France, as in a bird-eye landscape of a promised land' (viii. 115). Inscribed in Burke's heavy irony and threatening to undercut it is the comic narrative of the Israelites' release from bondage in Egypt and their journey to the Promised Land. The more he gives it a voice, the more this barely submerged subplot or countercurrent to his argument grows in force, especially at this early stage in the propaganda war when public opinion had not hardened and

[25] Paulson, *Representations of Revolution*, 58.

become polarized. As James Mackintosh, one of Burke's most eloquent critics, notes in *Vindiciae Gallicae* (1791), '[Burke] affects to despise those whom he appears to dread. His anger exalts those whom his ridicule would vilify.' James Boulton points out a parallel with Pope's treatment of the dunces in his *Dunciad*, which threatened, as Swift had warned, to confer immortality upon those he wished to consign to oblivion.[26] Similarly, the millenarian optimism of Price and his followers, which Burke had sought to dismiss as the 'importunate chink' of the 'little shrivelled, meagre, hopping . . . insects of the hour' (viii. 136), glows with an unprecedented prominence and credibility in the reflected heat of his denunciatory passion.

A prominent feature of Price's revolutionary comedy (as, indeed, of all eighteenth-century political counter-theatre) is inversion, the world turned upside-down: a king is enslaved and slaves are made kings, or, in the words of another well-wisher to the Revolution quoted by Burke, '*A King* [is] *dragged in submissive triumph by his conquering subjects*' (viii. 116 n.). In a truly apocalyptic world, such reversals are permanent features of the landscape: the first have come last, the last are first, and the lion lies down with the lamb. But inversion is a much more powerful device in contexts where hierarchies and power structures retain their force: hence, its durability as 'a central and ancient principle' of all comedy.[27] The typical comic plot, as Northrop Frye has noted, involves a generational conflict in which the desires of the younger characters are resisted by paternal or otherwise entrenched interests; the resolution of this opposition 'causes a new society to crystallize' around the resourceful protagonists.[28] In this connection Burke's persistent characterization of the French Revolution as the usurpation of paternal authority and age by youthful, insolent parvenus recapitulates the classic conventions of comedy, 'with its clever children, wives, and servants pitted against dim-witted fathers, pedants, husbands, and masters'.[29] Yet the same events that

---

[26] James Mackintosh, *Vindiciae Gallicae* (London, 1791), 293; Boulton, *Language of Politics*, 165.
[27] Barbara A. Babcock, *The Reversible World: Symbolic Inversion in Art and Society* (Ithaca, NY, 1978), 17.
[28] Northrop Frye, *Anatomy of Criticism* (Princeton, 1957), 163.
[29] Ian Donaldson, *The World Upside-Down: Comedy from Jonson to Fielding* (Oxford, 1970), 6.

project a comic shape when seen from below are tragic in their outlines when viewed from above. Thus, Burke identifies himself in his writings on the Revolution with the perspective of King Lear—age and authority beset by insolent youth, evil virility, and ruthless ambition. (When he turned on his political foes in the House of Commons, who ridiculed the vehemence of his opposition to the French Revolution, it was the words of Lear that he is revealingly said to have quoted: 'the little dogs, and all, | Tray, Blanche, and Sweetheart. See, they bark at me!'[30])

Perhaps the most striking illustration of this altered perspective is Burke's accusation in *A Letter to a Member of the National Assembly* that the French legislature is promoting the subversion of the family and the overthrow of paternal authority: 'the females of the first families in France may become an easy prey to dancing-masters, fidlers, pattern-drawers, friseurs, and valets de chambre, and other active citizens of that description, who having the entry into your houses, and being half-domesticated by their situation, may be blended with you by regular and irregular relations' (viii. 317). A situation that in another context might furnish the scenario for a farcical *opera buffa* here poses a fundamental threat to the social order; the Assembly 'propagate principles by which every servant may think it, if not his duty, at least his privilege, to betray his master' (viii. 319). Burke's expression of fear for the first families of France rehearses, in a slightly different key, the pattern of events narrated in the *Reflections*, where the revolutionary mob shatters the domestic tranquillity of France's royal family. But the demonic turn these events have taken signals that this is no *opera buffa*: the traditional reconciliation of opposing forces with which comedy concludes is shattered by a revolutionary conception of comedy which promises to make permanent the inversions of hierarchy that traditional comedy provisionally

---

[30] This incident reportedly occurred during the famous debates on the Quebec bill in May 1791 when Burke publicly renounced his association and friendship with Charles James Fox. In *The Life and Correspondence of the Right Honourable Henry Addington, First Viscount Sidmouth* (London, 1847), i. 84–5, George Pellew alludes to the debate and recounts the story, indicating it to be a previously unreported anecdote.

enacts. From Burke's perspective such a theatrical representation can only be tragic in its final outcome.

Accordingly, the bitter end, rather than the joyous beginning, of Christ's earthly life furnishes the paradigm for Burke's reading of the events of 5–6 October. Dr Price's *'leading in triumph'*—now 'the most horrid, atrocious, and afflicting spectacle, that perhaps ever was exhibited to the pity and indignation of mankind' (viii. 117)—becomes a latter-day *Via Dolorosa*, with the King and Queen of France retracing Christ's steps to their own Calvary: 'After they had been made to taste, drop by drop, more than the bitterness of death, in the slow torture of a journey of twelve miles, protracted to six hours, they were, under a guard, composed of those very soldiers who had thus conducted them through this famous triumph, lodged in one of the old palaces of Paris, now converted into a Bastile for kings' (viii. 122). Recalling Christ's agony in the Garden of Gethsemane, Burke describes the king as taking 'the cup of human misery full to the brim' and drinking it 'to the dregs' (viii. 121). Moreover, echoes of Restoration and eighteenth-century sentimental tragedy reverberate in the events he recounts: the violent assault, amounting to rape, upon the queen; her escape 'to seek refuge at the feet of a king and husband'; and the 'unprovoked, unresisted, promiscuous slaughter' of the king's loyal retainers (viii. 122). To complete this sensational, sentimental drama, he casts Marie Antoinette as a tragic heroine who bears up under her sufferings, humiliation, and captivity 'with the dignity of a Roman matron', that is, 'in a manner suited to her rank and race, and becoming the offspring of a sovereign distinguished for her piety and her courage'. In the final extremity, avers Burke, 'she will save herself from the last disgrace' and die like a Roman; 'if she must fall, she will fall by no ignoble hand' (viii. 126).

This contention of discourses between Price and Burke cannot be regarded merely as a rhetorical clash or simply an opposition of generic archetypes, but must be understood as a historicized conflict, in which the form that each chooses for his discourse is profoundly determined by historical circumstance. Burke acknowledges this when he seeks to account for Price's seemingly inexplicable 'fit of unguarded transport' in his sermon: 'I allow this prophet to break forth into hymns of joy and thanksgiving on an event which appears like the precursor of the Millenium, and the projected fifth monarchy' (viii. 123). In referring to the fifth monarchy he alludes to the last of the five empires foreseen by the prophet Daniel in his apocalyptic interpretation of King Nebuchadnezzar's dream (Daniel 2: 44); during the English Revolution the chiliastic sect known as the Fifth Monarchy Men, together with other millenarians, identified this fifth kingdom with the new era heralded by the execution of Charles I.

Burke thus traces Price's apocalyptic language back to the tumultuous days of Charles's trial and execution, citing a passage in a sermon delivered at Whitehall after the trial had commenced, in which the preacher, the radical Independent divine Hugh Peter, greeted the imminent deposition of the king with the same words of Simeon that echo in Price's sermon some 140 years later (viii. 116).[31] Moreover, Burke charges, Price's ecstatic description of the French king 'led in triumph' by his people constitutes a kind of plagiarism of the symbolically charged actions of the Reverend Hugh Peter who, according to a witness at his trial for high treason in 1660, triumphantly led the procession bringing Charles I to his first day in court. Burke quotes the testimony of Thomas Walkeley in the *State Trials:* 'I saw his Majesty in his Coach with Six Horses, and *Peters,* like Bishop *Almoner,* riding before the King triumphing.'[32]

Burke might equally have pointed to another of Peter's sermons, preached before the House of Commons a month before the trial, which takes up the same typology of the Exodus that is later ironically invoked in the *Reflections*: 'the subject of his Sermon was, *Moses leading the Israelites out of Egypt,* which he applied to the Leaders of this Army whose design is *to lead the people out of Aegyptian bondage: But how must this be done? . . . This Army must root up Monarchy, not only here, but in* France, *and other Kingdoms round about; this is to bring you out of Aegypt: This Army is that Corner stone cut out of the Mountain, which must dash the powers of the earth to pieces.*'[33]

---

[31] *A Complete Collection of State Trials, and Proceedings for High-Treason, and other Crimes and Misdemeanours,* 4th edn. (London, 1776–81), ii. 360 (hereafter cited as *State Trials*).   [32] Ibid. 360.
[33] Quoted in Raymond Phineas Stearns, *The Strenuous Puritan* (Urbana, Ill., 1954), 330.

In Burke's eyes, Price is a plagiarist of history: his narrative 'only follows a precedent' (viii. 116), drawing out unwelcome parallels between the French Revolution and the English Civil War. His mimicking of Peter's millenarian sermon is indeed striking, though the texts and tropes of dissenting apocalyptic discourse remained in wide use throughout the eighteenth century. None the less, in an earlier sermon Price had hailed the advent of a more enlightened and progressive age in language that links him directly with his Puritan forebear: 'The stone which was cut out of the mountain without human force is hereafter to fill the whole earth, and the kingdom of the Messiah to become universal. . . . A disdain of the restraints imposed by tyrants on human reason prevails.'[34] The millenarian language of Price's forefathers is assimilated to the enlightenment discourse of progress.

By establishing the regicide Peter as the 'precursor' (viii. 116) or originator of Price's discourse, Burke imposes on the latter's unfinished comic narrative an inevitable, if as yet unacted, tragic conclusion: 'The actual murder of the king and queen, and their child, was wanting to the other auspicious circumstances of this *"beautiful day."*. . . A groupe of regicide and sacrilegious slaughter, was indeed boldly sketched, but it was only sketched. It unhappily was left unfinished, in this great history-piece of the massacre of innocents' (viii. 123). But in accusing the dissenters of reviving the dreadful apparition of regicide, he projects onto his opponents his own most deep-seated nightmare of historical memory. If Price's sermon betrays him as nothing more than an imitator, a thrall to a false pattern of history, Burke's tragic version of events is scarcely more original. The *Via Dolorosa* Louis XVI traverses in Burke's account of his return from Versailles to Paris echoes the pattern Charles's contemporaries observed in his trial and execution. One writer after another emphasized the king's last days as a Christ-like passion and martyrdom:

After Sentence, The King being hurried from their Bar, as he passed down the stairs, The common Souldiers . . . scoffed at him, casting the

---

[34] Richard Price, *The Evidence for a Future Period of Improvement in the State of Mankind*, in D. O. Thomas (ed.), *Political Writings* (Cambridge, 1991), 173.

smoak of their stinking Tobacco in his face. . . . But one more insolent than the rest, defiled his venerable Face with his spittle, for his Majestie was observed with much patience to wipe it off with his Handkerchief, and as he passed, hearing them crie out Justice, Justice, *Poor soule* (said he) *for a peece of money, they would doe so for their Commanders.*[35]

The ritual humiliations associated with Christ's passion—scoffing and spitting—and Judas's betrayal of his master for thirty pieces of silver are recalled in this passage; other accounts stigmatized the king's persecutors as latter-day Pharisees and Pilates, and memorialized the scaffold at Whitehall as the king's Calvary. The parallels with the Passion story are almost irresistible: the death of King Charles, and now the 'persecution' of Louis XVI, assume the contours of what Herbert Lindenberger calls a 'martyr play, [which,] whether about a saint, a monarch, or simply some exemplary individual, can never completely escape being an imitation of Christ'.[36]

Hugh Peter is accorded a prominent role in this '*Passion-Tragedie*', as it was frequently called. The prosecutor at Peter's trial identified him as 'the Person that stirred up the Soldiery below to cry for Justice' and portrayed him as a 'Principle Actor in this sad Tragedy'.[37] With the Restoration of the monarchy, Charles's suffering and death were increasingly figures as heroic tragedy. Thus, Royalist apologists referred to the High Court of Justice at Westminster Hall, where the king was tried, as a 'Bloody Theater', and the scaffold on which he mounted 'the Theatre of his Murther'.[38] Andrew Marvell sets the scene, with typical restraint, in his 'Horatian Ode':

> That thence the royal actor borne,
> The tragic scaffold might adorn;
> While round the armed bands
> Did clap their bloody hands.

---

[35] *England's Black Tribunall. Set Forth in the Triall of K. Charles, I* (London, 1660), 62. The author of *A Hand-kirchife for Loyall Mourners, or a Cordiall for Drooping Spirits* (London, 1649) develops the parallels with the Passion story in some detail (see esp. 5–6). See also C. V. Wedgwood, *The Trial of Charles I* (London, 1964), 206–12.
[36] Herbert Lindenberger, *Historical Drama: The Relation of Literature and Reality* (Chicago, 1975), 45.   [37] *State Trials*, ii. 357.
[38] William Dugdale, *A Short View of the Late Troubles in England* (Oxford, 1681), 370; Richard Perrinchiefe, *The Life of Charles I*, in *The Workes of King Charles the Martyr* (London, 1662), i. 91.

Richard Perrinchiefe's *Life of Charles I* exploits this discourse much more shamelessly (as does Burke, with more skill, in the *Reflections*):

> the *King*, after He had finished his Supplications, was through the *Banqueting*-House brought to the Scaffold, which was dress'd to terrour, for it was all hung with Black. ... But it prevailed not to affright Him whose Soul was already panting after another Life. And therefore he entred this ignominious and gastly Theatre with the same minde as He used to carry to His Throne, shewing no fear of death.... *He that had nothing Common or Ordinary in His Life and Fortune is almost profaned by a Vulgar pen. The attempt, I confess, admits no Apology but this, That it was fit that Posterity, when they read his Works ... should also be told that His Actions were as Heroick as his Writings, and His Life more Elegant than His Style.*[39]

The overwrought, hagiographic tone of this passage is echoed in the famous 'purple prose', especially the celebrated (or notorious) apostrophe to Marie Antoinette and the lament for the passing of the age of chivalry, that suddenly bursts forth from Burke's pen in response to Price's comic optimism. (Conor Cruise O'Brien shrewdly calls this extravagant style Burke's 'Jacobite' manner.)[40] All readers of the *Reflections*, beginning with Thomas Paine, have recognized these great set-pieces as the climax of the text, determining the shape of everything that precedes and follows. In his vehemence to exorcize Dr Price's comic visions, Burke reaches deeply into his historic memory to uncover a language capable of voicing his response to an event that had shaken the foundations of his world.

V

By resituating the *Reflections* in its historical context, we come to recognize, as Burke himself did, how inextricably his treatise is implicated in historical process. His choice of tragedy as the fundamental literary form for his political discourse signals his awareness that the historical changes he is witnessing in France may render tragedy obsolete, just as the heroic forms of classical epic had become increasingly remote and problematic in the

---

[39] Perrinchiefe, ibid. 92, 118.
[40] O'Brien, Introduction to *Reflections*, 43.

eighteenth century. With the final passing of the age of chivalry the social conditions that have underpinned the traditional conception of tragedy are to be swept away: 'On [the new] scheme of things, a king is but a man; a queen is but a woman; a woman is but an animal; and an animal not of the highest order. ... Regicide, and parricide, and sacrilege, are but fictions of superstition, corrupting jurisprudence by destroying its simplicity. The murder of a king, or a queen, or a bishop, or a father, are only common homicide' (viii. 128). If kings, queens, and bishops no longer retain so much as a symbolic pre-eminence over their peoples; if, as Price affirms, 'the dominion of kings [is] changed for the dominion of laws, and the dominion of priests giv[es] way to the dominion of reason and conscience', then tragedy, at least of the kind conceived by Aristotle or Shakespeare, is no longer available as a mode of literary discourse.[41]

Consequently, the tragic idiom that apotheosized Charles I sounds a note of extravagance and 'romance' when applied to Louis XVI and Marie Antoinette, as even some of Burke's friends, among them Philip Francis, pointed out to him. 'In my opinion all that you say of the Queen is pure foppery,' wrote Francis to Burke on 19 February 1790 (*Corr.* vi. 86). Not unexpectedly, Thomas Paine offers the most memorable dismissal of Burke's heroical-sentimental flights: 'He pities the plumage, but forgets the dying bird. . . . His hero or his heroine must be a tragedy-victim expiring in show, and not the real prisoner of misery, sliding into death in the silence of a dungeon.'[42] Though they acknowledge the undeniable rhetorical power and skill of Burke's central tragic narrative, these two readers express their unease at the almost mock-heroic disparity of form and subject-matter in his description of the royal family. Their perception of this ironic gap (in contrast with the acceptableness of the same discourse a century and a half earlier) points to fundamental shifts in social and political awareness which resonate in the changing relations of literary genres to one another, with the emergence of new forms and the internal transformations of pre-existing kinds.

---

[41] Richard Price, *A Discourse on the Love of our Country*, in Thomas (ed.), *Political Writings*, 195. [42] Paine, *Rights of Man*, 73.

The depth of Burke's commitment to his version of events and the ideological significance of that commitment can be measured by the theoretical discussion of tragedy—one of his most revealing explorations of the subject—that follows upon his narrative of the queen's humiliation. As if conscious that his manner of proceeding requires some explanation, he apologizes for having 'dwelt too long on the atrocious spectacle of the sixth of October 1789' (viii. 131) and launches into a vigorous defence of his response to the Revolution. Posing himself the question, 'Why do I feel so differently from the Reverend Dr. Price?' he replies:

> For this plain reason—because it is *natural* I should; because we are so made as to be affected at such spectacles with melancholy sentiments upon the unstable condition of mortal prosperity, and the tremendous uncertainty of human greatness; because in those natural feelings we learn great lessons; because in events like these our passions instruct our reason; because when kings are hurl'd from their thrones by the Supreme Director of this great drama, and become the objects of insult to the base, and of pity to the good, we behold such disasters in the moral, as we should behold a miracle in the physical order of things. We are alarmed into reflexion; our minds (as it has long since been observed) are purified by terror and pity; our weak unthinking pride is humbled, under the dispensations of a mysterious wisdom. (viii. 131-2)

With a nod to Aristotle's doctrine of catharsis, he unfolds a theory of tragedy in the midst of his political treatise, a move not so unexpected, perhaps, in a period that regarded tragedy as a profoundly political genre, but sufficiently unusual from a late twentieth-century perspective to prompt the question why he should do so.

Joseph Addison's *Spectator* provides a context for Burke's political conception of tragedy. In *Spectator* 219 the reader is offered, as Ronald Paulson notes, two 'alternative models of providential design'.[43] On the one hand, 'Men in Scripture are called *Strangers and Sojourners upon Earth*, and Life a *Pilgrimage*', but on the other, as Epictetus suggests, the world is very much like 'a Theatre, where every one has a Part allotted to him'. Addison finds himself predisposed to the latter metaphor, 'which is', he states, 'very beautiful, and wonderfully proper to

---

[43] Paulson, *Popular and Polite Art*, 115.

incline us to be satisfyed with the Post in which Providence has placed us'. Our great responsibility is 'to excell in the Part which is given us. If it be an improper one the Fault is not in us, but in him who has *cast* our several Parts, and is the great Disposer of the Drama.'[44] To describe life as a pilgrimage is to emphasize one's beginning and one's end—a genetic and teleological metaphor. By contrast, Epictetus's theatrical analogy stresses life's arbitrariness, inscrutability, and uncertainty. Addison's preference for thinking of life as a spectacle or scene rather than a journey is revealing in a number of ways. Paulson observes, 'For Addison, the theatrical scene seems necessary to replace the determinedly teleological pilgrimage with a series of provisional structures, roles, and scenes, which are more appropriate to man's life in society.'[45] Addison's conservative commitment to an essentially static, hierarchical social order is in evidence, as is (perhaps less obviously) England's traumatic collective memory of its civil war, in which the roles that Englishmen were called upon to play had been fiercely contested.

Addison's conception of life as theatre is equally congenial to Burke, who likewise emphasizes the inscrutability of the 'Supreme Director of this great drama' and the necessity of submission to the incalculable ways of providence—'the dispensations of a mysterious wisdom'. The feelings a person experiences upon witnessing a sudden reversal of fortune yield intuitive insights, chiefly the awareness that human greatness is dangerous and uncertain. Such lessons have the effect of enforcing submission to existing social and political structures: the existing social order is explicitly linked to the eternal disposition of things. As the Earl of Shaftesbury had observed earlier in the century, 'The genius of [tragedy] consists in the lively representation of the disorders and misery of the great; to the end that the people and those of a lower condition may be taught the better to content themselves with privacy, enjoy their safer state, and prize the equality and justice of their guardian laws.'[46] Tragedy promotes social harmony by enforcing the lessons and underscoring the benefits of the social contract.

---

[44] Joseph Addison and Richard Steele, *The Spectator*, ed. Donald F. Bond (Oxford, 1965), ii. 353.   [45] Paulson, *Popular and Polite Art*, 116–17.
[46] Anthony Ashley Cooper, third Earl of Shaftesbury, *Characteristics of Men, Manners, Opinions, Times*, ed. John M. Robertson (Indianapolis, 1964) i. 143.

Harvey Mansfield argues that this is precisely the function of tragedy in Burke's political discourse: the experience of tragedy and the fall of great heroes (which Burke deliberately reproduces in his central narrative in the *Reflections*), by reminding individuals of the benefits of civil security, serve as a re-enactment of the original social contract, when the individual gave up the right 'to assert his own cause'. Lessons such as these also seemed uppermost in Burke's mind when he revived the problem of tragedy in the context of the impeachment proceedings against Warren Hastings: 'It is wisely provided in the constitution of our heart that we should interest ourselves in the fate of great personages. They are, therefore, made everywhere the objects of tragedy, which addresses itself directly to our passions and our feelings. And why? Because men of great place, men of great rank, men of great hereditary authority, cannot fall without a horrible crash upon all about them. Such towers cannot tumble without ruining their dependent cottages' (Bohn, viii. 59). Glossing Burke's remarks, Mansfield comments, 'The result of the realization that human greatness is uncertain is a natural feeling of awe; it makes men content with the little things that they have and eager to conserve that much. Love of finite things begins with the demonstration that love of greatness brings disaster. Tragedy, in Burke's theory, teaches the lesson that is taught by the natural right of self-preservation, in Hobbes's theory—the lesson that human vanity must be conquered to make human society possible.'[47]

Burke's insistence on inculcating a doctrine of 'tragic submission' in his account of events in France is closely bound up with his ambivalent attitude towards history. Though committed, as has already been noted, to a traditional, humanistic conception of history as 'a great improver of the understanding' (viii. 498), he fears that its reservoir of precepts has been irretrievably contaminated by modernity with its doctrinally and theoretically driven conflicts. Bruce James Smith describes the consequences that have followed from this fragmentation of tradition: 'Abstract theory had become "armed doctrine" by insinuating itself into history and thus entering the realm of possibility....

---

[47] Burke, *Speech in General Reply, Third Day*; Mansfield, *Statesmanship and Party Government*, 218.

Tradition had spoken with one voice, but the discovery of history had made the past problematic. Radicals and dissenters now had "predecessors." History was full of rebellious, even regicidal, "precept." The past had become a place of terror.'[48]

The ineradicable historical fact that Burke accuses the dissenters of reviving (and to which he himself compulsively adverted) is, of course, the execution of Charles I, but in France other historical images are being conjured up for equally revolutionary purposes. The 'infamous massacre of St. Bartholomew' (viii. 190–1) is performed on the Parisian stage in order to sharpen the ideological instincts and sanguinary impulses of its audience:

> In this tragic farce they produced the cardinal of Lorraine in his robes of function, ordering general slaughter. Was this spectacle intended to make the Parisians abhor persecution, and loath the effusion of blood?—No, it was to teach them to persecute their own pastors; it was to excite them, by raising a disgust and horror of their clergy, to an alacrity in hunting [them] down to destruction. (viii. 191)

This revolutionary appropriation of history in the form of political theatre catches Burke on the horns of a dilemma: though he wishes to erase horrors such as these from the rolls of history, he cannot give up the past, which alone stands in the way of unbridled innovation and social disintegration.

Smith argues that Burke's way out of this dilemma is to obliterate historical difference through an appeal to custom: 'if we are to save the future, we must hide the fact that the present is not like the past'. Henceforth, history is to be studied as the origin of 'habit' rather than as a source of 'precept': 'an exercise to strengthen the mind, as furnishing materials to enlarge and enrich it, not as a repertory of cases and precedents for a lawyer' (viii. 498).[49] Historians must 'stand upon that elevation of reason, which places centuries under our eye, and brings things to the true point of comparison, which obscures little names, and effaces the colours of little parties, and to which nothing can ascend but the spirit and moral quality of human actions' (viii.

---

[48] Bruce James Smith, *Politics and Remembrance: Republican Themes in Machiavelli, Burke, and Tocqueville* (Princeton, 1985), 111.
[49] Ibid. 116.

192). One means of ensuring that the right lessons are learned in the study of history is to distance oneself from the welter of facts and events in order to discern the true shape, the recurrent pattern lying behind them. Thus, the tragic outline of Charles I's capture and execution in the 1640s repeats itself in the unfolding struggle of the French Revolution. Though the dramatis personae and the contingent circumstances undergo change, the essential character of the historical narrative stands unaltered. The fall of kings will always prove to be tragic, a persuasion that dictates Burke's choice of narrative form in the *Reflections* and explains its proleptic intensity—its prophetic anticipation, almost three years before the event, of Louis XVI's execution.

By contrast, the narrative structure of pilgrimage insists on the process of change and throws the audience's attention forward to its final outcome. Thus, the end of the journey in Bunyan's famous pilgrimage narrative, *Pilgrim's Progress*, brings Christian to the gates of the Celestial City, the new Jerusalem foretold in the Book of Revelation. The word 'progress' in Bunyan's title conveys the primary sense of a journey, but the completion of the title—*from This World to That Which Is to Come*—imparts to the term, as Raymond Williams argues, a significant new shade of meaning: 'the sense of a manifest destiny and *future* ... [which] was soon to be secularized and given a wholly new content'.[50] The prophetic typology of the Book of Revelation which had inspired the Puritan radicals of the seventeenth century was increasingly recognized in the eighteenth century as finding its fulfilling antitype in the gathering momentum of progress, a secular heaven-on-earth prognosticated by the linear, forward movement of history in the direction of social and political improvement.[51] The title of Richard Price's millenarian sermon *The Evidence for a Future Period of Improvement in the State of Mankind*, delivered at the Old Jewry in April, 1787, testifies to his belief in the momentum of enlightened progress.

---

[50] R. Williams, *Keywords: A Vocabulary of Culture and Society* (New York, 1983), 206.
[51] See David Spadafora, *The Idea of Progress in Eighteenth-Century Britain* (New Haven, 1990), 104–32.

Burke was by no means an enemy of the idea of progress, but his metaphors of change—such as his celebrated characterization of the British political system as a perpetual cycle of 'decay, fall, renovation, and progression' (viii. 84)—continue to associate change with the cyclical rhythms of nature. Though he recognized the inevitability of change, he sought to minimize its corrosive influence by arguing for the preservation of the old and a reversion to or renovation of the past in the promulgation of the new. His obsessive concern to portray the French Revolution as a tragedy reflects, as Ronald Paulson notes, this desire to manage change: 'The basic mythos of tragedy or comedy, with the dichotomies of youth and age, birth–death, and rise–decline, has always been used by man to keep mutability under control. Progress was one deviation from this basic metaphor, and for that reason ominous.'[52] Burke was among the first to recognize that the French Revolution was not a revolution in the traditional sense of a return to a point of origin or to ancient liberties but rather an irreversible rising movement generated from below. The circular motion implied in the older definition recalls the venerable metaphor of the Wheel of Fortune, which figured so largely in medieval and Renaissance conceptions of tragedy: this language of fortune was shared by political writers of the seventeenth and eighteenth centuries, who continued to see some version of the Machiavellian opposition between virtue and fortune or virtue and corruption as the fundamental tension of human social existence.[53] The counter-theatre of the Revolution proclaims the final overthrow of this essentially tragic conception of history: a 'revolution in sentiments, manners, and moral opinions' (viii. 131) will ensure the onward march of virtue and the realization of a Rousseauian vision of human perfectibility.

VI

In *A Letter to a Member of the National Assembly*, Burke identifies the philosophical doctrines of Rousseau as the

---

[52] Paulson, *Representations of Revolution*, 48.
[53] See Pocock, *Machiavellian Revolution*, passim.

theoretical driving-force behind the counter-theatre of the French Revolution:

> Under this philosophic instructor in *the ethics of vanity*, they have attempted in France a regeneration of the moral constitution of man. Statesmen, like your present rulers, exist by every thing which is spurious, fictitious, and false; by every thing which takes the man from his house, and sets him on a stage, which makes him up an artificial creature, with painted theatric sentiments, fit to be seen by the glare of candlelight, and formed to be contemplated at a due distance.
>
> (viii. 315).

Rousseau's sentimentalism, together with his utopian faith that humanity's natural goodness will reassert itself with the transformation of the institutions that constrain and corrupt it, provides the basis for a theatre that celebrates the overthrow of false social and political establishments and the emancipation of the previously repressed human soul.

Thus, the emotional release expressed in the counter-theatrical demonstrations of the French Revolution strikes Burke as contrived and spurious: the theory of human character and motivation that undergirds this revolutionary counter-theatre is both factitious and fictitious. Such a charge of false artificiality sounds a jarring note, coming as it does from a writer who affirms in one of his most famous aphorisms that 'Art is man's nature'. Indeed, he acknowledges the indispensable artifice, role-playing, and theatricality of the old order—the fiction of an 'age of chivalry' with its 'pleasing illusions, which made power gentle, and obedience liberal', an age costumed in the 'decent drapery of life . . . [and] the superadded ideas, furnished from the wardrobe of a moral imagination'. This elaborate ceremonial is now to be 'exploded as a ridiculous, absurd, and antiquated fashion' (viii. 127–8), a formulation that, in its essentials, reverses back upon himself the charge he levels against his opponents in the above-quoted *Letter*.

Burke anticipates the contradiction in which he threatens to entangle himself by arguing, in effect, for a distinction between theatrical 'art' and counter-theatrical 'artifice'. The former differs from the latter in its emotional authenticity, which can be tested only by the intuitive, feeling response to real-life experience. The latter spurns humanity's 'natural feelings', playing instead on its potential for greed, vanity, rapacity, and insolence—precisely those tendencies in the human character which civil society was originally instituted to control. For Burke, 'Art is man's nature' precisely because human nature requires the external, monitory check of society to harness and repress its baser instincts and encourage its more altruistic impulses.

The experience of tragedy plays an important role in this process of socialization. The power of tragedy derives from the fact that it engages some of the most deep-seated impulses of human nature: the instincts of self-preservation, fear, and sympathy. The death of an individual, for instance, even the execution of a criminal, normally arouses an instinctive response of sympathy, rather than blood-lust: this fundamental response accounts for the powerful effect of tragedy on an audience.[54] Given this intimate connection, Burke can analyse his reaction to the humiliation of Louis XVI in terms of his own theory of tragic sympathy: 'Some tears might be drawn from me, if such a spectacle were exhibited on the stage. I should be truly ashamed of finding in myself that superficial, theatric sense of painted distress, whilst I could exult over it in real life. With such a perverted mind, I could never venture to shew my face at a tragedy' (viii. 132). The theatre functions for Burke as a moral touchstone: if a tragic drama can elicit tears from a spectator, the same response should be forthcoming in real life. In fact, his theory of tragedy in the *Reflections* is remarkably literal-minded, almost completely ignoring the distinction between tragic events in real life and dramatic tragedy as an *imitation* of reality. This denial of aesthetic distance was already apparent in his earliest consideration (in his *Philosophical Enquiry*) of the effects of tragic representations on a theatre audience:

Chuse a day on which to represent the most sublime and affecting tragedy we have ... and when you have collected your audience, just at the moment when their minds are erect with expectation, let it be reported that a state criminal of high rank is on the point of being executed in the adjoining square; in a moment the emptiness of the

---

[54] See *Philosophical Enquiry*, ed. Boulton, 44–6.

theatre would demonstrate the comparative weakness of the imitative arts, and proclaim the triumph of the real sympathy.[55]

In contrast, the artificial counter-theatre of Dr Price and the French revolutionaries displays a profound 'dissociation of sensibility'—an estrangement of thought from feeling—which carries in its wake a confusion of moral ends and means:

> Poets, who have to deal with an audience not yet graduated in the school of the rights of men, and who must apply themselves to the moral constitution of the heart, would not dare to produce such a triumph as a matter of exultation. . . . They would reject [the odious maxims of a Machiavellian policy] on the modern, as they once did on the antient stage, where they could not bear even the hypothetical proposition of such wickedness in the mouth of a personated tyrant, though suitable to the character he sustained. No theatric audience in Athens would bear what has been borne, in the midst of the real tragedy of this triumphal day; a principal actor weighing, as it were in scales hung in a shop of horrors,—so much actual crime against so much contingent advantage,—and after putting in and out weights, declaring that the balance was on the side of the advantages.
> (viii. 132).

The 'artifice' that Burke complains of—the 'painted' sentiments and distresses of the revolutionary stage—arises, in his opinion, from a fatal separation between abstract ideas, such as the conception of 'rights of man', and concrete actions and circumstances, such as 'the cruel and insulting triumph of Paris, and of Dr. Price' over the king (viii. 133). In order to make real its abstract creed (its 'contingent advantage'), the Revolution must stifle the natural sympathetic responses aroused by the suffering it inflicts ('so much actual crime') on flesh-and-blood individuals. If Louis XVI should in fact be innocent of any personal crimes, he must none the less undergo ritual humiliation because of his symbolic importance as the chief representative of a corrupt regime. In Burke's terms, revolutionary counter-theatre deliberately perverts the 'natural feelings' of its audience so as to inculcate in their place abstract, counter-intuitive beliefs. Thus, for instance, the National Assembly endorses a new, revolutionary morality by promulgating 'false and theatric' ceremonies in honour of Rousseau, who 'exhaust[ed] the stores

---

[55] *Philosophical Enquiry*, ed. Boulton, 47.

of his powerful rhetoric in the expression of universal benevolence; whilst his heart was incapable of harbouring one spark of common parental affection. Benevolence to the whole species, and want of feeling for every individual ... form the character of the new philosophy' (viii. 314).

But if Burke seeks to distinguish between political theatre and counter-theatre, art and artifice, on the basis of 'natural feelings', his argument is attacked on precisely the same grounds by Thomas Paine and Mary Wollstonecraft. That Burke should consider the execution of a *high-born* personage as the quintessential tragic moment, superior even to the greatest dramatic production, signals to his political opponents the extent to which his conception of tragedy in the *Reflections* is coloured by ideology, that is, by the assumption that certain social and political structures—in this instance, a hierarchical, aristocratic society—are the natural order. 'We fear God,' he affirms, 'we look up with awe to kings; with affection to parliaments; with duty to magistrates; with reverence to priests; and with respect to nobility ... [because] it is *natural* to be so affected; because all other feelings are false and spurious' (viii. 137–8). In short, as Michael Freedman mordantly observes, 'it is natural to be conservative, unnatural to be radical'.[56]

By contrast, the public execution that stirs deep feelings of terror and pity in Burke arouses only fear and loathing in Paine. 'Who does not remember the execution of Damien, torn to pieces by horses?' he asks. 'The effect of those cruel spectacles exhibited to the populace, is to destroy tenderness, or to excite revenge.' The example of the attempted regicide Robert Francis Damiens, who attacked Louis XV in 1757 and was put to death by *écartelement* after suffering unspeakable tortures, is alluded to in Burke's *Philosophical Enquiry* (p. 39). Damiens's fate excited great interest in England and may have been one of several instances (the execution of Lord Lovat in 1747 being another) that prompted Burke's reference to the rites of execution in his discussion of tragic sympathy. But the sublime terror that is meant to inculcate salutary lessons at such events strikes Paine as a 'base and false idea of governing men'.[57] This

---

[56] Michael Freeman, *Edmund Burke and the Critique of Political Radicalism* (Chicago, 1980), 40.   [57] Paine, *Rights of Man*, 80.

flat rejection of Burke's position forms part of a larger refutation of the latter's tragic narrative in the *Reflections*.

Burke's condemnation of the Parisians' revolutionary counter-theatre had centred, as Paine notes, on the bloody moment during the return to Paris from Versailles when several of the king's officials were beheaded and their heads carried about upon spikes: 'It is upon this mode of punishment that Mr Burke builds a great part of his tragic scene.' In response Paine inquires blandly as to the inspiration for the crowd's sanguinary counter-theatrical demonstration. 'They learn it', he asserts, 'from the governments they live under, and retaliate the punishments they have been accustomed to behold. The heads stuck upon spikes, which remained for years upon Temple-bar, differed nothing in the horror of the scene from those carried about upon spikes at Paris: yet this was done by the English government.'[58] The theatrical rituals by which official authority awed the populace and kept it in check have been turned back on the ruling élite with a vengeance.

If, as E. P. Thompson argues in the case of eighteenth-century English counter-theatre, 'There is a sense in which rulers and crowd needed each other, watched each other, performed theater and countertheater in each other's auditorium, moderated each other's political behavior', this 'active and reciprocal relation', this balance between ruler and ruled, is altogether absent in France. Instead, reports Paine, 'A vast mass of mankind are degradedly thrown into the background of the human picture, to bring forward with greater glare, the puppet-show of state and aristocracy.'[59] The consequence is that the counter-theatrical discourse of revolutionary France turns destructively violent in a savage redressing of the balance. Whereas plebeian crowd rituals had previously only mimicked official actions, they now move from mimesis to literal enactment, thus ironically fulfilling Burke's criterion for dramatic intensity by abandoning fiction in favour of a grisly reality. Yet, in some sense the crowd's behaviour remained symbolic, even though it had spilled over into direct action, in that the violence was limited, as Paine points out, to a few

---

[58] Paine, *Rights of Man*, 79.
[59] E. P. Thompson, 'Patrician and Plebeian' 402; Paine, *Rights of Man*, 81.

carefully chosen targets, among them the Governor of the Bastille and the Mayor of Paris: 'It is to the honour of the National Assembly, and the city of Paris, that during such a tremendous scene of arms and confusion . . . they have been able . . . to restrain so much.'[60]

Both Paine and Wollstonecraft attack Burke's conception of theatre at its theoretical foundations, namely, its insistence that a certain class of feelings is authentic, whereas all others are unnatural and spurious. Paine argues that the rites of official theatre may arouse unwelcome and unexpected emotions, feelings different from the anticipated responses of sublime awe, astonishment, and terror. Referring to the custom of mounting traitors' heads on Temple Bar, he writes, 'It may perhaps be said, that it signifies nothing to a man what is done to him after he is dead; but it signifies much to the living: it either tortures their feelings, or hardens their hearts; and in either case, it instructs them how to punish when power falls into their hands.'[61] For her part, Wollstonecraft insists that in his analysis of the French Revolution as a regal tragedy, Burke has deliberately banished an entire world of objects and experiences from the purview of his compassion and sympathy:

a *gentleman* of lively imagination must borrow some drapery from fancy before he can love or pity a *man*. Misery, to reach your heart, I perceive, must have its cap and bells; your tears are reserved . . . for the declamation of the theatre, or for the downfall of queens, whose rank alters the nature of folly, and throws a graceful veil over vices that degrade humanity; whilst the distress of many industrious mothers, whose *helpmates* have been torn from them, and the hungry cry of helpless babes, were vulgar sorrows that could not move your commiseration, though they might extort an alms.[62]

Though more impressionistic, Wollstonecraft's refutation of Burke is in some respects more shrewd than Paine's. She recognizes the fundamental subjectivity of his appeals to a universal standard of intuitive moral sensibility, and she locates the source of his doctrine of natural feelings in his ideological convictions: 'your respect for rank has swallowed up the

---

[60] Paine, ibid. 81.   [61] Ibid. 79.
[62] Mary Wollstonecraft, *A Vindication of the Rights of Men*, in *Works*, v. 15–16.

common feelings of humanity' (VM 17). Moreover, she attacks the basis for his affective analysis of drama's moral power—its status as a 'school of moral sentiments' (viii. 132)—by questioning the value of an intuitive response to scenes of distress. Such responses, she argues, engender moral self-complacency without inciting the individual to virtuous action:

> the being who is not spurred on to any virtuous act, still thinks itself of consequence, and boasts of its feelings. Why? Because the sight of distress, or an affecting narrative, made its blood flow with more velocity, and the heart, literally speaking, beat with sympathetic emotion. We ought to beware of confounding mechanical instinctive sensations with emotions that reason deepens, and justly terms the feelings of *humanity*. This word discriminates the active exertions of virtue from the vague declamation of sensibility (VM 53).

Her insistence on rational judgement as an essential part of the act of moral and aesthetic apprehension entails not only a revision of Burke's conception of official theatre and his affective narrative of political events, but also a rejection, ultimately, of political theatre of any kind as an inadequate, misleading mode of political discourse.

Perhaps Wollstonecraft's most penetrating insight into the tragic theatre of the *Reflections* is her recognition of its intimate connection with Burke's theory of aesthetic response, outlined in his *Philosophical Enquiry*. In that early treatise Burke had distinguished sharply between the experience of sublimity and the apprehension of beauty, arguing for the superior intensity of the former (which turns on pain and danger and is characterized by terror, awe, and astonishment) over the latter (which is actuated by pleasure and is distinguished by responses of love, tenderness, and affection). Wollstonecraft observes that this is not only a philosophical but also a hierarchical distinction: in valuing sublimity over beauty, Burke esteems heroism over tenderness, tragedy over comedy, masculinity over femininity, and the 'exalted qualities [of] fortitude, justice, wisdom, and truth' over compassion, kindness and liberality (VM 45).

This hierarchy has a crucial political dimension as well, as is obvious in Burke's association of the sublime emotions with the institutions of the *ancien régime*: *fear* of God, *awe* towards kings, *duty* to magistrates, *reverence* to priests, and *respect* to nobility. Wollstonecraft objects that this privileging of certain feelings, experiences, and institutions over others devalues the aspirations of the greater part of humanity. She points to the example of women, admonishing Burke, 'you have clearly proved that one half of the human species, at least, have not souls; and that Nature, by making women *little, smooth, delicate, fair* creatures, never designed that they should exercise their reason. ... The affection they excite ... should not be tinctured with the respect which moral virtues inspire, lest pain should be blended with pleasure, and admiration disturb the soft intimacy of love' (*VM* 45–6). Similarly, by denying any sublime dignity to the feelings that the counter-theatrical rituals of the crowd seek to express, by dismissing them as 'a servile, licentious, and abandoned insolence, to be our low sport for a few holidays' (viii. 138), Burke marginalizes the genuine grievances expressed through this inarticulate, often inchoate symbolic discourse.

The official theatre that Burke seeks to defend in the *Reflections* finds its apotheosis in his ecstatic paean to the state as an object of religious worship:

> They who are convinced of this his [God's] will, which is the law of laws and the sovereign of sovereigns, cannot think it reprehensible, that this our corporate fealty and homage, that this our recognition of a signiory paramount, I had almost said this oblation of the state itself, as a worthy offering on the high altar of universal praise, should be performed as all publick solemn acts are performed, in buildings, in musick, in decoration, in speech, in the dignity of persons, according to the customs of mankind, taught by their nature; that is, with modest splendour, with unassuming state, with mild majesty and sober pomp. (viii. 148)

In this passage he moves far beyond the crude didacticism or overt intimidation of eighteenth-century ceremonies of justice and royal pomp. Instead, he celebrates official theatre as affording the participant an experience of transcendence, of an eternal harmony which ratifies the existing order and the individual's place in it. The stability of society crucially depends on this affirmation, for the fundamental characteristic of the social order is inequality, a reality that can be defended only within the larger perspective of divine justice. Thus, the people 'must labour to obtain what by labour can be obtained; and when they find, as they commonly do, the success disproportioned to the endeavour, they must be taught their consolation in the final proportions of eternal justice' (viii. 290). This consolation is taught through the tragic doctrine of poetic justice—the view that tragic drama must offer a mirror of divine justice: the good must be rewarded and the evil punished. Through the observance of this critical principle, the enforcement of submission to existing social and political hierarchies and to the mysterious dispensations of providence is overtly integrated into the formal structure of tragic drama. Burke's choice of tragedy as the central narrative pattern of his *Reflections*, therefore, signals his awareness of its ideological and didactic potency on behalf of the counter-revolutionary cause that he espouses. The narrative structure of his treatise is nothing less, finally, than the embodiment of his passionate argument.

5
Burke's Dunciad: *The* Letters on a Regicide Peace *and Scriblerian Satire*

> This morning [was] publish'd Burke's primitive Thoughts
> On a Regicide Peace, and its palpable faults;
> These Thoughts to be sure are grown musty and stale,
> And may justly be clas'd with a Gulliver's tale;
> With a Tale of a Tub, with a Fable of Greece,
> But yet I will give you, the Regicide Peace.[1]

> The rage of *Juvenil*, and the playful levity of *Horace*, are not sufficient; and Billingsgate and the shambles are forced into alliance with the muses, the classics, and the sciences, to supply him with terms and metaphors sufficiently forcible to express the mighty hatred with which he labours.
>
> John Thelwall[2]

A. METAMORPHOSIS AND MASQUERADE

Burke's four *Letters on the Proposals for Peace with the Regicide Directory of France* (1795–7) are his swan-song, the final notes of a dying man beset by personal bereavement and public despair. Isolated from his former political associates,

---

[1] *Letters from Simkin the Second to his Brother Simon, in Wales; Dedicated without Permission, to the Ancient and Respectable Family of the Grunters* (London, 1796), 2.

[2] John Thelwall, *Sober Reflections on the Seditious and Inflammatory Letter of the Right Hon. Edmund Burke, to a Noble Lord* (London, 1796), 30. Though Thelwall is referring to *A Letter to a Noble Lord*, his observation describes the *Letters on a Regicide Peace* with equal aptness.

paralysed with grief at the untimely death of his only son, and deeply disturbed with the troubled course of the anti-revolutionary struggle against France, Burke characterizes himself in the preliminary correspondence to the *Fourth Letter* as a broken and condemned sea vessel: 'To have an idea of that vessel you must call to mind what you have often seen on the Kentish road. Those planks of tough and hardy oak, that used for years to brave the buffets of the Bay of Biscay, are now turned with their warped grain and empty trunnion-holes into very wretched pales for the inclosure of a wretched farmyard' (*Corr.* viii. 334; Bohn, v. 356). Arthur Young, who visited Burke on 1 May 1796, voiced considerable shock 'to see him so broken, so low, and with such expressions of melancholy'.[3]

Not surprisingly, the temptation has arisen, for critics and biographers alike, to read the catastrophic circumstances of those final years into the high-strung and often overwrought prose of the *Letters*—to characterize them, for instance, as a 'wild jeremiad of a mind at the end of its tether'[4] or, more frequently, to ignore them altogether. Gerald Chapman outlines trenchantly the image of Burke that such a reading conjures up from the pages of the *Regicide Peace* tracts, a reading, one should add, that he rejects as misleading:

[Burke] reminds us of the astronomer in *Rasselas* who thought himself secretly in control of the weather and was almost distraught with the terrible responsibility. . . . The last of neoclassic giants survives his proper day; in heroic despair, testifies to wicked change. Everywhere the sarcasm, the tone like a mocking bow, everywhere the frantic fancies and acrimonious cartoons, party, obsession, and the anxiety (such as commonly troubles an old man who has lost, or is losing, his power) that sees historical change as conspiracy. . . . We get an image of false heroics finally exhausted, and shrinking, alas, very much against his wish, in mock-heroic.[5]

To dismiss the *Letters*, however, as 'heated philippics' or to describe the rhetoric Burke employs as 'gulfs of empty words,

---

[3] Arthur Young, *The Autobiography of Arthur Young with Selections from his Correspondence*, ed. M. Betham-Edwards (London, 1898), 257.

[4] J. G. A. Pocock, 'The Political Economy of Burke's Analysis of the French Revolution', in *Virtue, Commerce, and History* (Cambridge, 1985) 205.

[5] G. W. Chapman, *Edmund Burke: The Practical Imagination* (Cambridge, Mass., 1967), 216–17.

reckless phrases, and senseless vituperations that surge and boil' (John Morley's assessment in the late nineteenth century) is not particularly illuminating.[6] An apt parallel is suggested by the incomprehending and even hostile responses of nineteenth-century readers to other fiercely satiric and denunciatory texts of the eighteenth century, such as Alexander Pope's *Dunciad* or Jonathan Swift's *Gulliver's Travels*. These works were not only largely misunderstood but also (especially in the case of *Gulliver's Travels*) systematically reviled, sometimes in terms much stronger than those Morley here reserves for Burke.[7] In the present century a drastic change in what Hans Robert Jauss terms the 'horizon' of readerly expectations has enabled modern readers to recover and revalue what previous generations had rejected. The grim historical experience of recent times has created a readership much more receptive to the fragmentariness, playfulness, irony, and pessimism of early eighteenth-century satire than were the Victorians with their self-confident faith in material and human progress. Moreover, the literary scholarship of the last fifty years has largely reconstructed the eighteenth-century horizon of expectations within which the writings of Pope and Swift were created and received, enabling us, in Jauss's words, 'to pose questions that the text gave an answer to, and thereby to discover how the contemporary reader could have viewed and understood the work'.[8]

This juxtaposition of Burke with Pope and Swift on the question of aesthetic reception is not as arbitrary as it might seem because Burke's rhetorical strategy in *Letters on a Regicide Peace* is deeply indebted to the satiric discourse of his illustrious predecessors. We are now better equipped to appreciate the literary and rhetorical dimensions of Burke's political language and to grasp how closely the literary and political discourses in

---

[6] Sir Philip Magnus, *Edmund Burke: A Life* (London, 1939), 286; John Morley, *Burke* (London, 1879), 201.

[7] On the subject of Pope's posthumous reputation, see James Reeves, *The Reputation and Writings of Alexander Pope* (New York, 1976). See also the Introduction and bibliography to Kathleen Williams (ed.), *Swift: The Critical Heritage* (London, 1970) for materials bearing on the reception of Swift after his death.

[8] Hans Robert Jauss, *Toward an Aesthetic of Reception*, trans. Timothy Bahti (Minneapolis, 1982), 28.

the *Letters* are connected. At issue is not so much the argument or intellectual content of the *Letters,* though this naturally occasioned outraged disagreement and rebuttal when they were published, but rather the sustained vehemence, the hyperbole of Burke's expression. F. P. Lock, for example, draws an unfavourable comparison between *Reflections on the Revolution in France,* in which short, climactic passages of emotional intensity alternate with much longer sections written in a more neutral style, and the 'overwritten' *Regicide Peace* letters, where Burke is perpetually on the stretch and the 'occasional rhetorical fireworks . . . cease to be spectacular and . . . become tiresome'.[9]

Questions of style aside, the thrust of Burke's polemic is obvious enough. He urges the view that the ideological nature of the current war with revolutionary France makes it a struggle fundamentally different from previous European conflicts. As corollaries to this central thesis he argues that there is no basis for reasonable negotiation with the *'armed doctrine'* of the 'Regicide republic' and that the inevitable prospect following from this realization is one of continued, protracted conflict (ix. 199). Britain possesses ample resources to prosecute the war successfully, Burke concludes, if only she can be persuaded to exert the necessary will and leadership for a decisive struggle. On this last score, however, he is gloomy, sometimes to the point of despair.

But, of course, style cannot be divorced from polemical content in the *Letters on a Regicide Peace.* Far from representing a spontaneous overflow of powerful feelings, Burke's imaginative flights, rhetorical set-pieces, and streams of invective are in their very form argumentative, tendentious, and carefully calculated. The idiom he most persistently employs is that of Scriblerian satire—evident in his dismissal of the revolutionaries as atheists, enthusiasts, projectors, and speculators; his characterization of the Jacobins in the carnivalesque terms of the masquerade, opera, public fairs, processions, and popular theatre (harlequinades, raree shows, pantomimes); his contrast of the heroic with the burlesque and mock-heroic, the high with the low, the courtly with the criminal; his gendered attack on his opponents

---

[9] F. P. Lock, *Burke's* Reflections on the Revolution in France (London, 1985) 124–5.

as effeminate and sexually suspect; and his recourse to the themes and imagery of metamorphosis, unnatural transformations, and the monstrous. These parallels are pervasive and easily documented; more complex is the question of what the presence of this Scriblerian discourse in the *Letters* signifies.

A few generalizations may be ventured at the outset, though they will be subject to refinement and revision as we proceed. It is clear that in drawing on the apocalyptic idiom of *The Dunciad*, with its gloomy prophecy of the return of Chaos, as '*Art* after *Art* goes out, and all is Night', Burke is groping for a language adequate to express his sense of the unprecedented, unassimilable character of the historic events in France, an 'answerable style' to convey his conviction of the far-reaching ideological significance of the Revolution. If anything, this borrowed mode of dark foreboding rings imaginatively more true in the revolutionary context of the 1790s than in the cultural environment that originally inspired it. The same anxiety about cultural upheaval and historical discontinuity that galvanized Pope and Swift animates the pages of Burke's treatise. Viewed in this light, there is nothing odd or accidental about the language of the *Letters*: those passages sometimes dismissed as rhetorical excrescences constitute the emotional and intellectual core of Burke's indictment of revolutionary France.

I

A number of important objections might well be raised against too glibly constructing a genealogy linking Burke to Pope and Swift. First, if viewed purely in their political context, the writings of the Tory satirists might not seem to have much to offer the staunchly Whiggish Burke. In the first of the *Regicide Peace* letters, Burke recalls the battle that raged in the press during the 1730s over the advisability of waging war with Spain, a confrontation that Sir Robert Walpole deprecated and the opposition loudly sought. 'For that war', remembers Burke, 'Pope sung his dying notes' (ix, 226). He pointedly remarks on the disparity between the impassioned tone of the controversial literature at the time and the comparative insignificance of the issues under debate: 'The events of that aera seemed then of magnitude, which the revolutions of our time have reduced to parochial importance; and the debates, which then shook the nation, now appear of no higher moment than a discussion in a vestry. When I was very young, a general fashion told me I was to admire some of the writings against that Minister [Walpole]; a little more maturity taught me as much to despise them' (ix, 227). Though Burke is referring specifically to the paper controversy surrounding the War of Jenkin's Ear, his observation can easily be extended to the wider cultural critique of Walpole's England with which Swift and Pope were associated. From the perspective that the lapse of half a century afforded, the political achievements of the *Pax Walpoleana* loomed considerably larger than they did in the 1730s, when dire prophecies of cultural dissolution and fiery denunciations of political corruption carried considerable weight; and Burke unhesitatingly aligns himself with his great Whig forebear.

An example may serve to illustrate the problem of Burke's precise relation to the Scriblerian discourse of the previous half-century. J. G. A. Pocock observes that in Burke's diagnosis of the French Revolution as a conspiracy of the monied against the landed interest, he reverts to a political discourse 'drawn straight from the vocabulary of Queen Anne Toryism ... a language first created to attack the foundations of the Whig order he is concerned to defend'.[10] And yet, in contrast with such Tory apologists as Swift, Burke was far from denying the value to society of a vigorous monied interest, together with its instruments of banks, paper credit, interest charges, public debt, and stocks and bonds:

Monied men ought to be allowed to set a value on their money. . . . The love of lucre, though sometimes carried to a ridiculous, sometimes to a vicious excess, is the grand cause of prosperity to all States. In this natural, this reasonable, this powerful, this prolifick principle, it is for the satyrist to expose the ridiculous; it is for the moralist to censure the vicious; it is for the sympathetick heart to reprobate the hard and cruel; it is for the Judge to animadvert on the fraud, the extortion, and the oppression: but it is for the Statesman to employ it as he finds it, with all it's [sic] concomitant excellencies, with all it's imperfections on it's head. (ix. 347)

---

[10] J. G. A. Pocock, 'Burke's Analysis of the French Revolution', *Virtue, Commerce, and History*, 200.

As a prosecutor in the impeachment of Warren Hastings, Burke repeatedly 'animadverted' on the fraud, extortion, and oppression of unbridled greed. But his moral indignation was often tempered by the high level of sophistication he brought to his analyses of economic forces (mechanisms, it must be remembered, that were very new in the early decades of the century). This complexity of understanding did not permit him, like Swift in the time of Queen Anne, to draw the opposition between land and credit in stark black-and-white terms—though in the white heat of polemical debate he sometimes expressed himself more categorically than otherwise.

This example serves as a reminder that literary and rhetorical features in one genre of writing and historical period cannot be assumed to function equivalently in a different historical and generic context. Burke expresses precisely such a contextual awareness in this passage when he discriminates among the points of view that the satirist, the moralist, the jurist, and the statesman—each employing a distinct discourse—would necessarily bring to the subject of money. (Indeed, he adopts each of these roles by turns in the course of his voluminous writings.) Moreover, the recognition that writers are the inheritors of preexisting literary and political languages tends to underscore continuities between them and their predecessors, while undervaluing the reality of historical change and innovation, manifested at the formal level in new combinations of existing literary features or a reordering of linguistic and generic elements. Certainly Burke, at the crucial historical juncture of the French Revolution, is driven to press inherited and, by his time, moribund forms into radical new service. A sensitivity to differences, as well as similarities, between Burke and his 'Augustan' predecessors, an awareness, furthermore, that both he and they often have recourse to even earlier strata of discourse such as the polemics of the English Civil War, is essential if we are to avoid misrepresenting the distinctive literary and political mode of the *Letters on a Regicide Peace*.

One important difference to be borne in mind is that of genre. The discursive forms Burke most often uses—the parliamentary speech, the public letter—raise questions about audience, occasions, and authorial control and function that the literary criticism of the twentieth century, working from a primarily belletristic conception of literature, has tended until recently to ignore. In the last two decades, however, the development of a broader, more inclusive conception of literary discourse and the emergence of new theoretical approaches such as cultural studies have greatly extended our understanding of the literary and have kindled a revival in literary scholarship devoted to Burke. These critical debates have challenged the narrow dichotomy between factual and imaginative discourse that has, since the Romantic period, delimited the field of literature. One effect of this critical ferment has been to revive the eighteenth-century sense of a continuity among forms of literary endeavour, restoring, in the process, a political writer such as Burke to what his contemporaries would have regarded as his rightful place in the literary pantheon. For in the eighteenth century a separation between fact and fiction or reality and imagination as a basis for defining 'literature' in opposition to other forms of discourse was simply not recognized as yet in any systematic or exclusive sense.

Raymond Williams points out that the modern, specialized concept of literature as 'creative' or 'imaginative' writing leads to several important consequences, among them the isolation of literary texts from the social reality surrounding them and the exclusion of non-literary texts from any interrogation of their processes of production and composition.[11] The first of these tendencies, the isolation or aestheticization of the literary text, has had a deleterious effect on Pope and Swift criticism, underplaying the broad political and cultural import of their writings, especially their satires. More specifically, critical understanding of Scriblerian satire has in the past been impeded by a definition of the literary that precludes an examination of conditions of production (evidence of which Pope himself worked hard to efface) or by a generalized conception of satire that overlooks its rootedness in circumstantial political and cultural reality.[12] The case of Burke falls in with the second

---

[11] Raymond Williams, *Politics and Letters* (London, 1979), 326. On this point see also C. Reid, *Edmund Burke and the Practice of Political Writing* (Dublin, 1985), 12–14.

[12] In *The Function of Criticism from* The Spectator *to Post-Structuralism* (London, 1984), 25, Terry Eagleton comments on the embarrassment 18th-c. Tory

point Williams raises: to regard him exclusively as a factual political and intellectual writer is to disregard his profound indebtedness to the prevailing forms of eighteenth-century literary discourse.

The example of another celebrated eighteenth-century political writer Lord Bolingbroke illustrates the period's habit of mixing literary and political discourse. As early as 1727 in the unmistakably political forum of *The Craftsman*, Bolingbroke adumbrated the major theme of Pope's 1743 *Dunciad*, in which political corruption is linked to the decay of learning and cultural standards:

> when no regard is had, in the disposition of offices and favours, to the *fitness* or *unfitness* of men; when ability, merit, and former services are of no weight in the scale; when all useful Arts and Sciences are held in contempt; when the Muses pine in obscurity, and Learning is look'd on as a disqualification, rather than a valuable endowment . . . then, I say, men of merit and ability have just reason to complain, remonstrate and protest; and it is ridiculous to expect that Arts, Wit or Learning should flourish, in any degree, under such a rapacious, selfish and usurious Administration.[13]

Many other familiar Scriblerian themes echo in the pages of *The Craftsman*: ridicule of the popular delight in operas and freak shows; satiric sallies in imitation of *Gulliver's Travels* (such as a proposal to sell identifying '*Court Ear-Knots* for *Pensioners* and *Hirelings*'); lampoons characterizing Walpole as a lowly peddler; parodies of Orator Henley's popular sermons; and a mock-history of harlequinades, including a sketch of a new dramatic production entitled, 'The Mock Minister; or Harlequin turn'd Statesman'.[14] This list of examples (by no means exhaustive) suffices to illustrate how readily those satiric elements that tend to be identified closely with *The Dunciad* are transposed from one generic context to another, in this instance appearing in the context of polemical journalism. The journalistic practice of the period blurred the line between factual and imaginative discourse

satire has posed to 'the later custodians of the literary: are not Swift's prose and *The Dunciad* marred as artefacts by their pathological spleen? The literary is the vanishing point of the political, its dissolution and reconstitution into polite letters.'

[13] *The Craftsman*, 20 (13 Feb. 1727).
[14] See *The Craftsman*, 29 (17 Mar. 1727), 36 (10 Apr. 1727), 55 (22 July 1727), 62 (9 Sept. 1727), 74 (2 Dec. 1727), 110 (10 Aug. 1728), 141 (15 Mar. 1729).

even further by employing allegories, fables, and other fictional devices as vehicles for political argument; thus, for example, *The Craftsman*, no. 159, offers an epistle from 'Usbeck to Rustan at Ispahan' in imitation of Montesquieu's fictional *Lettres persanes*.

Perhaps the most useful way of cutting through the methodological problems that have been set forth in the preceding pages is to approach Burke's *Letters on a Regicide Peace* from the perspective of intertextuality. Instead of concerning itself with questions of conscious allusion and specific influence, intertextuality conceives of a text as drawing upon the sum of all the signifying practices of a culture, including non-verbal ones, that together constitute the discursive space which underlies and enables all textual signification. Some of the non-verbal signifying systems employed by Pope, for instance, in *The Dunciad* and subsequently revived by Burke are the masquerade, the public pageant, and the urban topography of London and Westminster. To argue that Burke's citation of these cultural discourses points irresistibly and exclusively back to Pope and Swift is to ignore how widely dispersed these and other languages are through the entire range of eighteenth-century texts available to him. Thus, the author of *Harlequin-Horace: or, the Art of Modern Poetry* (1731) invokes the masquerade as a sign of economic corruption and social inversion—precisely the connotations that Burke's subsequent use of the term seeks to revive:

> Since *South-Sea Schemes* have so inrich'd the Land,
> That *Footmen* 'gainst their *Lords* for *Boroughs* stand;
> Since *Masquerades* and *Opera's* made their Entry,
> And *Heydegger* and *Handell* rul'd our Gentry.[15]

The poem from which these lines are cited, an extensive parody of Horace's *De Arte Poetica*, rehearses the whole gamut of Scriblerian tropes enumerated at the beginning of this chapter.

Another instance that illustrates how pervasive the language of cultural decline had become is cited in the opening pages of the *First Letter on a Regicide Peace*. Burke recalls John Brown, the author of *An Estimate of the Manners and Principles of the*

---

[15] James Miller, *Harlequin-Horace: or, the Art of Modern Poetry* (London, 1731), 29.

Times (1757), a popular social critique of England in the 1750s that fastened upon the same symptoms of cultural decay as those highlighted in the Tory satires of Walpole's day. Brown rounds up the usual cultural suspects (operas, masquerades, farces) and denounces his contemporaries' degeneracy of taste, concluding gloomily that England's unprecedented wealth and luxury have produced an enervating effeminacy in the national character. His diagnosis falls in with Pope's gender-based identification of the collapse of cultural standards with the female figure of Queen Dulness. Despite the pedestrian unoriginality of Brown's analysis, it was, as Burke acknowledges, enormously popular at the time as an explanation for the reverses England experienced at the beginning of the Seven Years' War. Yet just at the moment when Brown's speculations captured the public imagination, events conspired to prove them false: 'Never did the masculine spirit of England display itself with more energy ... than at the time when frivolity and effeminacy had been at least tacitly acknowledged as their national character, by the good people of this kingdom' (ix. 192–3).

The case of 'Estimate' Brown supports an intertextual reading of the *Letters on a Regicide Peace* in so far as it demonstrates how widely dispersed the discourse associated with Scriblerian satire actually proved to be in eighteenth-century Britain. But it also suggests the limitations of such a reading. If intertexuality, in its theoretically most radical acceptation, subverts the imposition of any contextual limitations on the meaning of a given text, a practical application of the concept to a given text nevertheless involves an inevitable reduction in the seemingly infinite range of intertextual possibilities. Certain intertextual relations (such as those between Burke's political discourse and Scriblerian satire in the present study) are foregrounded and privileged at the expense of others. Here generic considerations come into play, for while Brown explicitly rejects any satiric deployment of his 'Scriblerian' cultural themes, Burke positively relishes the satiric virtuosity with which Swift and Pope make use of the same discourse and follows their example, rather than Brown's, in his discursive practice. The value of intertextuality as a concept, then, is not so much in its immediate applicability to specific textual analysis, where it tends to mutate into a more traditional critical operation, but 'as a way of teeing-up the methodological approach' to a text.[16] In other words, by considering how a broad array of languages 'speak' through a text, rather than emphasizing an author's conscious efforts to control the text's articulations, we become aware of the rich array of cultural and linguistic resources that must be attended to in reading and understanding any text: we resist a premature foreclosure of the range of contexts within which a text resonates.

None the less, some contexts seem clearly more equal than others. The evidence that Burke's own corpus affords of his lifelong habits as a writer, for instance, must be given particular weight. In this connection, it is noteworthy that his writings (in contrast with Brown's *Estimate*) show a marked tonal and rhetorical affinity with the ironic, Juvenalian discourse of Pope and Swift, rather than the candid, analytical stance of Brown's essay. Evidence of this affinity can be traced back to the period of his literary apprenticeship as an undergraduate at Trinity College, Dublin. His youthful contributions to *The Reformer*, a short-lived periodical paper published during the early months of 1748, indicate his early familiarity with the discourse of dullness that had recently found its most memorable expression in Pope's four-book *Dunciad* (published in 1743). In the very first number of *The Reformer*, dated 28 January 1747–8, Burke announces as the purpose of his paper the expulsion of the forces of 'Dulness' from the shores of Ireland. 'If we may judge of the Empire of *Dulness* by other great ones, whose Unwieldiness brought on their Ruin, this is certainly its Time: for... the morals of a Nation have so great a Dependance on their taste and Writings, that the fixing the latter, seems the first and surest Method of establishing the former.' The verse 'Proclamation' with which he concludes his introductory number points even more explicitly to the familiar outlines of Pope's *Dunciad*:

> O yes! O yes! if any Man can tell
> Where WIT or SENSE are fled, or where they dwell;
> Let him stand forth.
> . . . .

---

[16] Brean S. Hammond, 'The Intertext of an Adaptation: Bond's *Lear* and *King Lear*', *Études Anglaises*, 40 (1987), 280.

> Ye modern *Poets*! who soft Lays indite,
> And without either make a shift to write
> . . . .
> Ye *Courtiers* gay! who more to Poets owe
> For witty Fragments, than to Birth-day shew:
> Ye *Play'rs*! who like Parrots, jabber Wit,
> Who speak the Words, but can't the Meaning hit:
> Ye *Cits*! who Cozenage reduce to Rules,
> And prove yourselves, tho' dull, yet cunning Fools:
> Ye *Students*! who to Colleges do run,
> Not to learn Wit or Wisdom, but to shun;
> Say! if by clubbing each his Blockhead's Head,
> Any can tell me whither WIT is fled.[17]

Burke's correspondence with his childhood friend Richard Shackleton further attests to his early fascination with Pope's pessimistic cultural auguries: 'beleive me Dear Dick we are just on the verge of Darkness and one push drives us in—we shall all live If we live long to see the prophesy of the Dunciad fullfilled and the age of ignorance come round once more—redeunt Saturnia regna magnus ab integro seclorum nasciur ordo' (*Corr*. i. 74).

Looking ahead to the end of Burke's career, we see the same themes resurface on the eve of the French Revolution in Burke's speeches on the Regency Crisis precipitated by the king's mental incapacity and apparent madness. The powerful spectacle of a mad king prompted Burke, as Christopher Reid shows, to figure the accompanying political crisis as an irruption of the forms and idioms of grotesque madness (familiar to readers of *The Dunciad*) into the rational, ordered world of court and parliament. Placing the Regency Crisis in the Scriblerian cultural context of a decline in learning—'The learning of this day was bad learning, which was the worst sort of ignorance'—Burke concludes one of his speeches during the crisis with a dramatic citation from the apocalyptic concluding lines of *The Dunciad*: 'Star after star goes out, and all is night.'[18] These and numerous

---

[17] A. P. I. Samuels, *Early Life of Burke* (Cambridge, 1923), 297–9.

[18] Burke, *Speeches . . . in the House of Commons* (London, 1816), iii. 415. Burke's allusion to Pope was noted in the *General Evening Post* (cited in Christopher Reid, 'Burke, the Regency Crisis, and the "Antagonist World of Madness"', *Eighteenth-Century Life*, 16/2 (1992), 72–3). Burke misquotes Pope; the original reads, '*Art* after *Art* goes out, and all is Night' (*Dunciad* IV. 640).

other instances suggest that while Burke's writings are deeply implicated in a popular and widespread discourse of cultural decay, he none the less chooses consciously to imitate a literary, high-cultural variant of that discourse.

In more general terms, the case of Burke serves as a reminder that to regard linguistic activity only as the manipulation or transformation of a pre-existing system is, as Raymond Williams observes, 'very far from the whole truth'. Individuals in fact exist in a complex dialectical relation to language, 'both producing and being produced by it'.[19] Burke's conscious imitation of Pope and Swift, representatives of a high-cultural, humanist intellectual and literary tradition, is a choice dictated by what he feels to be at stake in the French Revolution. His polemics on the Revolution struggle for the linguistic and cultural high ground against opposing views, which, as the epigraphs to this chapter indicate, also have the discourse of Scriblerian satire available to them.

The conflicts in which much of Burke's political writings are immersed serve to illustrate what Mikhail Bakhtin terms the 'heteroglot' potential of language, its capacity to juxtapose and articulate competing versions of experience. Burke's extraordinary writings on the French Revolution, in particular, dramatize one of the enabling conditions of heteroglossia, namely its emergence in periods of cultural turmoil, when the social, political, and ideological authority of an agreed-upon discourse is called into question and a stable language becomes contested ground. Burke's *Letters on a Regicide Peace* participate in precisely such a contest, and in so doing they inevitably give voice, even if only in a dismissive or parodic manner, to opposing views. In this respect the *Letters* share the heteroglot character of Pope's and Swift's satires, which were likewise written under the pressure of a perceived disintegration in cultural standards. But in assimilating the heteroglot discourse of Scriblerian satire, Burke also infuses it with his own intentions, creating a new language that bursts forth under the pressure of extraordinary political circumstances. The language of Scriblerian satire may indeed speak through Burke, but it is

---

[19] Williams, *Politics and Letters*, 330–1.

equally reshaped by him in response to a crucial historical moment.

II

A passage in Pat Rogers's study of the sociology or historical topography of Scriblerian satire, *Grub Street: Studies in a Subculture*, offers a useful way into the intertextual relation between Burke and his Augustan forebears. Rogers draws attention to Pope's imaginative reconstruction in *The Dunciad* of the recurring patterns of an eighteenth-century urban riot. He points in particular to Book IV, lines 73–134, which he sets against Gustave Le Bon's pioneering analysis of the crowd in action. As George Rudé observes, in summarizing Le Bon's generalized conception of the crowd,

> he was inclined to treat the crowd in *a priori* terms: as irrational, fickle, and destructive, as intellectually inferior to its components; as primitive or tending to revert to an animal condition. His prejudices led him to equate the 'mob' with the lower classes in society; and ... he took from [Taine] his fanciful picture of the French revolutionary crowd, which (as Le Bon claimed) tended to be formed of criminal elements, degenerates, and persons with destructive instincts, who blindly responded to the siren voices of 'leaders' or 'demagogues.'[20]

The corresponding passage in *The Dunciad*, describing the mob of dunces who answer the summons of the goddess Dulness, emphasizes the crowd's irresistible movement as it sweeps along gathering reinforcements, its heterogeneous social composition, its mob instinct 'intellectually inferior to its components', its destructive force, its susceptibility to the siren call of the goddess, its symbolic battle-standards of effigies and trophies, and its highly selective choice of targets and victims:

> The gath'ring number, as it moves along,
> Involves a vast involuntary throng,
> Who gently drawn, and struggling less and less,
> Roll in her Vortex, and her pow'r confess.
> . . . .

---

[20] G. Rudé, *The Crowd in History 1730–1848* (1964; London, 1981), 9. See also Pat Rogers, *Grub Street: Studies in a Subculture* (London, 1972), 99–126.

> There march'd the bard and blockhead, side by side,
> Who rhym'd for hire, and patroniz'd for pride.
> . . . .
> When Dulness, smiling—'Thus revive the Wits!
> But murder first, and mince them all to bits
> . . . .
> Let standard-Authors, thus, like trophies born,
> 'Appear more glorious as more hack'd and torn,
> And you, my Critics! in the chequer'd shade,
> Admire new light thro' holes yourselves have made.
> 'Leave not a foot of verse, a foot of stone,
> A Page, a Grave, that they can call their own;
> But spread, my sons, your glory thin or thick,
> On passive paper, or on solid brick.
> So by each Bard an Alderman shall sit,
> A heavy Lord shall hang at ev'ry Wit,
> And while on Fame's triumphal Car they ride,
> Some Slave of mine be pinion'd to their side.'
>
> (IV. 81–34)

The cumulative picture that emerges from the details of this passage corresponds remarkably to the paradigm that historians have developed of the eighteenth-century crowd and riot. Rogers suggests that Pope's description can be read as a proleptic warning of the two great civil affrays that were to convulse London in the second half of the century: the Wilkite demonstrations and the Gordon riots. Thus, to draw attention to one detail among many, Pope's mention of the aldermen who sit by 'each Bard' points to the role that the city fathers of London often played in riots, manipulating the crowd for their own political ends. The Wilkite demonstrations, to which Burke was a witness, were particularly rich in the symbolism and ritual of social protest that Pope alludes to in *The Dunciad*, but Rogers points especially to the Gordon Riots of 1780 as supplying 'the most striking authentication' of Pope's imaginative portrayal of populist activity:

I do not mean that Pope literally divined the shape of things to come, as Burke perhaps did in the case of French history. I am suggesting rather that the poet's creative mind shaped events along lines that were, so to speak, already immanent in history. His poem acts out fictively a myth of social disorder, which the anti-popery riots chance to follow with curious mimicry.... Events come to his support so often because he went so often (and at such an early imaginative stage) *to* events in the devising of his myth.[21]

Without actually naming or defining it, Rogers comes close here to a concept of intertextuality in his account of the link between Pope and the subsequent authenticating historical event. The connection is the ceremonial, ritual forms of public celebration and protest in eighteenth-century England, which constituted a complex and widely dispersed signifying system, as historians increasingly recognize.

Some important aspects of the ritual, symbolic character of crowd behaviour (identified in studies by John Brewer, Robert Malcolmson, George Rudé, E. P. Thompson and others as self-conscious political theatre, rather than simply unfocused, destructive anarchy) have been the focus of the previous chapter. In the present context, however, I should like to explore the parallels between Pope's and Burke's characterizations of the crowd, particularly their sense of its composition and its parodic modes of self-realization. *The Dunciad*, for instance, abounds with denigrating epithets for its population of dullards: 'rabble' (IV. 209), 'desp'rate pack' (II. 305), 'vulgar herd' (IV. 525), 'clam'rous crowd' (II. 385), a tribe 'thick as Locusts black'ning all the ground' (IV. 397–8), and so on. The cumulative effect of such terms is to associate the assembled dunces with the dregs of society (prostitutes, pimps, thieves, pickpockets), whose numbers were popularly thought to predominate at any unruly London gathering, and ultimately to reduce them to an undifferentiated mass.[22] The reality, as Pope acknowledges elsewhere in the poem, was considerably more complex: his description of the 'endless Band' who answer the summons of Dulness indicates the social composition of the crowd to be widely varied:

> A motley mixture! in long wigs, in bags,
> In silks, in crapes, in Garters, and in rags,
> From drawing rooms, from colleges, from garrets,
> On horse, on foot, in hacks, and gilded chariots.
>   (II. 21–4)

---

[21] Rogers, *Grub Street*, 117–18.
[22] See e.g. M. Dorothy George, *London Life in the Eighteenth Century* (London, 1925); and Dorothy Marshall, *Dr Johnson's London* (New York, 1968).

Burke's rhetoric similarly reduces the revolutionary crowd of France to the sediment of its most undesirable elements; the new French nation is described in the *Letters* as an 'infamous ... brothel ... a night cellar for such thieves, murderers, and house-breakers, as never infested the world' (ix. 251). Paris has become 'a lewd tavern for the revels and debauches of banditti, assassins, bravos, smugglers, and their more desperate paramours, mixed with bombastick players, the refuse and rejected offal of strolling theatres' (ix. 247). Here, too, the reality diverges widely from Burke's Swiftian invective: to cite just one example, Rudé points out that the participants in the October 1789 march on Versailles included women of all social classes, 'both fishwives and stall-holders of the markets, working women of the *faubourg*, smartly dressed *bourgeoises*, and "des femmes à chapeau" '—a far cry from Burke's 'furies of hell' and 'vilest of women'. The same was true of the crowds that rioted periodically on the streets of eighteenth-century London. Certainly, criminal and vagrant elements were present at any civil disturbance, but, as Dorothy Marshall concludes, 'historical investigation has shown that they were not its core. After the incident had been contained and arrests made, the trials of the rioters again and again established the fact that many of them were respectable members of the wage-earning population—apprentices, journeymen, even small shopkeepers.'[23]

Burke's sociological representation (or misrepresentation) of the revolutionary 'mob' in France undoubtedly draws, as I have already argued, on his personal experience of London's often tumultuous urban life. As the revolution progressed, however, and those elements that Burke liked to dismiss as 'la boue de Paris' (ix. 177) swept to power with the onrushing tide of revolution, he found himself observing an altogether unprecedented scene—one that suggested no answering counterpart in his own experience. Earlier, in *Reflections on the Revolution in France*, when he denounced the National Assembly for having become unduly submissive to the demands of popular opinion, he turned for an illustration to the popular culture of London's streets, characterizing the Assembly as 'the comedians of a fair

---

[23] George Rudé, *The Crowd in the French Revolution* (Oxford, 1959), 73. Marshall, *Dr. Johnson's London*, 237.

before a riotous audience'. The analogy of the fair or carnival suggests a temporary suspension of normal rules and hierarchies, the limited licence of the Lord of Misrule, who presides in this instance over a mock-legislature: 'As they have inverted order in all things, the gallery is in the place of the house' (viii. 119). But by 1796, after the horrors of the recent Terror, followed by the installation of a 'Directory of Regicide' at the helm of the French republic, the Lord of Misrule showed an altogether more sinister aspect and appeared to Burke to have extended his reign indefinitely.

In these seemingly unprecedented circumstances, Burke finds his imagination haunted by a nightmare of apocalyptic, but also, paradoxically, farcical proportions: the image, in Gerald Chapman's phrase, 'of a profane, mock-heroic procession, a farcical march of triumph upon the bastions of church and nobility'.[24] Thus, in a scene inspired equally by the urban topography of London and by Pope's poetic vision of 'the Removal of the imperial seat of Dulness from the City to the polite world', Burke imagines his countrymen's reception of Antoine-Joseph Santerre as the first ambassador of the new French regime:

I anticipate the day of his arrival. He will make his publick entry into London on one of the pale horses of his brewery. As he knows, that we are pleased with the Paris taste for the orders of Knighthood, he will fling a bloody sash across his shoulders with the order of the Holy Guillotine, surmounting the Crown, appendant to the ribband. Thus adorned he will proceed from Whitechapel to the further end of Pall-Mall, all the musick of London playing the Marseillois Hymn before him, and escorted by a chosen detachment of the *Legion de l'Echaffaud*. It were only to be wished, that no ill-fated loyalist for the imprudence of his zeal may stand in the pillory at Charing-Cross, under the statue of King Charles the First, at the time of this grand procession, lest some of the rotten eggs, which the Constitutional Society shall let fly at his indiscreet head, may hit the virtuous murderer of his King. They might soil the state dress, which the Ministers of so many crowned heads have admired, and in which Sir Clement Cotterel is to introduce him at St. James's. (ix. 112)

Santerre's progress from London's East End to the royal precincts of Westminster recalls the westward movement of

[24] Chapman, *Edmund Burke*, 237.

Pope's dunces from their strongholds of Smithfield and Grub Street to the palace where the goddess Dulness receives her votaries, a progress that in turn mimics, as Aubrey Williams has shown, the annual procession of the Lord Mayor to Westminster Hall, where he took his oath of office.[25] (This is by no means Burke's first use of the progress as a structural motif in his writings: the 'action' of the *Reflections on the Revolution in France* centres upon the 'procession' of the women of Paris to Versailles on 5–6 October 1789.)

The connection with *The Dunciad* is made explicit on the next page, when Burke describes the press of people at the grand ball to be given in commemoration of the execution of Louis XVI: 'Then what a hurly-burly;—what a crowding;—what a glare of a thousand flambeaus in the square;—what a clamour of footmen contending at the door;—what a rattling of a thousand coaches of Duchesses, Countesses, and Lady Marys' (ix. 113). Here he alludes to a passage in the second book of *The Dunciad* (II. 127–8)—'Whence hapless Monsieur much complains at Paris | Of wrongs from Duchesses and Lady Mary's'—in which Pope aims a satiric dart at Lady Mary Wortley Montagu, an erstwhile friend, but by now a longtime personal enemy. Once again, as in the portrayal of Santerre and the French revolutionaries generally, inversions of high and low are exploited here, as 'Duchesses and Lady Mary's' are revealed to be nothing more than 'Whores and Cheats under the name of Ladies'.[26]

Like Pope, Burke has mastered the art of marshalling a wealth of realistic, factual detail into an imaginative order that simultaneously parodies the dignity of official ceremony and invokes, through allusion, an external standard by which the vividly realized scene thus conjured up is to be judged. In the imagined triumphal entry of Santerre into London, much of the episode's satiric force derives from Burke's manipulation of the facts of Santerre's career. Thus, his ownership of a brewery in the east-end Paris working-class *faubourg* of Saint-Antoine is

---

[25] Aubrey Williams, *Pope's* Dunciad: *A Study of Its Meaning* (Baton Rouge, 1955), 29–41.
[26] Alexander Pope, *The Dunciad*, in *The Twickenham Edition of the Poems of Alexander Page*, ed. John Butt *et al.* (London, 1939–69), v. 112, ll. 127–8 n.

translated into topographical and sociological terms that Burke's London readers can readily interpret: hence, the procession's starting-point in the poor and often disaffected east-end district of Whitechapel. Similarly, Santerre's westward progress to the Court of St James, while clearly echoing Popean literary precedent, acquires much of its topical satiric point through its re-enactment on English soil of the notorious Paris demonstration of 20 June 1792, in which Santerre led a march from Saint-Antoine to the palace of the Tuileries, where the gathered crowd angrily confronted their embattled monarch.

Burke's burlesque rendering of the *déclassé* Santerre has a furious edge to it that Pope's more comic depiction of the dunces often lacks, at least in his original, three-book *Dunciad*. The account of Santerre's entry on horseback, for instance, recalls the latter's acknowledged skill as an equestrian and his position as Commandant of the National Guard, but in a savage transformation of these journalistic details, Burke describes Santerre's mount as a 'pale' horse, thereby identifying its rider unmistakably with the fourth horseman of the apocalypse in Revelation 6: 8: 'And I looked, and behold a pale horse: and his name that sat upon him was Death; and Hell followed with him'. This sudden metamorphosis of Santerre and his train from a comic imitation of the Lord Mayor's parade into a procession from hell harks back to Pope's vision of the final triumph of Dulness in Book IV of *The Dunciad*, rather than the more farcical events of the first three books: 'She comes! she comes! the sable Throne behold | Of *Night* Primæval, and of *Chaos* old!' (IV. 629–30). Both writers invoke an apocalyptic idiom that links the events they are describing to the final end of things—an end, however, that for Burke heralds the restoration of chaos rather than the promise of a new heaven and a new earth previously foreseen by many well-wishers of the Revolution, such as Richard Price. Burke further refers to what might be called the historical (as opposed to biblical or theological) apocalypse in the imagined encounter of the mounted Santerre with the equestrian statue of Charles I at Charing Cross. In a moment heavy with irony, Santerre, who assisted at the execution of Louis XVI, passes by a memorial to King Charles the Martyr, Louis's typological forebear. More extended allusions are unnecessary: the briefest of references suffices to provide the normative historical and cultural standard by which Santerre and his fellows are to be judged—very much in the manner of Pope's Virgilian and Miltonic allusions in *The Dunciad*, which supply the yardstick by which the dunces and their works are to be measured.

In setting the action of *The Dunciad* on the Lord Mayor's Day, Pope seeks, as recent scholarship amply demonstrates, to exploit the event's ambiguous associations with both high life and low life, official culture and popular culture: 'the Lord Mayor's Day is a ready-made paradox in which order and disorder—reason and unreason—share a single image'.[27] Ned Ward, who was unfortunate enough to become one of Pope's dunces, describes this often grotesque juxtaposition in his racy narrative of London life, *The London Spy*: 'In every Interval between *Pageant* and *Pageant* the *Mob* had still a new Project to put on Foot. By this time they had got a piece of Cloth of a Yard or more Square, this they dipt in the Kennel, till they had made it fit for their purpose, then tost it about, it Expending it self in the Air, and falling on the Heads of two or three at once.'[28] By associating the characters in their respective narratives with this dubious pageantry of London street life, both Pope and Burke intend for some of the crowd's dirt to adhere to their literary and political dunces. This fact did not go unnoticed on the opposing side of the debate. Thus, as Mona Ozouf notes, the French authorities in the 1790s were eager to present their festivals as rational observances—not only dedicated to Reason but also conducted with order and decency. The latter point was underscored with evident satisfaction in official accounts: 'there was no sign of those indecent forms familiar from the ancien régime, madness did not brandish its flaming torch'.[29] Madness, misrule, grossness, vulgarity—all these symptoms of social pathology from which polite society in the eighteenth century had progressively sought to distance itself are seen here, ironically, as the inevitable products of that very society: the

---

[27] David B. Morris, *Alexander Pope: The Genius of Sense* (Cambridge, Mass., 1984), 276.
[28] Edward Ward, *The London-Spy* (1700; repr. London, 1924), 300–1.
[29] Official account of the municipality of Foix, quoted in Mona Ozouf, *Festivals and the French Revolution*, trans. Alan Sheridan (Cambridge, Mass., 1988), 86.

satiric weapons of the *ancien régime* are trained back upon their originators.[30]

III

One element in Burke's description of Santerre, his reliance on strategies of transformation and metamorphosis, calls for further examination, for it constitutes perhaps *the* governing trope of the *Letters on a Regicide Peace*, as, indeed, of all Scriblerian satire. (Certainly, metamorphosis is closely linked to another pervasive figurative pattern critics have located in the *Letters*, namely, the theatrical metaphor.) A prominent instance of Burke's preoccupation with unnatural transformations appears a few pages earlier in the fourth *Letter*, when he describes the unnatural alliance recently formed between France and Spain:

> Here we have, formed, a new, unlooked-for, monstrous, heterogeneous alliance; a double-natured Monster; Republick above and Monarchy below. There is no Centaur of fiction, no poetic Satyr of the Woods; nothing short of the Hieroglyphick Monsters of Ægypt, Dog in Head and Man in Body, that can give an idea of it. None of these things can subsist in nature (so at least it is thought); but the moral world admits Monsters which the physical rejects. (ix. 96)

This diplomatic *mélange* is explicitly referred to as a 'Metamorphosis', and it calls to mind Milton's description of the outer regions of Hell in *Paradise Lost*—that 'Universe of death',

> Where all life dies, death lives, and Nature breeds,
> Perverse, all monstrous, all prodigious things,
> Abominable, inutterable, and worse
> Than Fables yet have feign'd, or fear conceiv'd,
> Gorgons and Hydras, and Chimeras dire.
>   (*PL* ll. 622–8)

---

[30] The history of madness in 18th-c. England is told in Roy Porter's *Mind-Forg'd Manacles: A History of Madness in England from the Restoration to the Regency* (London, 1987). For discussions of Pope's satiric and thematic uses of madness in *The Dunciad*, see Max Byrd, *Visits to Bedlam: Madness and Literature in the Eighteenth Century* (Columbia, SC, 1974), 12–57; and Morris, *Alexander Pope*, 270–95.

The systematically parodic anti-creation that is Hell in Milton's poem furnished the Scriblerians (especially Pope), and Burke after them, with a powerful model for their own prophetic visions of uncreation. Yet the appeal of Milton's demonic 'anti-epic' for these writers goes well beyond its theological significance. Indeed, the principles of parody, metamorphosis, and unnatural transformation that underlie his conception of Hell resonate on many cultural levels in the eighteenth century, from the philosophical and literary to the social, popular, and ritualistic.

In a broadly philosophical or metaphysical sense, the fascination with transformation in the writings of Pope and his contemporaries is a response to a world that is increasingly understood as dynamic and subject to change. Ralph Cohen argues, for instance, that such poems as *The Rape of the Lock* and *The Dunciad* are centrally concerned with the problem of cultural and historical change. In these poems Pope articulates the tension between 'a faded past and a changing present' in terms of 'natural or normal change and unnatural or artificial and grotesque change'.[31] The former is represented in *The Rape of the Lock* by the natural processes of growing old and losing one's beauty, whereas the latter is exemplified in the grotesque transformations in the Cave of Spleen: men bearing children and maids turning into bottles and teapots.

In a world of dynamic and accelerating change, it becomes crucial to retain a clear sense of a norm against which deviations can be judged and the value of change assessed. Thus, in distinguishing natural from unnatural transformations, both Pope and Burke seek to preserve their sense of Nature as a normative concept ('Unerring NATURE, still divinely bright') while conceding that within certain norms, change is not only inevitable, but desirable and natural. This accommodation between permanence and change—between a belief in God's 'divine tactic' and a growing awareness of historical contingency—is a recurring dynamic in Burke's writings. In *Reflections on the Revolution in France*, when the possibility of a legitimate and necessary revolution is broached, Burke goes to

---

[31] Ralph Cohen, 'Transformation in *The Rape of the Lock*', *Eighteenth-Century Studies*, 2 (1968–9), 206–7.

extraordinary lengths to insist that any legitimate recourse to violence is an instinctive response, anchored in the natural order, which seeks as its object only the restoration of that order:

> It is the first and supreme necessity only, a necessity that is not chosen but chooses, a necessity paramount to deliberation, that admits no discussion, and demands no evidence. . . . This necessity is no exception to the rule; because this necessity itself is a part too of that moral and physical disposition of things to which man must be obedient by consent or force; but if that which is only submission to necessity should be made the object of choice, the law is broken, nature is disobeyed, and the rebellious are outlawed, cast forth, and exiled, from this world of reason, and order, and peace, and virtue, and fruitful penitence, into the antagonist world of madness, discord, vice, confusion, and unavailing sorrow. (viii. 147)

The binary oppositions voiced in this passage—reason as opposed to madness, order versus discord, and so on—make explicit and give meaning to the Scriblerian satiric dynamic of high and low or the natural and the monstrous. This dynamic is reflected in the dichotomy between natural and unnatural change that pervades the *Letters on a Regicide Peace*. Thus, Burke writes that the new political institutions of revolutionary France have no analogue in the natural world—'None of these things can subsist in nature'—but he qualifies his assertion significantly by observing that 'the moral world admits Monsters which the physical rejects'.

That qualification is crucial, for like Pope, Burke sees unnatural transformations as the consequence of human agency (rather than as *lusus naturae*), and he locates them in the social and moral, rather than physical world. The seemingly fanciful or mock-mythological metamorphoses that both writers habitually employ point to underlying social and ethical pathologies. In the case of *The Rape of the Lock*, for instance, 'artificial or inappropriate changes result from humans competing with nature or from embracing changes without embracing the decorum and significance appropriate to them. Thus a society can formally adhere to social games or religious rites without giving them appropriate social or religious meaning.'[32] In *The*

---

[32] Ibid., 209.

Dunciad unnatural transformation is equally the outcome of human moral failure, of the dunces' lack of wisdom, judgement, and self-knowledge. In Book III a Miltonic world of monsters appears, not created by divine curse 'for evil only good', but called forth by the vulgar hand of the theatre impresario John Rich:

> All sudden, Gorgons hiss, and Dragons glare,
> And ten-horn'd fiends and Giants rush to war.
> Hell rises, Heav'n descends, and dance on Earth:
> Gods, imps, and monsters, music, rage, and mirth.
> (III. 235–8)

Similarly, the policy pursued by the diplomatic impresarios of revolutionary France produces a grotesquely hybrid alliance: 'a double-natured Monster; Republick above and Monarchy below'. This human anti-creation contrasts with the natural, organic political order of Great Britain, which, as Burke points out in the *Reflections*, is built 'after the pattern of nature':

Our political system is placed in a just correspondence and symmetry with the order of the world, and with the mode of existence decreed to a permanent body composed of transitory parts; wherein, by the disposition of a stupendous wisdom, moulding together the great mysterious incorporation of the human race, the whole, at one time, is never old, or middle-aged, or young, but in a condition of unchangeable constancy, moves on through the varied tenour of perpetual decay, fall, renovation, and progression. (viii. 84)

As a metaphor for change, the natural cycle provides a reassuring sense of continuity within change, a boundary to the range of possibilities for alterations in the natural order. Active human intervention in this cyclical rhythm produces an unnatural, and seemingly irreversible, linear breach—in this instance, a 'double-natured Monster' that can no longer be reintegrated into the natural diplomatic order of Europe.

At the literary level, the world of monsters conjured up in turn by Milton, Pope, and Burke owes its inspiration to, among other sources, Ovid's *Metamorphoses*, a work that adopts as its unifying thread the recurrent transformations recorded in classical mythology. The vivid scene in *Paradise Lost*, for example, when Satan and his hosts are transformed into serpents—

> dreadful was the din
> Of hissing through the Hall, thick swarming now
> With complicated monsters, head and tail,
> Scorpion and Asp, and *Amphisbæna* dire
>
> (PL X. 521–4)

—recalls the metamorphosis of Cadmus into a snake in *Metamorphoses*, 4. As with the other cited instances, this unnatural transformation is the consequence of individual choice, of deeply personal moral failure; thus, Satan is 'punisht in the shape he sinn'd, | According to his doom'. More suggestive, however, is Pope's Ovidian sketch, quoted above, of John Rich and his bag of theatrical tricks. Pope's own commentary on this dazzling scene, indicates the larger significance of Ovidian metamorphosis as a satiric device:

> Thence a new world to Nature's laws unknown,
> Breaks out refulgent, with a heav'n its own:
> Another Cynthia her new journey runs,
> And other planets circle other suns.
> The forests dance, the rivers upward rise,
> Whales sport in woods, and dolphins in the skies;
> And last, to give the whole creation grace,
> Lo! one vast Egg produces human race.
>
> (III. 241–8)

The image of whales and dolphins disporting in the trees is a borrowing from Horace's *De Arte Poetica*, where it serves to illustrate the ineptitude of writers who inappropriately vary their subject-matter, but, as Howard Erskine-Hill shows, the passage as a whole, with its 'recipe for the incompetent and absurd', finds its full-scale realization in Ovid's account of Deucalion and the flood in *Metamorphoses*, 1. Ovid describes boats sailing over fields and the roofs of houses, seals drowsing where goats had previously grazed, mermaids gazing into cities, and 'leaping dolphins' splashing their sides 'against oak bough and tree'.[33] That Pope was thinking principally of Ovid in this context is further confirmed by the early Scriblerian collaboration, *Three Hours after Marriage*, which is, in the view of its

---

[33] Ovid, *The Metamorphoses*, trans. Horace Gregory (New York, 1958), 11–12. See also, Howard Erskine-Hill, *Pope: The Dunciad* (London, 1972), 28–9.

modern editors, an extended allusion to Ovid: 'Emotions, ideas, things and people are systematically transmuted into what they are not.' The centrepiece in this mad comedy of Ovidian transformation is Phoebe Clinkit's absurd dramatic rendering of the story of Deucalion, Pyrrha, and the universal deluge: 'The raging seas o'er the tall Woods have broke, | Now perch, thou Whale, upon the sturdy Oak.'[34]

In *Three Hours after Marriage*, the motif of metamorphosis serves primarily as a comic gloss on the debasement of learning and letters, which is exhibited in the pedantic intellectual activities of the play's characters. Their eccentricities and the transmutations these give rise to are the external signs of their fundamental misconception of human reason and its purposes, as summed up in Pope's humanistic dictum, 'Know then thyself, presume not God to scan; | The proper study of Mankind is Man' (*Essay on Man*, II. 1–2). In *The Dunciad*, however, Pope casts a wider satirical net. The transformations brought about by Rich produce a world 'to Nature's laws unknown': the theatre manager has, in effect, arrogated to himself the Godlike function of creation, but the world he conjures into being is a cosmic bungle, a creation built on the principles of absurdity and disorder. Thus, by invoking the trope of metamorphosis, Pope (and subsequently Burke) broaden their attacks to call into question their opponents' grasp of fundamental philosophical and religious principles. The dunces' misapprehension of reality is to be measured not only on an ethical but also on a metaphysical scale. In *The Dunciad* these dark implications are held in check by the poem's prevailing spirit of anarchic comedy, but Burke finds occasion to realize fully the tragic potential of Pope's satiric discourse.

At the literary level this chaos of reason is mirrored in an anarchy of style, as in the productions of Pope's dunces, where 'Tragedy and Comedy embrace' and 'Farce and Epic get a jumbled race' (I. 69–70). Burke exploits this theme to devastating effect in discrediting the writings of his political opponents. Indeed, the fourth *Regicide Peace* letter is conceived as a literary

---

[34] John Gay, Alexander Pope, and John Arbuthnot, *Three Hours after Marriage*, ed. Richard Morton and William M. Peterson, Lake Erie College Studies, 1 (Painesville, Ohio, 1961), pp. xi–xiv, 8.

and critical arraignment of a political pamphlet by Lord Auckland: the hapless peer plays the unwilling role in the *Letter* of a political dunce whose appearance—'a gentleman in the fag end of October, dripping with the fogs of that humid and uncertain season' (ix. 55)—matches the cloudy and obscure state of his ideas and his style. Of more immediate relevance, however, is the social and political dimension suggested by the topsy-turvy transformations of dolphins into birds and forests into dancing crowds. Pope is drawing on a subject of longstanding popular fascination, namely, the broadsheet and chapbook theme of the world upside-down. These catchpenny prints typically comprised a series of panels or motifs depicting various inversions of normal social and natural hierarchies, from servants who become masters and hunters who are attacked by their prey, to fish that fly and attack birds in the sea.[35]

The imagery of inversion represented in the world upside-down motif is only one of the many rituals of rebellion or role reversal observed by anthropologists across a wide variety of human cultures. Barbara Babcock has coined the term 'symbolic inversion' to describe the expressive purpose of these rebellious rituals. Symbolic inversion, she writes, 'may be broadly defined as any act of expressive behavior which inverts, contradicts, abrogates, or in some fashion presents an alternative to commonly held cultural codes, values, and norms be they linguistic, literary or artistic, religious, or social and political'.[36] One of the most important of these rituals in eighteenth-century England was the masquerade, in which participants enact role reversals and inversions through the disguises they assume. In his verse satire 'On the Masquerades', Christopher Pitt draws a Dunciad-like portrait of the ensuing social confusion:

> So many various changes to impart,
> Would tire an Ovid's or a Proteus' art,
> Where, lost in one promiscuous whim, we see
> Sex, age, condition, quality, degree.—

---

[35] See Erskine-Hill, *Dunciad*, 29. See also David Kunzle, 'World Upside Down: The Iconography of a European Broadsheet Type', in B. A. Babcock (ed.), *The Reversible World* (Ithaca, NY, 1978) 41.
[36] Babcock, Introduction to *Reversible World*, 14.

> Where the facetious crowd themselves lay down,
> And take up ev'ry person but their own;
> Fools, dukes, rakes, cardinals, fops, Indian queens,
> Belles in tiewigs and lords in Harlequins,
> Troops of right honorable porters come,
> And garter'd small-coal merchants crowd the room,
> Valets adorn'd with coronets appear,
> Lacquies of state and footmen with a star,
> Sailors of quality with judges mix,—
> And chimney-sweepers drive their coach-and-six.
> . . . .
> Where sexes blend in one confus'd intrigue,
> Where the girls ravish and the men grow big.[37]
> (25–38, 51–2)

Not only have social roles been systematically reversed in this unnatural conjunction, but the prevailing social promiscuity also spills over into the sexual realm, as 'the girls ravish and the men grow big' in a grotesque literalization of Pope's Cave of Spleen, where 'Men prove with Child, as pow'rful Fancy works' (IV. 53). Social transformation threatens to end in the emergence of a world of monsters.

IV

It is not difficult to understand why this imagery of transformation and masquerade becomes one of Burke's chief rhetorical weapons in his denunciations of the French Revolution. Terry Castle sums up succinctly its semiotic appeal: 'When eighteenth-century satirists wished to depict a larger cultural sickness—the morbid state of civilization itself—the masquerade, not surprisingly, offered an image of universal corruption.'[38] Burke's most extended use of carnivalesque imagery appears in his satiric account of the inauguration of the new French constitution of 1795, which, in the sanguine hopes of many observers, augured a return to political stability in France and an abatement of revolutionary violence. Burke rejects such expressions of optimism as self-deluding: beneath the powders, perfumes,

---

[37] Christopher Pitt, 'On the Masquerades', quoted in T. Castle, *Masquerade and Civilization: The Carnivalesque in Eighteenth-Century English Culture and Fiction* (London, 1986), 83–4. [38] Castle, *Masquerade and Civilization*, 85.

ribbons, sashes, and plumes of the Directory's costumes he detects 'the very same Ruffians, Thieves, Assassins, and Regicides, that they were from the beginning' (ix. 72). More alarming still than these flimsy disguises are the costumes worn by Europe's diplomatic representatives at the inauguration—social slumming on a grand scale:

> Good God! in what habits did the Representatives of the crowned heads of Europe appear, when they came to swell the pomp of their humiliation, and attended in solemn function this inauguration of Regicide? That would be the curiosity. Under what robes did they cover the disgrace and degradation of the whole College of Kings? What warehouses of masks and dominos furnished a cover to the nakedness of their shame? The shop ought to be known; it will soon have a good trade. (ix. 74)

The full significance of the mock-diplomatic spectacle Burke sketches here can best be grasped by placing the scene against the background of the normal symbolic dynamics of masquerade in the period. Typically, the hierarchic inversions of the masquerade involved either a burlesque imitation of their inferiors by the rich and powerful ('lords in Harlequins', for instance, or ladies as shepherdesses) or a mock-heroic assumption of exalted social and political roles by the lower orders ('Valets adorn'd with coronets'). Though the first of these modes of impersonation was regarded as harmless and amusing, the second often excited contempt and alarm. Thus, Burke characterizes the members of the Directory ('the managers of their burlesque Government') at the inauguration as objects of derision to their countrymen:

> The Diplomacy, who were a sort of strangers, were quite awe struck with the 'pride, pomp, and circumstance' of this majestick Senate; whilst the Sansculotte Gallery instantly recognized their old insurrectionary acquaintance, burst out into a horse laugh at their absurd finery, and held them in infinitely greater contempt than whilst they prowled about the streets in the pantaloons of the last years Constitution when their Legislators appeared honestly, with their daggers in their belts and their pistols peeping out of their side pocket holes, like a bold brave Banditti, as they are. (ix. 73)

In accounting for this response, Burke recalls a conversation he once had with his friend, the actor David Garrick.

I asked him, how it happened that whenever a Senate appeared on the Stage, the Audience seemed always disposed to laughter? He said the reason was plain; the Audience was well acquainted with the faces of most of the Senators. They knew, that they were no other than candle-snuffers, revolutionary scene-shifters, second and third mob, prompters, clerks, executioners, who stand with their axe on their shoulders by the wheel, grinners in the Pantomime, murderers in Tragedies, who make ugly faces under black wigs; in short, the very scum and refuse of the Theatre; and it was of course, that the contrast of the vileness of the Actors with the pomp of their Habits naturally excited ideas of contempt and ridicule. (ix. 73)

Here he conflates a largely theoretical anxiety over the threat posed by a temporary, parodic assumption of the sumptuary trappings of authority in the eighteenth-century masquerade with the spectacle of executioners and revolutionaries casting themselves permanently in the roles of senators and governors.

The full extent of Burke's fear is revealed in his comment on the political pageant he has so vividly brought to life: 'The Parisians, (and I am much of their mind) think that a thief with a crape on his visage, is much worse than a bare-faced knave; and that such robbers richly deserve all the penalties of all the black Acts' (ix. 73–4). The 'black Acts' to which he refers were a cruel eighteenth-century manifestation of the time-honoured practice of sumptuary regulation. The Black Act of 1723 prescribed the death penalty for a person or persons caught poaching while armed and 'having his or their faces blacked, or being otherwise disguised'.[39] Successive judicial judgments quickly enlarged the scope of the Act, so that the action of blacking or appearing in disguise could in itself constitute a capital offence. As Castle points out, observers in the 1720s were not blind to the irony that members of the general public could be arrested for an act that fashionable people at a masquerade could perform with impunity. In the words of one writer,

by the late Act made against the *Blacks of Waltham*, it is no less than a Felony to go in any sort of disguise ... and it is well known [Charles Towers] was executed for the same, not without making some Reflections and Complaints, that he suffered Death for the same Thing,

---

[39] E. P. Thompson, *Whigs and Hunters: The Origin of the Black Act* (New York, 1975), 21–4, 271.

which some Hundreds of People practised at the Hay-Market, without being call'd to an Account for, whereby he would insinuate as if those lewd Assemblies were conniv'd at.[40]

The ferocity of the penalties prescribed in the Black Act for any illegal recourse to disguise suggests how deeply threatening and unsettling sartorial transformations were to the authorities in the eighteenth century. The ruling élite in the period viewed counter-theatrical appropriations of the official trappings and rituals of authority with alarm, a concern grounded in the fear that such symbolic arrogations would undermine the hierarchical structure of eighteenth-century society. A similar fear underlay the authorities' suspicion of disguise and masquerade, particularly when practised by the lower orders. Not only was the mimicking of one's social 'betters' felt to incite envy for the perquisites of rank and dissatisfaction with one's appointed station in life, but also, as the century wore on, it was increasingly seen as encouraging the revolutionary notion that 'rank itself could be altered as easily as its outward signs'. Not surprisingly, then, as social unrest grew in the later decades of the century, attacks on masquerading more and more emphasized its deleterious political (as well as moral) consequences, its tendency, for example, 'to diffuse a *spirit of liberty*, by reducing all men to an equality'.[41]

For observers in the period the unsettling political symbolism of the masquerade was ultimately grounded in the historical example of the English Revolution, the surpassing instance of masquerade in English political history. All the sinister associations Burke calls forth in characterizing the French revolutionaries as masqueraders coalesce in the figure of Cromwell, who was regarded as second only to the Devil himself in his capacity for dissimulation. Richard Flecknoe noted that Cromwell's reputation as 'the greatest dissembler living' (in Clarendon's phrase) was underscored for many by his masquerade of kingship: at his investiture, wrote Edmund Ludlow, 'The pretended Protector was clothed with a purple robe lined with ermins', and he was presented with 'a sword, a scepter, and a

---

[40] *Weekly Journal*, 10 April 1725, quoted in Castle, *Masquerade and Civilization*, 356–7, n. 51.
[41] Castle, *Masquerade and Civilization*, 92–3.

Bible', emblems of royal power and authority.[42] But, Cromwell's detractors were quick to point out, beneath these symbols and caparisons of monarchy (as Burke subsequently noted of the newly 'powdered, and perfumed, and ribanded' Directory of France) beat the heart of a thief, usurper, and regicide. In this instance, as so often in Burke's polemics on the French Revolution, the English Civil War stands as the historical *terminus a quo*, the interpretative point of origin that anchors his polemical fury. In this, as in so many other respects, his satiric vision harks back to that of his Scriblerian predecessors, especially Swift.

Burke's repeated characterizations of the Directory as a burlesque circus and tawdry masquerade are motivated by his concern to unmask or demystify an elaborate political ceremonial, whose symbolism the new French government is clearly prepared to exploit for its own ends.[43] The vociferousness of his attack is perhaps the supreme compliment of one master propagandist to another, for he notes with alarm that some of his countrymen have allowed themselves to be taken in by the constitutional and ceremonial trappings with which the Directory (after the manner of Cromwell) is seeking to clothe its illegitimacy. He cites a Whig pamphlet published in 1796, in which the writer comments with satisfaction on the complexion of the new French constitution, comparing it favourably with Britain's:

We see ... two chambers, which in their comparative numbers and modes of conducting public business, bear no very distant resemblance to the two Houses of Parliament. The regal dignity and functions, without its title, are committed to the 'executive directory;' or in more correct language, the crown is put into commission. In the 'Costume'

---

[42] Edmund Ludlow, *The Memoirs of Edmund Ludlow, Esq., Lieutenant-General of the Horse in the Army of the Commonwealth of England, 1625–1672*, ed. Charles H. Firth (Oxford, 1894), ii. 29.

[43] That Burke should be attempting to demystify the dress and ceremonial of the French republic is supremely ironic, for, as Stephen Blakemore argues, one of the goals of the Revolution was to expose the reality of oppression that was obscured by the garments and drapery of the *ancien régime*: 'To the revolutionaries ... metaphors of drapery, clothes, and veils are artificial and deceptive "masks," and their criticism corresponds to "the unmasking trend" of modern political and sociological criticism' (*Burke and the Fall of Language: The French Revolution as Linguistic Event* (Hanover, NH, 1988), 73–4).

assumed by the members of the legislative body, we almost behold the revival of the extinguished insignia of knighthood. Louis the Fourteenth never gave audience at Versailles, with more affectation of pageantry and splendor, than the 'directory' recently exhibited at the Palace of the Luxembourg, on the first presentation of the foreign ambassadors. . . . Every thing announces the decline of anarchy, and the termination of those sanguinary scenes, which have almost obliterated in atrocity the massacre of St. Bartholomew.[44]

The *naïveté* and superficiality of this commentator in judging the legitimacy of the new political order by the cut of its costume and its punctiliousness in observing the forms are easily dispatched by a broadside of sarcasm:

Are they not the very same Ruffians, Thieves, Assassins, and Regicides, that they were from the beginning? . . . Oh! but I shall be answered, it is now quite another thing:—They are all changed:—You have not seen them in their state dresses:—This makes an amazing difference:—The new Habit of the Directory is so charmingly fancied, that it is impossible not to fall in love with so well dressed a Constitution:—The *Costume* of the Sansculotte Constitution of 1793 was absolutely insufferable. The Committee for foreign Affairs were such slovens, and stunk so abominably, that no *Muscadin* Ambassador of the smallest degree of delicacy of nerves could come within ten yards of them:—but . . . as they now appear, there is something in it more grand and noble, something more suitable to an awful Roman Senate, receiving the homage of dependant Tetrarchs. (ix. 72)

Burke's characterization of this miraculous sartorial transformation recalls Pope's humorous advice in *Peri Bathous* on the 'method of turning a vicious Man into a Hero'. The approved political means of transforming a scoundrel into a great man, Pope advises, is to decorate him with a red, green, or blue ribbon—the 'dress' of English knighthood. (This is also the means of Santerre's transformation from a regicide into a statesman: he enters London wearing a 'bloody sash across his shoulders with the order of the Holy Guillotine' (ix. 112). The satiric conferral of a knighthood on Santerre is Burke's rejoinder, as he indicates in a footnote, to the Whig writer's optimism about 'the revival of the extinguished insignia of

---

[44] *A View of the Relative State of Great Britain and France, at the Commencement of the Year 1796* (London, 1796), 45–6. Burke's citation of this pamphlet can be found in ix. 112.

knighthood'.) But the rehabilitation of the vicious man, Pope explains, has an important rhetorical, as well as sartorial, dimension: 'The first and chief rule is *the Golden Rule* of *Transformation*, which consists in converting Vices into their bordering Virtues. A Man who is a Spendthrift, and will not pay a just Debt, may have his Injustice *transform'd* into Liberality; Cowardice may be metamorphos'd into Prudence... Corruption into Patriotism.'[45] Rhetorical transformation and misrepresentation are, as will become apparent in the next section of this chapter, *the* central preoccupation of the Scriblerians, the chief symptom for them of Britain's political and cultural degeneration. If 'Expression is the *Dress* of *Thought*', as Pope affirms in *An Essay on Criticism*, then the linguistic code is as vulnerable to distortion as the code of dress: language *clothes*, rather than *embodies*, truth, just as dress is the discardable sign rather than the materialization of the wearer's social and inner self.

Burke's sarcasm in his fanciful description of the Directory is motivated by the recognition that a society like his, which invests clothing with enormous symbolic value, is particularly susceptible to the cultural messages encoded in dress—is especially apt, in short, to accept at face value the dictum that clothes make the man or woman. The person he imagines as fatuously exclaiming, 'it is impossible not to fall in love with so well dressed a Constitution', reminds one of the Grub Street hack in Swift's *A Tale of a Tub*, who prefers externals and surfaces over 'that pretended Philosophy which enters into the Depth of Things'. An expensive suit of clothes impresses the hack much more than the character of the person wearing it: 'Yesterday I ordered the Carcass of a *Beau* to be stript in my Presence; when we were all amazed to find so many unsuspected Faults under one Suit of Cloaths.'[46] The credulous astonishment of the hack is an extreme instance of the all-too-human tendency to accept as natural, transparent, and legible those cultural codes (like dress) that prove, upon examination, to be thoroughly conventional and therefore potentially misleading.

A passage in *A Letter to a Noble Lord*, written at about the

---

[45] Alexander Pope, *Peri Bathous*, in *The Prose Works of Alexander Pope* ii. *The Major Works 1725–44*, ed. R. Cowler (Oxford, 1986), 227.

[46] Jonathan Swift, *Tale of a Tub*, in *The Prose Works* of Jonathan Swift, ed. Herbert Davis (Oxford, 1937–68), i. 109.

same time as the *Letters on a Regicide Peace*, furnishes an illuminating political gloss on Burke's preoccupation with masquerade, disguise, and sartorial transformation. In the opening paragraphs of the *Letter*, he apologizes ironically for not treating the Duke of Bedford with the deference owing to a man of his station, but he excuses himself by observing 'that a confusion of characters may produce mistakes; that, in the masquerades of the grand carnival of our age, whimsical adventures happen' (ix. 149). If Bedford and Lauderdale insist on assuming the *sans-culotte* garb of French republicanism, Burke asks innocently, then how is one to avoid confusing them with 'the Dukes and Earls of Brentford' (ix. 149)—the anti-heroes of Buckingham's burlesque play *The Rehearsal*? Similarly, forms of government in revolutionary France have become as numerous and ephemeral as the latest fashions, to be put on and discarded like a suit of clothes:

Abbé Sieyes has whole nests of pigeon-holes full of constitutions ready made, ticketed, sorted, and numbered; suited to every season and every fancy; some with the top of the pattern at the bottom, and some with the bottom at the top; some plain, some flowered; some distinguished for their simplicity; others for their complexity; some of blood colour, some of *boue de Paris* ... Some in long coats, and some in short cloaks; some with pantaloons; some without breeches. Some with five shilling qualifications; some totally unqualified. So that no constitution-fancier may go unsuited from his shop, provided he loves a pattern of pillage, oppression, arbitrary imprisonment, confiscation, exile, revolutionary judgment, and legalised premeditated murder, in any shapes into which they can be put. (ix. 177–8)

In this Swiftian catalogue, Burke contemplates satirically the consequences of that cavalier attitude which regards constitutional arrangements as extraneous and interchangeable, in stark contrast with his own view that the political institutions of a country must grow and accommodate themselves to the prejudices and historical experience of its people.

Burke's conception of constitutional change recalls the analogy of the magical coats in Swift's *A Tale of a Tub*, garments that '*will grow*', the Father informs the three brothers, '*in the same proportion with your Bodies, lengthning and widening of themselves, so as to be always fit*'.[47] But, as Paul

[47] Ibid. 44.

Fussell points out in his discussion of the clothing metaphor in *The Rhetorical World of Augustan Humanism*, the world as we know it is very different from the folktale world of the brothers' magical coats: in our world, 'clothing, unlike skin, is static and inorganic'. Fussell points out that when clothing is treated symbolically, it becomes semantically unstable, like any other symbolic system: 'always in extremes, man is given to symbolizing either too little or too much. If he oversymbolizes, the clothing seems to become absolutely synonymous with its wearer; and if he undersymbolizes, he approaches the condition of the Houyhnhnm [in *Gulliver's Travels*, Book IV] who conceives of man as entirely distinct from clothing and who fails to understand why he wears it.'[48]

In eyeing the latest political fashions, the constitution fancier in the Abbé's shop is guilty, in Burke's eyes, of 'undersymbolizing' (to borrow Fussell's terminology). But Burke himself tends to the opposite extreme, attempting to treat as metaphysical necessities that which he admits, in *Reflections on the Revolution in France*, to be nothing more than the 'pleasing illusions' of politics: 'All the decent drapery of life is to be rudely torn off. All the superadded ideas, furnished from the wardrobe of a moral imagination, which the heart owns, and the understanding ratifies, as necessary to cover the defects of our naked shivering nature, and to raise it to dignity in our own estimation, are to be exploded as a ridiculous, absurd, and antiquated fashion' (viii. 128). The vehicle of Burke's metaphor proves too slippery, too unstable, to bear the weight of the political vision he is trying to convey, for if political traditions are like the clothes that 'unaccommodated man' requires to cover his 'naked shivering nature', then the subversive thought occurs that one suit of clothes can keep out the weather as well as another. He appears to have forgotten his own cautionary note at the beginning of the *Letters on a Regicide Peace*, 'Parallels of this sort rather furnish similitudes to illustrate or to adorn, than supply analogies from whence to reason' (ix. 188). As is so often the case in the idiom of Scriblerian satire, the appropriation of a particular metaphor or mode of expression

---

[48] P. Fussell, *The Rhetorical World of Augustan Humanism* (Oxford, 1965), 218, 212–13.

pays covert tribute to a view the writer is attempting to exorcize—in this instance, the unwilling acknowledgement that the reality of historical change will inevitably lead to alterations in political as well as sartorial fashions. The trope of transformation in general (and of masquerade in particular), with which Burke attempts to castigate the French Directory, is suffused with this deconstructive symbolic recognition, bespeaking, in Castle's words, 'the possibility of astonishing transfigurations, and of a world perennially open to reconstitution'.[49]

Finally, it is noteworthy to observe how Burke's vision of the ceremonial inauguration of the Directory opens out into a wider pageant resembling the dream-like levee or assembly in Book IV of *The Dunciad*, at which the goddess Dulness confirms her sway and accepts the tributes of her followers:

> Now crowds on crowds around the Goddess press,
> Each eager to present the first Address.
> Dunce scorning Dunce beholds the next advance,
> But Fop shews Fop superior complaisance.
>   (IV. 135–8)

The votaries of Dulness in Burke's account are the 'diplomatic rabble' of Europe, who have prostituted themselves by answering the arrogant summons of the Directory:

They called them out by a sort of roll of their Nations, one after another, much in the manner, in which they called wretches out of their prison to the guillotine. When these Ambassadors of Infamy appeared before them, the chief Director, in the name of the rest, treated each of them with a short, affected, pedantic, insolent, theatric laconium; a sort of epigram of contempt. When they had thus insulted them in a style and language, which never before was heard . . . to finish their outrage, they drummed and trumpeted the wretches out of their Hall of Audience. (ix. 75–6)

The diplomatic gathering is adorned by some archetypal specimens of duncehood, including an 'atheistick coxcomb' and 'miserable fop' representing Austria, whom the Directory, after the manner of Pope's Queen of Dulness, compliments 'on his matriculation into *their* Philosophy' (ix. 76–7). The entire

---

[49] Castle, *Masquerade and Civilization*, 55.

assembly reminds Burke of a previous political sideshow in revolutionary France, Anacharsis Clootz's masquerade embassy to the Constituent Assembly on 19 June 1790—a motley delegation of representatives from the 'oppressed nations of the universe' (all appropriately decked out in the national costumes of their countries) who congratulated the legislators for having 'restored primitive equality among men'.[50] 'Were the dresses of the Ministers ... who attended on [the Directory]', he asks, 'taken from the wardrobe of that property man at the Opera, from whence my old acquaintance, *Anacharsis* Cloots, some years ago, equipped a body of Ambassadors, whom he conducted, as from all the Nations of the World, to the bar of what was called the Constituent Assembly' (ix. 74). Clootz's theatrical gesture drew on the precedent of a century's masquerading, as the remarks of an observer at a London masked ball in 1718 testify: 'By the vast variety of Dresses (many of them very rich), you would fancy it a Congress of the principal Persons of all Nations in the World, as Turks, Italians, Indians, Polanders, Venetians, &c.'[51]

Burke sees the current inaugural ceremonial of the Directory as going much further than the 'insolent mummery' of Clootz's fantastic pageant: 'Anacharsis himself, all fanatic as he was, could not have imagined, that his Opera procession should have been the prototype of the real appearance of the Representatives of all the Sovereigns of Europe themselves' (ix. 75). The movement is from burlesque spectacle to a literalization of the burlesque as a permanent feature of the political landscape. The 'mummery' of Clootz's deputation bears the same relation to the 'plumed' splendour of the Directory as the comic, mock-epic attitude of *The Rape of the Lock* does to the anti-epic stance of *The Dunciad*. In both cases a masquerade in costumes and cultural forms hilariously unsuited to the wearers gives way to an implicit denial of those differences (in social class and literary

---

[50] See Simon Schama, *Citizens: A Chronicle of the French Revolution* (Toronto, 1989), 474.
[51] Mist's *Weekly Journal*, 15 Feb. 1718. Quoted in Pat Rogers, *Literature and Popular Culture in Eighteenth Century England* (Sussex, 1985), 56. Rogers offers a short overview of masquerade in 18th-c. England on 54–64.

genre, for example) that give meaning to the kind of travesty enacted by a Clootz or a Belinda.

Fredric Bogel argues that *The Dunciad* is an exploration of the erasing of meaning through the denial of difference and the need for distinctions: 'Pope's goal is an image not of the unstructured but of the undoing of structure by undifferentiation: not of meaninglessness but of the partial subversion of meaning.'[52] The same loss of distinction, with a consequent erosion of meaning, is at work in the sartorial transformations of the Directory. If, as Adam Ferguson points out, a hierarchical society requires external markings to indicate to the individual 'the relation in which he stands to his fellow subjects, or distinguish the numberless ranks that fill up the interval between the state of the sovereign and that of the peasant',[53] then the transformations imagined by Burke—the collapse of difference into tautology and similitude—enact nothing less than the dissolution of the social order. In spite of the imaginative colouring he has used in recounting the inauguration of the Directory, Burke is at pains to insist that his satiric account portrays a mode of conduct 'perfectly systematick in every particular'. As he explains, 'it appears absurd only as it is strange and uncouth. . . . When by insult after insult they have rendered the character of Sovereigns vile in the eyes of their subjects, they know there is but one step more to their utter destruction. All authority, in a great degree, exists in opinion: royal authority most of all. The supreme majesty of a Monarch cannot be allied with contempt' (ix. 79). Thus, the deliberate sartorial reversals of the 'new-robed Directory' operate simultaneously on two levels: not only do they disrobe and demystify monarchy and obliterate the distinctions of the old order, but, at the same time, with the powerful illogic of the effective propagandist, they claim for the new order the outward splendour and authority of the old.

---

[52] Fredric Bogel, 'Dulness Unbound: Rhetoric and Pope's Dunciad', *PMLA* 97 (1982), 847. For a discussion of *The Dunciad* as 'anti-epic', see John E. Sitter, *The Poetry of Pope's* Dunciad (Minneapolis, 1971), 51–65.

[53] Adam Ferguson, *Essay on the History of Civil Society* (1767; repr. Philadelphia, 1819) 126.

B. LANGUAGE, GENRE, AND CANON

I

Fredric Bogel identifies meaning as perhaps *the* central thematic preoccupation of *The Dunciad*—particularly the subversion of the possibility of meaning through the dunces' persistent denial of difference as an indispensable element in the structure of meaning. He quotes Scriblerus in *Peri Bathous*, who affirms, 'A great Genius takes things in the lump, without stopping at minute considerations'; 'Choice and distinction are . . . a curb to the spirit.'[54] The literary and cultural consequences of this reckless disregard are sketched out in the opening Book of *The Dunciad*, when the Queen of Dulness contemplates her 'wild creation':

> Here she beholds the Chaos dark and deep,
> Where nameless Somethings in their causes sleep,
> 'Till genial Jacob, or a warm Third day,
> Call forth each mass, a Poem, or a Play.
> . . . .
> There motley Images her fancy strike,
> Figures ill pair'd, and Similes unlike.
> She sees a Mob of Metaphors advance,
> Pleas'd with the madness of the mazy dance:
> How Tragedy and Comedy embrace;
> How Farce and Epic get a jumbled race;
> How Time himself stands still at her command,
> Realms shift their place, and Ocean turns to land.
> Here gay description Ægypt glads with show'rs,
> Or gives to Zembla fruits, to Barca flow'rs;
> Glitt'ring with ice here hoary hills are seen,
> There painted vallies of eternal green,
> In cold December fragrant chaplets blow,
> And heavy harvests nod beneath the snow.
>   (I. 55–8, 65–78)

Confusion reigns supreme in this passage, from bathetic diction and ill-assorted metaphors to the large-scale blurring of generic boundaries. The verbal anarchy spawned by the goddess is imagistically underscored, as John Sitter and others note, by

---

[54] See Bogel, 'Dulness Unbound', 846; Pope, *Peri Bathous* 199, 200.

Pope's repeated references in Book I to abortive births, promiscuous couplings, and monstrous and amorphous offspring. The effect is to link the breakdown of artistic decorum with the grossest reversals of the normal course of nature.

Sitter remarks on the imagistic 'logic' behind Pope's mythologizing of bad writers and bad writing as a 'grotesque, misshapen and absurd genesis'. The poet's strategy allows him to link vastly disparate verbal and conceptual levels without reducing his discourse to shrill invective:

> In this heavy atmosphere of embryo, abortion, and all the other 'sooterkins' of dull wit, Pope is able to range back and forth between the most metaphysical and most grossly physical extensions of the 'mass of Nonsense' which includes all the progeny of Dulness, both the persons and the productions of the dunces. It is this essential imagistic logic, embracing all varieties of confusion and gradually equating them, that provides much of the 'point' of Pope's humor at every level.[55]

These violations of the laws of nature, which signal a corresponding ignorance of philosophical and rhetorical order, re-enact on a broader scale the social confusion mirrored in the sartorial metamorphoses of masquerade.

Burke exploits all these equivalencies or levels of discourse in the *Letters*, most notably in his characterization of Lord Auckland as a political dunce, and in his withering critical analysis of Auckland's attempt at political writing in a pamphlet entitled, *Some Remarks on the Apparent Circumstances of the War in the Fourth Week of October 1795*.[56] Auckland's pamphlet had intimated that in the existing stand-off between France's military power and Britain's naval superiority, an opportunity had arisen for a negotiated settlement between the two countries. The mere suggestion, however, that there could be a basis for co-existence with the French republic was deeply disturbing to Burke, and the proximate outcome of Auckland's

---

[55] Sitter, *Pope's* Dunciad, 22–3.
[56] William Eden, first Baron Auckland (1744–1814) was an ally of William Pitt, having left the Whig opposition in 1785 to serve Pitt as Britain's envoy to France. His extensive diplomatic experience is reflected in his pamphlet, which argues for a return to a traditional balance of power in Europe and places faith in the possibilities of diplomacy and negotiation.

proposal was Burke's own uncompromising polemic opposing any form of negotiation with the revolutionary usurpers of the legitimate French government.

Although Auckland's pamphlet provided the impetus for the *Letters on a Regicide Peace*, Burke soon abandoned his initial draft of a response to Auckland in favour of a more general critique of the government's diplomatic approaches to France, which he published as *Two Letters on a Regicide Peace*. (The reply to Auckland was never finished and was published after Burke's death as the fourth *Letter*, addressed to Lord Fitzwilliam.) However abortive Burke's response to Auckland, it none the less inaugurated the noteworthy strategy he was to pursue in the subsequent *Letters*, namely, to subject a series of political texts, government documents, and royal proclamations on the subject of France to a detailed rhetorical and literary analysis. The *Letters on a Regicide Peace* assimilate political analysis to literary criticism. A representative instance of Burke's critical procedure is his animadversion upon Auckland's unfortunate tendency towards rhetorical diminishment in his style:

> In the very womb of this last sentence, pregnant, as it should seem, with a Hercules, there is formed a little Bantling of the mortal race, a degenerate puny parenthesis, that totally frustrates our most sanguine views and expectations, and disgraces the whole gestation. Here is this destructive parenthesis, 'unless some adequate compensation be secured *to us*'—*To us*! The Christian world may shift for itself, Europe may groan in slavery . . . but all is well, provided the compensation *to us* be adequate. (ix. 93)

Readers familiar with Burke will not be surprised to find him applying literary and aesthetic criteria in this way to a political text. A previous text on the French Revolution, the *Letter to a Member of the National Assembly* (1791), had proved to be as much an exercise in literary criticism (of Rousseau) as political commentary. Of the passage just quoted Christopher Reid observes, 'There is a powerful fusion here of detailed textual criticism, classical allusion and passionate political conviction. Burke is evidently as much concerned with the style as with the substance of Auckland's argument. Indeed, he regards them as inseparable.'[57]

[57] Reid, *Edmund Burke*, 47.

Reid's assessment can, however, be carried a step farther. As this example indicates, Burke's censure of Auckland's style extends beyond literary criticism into the realm of satire. Deploying the same 'imagistic logic' as does Pope in *The Dunciad*, Burke dismisses Auckland's attempt at rhetorical grandeur as an abortive birth: the noble lord conceives and brings forth a mere 'Bantling of the mortal race, a degenerate puny parenthesis'. Auckland himself is variously characterized as a hapless projector, particularly in his attempts to vindicate the new constitutional arrangements in France (ix. 90–2), and as a fit candidate (together with his fellow political dunce, the Duke of Bedford) to join the diplomatic rabble of Europe at the inaugural levee of the Directory (ix. 78). Thus, Burke's ultimate judgement of Auckland is to consign him to a political realm of dunces patterned after Pope's original.

That fictitious realm was already well on the way to being peopled by the time Burke turned his attention to Auckland. Earlier in 1795 he had pursued an identical approach in his *Letter to William Elliot*, which he wrote in reply to an attack on the *Reflections* by the Duke of Norfolk. In an address to the House of Lords, Norfolk condemned both Burke's book and Paine's reply, *The Rights of Man* as having done 'infinite mischief'.[58] Burke remarks in the *Letter to Elliot* on his 'good or ill fortune' to have provoked at least two men, Paine and Norfolk, into publishing their opinions: 'I am not so great a leveller as to put these two great men on a par, either in the state, or the republick of letters: but, "the field of glory is a field for all" ' (ix. 31). The 'field of glory' to which he refers is that upon which Queen Dulness conducts her 'high heroic Games' in *The Dunciad* II, games of brute, if high-spirited physicality (see *Dunciad* II. 32), Burke is no longer content to allude to Pope's *Dunciad*: following his predecessor's lead, he literalizes his allusion by identifying specific individuals of his generation, including Auckland, Norfolk, Bedford, and Paine, as the current inhabitants of the Queen's Realm.

Much more than an attempt at rhetorical one-upmanship, Burke's satirical dismissal of Auckland is perfectly consistent

---

[58] W. Cobbett (ed.), *Parliamentary History of England . . . to the Year 1803*, xxxi., *1496–1501* (London, 1817).

with his passionate amalgam of political argument and literary criticism in his analysis of Auckland's pamphlet, given that the original *Dunciad* is itself a fusion of political, literary, and cultural criticism. The cultural issues that animate Pope's poem echo throughout Burke's writings on the French Revolution. Among these are a concern with the question of canonical writing, those authors and genres worthy of study and emulation, as opposed to the debased generic offspring of the present day; an evaluation of texts and ideas in terms of hierarchical oppositions between ancient and modern or high and low; and a preoccupation with the debasement of language and forms of expression. All these themes emerge, more or less explicitly, in Pope's contemplation of the anti-creation of Dulness and her children; to a surprising extent, they also form the intellectual structure of Burke's attack on Lord Auckland and numerous other political and philosophical foes.

In mounting his attack on the enfeebled discourse of Auckland's pamphlet, a political equivalent of the promiscuous embrace of tragedy and comedy in *The Dunciad*, Burke takes pains to signal his critical awareness of literary form by discriminating among the genres of political writing and their effects. Thus, at the outset he considers the possibilities of the dialogue form as a framework for his reply, before finally settling on a modified version of that genre, in which Auckland's own words will be allowed to speak for themselves: 'If the writer, who attacks another's notions, does not deal fairly with his adversary, the diligent reader has it always in his power, by resorting to the work examined, to do justice to the original author and to himself' (ix. 45). Further, as he begins his analysis of Auckland's pamphlet, he undertakes to observe the liberal critical procedures recommended in Pope's *Essay on Criticism*. Pope had recommended that a 'perfect judge' should,

> *read* each Work of Wit
> With the same Spirit that its Author *writ*,
> Survey the *Whole*, nor seek slight Faults to find,
> Where *Nature moves*, and *Rapture warms* the Mind.
> (ll. 233–6)

Taking his cue from Auckland's own appeal to his readers' critical generosity, Burke arraigns his opponent by applying to his work the selfsame critical doctrine to which he has appealed:

> Examining it part by part, it seems almost every where to contradict itself.... For this reason, amongst others, I follow the advice which the able writer gives in his last page, which is, 'to consider the *impression* of what he has urged, taken from the *whole*, and not from detached paragraphs.' That caution was not absolutely necessary. I should think it unfair to the author and to myself, to have proceeded otherwise. This author's *whole*, however, like every other whole, cannot be so well comprehended without some reference to the parts; but they shall be again referred to the whole. Without this latter attention, several of the passages would certainly remain covered with an impenetrable and truly oracular obscurity. (ix. 49)

Even the critical magnanimity advocated by Pope cannot rescue Auckland from censure. On the contrary, in a pattern familar to readers of Pope, Burke begins by invoking a critical standard that, when applied, ends in a satirical dismemberment of his opponent's writing. At this point, critical and political discourse have become almost indistinguishable.

An awareness of genre is for Burke both a matrix for ordering experience and a vital link with history by which his text is situated in a tradition of related texts sharing common formal and thematic features. By contrast, Auckland's political discourse is unmoored from any familiar cultural landmark and characterized only by its radical novelty:

> In the time I have lived to, I always seem to walk on enchanted ground. Every thing is new, and according to the fashionable phrase, revolutionary. In former days authors valued themselves upon the maturity and fullness of their deliberations. Accordingly, they predicted ... an eternal duration to their works. The quite contrary is our present fashion. Writers value themselves now on the instability of their opinions and the transitory life of their productions. ... They write for youth, and it is sufficient if the instruction 'lasts as long as a present love,—or as the painted silks and cottons of the season.'
> (ix. 45–6)

The pragmatic Johnsonian criterion for determining a literary classic—'length of duration and continuance of esteem'—has become meaningless in a context where the events and opinions of the previous month or year no longer retain any significance greater than the design of last year's fabrics. A full century after

Swift's *Tale of a Tub*, in which the hack author flaunts his cultural amnesia and proudly strives to keep abreast of the latest ephemeral literary fashion, Burke revives the terms of his predecessor's satiric critique of modern learning.

Burke's self-conscious assimilation of his political writings to traditional literary genres—his reliance on tragedy in the narrative structure of *Reflections on the Revolution in France*, for example—marks his commitment to a political and cultural consensus that is in the process of being swept away. A similar dynamic animates *The Dunciad*, in which the traces of epic that structure Pope's poem serve as fragments to be shored against the ruin threatened by the promiscuous, amorphous creations of the Dunces. The manner in which both writers manipulate literary genres implies a conception of literary kinds as an interrelated, hierarchical system in which the lesser forms (lyric, epigram, pastoral, etc.) are included in or subsumed by the greater (epic and tragedy), and from which certain forms of debased discourse are resolutely to be excluded. The hierarchy of genres is related to hierarchies of diction, social class, cultural practices, and authorship. And, as Burke's writings amply demonstrate, these hierarchies are an equally powerful and determining presence in political as in literary discourse.

All this becomes clear in Burke's analysis of Auckland's pamphlet. His chief political objection to Auckland's position is that the noble lord is too temporizing, too eager to see signs of moderation in the conduct of the French government and, upon these slender reeds, to base hopes for a negotiated peace between Britain and France. In refuting Auckland's views, however, he devotes as much attention to the writer's manner of expression as to the content of his argument. Auckland has failed abysmally to rise to the formal and stylistic requirements of his genre: his *Remarks* are 'a direct contradiction' to the requisite 'style of manly indignation' (ix. 53). The standard against which Burke measures Auckland's pamphlet is a royal declaration issued at Whitehall on 29 October 1793, which laid out Britain's reasons for embarking on a war against France. Of this declaration Burke affirms, in the words of Milton's *Lycidas*, ' "That strain I heard was of an higher mood" ':

That declaration of our Sovereign was worthy of his throne. It is in a style, which neither the pen of the writer of October, nor such a poor crow-quill as mine can ever hope to equal. I am happy to enrich my letter with this fragment of nervous and manly eloquence, which, if it had not emanated from the awful authority of a throne, if it were not recorded amongst the most valuable monuments of history, and consecrated in the archives of States, would be worthy as a private composition to live for ever in the memory of men. (ix. 54)

The King's declaration has achieved the status of an instant classic for Burke: he anticipates for it the duration and continued esteem that time confers upon all classics. He seals his approval by quoting a verse from Milton's *Lycidas* (l. 87) that acknowledges, significantly, a hierarchy of modes of expression in literary discourse.

The term 'classic' itself, which derives etymologically from the Latin *classicus*, meaning 'of the highest class of Roman citizens', implies a hierarchy of genres and authors. The criterion of model authorship was originally the grammatical criterion of 'correct speech'. Ernst Curtius has traced the term back to the Latin grammarian Aulus Gellius (fl. *c*.123–*c*.165), who referred problems of grammar to the arbitration of prominent writers. 'The thing to do is to follow the usage of a model author: "e cohorte illa dumtaxat antiquiore vel oratorum aliquis vel poetarum, id est classicus adsiduusque aliquis scriptor, non proletarius": "some one of the orators or poets, who at least belongs to the older band, that is, a first-class and tax-paying author, not a proletarian".'[59] The ranking of authors is based on social and military hierarchies: first-rank authors, like first-class, tax-paying citizens, are called *classici*.

These origins of the concept of the classical resurface in Burke's critique of Auckland. Though one suspects that he values the style of the royal declaration over that of Auckland's pamphlet primarily because the views expressed by the king coincide more closely with his own, he justifies his opinion by reference to the Gellian model of the classic. This is evident, first, in his dismissal of Auckland as a literary 'proletarian' in comparison to his royal superior: 'but in comes a gentleman in the fag end of October [who] . . . does not hesitate in Diameter to contradict this wise and just Royal declaration. . . . When I

---

[59] Ernst Robert Curtius, *European Literature and the Latin Middle Ages*, trans. Willard R. Trask (London, 1953), 249–50.

hear the Master and reason on one side, and the Servant and his single and unsupported assertion on the other, my part is taken' (ix. 55). The effect of Burke's argument is to assert (rather than to justify) his valuation of the royal declaration by situating it in terms of the hierarchical categories of high/low, master/servant, and reason/unsupported assertion.

Burke's dismissal of Auckland echoes his well-known denunciation of the writings of Rousseau in *A Letter to a Member of the National Assembly*, which similarly classes the Genevan philosopher as a lowly literary modern, against whose baneful influence only the lofty writings of the ancients can offer an adequate specific: 'We continue, as in the last two ages, to read more generally, than I believe is now done on the continent, the authors of sound antiquity. These occupy our minds. They give us another taste and turn; and will not suffer us to be more than transiently amused with [Rousseau's] paradoxical morality' (viii. 318). Burke's quarrel is with Rousseau's political and moral philosophy, but, once again, his dismissal of the writer's works takes the form of literary criticism: 'Rousseau, a writer of great force and vivacity, is totally destitute of taste in any sense of the word. . . . Amongst his irregularities, it must be reckoned, that he is sometimes moral, and moral in a very sublime strain. But the *general spirit and tendency* of his work is mischievous; and the more mischievous for this mixture: For, perfect depravity of sentiment is not reconcilable with eloquence' (viii. 316–18). Equally significant is his appeal to historical precedent in his reference to the intellectual habits of English readers of 'the last two ages'. The span of two generations carries him back to the time of Swift and Pope, for whom the debate over the relative merits of ancient and modern learning still dominated the intellectual landscape. That debate helped shape the modern conception both of the literary canon and of the 'aesthetic' as the defining characteristic of those texts that belong to the canon.[60] Auckland and Rousseau are, in Burke's view, writers without taste; their works lack the requisite aesthetic character that marks canonical writing, and in their novelty they deliberately turn their backs on the forms of ancient wisdom.

---

[60] D. L. Patey, 'The Eighteenth Century Invents the Canon', *Modern Language Studies*, 18 (1988), 20.

In assessing the soundness of political discourse in terms of the opposition between ancients and moderns, Burke appropriates one of the most important elements in the intellectual superstructure of Scriblerian satire. Pope's dunces, to say nothing of the moderns in Swift's *Battle of the Books*, are deficient in taste and in any historical sense of the tradition to which they belong. That deficiency is linked to their lack of education, which, in turn, is a function of their lowly social status. But the real threat, as Burke suggests in his censure of Rousseau, appears to be the overturning of traditional social hierarchies: like Pope, Burke recognizes a causal link between cultural and social revolution. Thus, the French National Assembly's canonization of Rousseau as a patron saint of the Revolution is, in Burke's eyes, a carefully calculated step in their campaign to abolish social distinctions:

> The rulers in the National Assembly are in good hopes that the females of the first families in France may become an easy prey to dancing-masters, fidlers, pattern-drawers, friseurs, and valets de chambre, and other active citizens of that description, who having the entry into your houses, and being half-domesticated by their situation, may be blended with you by regular and irregular relations. . . . I am certain that the writings of Rousseau lead directly to this kind of shameful evil.
>
> (viii. 317)

The indiscriminate mingling Burke imagines here, a compound of social and sexual promiscuity, vividly enacts the obliteration of difference that Pope identifies as the ultimate threat to England's cultural distinctiveness—indeed, to the possibility of culture itself.

Besides his instinctive categorization of Auckland in a literary hierarchy based on social rank, Burke justifies his preference for the royal declaration by comparing it to the acknowledged 'first-class' authors of his time. He first tests the declaration by the standard of the great rhetoricians of antiquity, and he judges the comparison a favourable one. Not only does it exhibit all the prescribed features of a classical rhetorical performance (Burke pronounces it 'the most eloquent and highly finished in the style, the most judicious in the choice of topicks, the most orderly in the arrangement . . . of any state-paper that has ever yet appeared' (ix. 220)), but it invites comparison with the productions of the greatest rhetoricians in history, such as

Cicero and Pericles, ' "the only orator that left stings in the minds of his hearers" ' (ix. 220).

It is to be expected that Burke would invoke the canonical masters of political discourse; rather more surprising are his far more insistent references to Virgil, Shakespeare, and Milton as the ultimate standard for judging political utterances. One of the most sustained examples of this kind of literary/political analysis is to be found in the third of the *Letters on a Regicide Peace*, in which Burke scrutinizes a more recent government declaration (dated 27 December 1796) outlining the latest stages in the relations between Britain and France, and proposing a course of action for the future. He is impressed by the government's summary of its tortuous efforts to open a diplomatic dialogue with France, and he praises the ministerial speech commenting on the declaration as a 'most eloquent and finished performance' which 'does credit to our official style' (ix. 301). He regards the minister's speech, indeed, as a tightly woven verbal tapestry of unparalleled quality:

> This Speech may stand for a model. Never, for the triumphal decoration of any theatre, not for the decoration of those of Athens and Rome . . . has there been sent any historick tissue, so truly drawn, so closely and so finely wrought, or in which the forms are brought out in the rich purple of such glowing and blushing colours. It puts me in mind of the piece of tapestry, with which Virgil proposed to adorn the theatre he was to erect to Augustus, upon the banks of the Mincio, who now hides his head in his reeds, and leads his slow and melancholy windings through banks wasted by the barbarians of Gaul. (ix. 302)

Here Burke invokes the ultimate cultural standard by which he deems political discourse must be judged: not the oratory of antiquity, but the discourse of imperial praise perfected by Virgil in the *Georgics* and the *Aeneid*.

Burke's compliment on the Virgilian splendour of the latest political declarations is double-edged, for he finds the eloquence and forthrightness with which the declaration details 'the indignities offered by the Directory of Regicide' to British diplomatic initiatives (ix. 301) strangely at odds with the unwillingness of the declaration's authors to propose forthright and courageous action. Indeed, the opulent verbal tapestry they have created is perhaps a little too similar to Virgil's. In the third

Book of the *Georgics*, the poet imagines a pageant in honour of Augustus Caesar's imperial exploits, in which, as Burke describes it,

> the figures of the conquered nations in his [Virgil's] tapestry are made to play their part, and are confounded in the machine:
>
> —utque
> Purpurea intexti tollant aulæa Britanni;
>
> Or, as Dryden translates it somewhat paraphrastically, but not less in the spirit of the Prophet than of the Poet,
>
> > Where the proud theatres disclose the scene,
> > Which, interwoven, Britons seem to raise,
> > And show the triumph which their shame displays.
> > (ix. 302)

The writers of the declaration similarly arraign themselves by their own eloquence: in documenting so memorably France's contemptuous treatment of Britain's repeated overtures of peace, they expose the inadequacy and pusillanimity of British policy towards France, ironically highlighting the 'triumph which their shame displays'.

What the British ministry needs, Burke appears to suggest, is a more able scriptwriter. They have chosen the right mode for their narrative—the heroic—but they are unable to compose an appropriately stirring conclusion for their epic. So Burke proposes to supply it for them, urging the prime minister to rise to the glory of the perilous occasion with which he is confronted:

> If he found his situation full of danger . . . he must feel that it is also full of glory; and that he is placed on a stage, than which no Muse of fire that had ascended the highest heaven of invention, could imagine any thing more awful and august. It was hoped, that in this swelling scene, in which he moved with some of the first Potentates of Europe for his fellow actors . . . like Ulysses, in the unravelling point of the epic story, he would have thrown off his patience and his rags together; and, stripped of unworthy disguises, he would have stood forth in the form, and in the attitude of an hero. On that day, it was thought he would have assumed the port of Mars; that he would bid to be brought forth from their hideous kennel . . . those impatient dogs of war, whose fierce regards affright even the Minister of Vengeance that feeds them.
> (ix. 311–12)

Burke's imagination conflates Homer's Ulysses with Shakespeare's Prince Hal—both characters at the point in their respective epic stories when mean disguises are thrown off to reveal to the world the decisive hero in his true colours. These allusions to the *Odyssey* and *Henry V* have a particular aptness to the circumstances as Burke sees them, especially the reference to Shakespeare, which recalls a more glorious chapter in English history when England's honour was fairly acquitted in the face of the French challenge at Agincourt. But the poets he invokes as models of political writing—Homer, Virgil, Shakespeare (at his most epic pitch), and Milton—are striking to the modern reader precisely because they represent the core of what the Anglo-American world has come to regard as the literary canon.

That Burke is explicitly invoking a historically constructed, but seemingly timeless, classical canon in his evaluation of the declaration is underscored by a comparison of its eloquence to the visual impact of a prized ancient sculpture, the Apollo Belvedere, a statue representing for the eighteenth century the apex of classical values:

Never was there a jar or discord, between genuine sentiment and sound policy. Never, no, never, did Nature say one thing and Wisdom say another. Nor are sentiments of elevation in themselves turgid and unnatural. Nature is never more truly herself, than in her grandest forms. The Apollo of Belvedere (if the universal robber has yet left him at Belvedere) is as much in Nature, as any figure from the pencil of Rembrandt, or any clown in the rustic revels of Teniers.   (ix. 313)

Like Winckelmann and later Goethe, Burke singles out this production as the embodiment of the most elevated and permanent aesthetic qualities that human art can achieve—in short, the epitome of sublime art. Yet the contrary judgement of the twentieth-century art historian Kenneth Clark ('in no other famous work of art are idea and execution more distressingly divorced') impels us to recognize just how thoroughly historicized Burke's sense of the classical canon is. He is powerfully committed, nevertheless, to the belief that the criterion of sublimity, by which the canon of classic art is defined, is an enduring attribute of Nature 'in her grandest forms' and a quality to which all persons, at all times and in all places, are psychologically fitted to respond. He is extending to the field of literary and art criticism his political principle, amounting to an axiom, that time-honoured methods and institutions, 'the general bank and capital of nations, and of ages' (viii. 138), are always to be favoured over untried, new-fashioned forms.

The unselfconscious ease with which Burke calls upon these aesthetic, and especially literary, touchstones in his *Letters on a Regicide Peace* can be explained in a number of ways. First, as I have noted, the lines of demarcation between imaginative literature and other modes of writing had not as yet been firmly drawn: Burke is therefore exercising a natural intellectual reflex in measuring the political discourse of his time by the greatest productions of literary art known to him. Moreover, eighteenth-century readers habitually read the texts of the great *epic* poets as political documents. Charles Gildon makes the point succinctly: 'the lessons taught by the epic poem are political, and direct the conduct of states and kingdoms'.[61] From Hobbes onwards, critics regarded the portrayal of epic heroism as a commentary on political leadership and statesmanship. John Newbery is typical in arguing that 'the *Odyssey* was written ... for the instruction of each particular [Greek] state separately considered ... and contains not only the duty of the prince and of the people, but the ill consequences which naturally ensue from a neglect of that duty'.[62] In his study of the eighteenth-century epic, Peter Hägin points out that both practitioners and theorists of epic in the period emphasized the function of the hero as a commander-in-chief, rather than as a warrior: 'As a character symbolizing the beliefs and endeavours of a whole people or culture, he had also to concern himself with the government of a state in its religious, political and cultural aspects.'[63]

Burke is the latest in a long line of readers to ponder the social

---

[61] Charles Gildon, *The Laws of Poetry* (London, 1721), 257
[62] John Newbery, *The Art of Poetry on a New Plan illustrated with a great Variety of Examples from the best English Poets* (London, 1762), ii. 233. Similarly, in a comment entitled, 'On Epic Poetry', a contributor to *The Gentleman's Magazine*, 5 (1735), 357, speculates that if Homer had lived in the time of Alexander the Great, his epic would have celebrated '*The irresistible Influence of Power in a wise and a brave Man's single Hand; and what benefits accrue to good Subjects, by Courage and Loyalty*'.
[63] Peter Hägin, *The Epic Hero and the Decline of Heroic Poetry: A Study of the Neoclassical English Epic with Special Reference to Milton's 'Paradise Lost'*, Cooper Monographs on English and American Language and Literature, 8 (Berne, 1964), 39.

and political uses of heroism. His attempt to rouse Pitt to epic heroism invokes the contemporary critical view of the epic genre just outlined. By accepting his destiny as defender of the traditional political, religious, and cultural order of Europe, the minister would command a rare historical moment in which a literary conception would literally be lifted off the printed page and brought to life. Here, as so often in his political polemics, Burke uses narrative structures as a means of imaginatively ordering, both for himself and his readers, an otherwise unassimilable welter of events, thereby cutting dramatically to the heart of the political issue that needs to be decided. But his choice of epic also relies on the familiar generic dynamic of the mock-heroic, which typically measures the gap between the inherited cultural values that the form emulates and their imperfect, parodic realization in the present day. By the time Pope came to write *The Dunciad* he perceived this gap in his own time to have become so great that its only hero could be the anti-hero Colley Cibber and its only epic, an anti-epic. English culture had become too degenerate and corrupt to merit the greatest literary legacy of antiquity. Burke's characterization of Pitt as a latter-day Henry V throws out a similar challenge to his contemporary: he dares Pitt to live up to the achievements of the society he professes to defend, and he taunts him with the ignoble prospect that, like Dryden in Swift's *Battle of the Books*, whose helmet in his skirmish with Virgil is 'nine times too large for the head', Pitt may prove pathetically unequal to the role he has been called upon to play.

Indeed, the course of negotiations have hitherto been burlesque rather than heroic, a farce so badly performed that Britain has been 'shamefully hissed off [the] stage' (ix. 299). The performance has wavered between slapstick and pathos:

The Regicides were more fatigued with giving blows than the callous cheek of British Diplomacy was hurt in receiving them. They had no way left for getting rid of this mendicant perseverance, but by sending for the Beadle, and forcibly driving our Embassy 'of shreds and patches,' with all it's mumping cant, from the inhospitable door of Cannibal Castle—

> Where the gaunt mastiff, growling at the gate,
> Affrights the beggar whom he longs to eat.

(ix. 301)

Burke imagines a kind of diplomatic Punch-and-Judy show with ambassadors dressed in a harlequin motley of 'shreds and patches', a costume that represented for Pope and his fellow Scriblerians the nadir of popular culture. The shreds and patches also signify *lèse-majesté* and illegitimate authority, for they are the dress that Hamlet associates with his usurping, regicide uncle, King Claudius (*Hamlet* III. iv. 102). But the scene, as is so often the case in Burke's representations of the French Revolution, modulates from burlesque to a tragicomic note, with the concluding reference to Pope's portrait of the miserly and socially irresponsible Cotta in the *Epistle to Bathurst*.[64]

The mock-heroic disparity between the Roman dignity that befits the representatives of British power and the ludicrous, indecorous scenes in which they find themselves participating is represented even more forcefully in an earlier scene of Burke's lengthy drama of 'the diplomacy of humiliation' (ix. 201). He recounts the government's intervention in the case of several French emigrés who had been accidentally thrown by a storm upon a French shore:

> Here was an opportunity . . . to open some sort of conversation, which . . . might lead to something like an accommodation. What was the event? A strange uncouth thing, a theatrical figure of the opera, his head shaded with three-coloured plumes, his body fantastically habited, strutted from the back scenes, and after a short speech, in the mock-heroic falsetto of stupid tragedy, delivered the gentleman who came to make the representation into the custody of a guard . . . and then ordered him to be sent from Paris in two hours. (ix. 202)

Here we find ourselves back in the world of masquerade, but equally in the world of popular entertainments and low art, which, in the discourse of Scriblerian satire, progressively threaten to invade and corrupt the sacred precincts of traditional, classic culture. High on the list of subversive entertainments is opera, a form whose foreign provenance, artifice, spectacle, incomprehensible language, and unnatural performers (castrati) make it an apt metaphor for the utter confusion of sound and sense in art, and the divorce of signifier and signified.

---

[64] Burke quotes ll. 197–8 of *Epistle to Bathurst*. In the posthumous edition of Pope's poetry edited by William Warburton (and in subsequent editions drawing on Warburton's work), this couplet appears as ll. 195–6.

In February 1723 John Gay complained in a letter to Swift that opera had displaced epic in the hierarchy of art: 'Theres nobody allow'd to say I sing but an Eunuch or an Italian Woman. . . . People have now forgot Homer, and Virgil & Caesar, or at least they have lost their ranks, for in London and Westminster in all polite conversation's Senesino is daily voted to be the greatest man that ever liv'd.'[65] Not only does opera displace the traditional exemplars of serious art, but, as a form of conspicuously foreign origin, it enacts Burke's suspicion of innovation and the influence of foreign ideas and ideology. 'Hitherto', he states, 'it seems we have put wax into our ears to shut them up against the tender, soothing strains, in the *affettuoso* of humanity, warbled from the throats of Reubel, Carnot, Tallien, and the whole chorus of Confiscators . . . Regicides, Assassins, Massacrers, and Septembrizers' (ix. 219). The operatic stars of the French government are figured as a band of latter-day Sirens, against whose seductive, destructive song the British, like Ulysses, must heroically stop their ears. A familiar opposition is played out in terms of gender, as heroic masculinity is beset by bewitching, insidiously enticing femininity. Moreover, in his dismissal of the French regime as the sponsor of an 'insolent and bloody theatre', in contrast with the 'temperate, natural majesty of a civilized court' (ix. 202), Burke reproduces the Scriblerian denigration of the court and ministry of George II (especially Walpole) as a band of side-show hucksters and demonic theatrical impresarios.

Burke does not limit himself to the example of opera in his unfavourable contrast of the high and the low, the classical and the popular. The whole range of Scriblerian targets is invoked, from street theatre, fairs, and raree shows, to the popular burlesque of the official panoply of state. Just as Pope and Swift habitually decried the debasement of the cultural marketplace in their time, with audiences demanding operas, stage spectaculars, harlequinades, and pantomimes instead of the serious dramatic genres of tragedy and comedy and with readers turning to novels and romances instead of epic, so too Burke notes with disgust the vitiation of cultural forms in revolutionary Paris. Among the political élite of France are to be found 'bombastick

---

[65] John Gay, *The Letters of John Gay*, ed. C. F. Burgess (Oxford, 1966), 43.

players, the refuse and rejected offal of strolling theatres, puffing out ill-sorted verses about virtue, mixed with the licentious and blasphemous songs, proper to the brutal and hardened course of life belonging to that sort of wretches' (ix. 247). This rhetoric of exclusion permeates the *Letters on a Regicide Peace* as much as it does *The Dunciad*; indeed, the vehemence of Burke's dismissal of these carnivalesque elements of the French Revolution testifies to their conceptual importance for him. If Mikhail Bakhtin has succeeded in reminding modern readers of the potency of 'carnival' as a symbolic order and activity, as a holiday from 'the prevailing truth of the established order ... [marking] the suspension of all hierarchical rank, privileges, norms and prohibitions', for Burke this knowledge was instinctive.[66] It may be argued, given what is at stake for him, that he takes carnival much more seriously than does Bakhtin, for he sees the pervasive carnivalesque elements of the French Revolution as signs of its success.

Peter Stallybrass and Allon White draw attention to the interpenetration of the high and the low in the literary culture of early modern and modern Europe. Taking as their starting point Bakhtin's contrast between the classical and the grotesque body, they argue that the one cannot be understood without reference to the other, that the low persistently troubles the high in European culture. For Bakhtin the classical body is defined by the image of the classical statue—Burke's Apollo Belvedere—which is finished, isolated, self-sufficient, raised upon a pedestal or plinth, in contrast with the grotesque, which is distinguished, as Stallybrass and White observe, by 'impurity (both in the sense of dirt and mixed categories), heterogeneity, masking, protuberant distension, disproportion, exorbitancy, clamour, decentred or eccentric arrangements, a focus upon gaps, orifices and symbolic filth ... physical needs and pleasures of the "lower bodily stratum", materiality and parody'.[67] Burke's writings on the French Revolution embrace this conception of the grotesque wholeheartedly; his portraits of the French revolutionaries employ this Bakhtinian palette liberally and exuberantly.

[66] M. Bakhtin, *Rabelais and his World*, trans. Helene Iswolsky (Cambridge, Mass., 1968), 10.
[67] Ibid. 24–9; Stallybrass and White, *Politics and Poetics*, 23.

Just as Gellius defines the term *classicus* by setting it in binary opposition to *proletarius* (ignoring the three intermediate social categories), so too Scriblerian satire defines its classical standard in exclusionary terms by rejecting the popular and *arriviste* culture of its time. Stallybrass and White set this satiric dynamic in the context of what Jürgen Habermas terms the emergence of a 'bourgeois public sphere' in early modern Europe: the creation of a public space, separate from court, Church, and marketplace, in which public opinion could flourish and private individuals could engage in rational discourse—in short, a space from which the grotesque, physical body has been banished as a sign of the new-found rationality, wit, and judgement of the emerging professional classes. Swift and Pope are present at a crucial moment in this realignment of discourses, as their writing, which simultaneously expresses and rejects the grotesque, persistently demonstrates:

> The Augustans laboured to translate what they were designating as grotesque (in Bakhtin's special sense) into discourse more in line with the classical: discourse which is elevated, serious, refined, tending to relate to genres of epic and tragedy, pure, homogeneous, closed, finished, proportioned, symmetrical, dignified and decorous. At the same time and just as important, they appropriated symbolic elements of the grotesque and deployed them as the focal imaginative and revivifying elements of their own discourse. This two-way transaction thus begins by creating a discursive hierarchy with itself at the top and a number of inferior realms beneath it where language is deemed to be 'grotesque': impure, vulgar, of lesser epistemological clarity, masked and muddied, irresponsibly protean, indecent and exorbitant.[68]

Pope and Swift invoke the grotesque continually in their satire but enfold it in a rhetoric of exclusion. Interestingly, the sphere of the grotesque, against which they demarcate their discourse of judgement and wit, is seen to threaten them on two sides simultaneously: not only Smithfield but also the Court (hitherto the patron of high art and learning) is contaminated by the carnivalesque, as the opening lines of *The Dunciad* testify:

> The Mighty Mother, and her Son who brings
> The Smithfield Muses to the ear of Kings,
> I sing.

---

[68] Stallybrass and White, *Politics and Poetics*, 108

The term 'Smithfield Muses' is a kind of oxymoron encapsulating the confounding of high and low that the Scriblerians professed to see on all sides. Ironically, it falls to Pope, as a *professional* author, to defend the traditional discourse and canons of classicism from the onslaught of the *déclassé* on the one side and the indifference of the privileged on the other. He labours mightily and, ultimately, unsuccessfully, to keep the high and the low separate and distinct, not least in his own poetry, which achieves its most memorable effects in the mixed, promiscuous form of satire, rather than the pure, elevated discourse of epic.

As a professional writer in his own right, Burke occupies a similarly ambiguous position *vis-à-vis* the rival political voices of his time. France, he conceives, has already irretrievably contaminated and confounded high and low: the burlesque of revolution has supplanted the 'temperate, natural majesty of a civilized court' (ix. 202). But he fears that the same hybridization of discourse is making progress in Britain; certainly, he finds ample evidence of it in Lord Auckland's pamphlet and the Duke of Bedford's speeches. Thus, he finds it necessary to advise the government on the form their public declarations should take: in this sense his insistence on a heroic stance in public pronouncements is as much a political as a rhetorical recommendation. The surest way, in his view, to guard against any irresolution in Britain's policy towards France is to promote a political discourse that will not permit the expression of revisionary sentiments. Yet Burke's own literary practice remains sharply at odds with his advocacy of an absolute purity of discourse; indeed, such transcendent purity proves an impossible ideal. His most memorable literary achievements, like those of his Augustan forebears, are brilliant, virtuoso confections of form—innovative generic mixtures created to address the new demands of a time of rapid change. Thus, even as Burke labours to expunge the grotesque, monstrous, excessive manifestations of revolution, he finds himself drawn (at least symbolically and verbally) to the self-same excesses he is committed to exorcize.

This contradiction is not a question of Burke's having to resort to violent and tortured language in order to convey the wrenching reality of the Revolution. Though he undoubtedly strains consciously for a language adequate to represent the unprecedented events on the Continent, an equally important factor contributing to the extraordinary style of the *Letters on a Regicide Peace* is the hierarchical theory of language and genre to which he is committed. The high and serious require the low and grotesque, if only as foils, as the means of defining themselves by a process of negation. And the more consciously and strenuously Burke attempts to project the low, vulgar, and burlesque onto the revolutionary 'other' in France, the more these features come to dominate his own discourse. Of course, such complaints about indecorous mixtures of language and genres were not uncommon in eighteenth-century literary criticism: Shakespeare was frequently singled out by critics in the period as a chief offender against literary propriety and decorum. But in comparison to the violent ruptures of tone, style, and form characteristic of Scriblerian satire and of Burke's anti-revolutionary writings, Shakespeare's mixtures of formal and informal language or comic and tragic modes seem unforced and natural. The sense of strain and unnaturalness arises when writers (and societies) become self-conscious about hierarchy, when the legitimacy of hierarchical order is itself called into question.

Stallybrass and White argue that the hybrid character of Scriblerian discourse results from its entanglement in the project of bourgeois self-definition and the assertion of a public sphere and role for the professional classes:

> This refined public sphere occupied the centre. That is to say, it carved out a domain between the realm of kings and the world of the alleyways and taverns, and it did so by forcing together the high and the low as contaminated equivalents, somehow in league with each other and part of a conspiracy of exchange and promiscuity in which the low was ebbing [sic] higher to flood the court and the court was sinking into the filthy ways and pastimes of the low.[69]

This analysis is at once illuminating and overly schematic. It is illuminating in its recognition of a process of literary change at work in the generic mixtures with which Pope, Swift, and their contemporaries habitually experimented—new combinations of literary features reflecting new social and cultural realities and

---

[69] Stallybrass and White, *Politics and Poetics*, 109.

the changing demands of the literary market-place. But it jumps too quickly from the complex interactions of linguistic and generic features to a single, overarching explanation for these intricate interrelations.

Indeed, when Burke deploys the same literary and linguistic resources in the *Letters*, the complexity of the relation between literary form and historical knowledge quickly becomes apparent. Though it is true that *A Letter to a Noble Lord* assumes something of the pattern outlined by Stallybrass and White, with the aristocratic dignity of the Duke of Bedford reduced to a burlesque farce ('the Dukes and Earls of Brentford' (ix. 149)), and with Burke, the professional writer and politician, asserting that same dignity, through merit, for himself and others of his class, the *Letters on a Regicide Peace*, by contrast, undertake explicitly to defend traditional hierarchy and the structure of meaning undergirded by that hierarchy. The objects of Burke's ridicule in the latter text are the upstarts who arrogate to themselves the symbols, panoply, and power of monarchy, rather than the old order itself or its actors. The representatives of aristocracy who fall victim to Burke's heavy irony do so because they have abandoned the roles that tradition has called upon them to play. A similar observation might be made about Pope and Swift, whose satires on royalty and nobility focus persistently on delinquent individuals, rather than the political and social structures these persons represent.

Burke goes so far as to disparage his own contribution to the ongoing political debate, placing himself among the tribe of hacks who are so often the object of Scriblerian mockery. When he attacks the newspapers for the irresponsible manner in which they reported the food shortages of 1796, he emphasizes the writers' misrepresentations of the pronouncements of Members of Parliament on the subject, their adoption of 'language, so ill suited to the persons to whom it has been attributed, and so unbecoming the place in which it is said to have been uttered', and he revealingly places himself in their ranks: 'I presume [this misrepresentation] is only to be ascribed to the intolerable licence with which the newspapers break not only the rules of decorum in real life, but even the dramatick decorum, when they personate great men, and, like bad poets, make the heroes of the piece talk more like us Grub-street scribblers, than in a style consonant to persons of gravity and importance in the State' (ix. 354). Elsewhere, Burke places his own writing (in comparison with the royal declaration of 1793) on the same low level as the scribblings of Lord Auckland, whose lucubrations he otherwise excoriates: 'That declaration of our Sovereign . . . is in a style, which neither the pen of the writer of October, nor such a poor crow-quill as mine can ever hope to equal' (ix. 54). He strikes a note of disingenuousness here, for in other contexts he shows no hesitation to vindicate his right and indeed his worthiness to deem himself equal to his 'betters' and to address whatever political issue he chooses. But in the *Letters on a Regicide Peace*, his attention is focused outwards rather than inwards: his overriding theme is the fate of Europe itself, not self-apology, as in *A Letter to a Noble Lord*. Once again, a parallel may be drawn with the contrasting focus of Pope's *An Epistle to Dr. Arbuthnot* and *The Dunciad*, the latter poem achieving a magisterial breadth of cultural vision, if not impersonality, that is absent from Pope's *apologia pro vita sua*.

Within this larger context, Burke's ritual self-abasement serves primarily an ideological function. He in no way believes himself to be a Grub-Street hack or literary dunce, but he allows this self-characterization to stand because his concern at this point is to uphold 'the rules of decorum', to maintain the integrity of the due degrees of order and position in his society. Or, to put it another way, he tactically conceals any brief he might have for himself and his class in order to press a more important principle, namely, the preservation of the structure by which order and meaning exists in his society. His argument is that the political debate to which he is contributing can have meaning only within the framework of differentiation that distinguishes him as a professional 'scribbler' from the 'great' men who employ him. This is perhaps the most important end that his elaborate use of the discourse of Scriblerian satire is meant to serve: his satirical characterizations, however heavy-handed and overwrought they may at times appear to be, reassign his political enemies to the roles and places their revolutionary ideology seeks to overthrow.

In the final analysis, Burke's use of Scriblerian discourse abandons entirely the strategies of satiric laughter upon which that discourse so often relies, transposing its parodic, derisive key into one that is altogether more sinister and demonic, as in the following passage:

> Whilst courts of justice were thrust out by revolutionary tribunals, and silent churches were only the funeral monuments of departed religion, there were no fewer than nineteen or twenty theatres, great and small, most of them kept open at the publick expence, and all of them crowded every night. Among the gaunt, hagard forms of famine and nakedness, amidst the yells of murder, the tears of affliction, and the cries of despair, the song, the dance, the mimick scene, the buffoon laughter, went on as regularly as in the gay hour of festive peace. I have it from good authority, that under the scaffold of judicial murder, and the gaping planks that poured down blood on the spectators, the space was hired out for a shew of dancing dogs. (ix. 246–7)

Here the violation of decorum, the promiscuous mixing of forms, is seen as a descent into unthinkable depths of savagery and depravity. The great public dramas of state—courts of justice, religious ritual, and criminal punishment—have been not only trivialized, but corrupted beyond imagination. In a typically eighteenth-century conflation of taste and morality, the collapse of the one is seen to go hand in hand with the breakdown of the other. At the end of the twentieth century, with the appalling benefit of hindsight, it is impossible not to see in the shadow of Burke's bloody scaffold the state-sponsored terror of our time, whose legacy defeats satiric laughter and can be confronted only by prophetic indignation.

II

Burke uses satirical discourse, then, as a means of renovating language and meaning, of repairing, as Steven Blakemore puts it, 'the radical split between word and thing, a split in which language no longer brings the real world into presence'. Blakemore argues that Burke viewed the French Revolution, like history generally, as a 'linguistic event', a linguistic struggle entailing, to be sure, momentous material consequences: 'Burke's great insight was that history, tradition, and reality are essentially linguistic and that the recovery of their presence resides in the recovery of their meaning through the inherited documents of the "written past," recreated and reaffirmed in present and future documents. From this follows his efforts to conserve the "real" authority and meaning of words.'[70] Blakemore traces these efforts in Burke's defence of the languages of patriarchy, origins, and constitutional traditions, but this reaffirmation of traditional political languages is, as we have seen, only part of the much larger process of linguistic and cultural recuperation embodied in the Scriblerian satirical project. Burke relies not only on inherited legal and political texts, but also on the long heritage of literary texts enshrined in the classical canon, which he then transforms into crucial political documents by his manner of reading and imitating them.

This preoccupation with the French Revolution as 'linguistic event' extends beyond the revalidation of traditional texts to a deep concern about the nature and use of language itself, and about the epistemological implications that flow from the linguistic revolution allegedly underway in France. In *The Dunciad* Pope adumbrates a similar theme with his alarm at the dunces' eagerness to separate words from thoughts or from their proper objects: '"Since|Man|from|beast by Words is known, | Words are Man's province, Words 'we|teach' alone"' (IV. 149–50). This debasement of language, the divorce of signifier and signified, is, for Pope, a development fraught with political significance, as his note to Book IV. 175 underscores:[71]

> The matter under debate is how to confine men to Words for life. The instructors of youth shew how well they do their parts; but complain that when men come into the world they are apt to forget their Learning, and turn themselves to useful Knowledge. ... And this the Goddess assures them will need a more extensive Tyranny than that of Grammar schools. She therefore points out to them the remedy, in her wishes for *arbitrary Power*; whose interest it being to keep men from the study of *things*, will encourage the propagation of *words* and *sounds*; and to make all sure, she wishes for another *Pedant Monarch*. ... Nothing can be juster than the observation here insinuated, that no branch of Learning thrives well under Arbitrary government but *Verbal*.

The Goddess Dulness is, in a sense, the lineal ancestor of the creators of Newspeak in George Orwell's *1984*. As David Nokes points out,

---

[70] Blakemore, *Burke and the Fall of Language*, 93.
[71] See *Twickenham Edition*, v. 358.

a significant characteristic of revolutionary prose ... has been its preoccupation with forging a new purified vocabulary and grammar, purged of the accumulated assumptions inherent in the language of a corrupt society. One of the revolutionary's first targets must always be language itself, cutting off at source the currency of established ideas and replacing them with his own ideal notions. The satirist, on the other hand, trades and revels in the rich accumulations of imaginative resources stored in the language of the past to confront the utopian schemes of the Aeolists, or the Newspeak of Oceania.[72]

The connection between political tyranny and linguistic arbitrariness is no less explicit for Burke, who notes in his *Preface to the Address of M. Brissot to His Constituents* that just as the Revolution has demanded a new canon of authors (Voltaire and Rousseau, instead of 'the authors of sound antiquity'), so too it requires a revolution in language. Thus, he notes, Brissot has deliberately abandoned the standard set by the French Academy: 'He writes with great force and vivacity; but the language, like every thing else in his country, has undergone a revolution' (viii. 521). Ironically, Burke's theme finds confirmation in the very pamphlet of Lord Auckland that he sets out to discredit in the *Letters*. Auckland lists numerous instances of the neologisms the Revolution has spawned: 'For example—"Nationaliser, fayettiser, féderaliser, démocratiser, démoraliser, municipaliser, lanterner, volcaniser, septembriser, guillotiner, décatholiser, fraterniser, désocialiser, desorganiser, férociser, sansculottiser, panthéoniser:—et les substantifs; Centralité, Civisme, Sansculottisme, Terrorisme, Républicanisme, Lezenation, Burocratie, Démonétisation, Baignade, Noyade, Fusillade, Rolandiste, Démocrate, Désorganisateur, Robespierriste, Ultra-révolutionaire, Terroriste, Septembriseur, Sansculottiste, &c. &c. &c." '[73]

Blakemore has documented extensively the French revolutionaries' own self-consciousness about the relation between language and ideology and of their revolution as a revolution in language—questions that need not be elaborated here. Two

---

[72] David Nokes, *Raillery and Rage: A Study of Eighteenth Century Satire* (Brighton, 1987), 19.
[73] *Some Remarks on the Apparent Circumstances of the War in the Fourth Week of October 1795* (London, 1795), 29.

points are worth emphasizing in the present context, however, the first being the extent to which Burke's own language is profoundly reshaped in response to the French Revolution. His defence of the traditional canon and genres of writing ironically involves him in significant generic innovation; the same effect can be observed in his rhetorical inventiveness and linguistic usage. Gerald Chapman has remarked on the numerous coinages and bizarre usages sprinkled through the prose of Burke's last years:

> It's as though he strained against the limits of language itself, as if he had abandoned all care for propriety in a desperate effort to shock his readers, or, more accurately perhaps, to shock his distraught vision into words—any words—as if words savage and strange enough might charm a savage, strange world into submission. *Genethliacon, dephlegmated, lixiviated, aulnager, exceptions* [sic], *quadrimanous, psephismata, delation, provocatives of cantharides, stum, dulcify, boulimia, diachylon, compurgation, founderous, turbinating*: the language of his last years is thick with odd, hard diction (many words, according to the *New English Dictionary*, appear in Burke's late writings for the first time in English).[74]

If, as Pope advises in *An Essay on Criticism*, propriety in diction implies a respect for traditional usage ('Be not the *first* by whom the *New* are try'd | Nor yet the *last* to lay the *Old* aside'), then Burke offends against taste and tradition as surely as any dunce or revolutionary polemicist. Once again, a central paradox of his political and historical vision reveals itself here: he upends tradition in the course of defending it, or at least redefines it ideologically (and radically) to serve the ends of counter-revolution.

The second point to be observed is the extent to which the debate about language is also a debate about education (and, ultimately, about ideology). Blakemore notes that the French Revolution marks the culmination of a long historical process in which Latin was displaced by the vernacular tongues of Europe as the language of education and the educated. Not unexpectedly, Burke champions the traditional emphasis of classical education on Latin and Greek, a position that places him squarely at odds with such educational theorists of the

---

[74] Chapman, *Edmund Burke*, 236.

Revolution as the Marquis de Condorcet. In his *Report on Education* (1792), the latter advocated a system of universal education with a practical, technical emphasis. In such a scheme Latin had no place, both because the effort of learning it was burdensome and of little utility (since it no longer was the 'universal language of scholars'), and because the knowledge contained in the classics was erroneous: 'In education we seek to make truths known, and these books are full of errors. We seek to train the mind, and these books may lead it astray. We are so far removed from the ancients, we are so far ahead of them on the road to truth, that we must have well-fortified minds if these precious relics are to enrich them without corrupting them.'[75]

The opposition between Condorcet and Burke is irreconcilable. The debate between them turns not only on the question of what constitutes useful and valuable knowledge, but also on the ideological issue of how education is meant to serve society. Burke's ideal of classical education is focused on the formation of an élite, a corps of gentlemen whose studies are meant to furnish them with a comprehensive, elevated, and disinterested view of nature and society, free of the narrow, biased perspective of the professional or specialist. This ideal animates, as we have seen, his repeated use of the prospect survey in his writings and speeches. But the practical effect of this classical education was, as Condorcet perceived, to erect barriers between classes (and sexes). Boys of privilege were taught Latin and Greek, the keys to social and political preferment; their servants and sisters were not.

This clash of views, underscored by Condorcet's dismissal of the longstanding debate on the merits of ancient versus modern learning (the issue for him has been overwhelmingly decided in favour of the latter), carries to its final conclusion the passionate debate over cultural values which animates so much of Scriblerian satire. But, as with the other features of the Scriblerian project adopted by Burke, the crucible of revolution has clarified and radicalized the terms of the debate. In the concluding book of *The Dunciad*, Pope depicts the pedantry of

---

[75] 'Report on the General Organization of Education' (20–1 April 1792), in John Hall Stewart (eds.), *A Documentary Survey of the French Revolution* (New York, 1951), 354.

contemporary education, exemplified in the brutal methods of Busby and Bentley, and excoriates the influence of the Grand Tour on the young gentleman, who returns to England having,

> saunter'd Europe round,
> And gather'd ev'ry Vice on Christian ground
> . . . .
> Dropt the dull lumber of the Latin store,
> Spoil'd his own language, and acquir'd no more;
> All Classic learning lost on Classic ground;
> And last turn'd *Air,* the Echo of a Sound.
> (IV. 311–12, 319–22)

Burke shrewdly adapts Pope's scathing portrait of the oblivious English youth corrupted by the allurements of the decadent Continent to the circumstances of the 1790s. Just as Pope's modern Aeneas explores the stews, fairs, and operas of Europe, so too the youth of revolutionary France are now to be tempted with every conceivable 'invention of seduction', from opera-houses and play-houses to brothels and casinos. In this manner, 'whilst they corrupt young minds through pleasure, they form them to crimes' (ix. 114). Not only is 'All Classic learning lost on Classic ground', but 'All elegance of mind and manners is banished' (ix. 114).

Burke questions the value of a Grand Tour conducted on this basis: 'Is it for this our youth of both sexes are to form themselves by travel? Is it for this that with expence and pains we form their lisping infant accents to the language of France?' (ix. 114). In Pope's portrayal the Grand Tour provides an easy occasion for corruption: the fault lies not with the conception of the Tour itself, but with the laxity and complaisance of parents and tutors. The 'lac'd Governor from France' accepts full responsibility for the dissolute character of his youthful charge ('Led by my hand, he saunter'd Europe round'): as Pope's notes make clear, the Governor himself participates enthusiastically in the sordid life to which he introduces his pupil (*Dunciad* IV. 272 n.). The focus, so characteristic of Pope and Swift, is squarely on the offender, who bears the responsibility for perverting an otherwise unexceptionable institution. The emphasis in *Letters on a Regicide Peace* is different. For Burke the Grand Tour must be abandoned because an entire society has mutated into an object without precedent in the annals of history. The French, for so long the cultural leaders of Europe, have become 'the enemies of all arts, all sciences, all civilization, and all commerce' (ix. 323). The corruption that Burke's satire seeks to expose is systemic and seemingly irreversible, like a biological mutation, rather than the sum of individual malfeasance.

A further sense of the way in which Burke radicalizes the satiric stance of his Scriblerian predecessors emerges from his adaptation of their favourite satiric butts, the projector and the virtuoso (such as Fossile in *Three Hours after Marriage* or the archetypal Martinus Scriblerus, whose mindless pursuit of arcane knowledge and worship of useless objects make them the personification of that central Scriblerian preoccupation, the abuse of knowledge and learning. In Pope and Swift, these virtuosi and speculative reasoners are objects of fun, like the antique coin collector, the florist, and the entomologist in *The Dunciad* IV or the mad scientists of the Grand Academy of Lagado in *Gulliver's Travels*. The speculative reasoners in Burke's pages, however, are an altogether more sinister lot. One need only compare the preposterous experimenters that people Swift's fanciful Academy with the 'grave, demure insidious, spring-nailed, velvet-pawed, green-eyed philosophers' of the French Revolution to detect a decisive shift in kind (and not simply tone) in the use Burke makes of the Scriblerian mode.

In *A Letter to a Noble Lord* he imagines the designs that the French projectors have on the Duke of Bedford's extensive estates:

he is a glorious subject for their experimental philosophy. He affords matter for an extensive analysis, in all the branches of their science, geometrical, physical, civil and political. . . . The geometricians, and the chymists bring, the one from the dry bones of their diagrams, and the other from the soot of their furnaces, dispositions that make them worse than indifferent about those feelings and habitudes, which are the supports of the moral world. . . . These philosophers, consider men in their experiments, no more than they do mice in an air pump, or in a recipient of mephitick gas. (ix. 176–7)

One source of the difference in Burke's characterization is the altered balance in the relative prestige of ancient and modern learning by the end of the eighteenth century, together with the gathering momentum of the idea of progress. In Swift's time the prestige of humanism and the renaissance revival of classical learning remained strong, though it was losing ground, but by the end of the century an observer such as Condorcet could declare categorically that modern thinkers had eclipsed the ancients. Thus, whereas Swift could still dismiss the projectors of his day as mad, deluded, and comical fools, Burke finds the speculative reasoners of the French Revolution far more formidable, both in their numbers and their influence. Their zeal is fuelled by the conviction that progress is possible and historical change inevitable: a revolution is no longer a return to the point of origin (to classical ground, as Burke would have preferred) but a linear trajectory into an unknown future. Accordingly, his satiric excoriation of them takes on an edge of urgency, desperation, and even hysteria: the heat of his prose is turned up to a fevered pitch.

Burke proceeds, like Swift, with a detailed account of the experiments that the 'Grand Academy' of France will perform on the Duke's estates. His Grace's lands are an open temptation to *agrarian* experiment', that is, to political speculation: 'There is scope for seven philosophers to proceed in their analytical experiments, upon Harington's seven different forms of republicks, in the acres of this one Duke' (ix. 177). The choice of James Harrington as the type of the political speculator is significant, for Harrington regarded himself as a pioneering political scientist, like the pioneering natural philosophers of his generation. Indeed, he consciously modelled his intellectual enterprise upon the career of the famous anatomist William Harvey, arguing that he was introducing a scientific methodology into the study of politics as surely as Harvey had revolutionized the science of anatomy.[76] For Burke, Harrington's credentials as a dangerous projector or abstract reasoner were confirmed by the enthusiasm with which the constitutional theorists of the French Revolution, especially the Abbé Sieyès, embraced his ideas. Like Harrington, Sieyès was hailed by his contemporaries

---

[76] See Felix Raab, *The English Face of Machiavelli: A Changing Interpretation 1500–1700* (London, 1964), 198–201; and Charles Blitzer, introduction to *The Political Writings of James Harrington: Representative Selections* (New York, 1955), pp. xxvi–xxx.

as a pioneering scientist in politics, a 'political Newton'.[77] In equating Harrington and Sieyès, Burke reproduces the Swiftian satiric typology linking projectors and other moderns with Puritan zealots of the English Revolution and their dissenting progeny. The Abbé, who has 'whole nests of pigeon-holes full of constitutions ready made, ticketed, sorted, and numbered' (ix. 177), combines the worst characteristics of Swift's intellectual and religious enthusiasts and Pope's dunces. Like a hill of ants, 'the Seieyes [sic], and the rest of the analytical legislators, and constitution-vendors, are . . . busy in their trade of decomposing organization, in forming his Grace's vassals into primary assemblies, national guards, first, second, and third requisitioners, committees of research, conductors of the travelling guillotine, judges of revolutionary tribunals, legislative hangmen, supervisors of domiciliary visitation, exactors of forced loans, and assessors of the maximum' (ix. 179).

These links are further insisted on when Burke moves from the 'School of political Projectors' (to borrow Swift's phrase) to the scientific wing of the revolutionary Academy. Here he imagines the experiments that the chemists of the Revolution, 'the Morveaux and Priestleys', might perform upon the Duke's estates. Their aim is to transform the mortar of Bedford's buildings into gunpowder to further the purposes of the Revolution:

They have calculated what quantity of matter convertible into nitre is to be found in Bedford House, in Woburn Abbey, and in what his Grace and his trustees have still suffered to stand of that foolish royalist Inigo Jones, in Covent Garden. Churches, play-houses, coffee-houses, all alike are destined to be mingled, and equalized, and blended into one common rubbish; and, well sifted, and lixiviated, to chrystalize into true, democratick explosive insurrectionary nitre. Their Academy del *Cimento* (per antiphrasin) with Morveau and Hassenfrats at it's head, have computed that the brave Sans-culottes may make war on all the aristocracy of Europe for a twelvemonth, out of the rubbish of the Duke of Bedford's buildings. (ix. 178–9)

Like Pope's busy dunces, the chemists obliterate all landmarks of cultural significance, including the architectural masterpieces

---

[77] Hugh F. R. Smith, *Harrington and His* Oceana: *A Study of a 17th Century Utopia and Its Influence in America* (Cambridge, 1914), 205.

of Inigo Jones, whose most celebrated building, the Whitehall Banqueting House (where Charles I was executed), stands as a great cultural monument to the classical values the French Revolution placed under siege. The implied equation in this passage, which fuses the mingled literary and political discourses of the *Letters*, insists on an analogy between political and cultural inheritance: hereditary monarchy, symbolizing the cumulative political wisdom of generations, is the political equivalent of the classical canon, which is the product of choices made by a long succession of readers.

The fusion of literary criticism and political analysis in the *Letters on a Regicide Peace* signals the high degree of critical self-consciousness Burke brings to all his writings. What follows from this recognition is the assumption that has guided our analysis in this chapter, namely, that the violence of Burke's writing, if not necessarily always well-advised or wholly successful, is nevertheless calculated and deeply meaningful. If the tone or rhetoric of the *Letters* often seems excessive, it is an excess that finds ample precedent in the satirical discourses upon which Burke continually draws. Whatever the responses of later generations, that of his contemporaries indicates that they understood what he was doing, for they paid him the compliment of buying up no fewer than thirteen editions of the *Letters*.

6
Epilogue: The Prophetic Burke

> I wished to warn the people against the greatest of all evils . . .
>
> Burke, *Letter to William Elliot* (ix. 40)

A study that seeks to demonstrate a writer's assimilation of an inherited literary discourse risks overemphasizing the debt the writer owes his or her forebears without paying due heed to the transformative power of historical change and the new uses succeeding generations make of their cultural legacy. Thus, Burke's recourse, in Pocock's phrase, to the 'vocabulary of Queen Anne Toryism' in his attacks on the French Revolution (a political language in which Scriblerian discourse is deeply implicated) by no means entitles us to view him as a Whig in Tory clothing. The terms, uses, and relations of this language are subtly (and sometimes radically) altered by the new contexts into which he marshalls them. Indeed, no one is more aware than Burke of the alterations that existing words and concepts can undergo: he himself observed that the terms 'Whig' and 'Tory', as they were understood at the beginning of the eighteenth century, had by his time become almost meaningless. 'Is it to the Whigs', he asks, 'we are to recommend the aggrandisement of France, and the subversion of the balance of power? Is it to the Tories we are to recommend our eagerness to cement ourselves with the enemies of Royalty and Religion?' (ix. 326). The pressure of changing historical circumstances exposes the superficiality of the divisions between the old Whigs and Tories and reveals their shared underlying values, which distinguish them sharply from new political groupings that 'have their roots in the present circumstances of the times' (ix. 326). Similarly, the creative transformation that Burke visits upon the discourse of Scriblerian satire goes considerably deeper than a rearrangement of the verbal furniture: he deploys the language of Pope and Swift in such a way as to unleash the full measure of its apocalyptic potential.

Some of Pope's modern readers, chiefly Aubrey Williams, have insisted that the theological and apocalyptic dimension of Scriblerian satire has always been paramount, especially in *The Dunciad*. According to this 'deep Intent' reading, Pope systematically employs a 'principle of inversion' (inversions and parodies of Christian themes and symbols), together with a matrix of allusion to Milton's *Paradise Lost*, in order to convey imaginatively the active principle of evil that animates Dulness and her followers.[1] Leo Damrosch cautions, however, that references to Milton or to parodic acts of uncreation do not of themselves constitute a systematic argument or chain of meaning: 'Without question the dunces often resemble Milton's devils. What is not obvious is that dulness is thereby shown to be sinful and "diabolical".' The dominant mode of *The Dunciad*, in short, is satire, not theology; Pope's poem affords the reader 'amusement rather than metaphysical horror'.[2]

If Damrosch offers a useful corrective to an unduly portentous or ponderous reading of *The Dunciad*, Burke's deployment of Scriblerian discourse in the *Letters on a Regicide Peace* would seem to vindicate Williams's stress on the weighty rather than the burlesque in the Scriblerian mode. But the apocalyptic violence Burke extracts, *in extremis*, from the Scriblerian language he borrows is not so much a dark interpretation of *The Dunciad* as a horrified reading of the French Revolution itself. After all, as he makes clear in the opening pages of the *Letters*, the 'dying notes' Pope uttered in opposition to Walpole seem, in retrospect, a disproportionate response to the controversies that occasioned them. Pope's language, even at its most fiercely denunciatory, always remains primarily satiric in impulse: a note of glee, however attenuated, can almost always be heard as the poet discomfits his enemies. Burke's apocalyptic turn, by contrast, enlists satire in aid of prophecy, a move that charges his language with precisely the metaphysical and historical significance Williams claims for *The Dunciad*.

---

[1] A. Williams, *Pope's Dunciad: A Study of Its Meaning* (Baton Rouge, 1955), 154–5.
[2] Leo Damrosch, *The Imaginative World of Alexander Pope* (Berkeley and Los Angeles, 1987), 264–5.

The move from satire to prophecy is by no means unprecedented, for the two modes have much in common and have been linked in various ways from the earliest times. Satire's origins in magical imprecations and curses show traces of this relationship,[3] as do the pronouncements of the biblical prophets, who often resorted to satire in their prophetic denunciations. A case in point is the prophet Isaiah's satire on female vanity in Isaiah 3. Even Milton recognized the affinity between satire and prophecy, pointing to the example of Elijah's mockery of the false prophets of Baal in 1 Kings 18. Milton asks whether Elijah's sarcasm on that occasion served merely 'to shew his wit, or to fulfill his humour', and responds, 'doubtlesse we cannot imagine that great servant of God had any other end . . . but to teach and instruct the poore misledde people'.[4] His observation betrays an ambivalence that persisted well into the eighteenth century about the appropriateness of satiric laughter and ridicule in sacred contexts or theological debates. Some of that same ambivalence is evident in the responses to the writings of Burke's final years: just as many readers of Swift's *Tale of a Tub* were deeply unsettled by his ironic treatment of religious controversy, so too Burke's vehement polemics provoked unease about the cogency of his views, the propriety of his expression, and even, ultimately, his sanity.

Evidence for the modal shift from satire to prophecy can be found everywhere in *Letters on a Regicide Peace*. Burke's irony, heavy at the best of times, gives way again and again to unrestrained denunciation, the prophetic spirit of Jeremiah: 'Should we not obtest Heaven, and whatever justice there is yet on Earth? Oppression makes wise men mad; but the distemper is still the madness of the wise, which is better than the sobriety of fools. Their cry is the voice of sacred misery, exalted, not into wild raving, but into the sanctified phrensy of prophecy and inspiration—in that bitterness of soul, in that indignation of suffering virtue, in that exaltation of despair, would not persecuted English Loyalty cry out, with an awful warning voice . . .?' (ix. 255). Like Jeremiah, who complains bitterly, 'I am in derision daily, everyone mocketh me', Burke sees himself

---

[3] See Robert C. Elliott, *The Power of Satire: Magic, Ritual, Art* (Princeton, 1960).
[4] John Milton, *An Apology against a Pamphlet*, in *Complete Prose Works of John Milton*, gen. ed. D. M. Wolfe (New Haven, 1953–82), i. 903.

isolated and set apart in his lonely crusade, yet he nevertheless feels compelled to speak out, as did his biblical precursor: '[God's] word was in mine heart as a burning fire shut up in my bones, and I was weary with forbearing, and I could not stay' (Jer. 20: 8–9). He had previously declared his prophetic vocation in his correspondence and in his *Letter to William Elliot*, where he writes,

> I would not wish to excite, or even to tolerate, that kind of evil spirit which evokes the powers of hell to rectify the disorders of the earth. No! I would add my voice with better, and I trust, more potent charms, to draw down justice and wisdom and fortitude from heaven, for the correction of human vice, and the recalling of human errour from the devious ways into which it has been betrayed. (ix. 42)[5]

Satire, in the writings of Burke's last years, including his great speeches in the impeachment of Warren Hastings, operates everywhere under the sign of prophecy, in marked contrast with Pope, who, with a few notable exceptions, such as the concluding lines of *The Dunciad*, writes satire in a judicial vein, arraigning individuals and modes of conduct, rather than denouncing his nation's apostasy from a sacred mission.

The jeremiad as a literary mode has been explored most fully by students of American literature, notably Perry Miller and Sacvan Bercovich. Bercovich argues that the American jeremiad can be sharply distinguished from its European counterpart: 'The European jeremiad developed within a static hierarchical order; the lessons it taught, about historical recurrence and the vanity of human wishes, amounted to a massive ritual reinforcement of tradition. Its function was to make social practice conform to a completed and perfected social ideal. The American Puritan jeremiad was the ritual of a culture on an errand ... it discarded the Old World ideal of stasis for a New World vision of the future.'[6] This analysis falls in with the

---

[5] See e.g. *Correspondence*, vii. 496–7.
[6] S. Bercovitch, *The American Jeremiad* (Madison, 1978), 23. See also Perry Miller, *The New England Mind: From Colony to Province* (Cambridge, 1953), 27–39. For further discussions of jeremiad, see Bercovitch, 'Horologicals to Chronometricals: The Rhetoric of the Jeremiad', in Eric Rothstein (ed.), *Literary Monographs*, 3 (1970), 1–124; and J. Egan, ' "This is a Lamentation and shall be for a Lamentation": Nathaniel Ward and the Rhetoric of the Jeremiad', *Proceedings of the American Philosophical Society*, 122 (1978), 400–10.

generic conflict dramatized in *Reflections on the Revolution in France*: the contrast between Burke's conception of tragedy as a genre designed to enforce existing social norms and Richard Price's optimistic, progressive conception of history as a comic pilgrimage. In both instances the fundamental contrast is between a discourse that is resolutely mundane, this-worldly, and one that is apocalyptic and teleological. Bercovitch emphasizes, for instance, the European jeremiad's focus on the city of man rather than the city of God: 'It required not conversion but moral obedience and civic virtue. At best, it held out the prospect of temporal, worldly success. At worst, it threatened not hellfire but secular calamity (disease, destruction, death).'[7] The American Puritan jeremiad differs, according to Bercovitch, in the note of affirmation it sounds: God's chastisement of the Puritans serves, paradoxically, to confirm their special status as his chosen people and to rededicate them to their divinely ordained mission.

This dichotomy offers some useful distinctions between European and American historical experience, yet it perhaps overstates the uniqueness of the American Puritan version of the jeremiad and undervalues the complexity of the form in its various British manifestations.[8] British jeremiads of the eighteenth century remained deeply rooted in biblical and Christian precedent, but their analyses drew more immediately upon classical sources, which tended to give them a more rationalistic and secular cast.[9] The typical jeremiad fastened variously upon factionalism, political corruption, and religious laxity as causes of national decline, but the chief suspect was always the parent vice of luxury. This view was grounded in a cyclical view of history inherited from classical times, which saw an inevitable progression from the virtuous industry that produces the arts of civilization to the satiation of need and desire in excessive

---

[7] Bercovitch, *American Jeremiad*, 9.
[8] Laura Lunger Knoppers argues that Puritan writers of the English Revolution, including Milton, used the jeremiad in complex ways that parallel the practice of their American contemporaries. See 'Milton's *The Readie and Easie Way* and the English Jeremiad', in David Loewenstein and James Grantham Turner (eds.), *Politics, Poetics, and Hermeneutics in Milton's Prose* (Cambridge, 1990), 213–25.
[9] See John Sekora, *Luxury: The Concept in Western Thought, Eden to Smollett* (Baltimore, 1977), 23–109.

wealth and luxury. The circle is completed by the corruption, enervation, and social collapse to which luxury was thought inevitably to lead. The paradox of this 'consumptive' view of history, as David Spadafora terms it, is that prosperity, a seemingly desirable social goal, carries with it the seeds of social and spiritual destruction.[10]

These litanies of woe tended to appear during times of military or economic crisis, such as the wars of the Spanish and Austrian successions, the South Sea Bubble, and the American and French Revolutions. One of the best-known of these jeremiads, John Brown's *Estimate of the Manners and Principles of the Time*, to which Burke refers at the beginning of the *Letters on a Regicide Peace*, was published during the inauspicious opening months of the Seven Years War. Though Burke rejects the determinism of Brown's cyclical model of historical change, declaring that he is 'not quite of the mind of those speculators, who seem assured, that necessarily, and by the constitution of things, all States have the same periods of infancy, manhood, and decrepitude, that are found in the individuals who compose them' (ix. 188), his etiology of the French Revolution relies on many of the same time-honoured arguments as Brown employs in his *Estimate*:

> [N]ever was so beautiful and so august a spectacle presented to the moral eye, as Europe afforded the day before the revolution in France. I knew indeed that this prosperity contained in itself the seeds of its own danger. In one part of the society it caused laxity and debility. In the other it produced bold spirits and dark designs. . . . General wealth loosened morals, relaxed vigilance, and increased presumption. . . . What a base and foolish thing is it for any consolidated body of authority to say, or to act as [the French government] said, 'I will put my trust not in my own virtue, but in your patience; I will indulge in effeminacy, in indolence, in corruption; I will give way to all my perverse and vitious humours, because you cannot punish me without the hazard of ruining yourselves?' (ix. 39–40)

Echoing the gendered terms of Brown's argument, Burke identifies excessive prosperity as the breeding ground of an

---

[10] David Spadafora, *The Idea of Progress in Eighteenth-Century Britain* (New Haven, 1990), 15.

effeminizing intellectual and moral licence, which can only be countered by a return to a manly 'republican spirit':

> By this which I call the true republican spirit, paradoxical as it may appear, monarchies alone can be rescued from the imbecillity of courts and the madness of the crowd. This republican spirit would not suffer men in high place to bring ruin on their country and on themselves. It would reform, not by destroying, but by saving, the great, the rich and the powerful. Such a republican spirit, we perhaps fondly conceive to have animated the distinguished heroes and patriots of old, who knew no mode of policy but religion and virtue. (ix. 42)

On the face of it, this analysis falls back on a familiar language of republican virtue which seeks to counter the centrifugal forces that threaten the polity—'the imbecillity of courts and the madness of the crowd'—with 'those moral riders which reason has appointed to govern every sort of ruder power' (ix. 42). The emphasis is on the preservation of hierarchy and tradition ('saving the great, the rich, and the powerful'), and the desire for radical change is conflated with corruption. Innovation of redefined as a form of luxury, a desire for more than is necessary to human existence.

If, in these important respects Burke's *Letters on a Regicide Peace* and the *Letter to William Elliot* display the characteristics of the European jeremiad, they also communicate the messianic urgency of the American jeremiad, inculcating an acute sense of crisis and recalling Britain to its divine errand: 'If ever there was a time that calls on us for no vulgar conception of things, and for exertions in no vulgar strain, it is the awful hour that Providence has now appointed to this nation' (ix. 313–14). The fact that Burke exerts himself to write the four lengthy *Letters* near the end of his life implies a hope that Britain can be recalled to a sense of her historic role and mission among the nations of Europe. 'I despair', he writes, 'neither of the publick fortune nor of the publick mind,' but he adds, ominously, 'Let us not deceive ourselves: we are at the beginning of great troubles' (ix. 193). Significantly, when he seeks for an example of the 'heroes and patriots of old' (ix. 42) who came to their country's rescue, he passes over the obvious figures of Greek and Roman history in favour of the Jewish hero Judas Maccabaeus: 'Why should not a Maccabeus and his brethren arise to assert the honour of the ancient law, and to defend the temple of their forefathers, with as ardent a spirit, as can inspire any innovator to destroy the monuments of the piety and the glory of antient ages?' (ix. 41). Revolutionary energy must be countered with a like spirit of radical struggle, for, 'when once things are gone out of their ordinary course, it is by acts out of the ordinary course they can alone be re-established' (ix. 41). Burke's turn to apocalyptic discourse is motivated by this insight. The decadence of pre-revolutionary France has led not to the anticipated consequence of disintegration, but to an unexpected mutation in the French body politic. It is precisely because the French Revolution is like no previous revolution (and Burke is among the very first to use the word 'revolution' in the modern sense of a radical upheaval in social structures, rather than a circular return to ancient values and liberties) that he feels compelled to counter one language of linear, irreversible change with another.

At one level at least, the urgent sense of mission Burke conveys has become thoroughly secularized. He reminds his readers of the dynastic wars in which England found herself embroiled at the end of the previous century.

'To what purpose', he asks, 'have I recalled your view to the end of the last century? It has been done to shew that the British Nation was then a great people—to point out how and by what means they came to be exalted above the vulgar level, and to take that lead which they assumed among mankind. To qualify us for that pre-eminence, we had then an high mind, and a constancy unconquerable. (ix. 236)

He credits a power from 'above' with infusing the sense of greatness and purpose that prevailed at the beginning of the century, but that power was secular and human, rather than sacred and transcendent: 'This force of character was inspired, as all such spirit must ever be, from above. Government gave the impulse' (ix. 236). Here the apocalyptic impulse remains an élitist one; there is no question of a biblical reversal, with the first becoming last, and the last first. Nevertheless, Burke's rhetoric registers an 'exceptionalist' strain, of the British as a special, chosen people, though their election is to temporal greatness, not divine. In fact, this marshalling of national greatness in the opening years of the eighteenth century was undertaken in the service of England's traditional geopolitical role: the preservation of the balance of power in Europe. This

EPILOGUE: THE PROPHETIC BURKE

secularized sense of prophecy is also present, as we have seen, in Burke's adaptation of the Miltonic prophetic voice in his georgic prospect views.

Burke's tone changes drastically, however, when he contemplates revolutionary France. The current conflict can no longer be understood in the traditional terms of European power diplomacy because France has rejected the framework of assumptions on which the 'Christian commonwealth' of Europe was founded. France is no longer a 'State' but a 'Faction', an 'evil spirit that possesses the body' of the country (ix. 264). Accordingly, Britain's sacred mission must be 'to preserve Europe from the return of barbarism, and the Universe from the subversion and anarchy with which it [is] threatened' (ix. 266). The war with revolutionary France is to be understood not as a conventional game of power politics, but as a 'civil war' (ix. 267), a war 'where light and darkness are struggling together' (ix. 345). 'It is a war between the partizans of the antient, civil, moral, and political order of Europe against a set of fanatical and ambitious atheists which means to change them all. It is not France extending a foreign empire over other nations: it is a sect aiming at universal empire, and beginning with the conquest of France' (ix. 267). Burke regards the present conflict as nothing less than a holy war, and he turns up the rhetorical temperature accordingly. France is the 'mother of monsters', a country inhabited by 'Amazonian and male cannibal[s]' and presided over by a legislature that is 'the Synagogue of Anti-Christ' and the 'forge and manufactory of all evil'. The god these cannibals worship is 'the grim Moloch of Regicide', and as votaries of Moloch they are described as consuming their victims with 'ravening maw' and 'drinking the blood of their victims' (ix. 223, 308, 243, 312, 206, 245). One hears in these outbursts the indignant voices of the Old Testament prophets denouncing the periodic apostasies of the children of Israel.

The climax of this rhetorical fusillade comes with Burke's Miltonic characterization of the *philosophes*, the intellectual and spiritual fathers of the revolution, as 'rebels to God' who 'perfectly abhor the Author of their being':

They hate him 'with all their heart, with all their mind, with all their soul, and with all their strength.' . . . They cannot strike the Sun out of

Heaven, but they are able to raise a smouldering smoke that obscures him from their own eyes. Not being able to revenge themselves on God, they have a delight in vicariously defacing, degrading, torturing, and tearing in pieces his image in man. ... [W]hen the possibility of dominion, lead, and propagation presented themselves, and that the ambition, which before had so often made them hypocrites, might rather gain than lose by a daring avowal of their sentiments, then the nature of this infernal spirit, which has 'evil for it's good' appeared in it's full perfection. (ix. 278–9)

By now we are well beyond the furthest reaches of apocalyptic foreboding in *The Dunciad*, though the rhetorical means Burke uses are similar. The crucial difference lies, as I have previously argued, in the tone and context of the two men's writings. If Pope's references to uncreation and the powers of darkness function satirically, in Burke, as in Milton, they function metaphysically, and on the generic level this shift can be measured by satire's transformation into the bordering mode of the jeremiad. This transformation is confirmed by the recurring imagery of the jeremiad in the *Letters* and in Burke's other writings on the French Revolution: imagery of light and darkness, of disease, decay, and ruin, of drought and storms, of family strife and filial disobedience, and of plagues, wilderness, and trackless desert.[11]

The transformation is, in the final analysis, inevitable. Burke recognizes with dreadful clarity that the struggle with revolutionary France is ideological in nature and that France's governors are akin to what we today might well characterize as terrorists, yet he lacks the political vocabulary to describe a then unprecedented reality. The conflict, in other words, is one about first principles, and he reverts to the traditional language of first (and last) things in order to describe and analyse a radically new political landscape. But in using this traditional idiom in a new context, he modifies it and innovates upon it. One dimension of that innovation lies ironically in the fact that the eschatalogical language he employs is normally associated with the oppressed

---

[11] See Emory Elliott, *Power and the Pulpit in Puritan New England* (Princeton, 1975), *passim*. For an analysis of some of these image patterns in *Reflections on the Revolution in France*, see J. T. Boulton, *The Language of Politics in the Age of Wilkes and Burke* (London, 1963), 97–133.

and downtrodden: it has more in common with the chiliastic visions of radical writers during the English Revolution of the 1640s than with the Whig tradition of which he is a part. This irony is compounded by the fact that the dissenters of Burke's day, including Price, nominally the spiritual heirs of the Puritan visionaries of the English Revolution, had long since assimilated their Christian eschatalogical outlook to an increasingly secularized enlightenment faith in progress.[12] In this context, apocalyptic discourse splits in two, with the optimistic, millenarian language of rebirth being appropriated by the likes of Price and other well-wishers of the Revolution and the grim, eschatalogical language of judgement and the last things becoming the idiom of conservative thinkers such as Burke.[13] Apocalyptic imagery could voice the desires and anxieties of the powerful as well as the powerless, of rulers as well as rebels. This recognition helps to explain how *Paradise Lost*, the production of a radical poet, could appeal to such cultural traditionalists as Pope and Burke: Milton bequeathed to the eighteenth and nineteenth centuries both a conservative and a radical cultural legacy.

Damrosch suggests that Burke's use of apocalyptic imagery represents a retreat from history, a reversion to 'an older notion of change as irrational and chaotic, explicable *only* on the assumption that Providence somehow directs it'. Rather than positing 'an intelligible development of tensions in French society', Burke's analysis of the Revolution reverts to ahistorical explanations that account for events as the product of evil forces.[14] Though it is certainly true that Burke's evolutionary sense of history as process is pressed to the breaking point by the events in France and that he has no ready explanation for the rapid changes unfolding there, it does not necessarily follow that he has retreated from history in his old age. On the contrary, he thought long and hard about historical causation and the

---

[12] Spadafora, *Idea of Progress*, 104–32 and 223–52.
[13] In his *Autonomy of Criticism* (Princeton, 1957), 141–50, Northrop Frye distinguishes between an apocalyptic language of human desire (God, heaven), which he calls 'apocalyptic imagery' proper, and an apocalyptic language of nightmare, pain, and bondage (Satan, hell), which he classifies as 'demonic imagery'.
[14] Leo Damrosch, *Fictions of Reality in the Age of Hume and Johnson* (Madison, 1989), 213.

problem of change: his preoccupation with the subject is itself an indication of the degree to which an awareness of history is central to his experience and thought. His occasional association of change with chance or providential interposition is not an abandonment of historical awareness, but a recognition that causation, from his empirical perspective, is so complex as to defy analysis or understanding. For Burke, social science is in its infancy, and a comprehensive understanding of states or commonwealths, which are 'the arbitrary productions of the human mind', is not yet possible: 'We are not yet acquainted with the laws which necessarily influence the stability of that kind of work made by that kind of agent. . . . I am far from denying the operation of such causes: But they are infinitely uncertain' (ix. 188–9). He is left with the novelist's sense of the infinite complexity of the fabric of human society: 'A common soldier, a child, a girl at the door of an inn, have changed the face of fortune, and almost of Nature' (ix. 189).

Yet uncertainty does not beget paralysis in the face of events. Burke realizes that he will not live to 'behold the unravelling of the intricate plot' in which the people of Europe are playing their parts; it would be impertinent of him, therefore, to write the drama or the history of what has not yet transpired (ix. 188). An attention to genre prevents this sort of misreading: Burke makes it clear that his *Letters* are 'testamentary', a 'dying declaration' addressed to a younger man who represents the generation that will carry on the struggle after he is gone (ix. 263). In this context the mode of the jeremiad is entirely appropriate, for, to cite once more the formulation of the New England jeremiadist Nicholas Noyes, '*Prophesie* is *Historie antedated*; and *Historie* is *Post-dated Prophesie*: the same thing is told in both.'[15] Far from lamenting the passing of an era or abandoning history, Burke seeks to write '*Historie antedated*', to influence the course of change and chart the direction of events. If change itself is finally inscrutable, action is nevertheless still possible: 'Not to lose ourselves in the infinite void of the conjectural world, our business is with what is likely to be affected for the better or the worse, by the wisdom or weakness

---

[15] *New-Englands Duty*, 43, quoted in *American Jeremiad*, 15. See above, Ch. 3, n. 24.

of our plans' (ix. 188). His jeremiad, then, moves beyond arraignment (the stance of Scriblerian satire) to an active intervention in the historical process—it too becomes 'the ritual of a culture on an errand'. Perhaps Burke, like that soldier, child, or girl at the inn door, can hope to shift the inertial weight of history with the fulcrum of his prophetic discourse.

The literary shape Burke confers upon the *Letters* and the generic innovations he grafts onto them mark his work as the products of specific historical circumstances, and we risk failing to understand what he has to say by ignoring the historical context that echoes in the cadences of his prose. Still, many readers have responded to a strain in his writings that claims a significance for his ideas transcending the immediate historical circumstances which occasioned them. One such reader was Sir Gilbert Elliot, who wrote to Burke on 6 November 1790 to express his admiration for the latter's *Reflections on the Revolution in France*:

> Your book contains the fundamental Elements of *all* Political knowledge, and lays clearly open to us the just foundations of *all* Social wisdom.... You have not been satisfied with unmasking and deposing Error, but you have unveiled Truth and set her in all her brightness on the vacant throne—I consider this book as the Rudiments in which we ought all to learn to read, and yet as the new and better Aristotle, in which we are to end our Study and prove our qualification to act and teach in our turn.... I do protest I could feel as if it came like the *word* like a *Revelation*, to save us when our own best wisdom or virtue could not suffice. (*Corr.* vi. 156)

As one of Burke's most devoted disciples, Elliot might be expected to accord him lavish praise, yet however one is inclined to judge the rhetorical excesses of Elliot's response, it identifies several features that Burke's writing shares with other works of political theory (as modern scholarship understands the term). Among these are Burke's self-conscious identification of a tradition within which he is writing, a sense of the work's genesis in a moment of supreme crisis, and a recognition of a prophetic strain in the work.

All these features figure prominently among the characteristics John Gunnell identifies in his analysis of political theory as a discrete genre. He defines the literature of political theory in terms of certain family resemblances which are shared by a sufficient number of works to justify their being grouped together provisionally as members of the genre of political theory. This approach is particularly useful for our purposes because it offers an explanatory context for those features of Burke's political œuvre that have been the primary focus of this study. One of these is the question of authorial persona—the voice and personality of the author as projected in the work. Gunnell notes that the theorist is often an individual who is debarred in some way from the normal sphere of political action and who regards his texts as a 'substitute for political action, or even a kind of political action itself'.[16] The theorist writes partly in self-justification and partly to erect a monument to his own literary fame. Gunnell's analysis most aptly describes Burke in the final years of his career—the Burke who emerges from the pages of his polemics on the French Revolution and his speeches in the impeachment of Warren Hastings—but it equally accounts for the oppositional stance, the voice of the outsider, that is discernible throughout his writings.

More interestingly, Gunnell identifies the moment of crisis, of social disintegration, as the enabling condition of the theorist, whose intervention is especially needed in such a time. The crisis of the theorist, who is in some way excluded from society, and the crisis of society at large are seen as closely bound up with each other:

> Although excluded from participation, [the theorist], like the Hebrew prophet, comes to see himself as the personification of the community. He feels the wounds of society more deeply partly because of this very exclusion and perceives more objectively, through his detachment, the condition of society. Although his attitude may at times appear to be almost one of hate and a willingness to do great violence to society . . . it is a hatred for what has befallen the polity. Machiavelli's statement that he loved his native city more than his own soul could well express the sentiment of most theorists. His position is one of suffering. He, like Socrates or the prophet, is the suffering servant, the pilgrim in a corrupt society who bears within himself the painful truth of the source of political disorder. Yet, as in all tragedy, suffering brings wisdom, and he views himself ultimately as the repository of a new idea of order, as the remnant of truth in society, and as the carrier of the secret of redemption.[17]

[16] Gunnell, *Political Theory*, 136, 141.   [17] Ibid. 143.

The nature of the crisis perceived by the theorist is often described in cosmic terms as a version of society's fall into history: a recognition that human society is transitory, mortal, and subject to destructive change. The theorist's response to this is to articulate a vision of political order that he sees as 'the answer to the basic problem of the human condition. The vision of the theorist reflects the experience of historical decline and cosmic crisis, and his vision is one of the restoration of order but a restoration that is informed by a new truth.'[18]

Gunnell's discussion offers an embracing generic paradigm within which the various literary strands of Burke's political discourse can be placed. For the distinctive characteristic of the theorist, as Gunnell conceives him, is that he deflects action into literary production, into the imaginative conceptualizing of a social order whose literal realization is uncertain. This is not to suggest that the theorist has abandoned practical political problems or turned his back on concrete action (certainly Burke never submitted to any such acknowledgement of defeat), but to recognize that action has become problematic or uncertain. Burke increasingly laboured under such uncertainty in the last fifteen years of his life, and his response was to elevate the language of ordinary political debate to a different plane altogether. The central manifestation of this strategy is the array of literary and cultural resources he marshalls in support of his vision in an effort to remind his compatriots of the inestimable riches they have inherited as citizens of the 'Christian commonwealth of Europe'. What has so arduously been won over many centuries, he laments, may be squandered through the pride, greed, and short-sightedness of a single generation.

[18] Ibid. 144. Cf. Steven Blakemore, who argues in *Burke and the Fall of Language* (Hanover, NH, 1988), 106, 'Burke depicts the French Revolution as a second Fall, a second Babel, a second Golgotha in which the cosmic ordering of the Logos, the sanctity and authority of the Word is also assaulted.'

Bibliography

AUTHORS PRE-1832

ADDISON, JOSEPH, and STEELE, RICHARD, *The Spectator*, ed. Donald F. Bond. 5 vols. Oxford, 1965.

An Authentic and Impartial Copy of the Trial of the Hon. Augustus Keppel . . . Taken in Short Hand, by a Person who attended during the whole Trial. And Printed by the Desire of a Society of Gentlemen. Portsmouth, 1779.

ANDERSON, JAMES, *Essays Relating to Agriculture and Rural Affairs*, iii. Edinburgh, 1796.

AUCKLAND, WILLIAM, EDEN, 1ST BARON, *Some Remarks on the Apparent Circumstances of War in the Fourth Week of October 1795* London, 1795.

BATCHELOR, THOMAS, *General View of the Agriculture of the County of Bedford*. London, 1808.

—— *Village Scenes, The Progress of Agriculture, and Other Poems*. London, 1804.

BLAKE, WILLIAM, *William Blake's Writings*, ed. G. E. Bentley, Jr. 2 vols. Oxford, 1978.

BLITH, WALTER, 'The Epistle to the Ingenious Reader', *The English Improver, or a New Survey of Husbandry*. London, 1649.

BOSWELL, JAMES, *Life of Johnson*, ed. George Birkbeck Hill and L. F. Powell. 6 vols. 1934; repr. Oxford, 1971.

BROWN, JOHN, *An Estimate of the Manners and Principles of the Times*. London, 1757.

BURKE, EDMUND, *The Correspondence of Edmund Burke*, ed. Thomas W. Copeland *et al.* 10 vols. Cambridge and Chicago, 1958–78.

—— *A Philosophical Enquiry into the Origin of Our Ideas of the Sublime and Beautiful*, ed. James T. Boulton (London, 1958).

—— *The Speeches of the Right Honourable Edmund Burke, in the House of Commons, and in Westminster Hall*. 4 vols. London, 1816.

—— *The Works of the Right Honourable Edmund Burke*, Bohn's British Classics. 8 vols. London, 1854–89.

—— *The Works of the Right Honourable Edmund Burke*, ed. French Laurence and Walter King. 16 vols. London, 1803–27.

—— *The Writings and Speeches of Edmund Burke*, ed. Paul Langford *et al.* Oxford, 1981– .

CHESTERFIELD, PHILIP DORMER STANHOPE, EARL OF, *Miscellaneous Works of the Late Philip Dormer Stanhope, Earl of Chesterfield.* 2 vols. London, 1777.
COBBETT, WILLIAM (ed.), *The Parliamentary History of England from the Earliest Period to the Year 1803.* London, 1817.
COLERIDGE, SAMUEL TAYLOR, *The Collected Works of Samuel Taylor Coleridge,* ed. Kathleen Coburn, Bollingen Series LXXV (projected at 16 vols.). Princeton, 1970– .
A Complete Collection of State Trials, and Proceedings for High-Treason, and other Crimes and Misdemeanours. 4th edn., 11 vols. London, 1776–81.
COWPER, WILLIAM, *The Poetical Works of William Cowper,* ed. Humphrey Summer Milford. 4th edn. London, 1934.
The Craftsman: Being a Critique on the Times. 14 vols. London, 1731–7.
DRYDEN, JOHN, *The Works of John Dryden,* ed, Edward Niles Hooker and H. T. Swedenberg (projected at 20 vols). Berkeley and Los Angeles, 1956– .
DUGDALE, WILLIAM, *A Short View of the Late Troubles in England.* Oxford, 1681.
England's Black Tribunall. Set Forth in the Triall of K. Charles, I. London, 1660.
FERGUSON, ADAM, *Essay on the History of Civil Society.* 1767; repr. Philadelphia, 1819.
FIELDING, HENRY, *An Enquiry into the Causes of the Late Increase of Robbers.* London, 1751.
—— *Joseph Andrews,* ed. Martin C. Battestin. Oxford, 1967.
GAY, JOHN, *The Letters of John Gay,* ed. C. F. Burgess. Oxford 1966.
—— POPE, ALEXANDER, and ARBUTHNOT, JOHN, *Three Hours after Marriage,* ed. Richard Morton and William M. Peterson, Lake Erie College Studies, 1. Painesville, Ohio, 1961.
The Gentleman's Magazine, 5 (1735).
GIBBON, EDWARD, *Memoirs of My Life,* ed. Georges A. Bonnard. London, 1966.
GILDON, CHARLES, *The Laws of Poetry.* London, 1721.
GODWIN, WILLIAM, *Enquiry Concerning Political Justice and Its Influence on Morals and Happiness,* ed. F. E. L. Priestley. 3 vols. Toronto, 1946.
GOLDSMITH, OLIVER, *The Poems of Thomas Gray, William Collins, Oliver Goldsmith,* ed. Roger Lonsdale. London, 1969
A Hand-kirchife for Loyall Mourners, or a Cordiall for Drooping Spirits. London, 1649.
HARTE, WALTER, *Essays on Husbandry.* 2 vols. London, 1764.

HUNTER, ALEXANDER, *Georgical Essays: in which The Food of Plants is particularly considered, Several new Composts recommended, and Other important Articles of Husbandry explained, Upon the Principles of Vegetation*. 4 vols. London, 1770–2.

JUVENAL AND PERSIUS, *Juvenal and Persius* (Loeb Classical Library), trans. G. G. Ramsay. Cambridge, Mass., 1979.

KAMES, HENRY HOME, LORD, *The Gentleman Farmer. Being an Attempt to Improve Agriculture, by Subjecting It to the Test of Rational Principles*. Edinburgh, 1779.

KENT, NATHANIEL, *Some Particulars of the King's Farm, at Windsor, in 1798*. Oxford, n.d.

LA TOUR DU PIN, HENRIETTA-LUCY, MME. DE, *Memoirs of Madame de La Tour du Pin*, ed. and trans. Felice Harcourt. London, 1985.

LEADBEATER, MARY [SHACKLETON], *The Leadbeater Papers*. 2 vols. London, 1862.

Letters from Simkin the Second to his Brother Simon, in Wales; Dedicated without Permission, to the Ancient and Respectable Family of the Grunters. London, 1796.

LUDLOW, EDMUND, *The Memoirs of Edmund Ludlow, Esq., Lieutenant-General of the Horse in the Army of the Commonwealth of England, 1625–1672*, ed. Charles H. Firth. 2 vols. Oxford, 1894.

MACAULAY, CATHARINE, *Observations on a Pamphlet, Entitled, Thoughts on the Cause of the Present Discontents*. London, 1770.

MACKINTOSH, JAMES, *Vindiciae Gallicae*. London, 1791.

MARSHALL, WILLIAM, *The Rural Economy of the West of England*. 2 vols. London, 1796.

MILLER, JAMES, *Harlequin-Horace: or, the Art of Modern Poetry*. London, 1731.

MILTON, JOHN, *Complete Poems and Major Prose*, ed. Merritt Y. Hughes. Indianapolis, 1957.

—— *Complete Prose Works of John Milton*, gen ed. D. M. Wolfe. 8 vols. New Haven, 1953–82.

Mist's *Weekly Journal*, 15 Feb. 1718.

MONTAGU, LADY MARY WORTLEY, *Complete Letters*, ed. Robert Halsband. 3 vols. Oxford, 1965–7.

NEWBERY, JOHN, *The Art of Poetry on a New Plan, illustrated with a great Variety of Examples from the best English Poets*. London, 1762.

OVID, *The Metamorphoses*, trans. Horace Gregory. New York, 1958.

PAINE, THOMAS, *Rights of Man*, ed. Henry Collins. Harmondsworth, 1969.

PERRINCHIEFE, RICHARD, *The Life of Charles I*, in *The Workes of King Charles the Martyr*. 2 vols. London, 1662.

Poems on Several Occasions. Dublin, 1748.
POPE, ALEXANDER, *The Prose Works of Alexander Pope*, ii. *The Major Works, 1725–44*, ed. Rosemary Cowler. Oxford, 1986.
—— *The Twickenham Edition of the Poems of Alexander Pope*, ed. John Butt *et al.* 11 vols. London and New Haven, 1939–69.
PRICE, RICHARD, *A Discourse on the Love of Our Country*, in D. O. Thomas (ed.), *Political Writings*. Cambridge, 1991
—— *The Evidence for a Future Period of Improvement in the State of Mankind*, in Thomas (ed.), *Political Writings*.
The Proceedings at Large of the Court-Martial, on the Trial of the Honourable Augustus Keppel . . . on Thursday, January 7th, 1779. . . . Taken in Short Hand, by W. Blanchard, for the Admiral, and Published by his Permission. London, 1779.
SHAFTESBURY, ANTHONY ASHLEY COOPER, 3RD EARL OF, *Characteristics of Men, Manners, Opinions, Times*, ed. John M. Robertson. 2 vols. Indianapolis, 1964.
SMITH, ADAM, *An Inquiry into the Nature and Causes of the Wealth of Nations*, ed. R. H. Campbell and A. S. Skinner. 2 vols. Oxford, 1976.
SWIFT, JONATHAN, *The Prose Works of Jonathan Swift*, ed. Herbert Davis. 16 vols. Oxford, 1941–74.
THELWALL, JOHN, *Sober Reflections on the Seditious and Inflammatory Letter of the Right Hon. Edmund Burke, to a Noble Lord*. London, 1796.
THOMSON, JAMES, *Liberty, The Castle of Indolence, and Other Poems*, ed. James Sambrook. Oxford, 1986.
—— *The Seasons*, ed. James Sambrook. Oxford, 1981.
A View of the Relative State of Great Britain and France, at the Commencement of the Year 1796. London, 1796.
VIRGIL, *The Works of Virgil Translated into English Prose*, trans. John Conington. London, 1890.
WALPOLE, HORACE, *The Correspondence of Horace Walpole*, ed. W. S. Lewis *et al.* 48 vols. New Haven, 1937–83.
WARD, EDWARD, *The London-Spy*. 1700; repr., London, 1924.
WOLLSTONECRAFT, MARY, *Vindication of the Rights of Woman*, in Janet Todd and Marilyn Butler (eds.), *The Works of Mary Wollstonecraft*, 7 vols. London, 1989.
—— *Vindication of the Rights of Men*, in Janet Todd and Marilyn Butler (eds.), *The Works of Mary Wollstonecraft*, 7 vols. London 1989.
YOUNG, ARTHUR, *Annals of Agriculture, and other Useful Arts*, ii. (1784), v. (1786), and xvii. (1792). London.
—— *The Autobiography of Arthur Young with Selections from his Correspondence*, ed. M. Betham-Edwards. London, 1898.

────── *The Farmer's Tour through the East of England*. 4 vols. London, 1771.
────── *Political Essays Concerning the Present State of the British Empire*. London, 1772.
────── *A Six Months Tour through the North of England*. 4 vols. London, 1770.
────── *Travels, During the Years 1787, 1788, and 1789. Undertaken more particularly with a View of ascertaining the Cultivation, Wealth, Resources, and National Prosperity, of the Kingdom of France*. Bury St Edmunds, 1792.

AUTHORS POST-1832

AERS, DAVID, 'Coleridge and the Egg that Burke Laid: Ideological Collusion and Opposition in the 1790s', *Literature and History*, 9 (1983), 152–63.
The Agrarian History of England and Wales, gen. ed. Joan Thirsk. 8 vols. Cambridge, 1967– .
ALLEN, R. T., 'The State and Civil Society as Objects of Aesthetic Appreciation', *British Journal of Aesthetics*, 16 (1976), 237–42.
ANDERSON, HOWARD, DAGHLIAN, PHILIP B., and EHRENPREIS, IRVIN, (eds.), *The Familiar Letter in the Eighteenth Century*. Lawrence, Kan., 1966.
AYLING, STANLEY, *Edmund Burke: His Life and Opinions*. London, 1988.
BABCOCK, BARBARA A. (ed.), *The Reversible World: Symbolic Inversion in Art and Society*. Ithaca, NY, 1978.
BAKHTIN, MIKHAIL, *Rabelais and His World*, trans. Helene Iswolsky. Cambridge, Mass., 1968.
BARRELL, JOHN. *English Literature in History, 1730–80: An Equal, Wide Survey*. London, 1983.
BARTHES, ROLAND, *Image, Music, Text*, trans. Stephen Heath. New York, 1977.
BECKETT, J. V., *The Agricultural Revolution*. Oxford, 1990.
────── *The Aristocracy in England: 1660–1914*. Oxford, 1986.
BERCOVITCH, SACVAN, *The American Jeremiad*. Madison, 1978.
────── 'Horologicals to Chronometricals: The Rhetoric of the Jeremiad', *Literary Monographs*, 3 (1970), 1–124.
BLAKEMORE, STEVEN, *Burke and the Fall of Language: The French Revolution as Linguistic Event*. Hanover, NH, 1988.
BLITZER, CHARLES, Introduction to *The Political Writings of James Harrington: Representative Selections*. New York, 1955.

BOGEL, FREDRIC, 'Dulness Unbound: Rhetoric and Pope's Dunciad', *PMLA* 97 (1982), 844–55.
BOULTON, JAMES T., 'Edmund Burke's *Letter to a Noble Lord*: Apologia and Manifesto', *Burke Newsletter*, 8 (1967), 695–702.
—— *The Language of Politics in the Age of Wilkes and Burke*. London, 1963.
—— 'The Letters of Edmund Burke: "Manly Liberty of Speech" ', in Anderson *et al* (eds.), *The Familiar Letter in the Eighteenth Century*. Lawrence, Kan., 1966
BREWER, JOHN, *Party Ideology and Popular Politics at the Accession of George III*. Cambridge, 1976.
BROMWICH, DAVID, *Politics by Other Means: Higher Education and Group Thinking*. New Haven, 1992.
BROWNE, STEPHEN H., *Edmund Burke and the Discourse of Virtue*. Tuscaloosa, Ala., 1993.
BRYANT, DONALD CROSS, *Edmund Burke and His Literary Friends*. St Louis, 1939.
BURKE, PETER, *The Public and Domestic Life of the Right Honourable Edmund Burke*. 2nd edn. London, 1854.
BUTTERFIELD, H., *George III, Lord North, and the People: 1779–80*. 1949; repr. New York, 1968.
BYRD, MAX, *Visits to Bedlam: Madness and Literature in the Eighteenth Century*. Columbia, SC, 1974.
CAIRNS, FRANCIS, *Generic Composition in Greek and Roman Poetry*. Edinburgh, 1972.
CANAVAN, FRANCIS P., *The Political Reason of Edmund Burke*. Durham, NC, 1960.
CASTLE, TERRY, *Masquerade and Civilization: The Carnivalesque in Eighteenth-Century English Culture and Fiction*. London and Stanford, Calif., 1986.
CHALKER, JOHN, *The English Georgic: A Study in the Development of a Form*. Baltimore, 1969.
CHAMBERS, J. D., 'Enclosure and Labour Supply in the Industrial Revolution', *Economic History Review*, 2nd ser., 5 (1953), 319–43.
—— and MINGAY, G. E., *The Agricultural Revolution: 1750–1880*. London, 1966.
CHAPMAN, GERALD W., *Edmund Burke: The Practical Imagination*. Cambridge, Mass., 1967.
CHRISTIE, I. R., *The End of North's Ministry: 1780–82*. London, 1958.
COHEN, RALPH, 'Historical Knowledge and Literary Understanding', *Papers in Language and Literature*, 14 (1978), 227–48.
—— 'Innovation and Variation: Literary Change and Georgic Poetry.' In Ralph Cohen and Murray Kreiger, *Literature and History: Papers*

Read at a Clark Library Seminar, March 3, 1973. Los Angeles, 1974, 3–42.

—— 'Literary History and the Ballad of George Barnwel', in Douglas L. Patey and Timothy Keegan (eds.), *Augustan Studies: Essays in Honor of Irvin Ehrenpreis.* Newark, Del., 1985, 13–31.

—— 'On the Interrelations of Eighteenth-Century Literary Forms', in Phillip Harth (ed.), *New Approaches to Eighteenth-Century Literature.* New York, 1974, 33–78.

—— 'Transformation in *The Rape of the Lock*', *Eighteenth-Century Studies*, 2 (1968–9), 205–24.

—— *The Unfolding of* The Seasons. Baltimore, 1970.

COLLINS, JAMES, *Interpreting Modern Philosophy.* Princeton, 1972.

CONDREN, CONAL, *The Status and Appraisal of Classic Texts: An Essay on Political Theory, Its Inheritance, and the History of Ideas.* Princeton, 1985.

CONE, CARL B., *Burke and the Nature of Politics.* 2 vols. Lexington, Ken., 1957–64.

—— 'Edmund Burke, the Farmer', *Agricultural History*, 19 (1945), 65–9.

CURTIUS, ERNST ROBERT, *European Literature and the Latin Middle Ages*, trans. Willard R. Trask. London, 1953

DAMROSCH, LEO, *The Imaginative World of Alexander Pope.* Berkeley and Los Angeles, 1987.

—— *Fictions of Reality in the Age of Hume and Johnson.* Madison, 1989.

DE BRUYN, FRANS, 'Edmund Burke's Gothic Romance: The Portrayal of Warren Hastings in Burke's Writings and Speeches on India', *Criticism*, 29 (1987), 415–38.

—— 'Edmund Burke's Natural Aristocrat: The "Man of Taste" as a Political Ideal', *Eighteenth-Century Life*, 11 (1987), 41–60.

DONALDSON, IAN, *The World Upside-Down: Comedy from Jonson to Fielding.* Oxford, 1970.

DOWNIE, J. A., *Robert Harley and the Press: Propaganda and Public Opinion in the Age of Swift and Defoe.* Cambridge, 1979.

DREYER, FREDERICK A., *Burke's Politics: A Study in Whig Orthodoxy.* Waterloo, Ont., 1979.

DURLING, DWIGHT L., *Georgic Tradition in English Poetry.* New York, 1934; repr. Port Washington, NY, 1964.

EAGLETON, TERRY, *The Function of Criticism from* The Spectator *to Post-Structuralism.* London, 1984.

EGAN, J., ' "This is a Lamentation and shall be for a Lamentation": Nathaniel Ward and the Rhetoric of the Jeremiad', *Proceedings of the American Philosophical Society*, 122 (1978), 400–10.

ELLIOTT, EMORY, *Power and the Pulpit in Puritan New England.* Princeton, 1975.
ELLIOTT, ROBERT C., *The Power of Satire: Magic, Ritual, Art.* Princeton, 1960.
ERSKINE-HILL, HOWARD, *Pope: The Dunciad.* London, 1972
FEINGOLD, RICHARD, *Nature and Society: Later Eighteenth-Century Uses of the Pastoral and Georgic.* New Brunswick, NJ, 1978.
FERRIS, INA, 'Thackeray and the Ideology of the Gentleman', in John J. Richetti (ed.), *The Columbia History of the British Novel.* New York, 1994.
FOUCAULT, MICHEL, *The Foucault Reader*, ed. Paul Rabinow. New York, 1984.
FOWLER, ROGER (ed.), *A Dictionary of Modern Critical Terms.* London and Boston, 1973.
FOX, HENRY RICHARD, 3RD BARON HOLLAND, *Memoirs of the Whig Party during My Time.* 2 vols. London, 1852–4.
FREEMAN, MICHAEL, *Edmund Burke and the Critique of Political Radicalism.* Chicago, 1980.
FRYE, NORTHROP, *Anatomy of Criticism.* Princeton, 1957.
FUCHS, MICHEL, 'Edmund Burke et Augustus Keppel', *Études Anglaises*, 18 (1965), 18–26.
FUSSELL, PAUL, *The Rhetorical World of Augustan Humanism: Ethics and Imagery from Swift to Burke.* Oxford, 1965.
GEORGE, M., DOROTHY, *London Life in the Eighteenth Century.* London, 1925.
GILMOUR, ROBIN, *The Idea of the Gentleman in the Victorian Novel.* London, 1981.
GRIFFIN, DUSTIN, *Alexander Pope: The Poet in the Poems.* Princeton, 1978.
GUNNELL, JOHN G., *Political Theory: Tradition and Interpretation.* Cambridge, Mass., 1979.
HÄGIN, PETER, *The Epic Hero and the Decline of Heroic Poetry: A Study of the Neoclassical English Epic with Special Reference to Milton's 'Paradise Lost'*, Cooper Monographs on English and American Language and Literature, 8. Berne, 1964.
HAMMOND, BREAN S., 'The Intertext of an Adaptation: Bond's *Lear* and *King Lear*', *Études Anglaises*, 40/3 (1987), 279–93.
—— *Pope.* Brighton, 1986.
HAMMOND, J. L. and BARBARA, *The Village Labourer, 1760–1832.* London, 1911.
HAY, DOUGLAS, LINEBAUGH, PETER, RULE, JOHN G., THOMPSON, E. P., and WINSLOW, CAL, *Albion's Fatal Tree: Crime and Society in Eighteenth-Century England.* New York, 1975.
HIRSCH, E. D., *The Aims of Interpretation.* Chicago, 1976.

HUERGON, JACQUES, Introduction to Varro, *Économie Rural [Res Rusticae]*. 2 vols. Paris, 1978.
JAMESON, FREDRIC, *Marxism and Form: Twentieth-Century Dialectical Theories of Literature*. Princeton, 1971.
—— *The Political Unconscious: Narrative as a Socially Symbolic Act*. Ithaca, NY, 1981.
JAUSS, HANS ROBERT, *Toward an Aesthetic of Reception*, trans. Timothy Bahti. Minneapolis, 1982.
JONES, E. L., 'Agriculture and Economic Growth in England, 1660–1750: Agricultural Change', *Journal of Economic History*, 25 (1965), 1–18. Repr. in W. E. Minchinton (ed.), *Essays in Agrarian History*, i. Newton Abbott, 1968, 203–20.
KENYON, J. P., (ed.), *The Stuart Constitution, 1603–88*. Cambridge, 1966.
KEPPEL, THOMAS, *The Life of Augustus Viscount Keppel*. 2 vols. London, 1842.
KERNAN, ALVIN, *Printing Technology, Letters, and Samuel Johnson*. Repr. as *Samuel Johnson and the Impact of Print*. Princeton, 1987.
KERRIDGE, ERIC, *The Agricultural Revolution*. London, 1967.
KNOPPERS, LAURA LUNGER, 'Milton's *The Readie and Easie Way* and the English Jeremiad', in David Loewenstein and James Grantham Turner (eds.), *Politics, Poetics, and Hermeneutics in Milton's Prose*. Cambridge, 1990, 213–25.
KRAMNICK, ISAAC, *The Rage of Edmund Burke: Portrait of an Ambivalent Conservative*. New York, 1977.
LANG, BEREL, *The Anatomy of Philosophical Style: Literary Philosophy and the Philosophy of Literature*. Oxford, 1990.
LESLIE, MICHAEL, and RAYLOR, TIMOTHY, (eds.), *Culture and Cultivation in Early Modern England: Writing and the Land*. Leicester and London, 1992.
LINDENBERGER, HERBERT, *Historical Drama: The Relation of Literature and Reality*. Chicago, 1975.
LOCK, F. P., *Burke's Reflections on the Revolution in France*. London, 1985.
LODGE, DAVID, 'The French Revolution and the Condition of England: Crowds and Power in the Early Victorian Novel', in Ceri Crossley and Ian Small (eds.), *The French Revolution and British Culture*. Oxford, 1989.
LOW, ANTHONY, *The Georgic Revolution*. Princeton, 1985.
MACK, MAYNARD, *Alexander Pope: A Life*. New York, 1986.
MCKENDRICK, NEIL, BREWER, JOHN, and PLUMB, J. H., *The Birth of a Consumer Society: The Commercialization of Eighteenth-Century England*. London, 1982.
MCKEON, MICHAEL, 'Historicizing *Absalom and Achitophel*', in

Felicity Nussbaum and Laura Brown (eds.), *The New Eighteenth Century: Theory, Politics, English Literature*, New York, 1987, 23–40.
MACLEAN, KENNETH, *Agrarian Age: A Background for Wordsworth*. New Haven, 1950.
MCLUHAN, MARSHALL, 'On Pope's *Dunciad*', in Eugene McNamara (ed.), *The Interior Landscape: The Literary Criticism of Marshall McLuhan 1943–1962*. New York, 1969, 169–79.
MACPHERSON, C. B., *Burke*. Oxford, 1980.
MAGNUS, SIR PHILIP, *Edmund Burke: A Life*. London, 1939.
MANSFIELD, HARVEY C., Jr., *Statesmanship and Party Government: A Study of Burke and Bolingbroke*. Chicago and London, 1965.
MARSHALL, DOROTHY, *Dr. Johnson's London*. New York, 1968.
MARX, KARL, *Capital: A Critique of Political Economy*, trans. Ben Fowkes. 3 vols. Harmondsworth, 1990.
MELVIN, PETER H., 'Burke on Theatricality and Revolution', *Journal of the History of Ideas*, 36 (1975), 447–68.
MILLER, PERRY, *The New England Mind: From Colony to Province*. Cambridge, 1953.
MINGAY, G. E. (ed.), *The Agricultural Revolution: Changes in Agriculture 1650–1880*. London, 1977.
—— *English Landed Society in the Eighteenth Century*. London, 1963.
—— *The Gentry: The Rise and Fall of a Ruling Class*. London, 1976.
MORLEY, JOHN, *Burke*. London, 1879.
MORRIS, DAVID B., *Alexander Pope: The Genius of Sense*. Cambridge, Mass., 1984.
NOKES, DAVID, *Raillery and Rage: A Study of Eighteenth Century Satire*. Brighton, 1987.
O'BRIEN, CONOR CRUISE, *The Great Melody: A Thematic Biography and Commented Anthology of Edmund Burke*. Chicago, 1992.
—— Introduction to Edmund Burke, *Reflections on the Revolution in France*. Harmondsworth, 1969.
O'GORMAN, FRANK, *Edmund Burke: His Political Philosophy*. London, 1973.
O HEHIR, BRENDAN, *Expans'd Hieroglyphicks: A Critical Edition of Sir John Denham's* Coopers Hill. Berkeley and Los Angeles, 1969.
OZOUF, MONA, *Festivals and the French Revolution*, trans. Alan Sheridan. Cambridge, Mass., 1988.
PARKIN, CHARLES, *The Moral Basis of Edmund Burke's Political Thought*. Cambridge, 1956.
PATEY, DOUGLAS LANE, 'The Eighteenth Century Invents the Canon', *Modern Language Studies*, 18 (1988): 17–37.

PAULSON, RONALD, *Popular and Polite Art in the Age of Hogarth and Fielding*. Notre Dame, Ind., 1979.
—— *Representations of Revolution (1789–1820)*. New Haven, 1983.
PELLEW, GEORGE, *The Life and Correspondence of the Right Honourable Henry Addington, First Viscount Sidmouth*. 3 vols. London, 1847.
POCOCK, J. G. A., Introduction to Edmund Burke, *Reflections on the Revolution in France*. Indianapolis, 1987.
—— *The Machiavellian Moment: Florentine Political Thought and the Atlantic Republican Tradition*. Princeton, 1975.
—— *Virtue, Commerce, and History: Essays on Political Thought and History, Chiefly in the Eighteenth Century*. Cambridge, 1985.
POOVEY, MARY, *The Proper Lady and the Woman Writer: Ideology as Style in the Works of Mary Wollstonecraft, Mary Shelley, and Jane Austen*. Chicago, 1984.
PORTER, ROY, *Mind-Forg'd Manacles: A History of Madness in England from the Restoration to the Regency*. London, 1987.
POWIS, JONATHAN, *Aristocracy*. Oxford, 1984.
PRIOR, JAMES, *Life of the Right Honourable Edmund Burke*. 3rd edn. London, 1839.
RAAB, FELIX, *The English Face of Machiavelli: A Changing Interpretation 1500–1700*. London, 1964.
REEVES, JAMES, *The Reputation and Writings of Alexander Pope*. New York, 1976.
REID, CHRISTOPHER, 'Burke, the Regency Crisis, and the "Antagonist World of Madness"', *Eighteenth-Century Life*, 16/2 (1992), 59–75.
—— *Edmund Burke and the Practice of Political Writing*. Dublin and New York, 1985.
RICHETTI, JOHN J., *Philosophical Writing: Locke, Berkeley, Hume*. Cambridge, Mass., 1983.
ROGERS, NICHOLAS, 'Popular Protest in Early Hanoverian London', *Past and Present*, 79 (May 1978), 70–100.
ROGERS, PAT, *Grub Street: Studies in a Subculture*. London, 1972.
—— *Literature and Popular Culture in Eighteenth Century England*. Sussex, 1985.
ROSCOE, E. S., *Between Thames and Chilterns: Being Literary and Historical Studies of the Country of Milton, Penn, Gray, Burke, and the Disraelis*. London, 1927.
RUDÉ, GEORGE, *The Crowd in the French Revolution*. Oxford, 1959.
—— *The Crowd in History: A Study of Popular Disturbances in France and England 1730–1848*. 1964; repr. London, 1981.
—— *Wilkes and Liberty: A Social Study of 1763 to 1774*. 1962; repr. London, 1983.
SAMBROOK, A. J., 'The English Lord and the Happy Husbandman',

Studies in Voltaire and the Eighteenth Century, 57 (1967), 1357–75.

SAMUELS, A. P. I., *The Early Life, Correspondence and Writings of the Rt. Hon. Edmund Burke*. Cambridge, 1923.

SARASON, BERTRAM, 'Edmund Burke's Burial Place', *Notes and Queries*, NS, 2/2 (February 1955), 69–70.

SCHAMA, SIMON, *Citizens: A Chronicle of the French Revolution*. Toronto, 1989.

SEKORA, JOHN, *Luxury: The Concept in Western Thought, Eden to Smollett*. Baltimore, 1977.

SITTER, JOHN E., *The Poetry of Pope's* Dunciad. Minneapolis. 1971.

SMITH, BRUCE JAMES, *Politics and Remembrance: Republican Themes in Machiavelli, Burke, and Tocqueville*. Princeton, 1985.

SMITH, HUGH F. R., *Harrington and His Oceana: A Study of a 17th Century Utopia and Its Influence in America*. Cambridge, 1914.

SMYTH, ALBERT H., 'Life of Burke', in *Edmund Burke's* Letter to a Noble Lord, ed. Smyth. Boston, 1898.

SPADAFORA, DAVID, *The Idea of Progress in Eighteenth-Century Britain*. New Haven, 1990.

SPATE, O. H. K., 'The Muse of Mecantilism: Jago, Grainger, and Dyer', in R. F. Brissenden (ed.), *Studies in the Eighteenth Century: Papers Presented at the David Nicol Smith Memorial Seminar*. Canberra 1966. Toronto 1968, 119–31.

STALLYBRASS, PETER, and WHITE, ALLON, *The Politics and Poetics of Transgression*. London, 1986.

STANLIS, PETER J., *Edmund Burke and the Natural Law*. Ann Arbor, 1958.

STEARNS, RAYMOND PHINEAS, *The Strenuous Puritan*. Urbana, Ill., 1954.

STEWART, JOHN HALL (ed.), *A Documentary Survey of the French Revolution*. New York, 1951.

STONE, LAWRENCE, and STONE, JEANNE C. FAWTIER, *An Open Élite? England 1540–1880*. Oxford, 1984.

STRAUSS, LEO, *Natural Right and History*. Chicago, 1953

TAWNEY, R. H., 'The Rise of the Gentry', *Economic History Review*, 11 (1941), 1–38.

THOMPSON, E. P., 'Patrician Society, Plebeian Culture', *Journal of Social History*, 7 (1974), 382–405.

—— *Whigs and Hunters: The Origin of the Black Act*. New York, 1975.

TODD, WILLIAM B., *A Bibliography of Edmund Burke*. London, 1964.

WATT, IAN, 'Two Historical Aspects of the Augustan Tradition', in R. F. Brissenden (ed.), *Studies in the Eighteenth Century: Papers*

Presented at the David Nichol Smith Memorial Seminar. Canberra, 1966. Toronto, 1968.
WEDGWOOD, C. V., *The Trial of Charles I.* London, 1964.
WEINBROT, HOWARD D., *Augustus Caesar in 'Augustan' England: The Decline of a Classical Norm.* Princeton, 1978.
WILKINS, BURLEIGH TAYLOR, *The Problem of Burke's Political Philosophy.* Oxford, 1967.
WILLIAMS, AUBREY, *Pope's* Dunciad: *A Study of Its Meaning.* Baton Rouge, 1955.
WILLIAMS, KATHLEEN (ed.), *Swift: The Critical Heritage.* London, 1970.
WILLIAMS, RAYMOND, *The Country and the City.* New York, 1973.
―― *Keywords: A Vocabulary of Culture and Society.* London, 1976.
―― *Politics and Letters.* London, 1979.
WOOD, NEAL, 'The Aesthetic Dimension of Burke's Political Thought', *Journal of British Studies*, 4 (1964), 41–64.

Index

Individual works and speeches by Edmund Burke (such as *Reflections on the Revolution in France* and *Speech on Conciliation with the Colonies*) are listed in this index as separate main entries. Works of other writers (such as John Milton's *Paradise Lost* or Alexander Pope's *Dunciad*) are listed as sub-entries under the main entry for the author.

Addison, Joseph 194–5
agriculture:
   agricultural revolution 68–71, 79–80
   improvement of 84, 86–8, 98–9
   as occupation of gentleman 62, 101–3
   see also improvement
American Revolution 112, 132–5, 138–9, 147
ancient vs. modern, *see* classic
anniversaries, *see* political calendar
Antoinette, Marie 137, 188, 192, 193
apocalypse, *see* biblical allusion; Scriblerian satire
Appeal from the New to the Old Whigs 114, 119–20, 124, 139–40, 141, 157
aristocrat 42–3, 47–9, 54–5, 58, 153, 156–7, 271
   and British constitution 60–1
   defined 113–14
   nobility defined 51–2, 114
   political ideal of 111–12
   redefined as natural aristocrat 119–21, 124, 127, 157
   see also gentleman, gentry
Auckland, William Eden, first Baron 251–9, 269, 272
authorship 34–7, 45–6
   and print culture 35
   professionalization of 25, 43–4, 49, 268–9, 271–2
   and social mobility 131–2
   writer as comprehensive observer 131, 137–8, 139–40, 164
   writer as gentleman 46, 132, 137–8, 139–40, 164

Batchelor, Thomas 71–2, 105–7

Bathurst, Allen, first Earl 138–9
Bedford, Francis Russell, fifth Duke of 20, 38–42, 47, 49, 54–5, 58, 103–5, 269, 271
   Bedford level 90–1
   as improver 105–7
biblical allusion:
   apocalyptic 185, 188–9, 198, 229
   birth of Christ 185
   gospels 142
   Judas Maccabeus 289–90
   millenarianism 189–90
   Moses 140–1, 159, 185
   passion of Christ 170, 188, 190–2
   prophecy 141, 285–6
   wisdom literature 116–17
   see also Milton
Black Acts 240–1
Blake, William 108
Bolingbroke, Henry St. John, Viscount 217–18
Brown, John 'Estimate'
   An Estimate of the Manners and Principles of the Time 218–20, 288
Bunyan, John 198
Burke, Edmund:
   and American Revolution 112, 134, 147
   as anti-revolutionary spokesman 20, 30–1, 44–5, 48
   and anti-selves 41–3
   authorial persona of 30–1, 36–7, 271–2
   canophobia of 187
   dynastic hopes of 47–9, 53
   education of 1, 2–5, 220–1
   farming activities of 61–2
   French Revolution, personal identification with 30–1, 44–5, 52, 212–13, 285–6, 296–7

Burke, Edmund (*cont.*)
  as gentleman 58, 61–2, 136–8, 157–8
  georgic poetry of 3–4, 72
  and Gordon Riots 171–2, 224
  independence of 23, 36–8, 42–5, 156–8
  and India 123, 143–7
  juvenile writings of 3–4, 220–1
  as landholder 61–2
  old age and impending death of 20–1, 30, 50–2, 187, 209–10, 294
  and patronage 28–9, 41, 44–5, 49, 156
  pension of 19–20, 44–5
  and Rockingham Whigs 28–9, 41, 54–5, 136–7, 153, 156–7, 209
  son's death 47, 50–1, 210
  as Whig 82, 128, 153, 213–15, 283
  see also under titles of individual works (such as *A Letter to a Noble Lord* and *Reflections on the Revolution in France*) *and under specific topics* (such as gentleman, improvement, patronage, Scriblerian satire)
canon, literary 254, 258–60, 262–3, 269, 274, 280
change, *see* historical change
Charles I 182, 184–5, 189–93, 197, 198, 227, 229
Chesterfield, Philip Dormer Stanhope, fourth Earl of 34, 37
Civil War, English, *see* English Revolution
class, *see* hierarchy
classic and classical 257–60, 262, 269, 278, 282
  ancient vs. modern 254, 255–6, 258–9, 276–7, 280
  classic vs. grotesque body 262, 267–8
  criteria of 255, 257, 262–3
clientage, *see* patronage
Clootz, Anacharsis 248–9
clothing 200, 239–49
  and sartorial transformation 239–45, 248
  symbolic significance of 241–2, 246–7
clubs 179–81
comedy:
  French Revolution figured as 168, 184–7

inversion in 185–7
comprehensiveness:
  as political ideal 120, 140, 144–5, 147
  as problematic concept 125–32, 149
  women and 161–4
  see also gentleman
Condorcet, Marquis de 277
constitution:
  changes in 81–2, 83–4, 94–7, 245–6
  as entailed inheritance 59–61, 63, 82
  estate as analogy for 59–61, 63, 98–9
  French 78, 242–3, 245–6, 281
  Revolution Society and 180
counter-theatre:
  defined 167–8, 200–1
  as parodying theatre of official authority 167–8, 174–5, 204, 227–9, 240
  political discourse of 176–7
  see also theatre
Country party 128, 151, 154, 213–15, 217–19, 283
Cowper, Abraham:
  The Task 63
Craftsman 217–18
credit, *see* money
crowd:
  figured as irrational mob 170–3, 176–7, 181–3, 187, 223, 225–6
  in French Revolution 172–3, 176–7, 223, 225–7
  gendered as female 172, 176
  in Gordon Riots 171–2, 174, 224
  London crowds, behaviour of 173, 224–5, 230
  in march on Versailles (October, 1789) 172–3, 176–7, 187, 204–5, 226
  parodic behaviour of 174–6
  and Wilkite disturbances 171, 178–9, 224
  see also public opinion

Defoe, Daniel 119
Compleat English Gentleman 124–5
Denham, John:
  Coopers Hill 90–2, 94–5, 99–101
dependence, *see* independence, patronage
disinterestedness:
  aesthetic 122–3

landownership as basis for 119, 122–3
  as political ideal 117, 122–3, 149–50, 155–6
  as problematic concept 125–32, 149, 154
  see also gentleman
dress, see clothing
dullness, see Scriblerian satire
dunce, see Scriblerian satire

economics, see georgic mode; improvement; money; property
effeminacy, see gender; Scriblerian satire
elegaic mode 50–4
Elliot, Gilbert 295
English Revolution or Civil War 52–3, 91–7, 182, 195, 197, 198, 215, 241–2
  parallels with French revolution 91–2, 97, 168, 182, 184–5, 189–92
  Roman Civil War as type of 92–3
entailment 59–63
  see also constitution; estate
epic 141, 143, 256
  and heroic mode 55–6, 134, 145–6, 191–2, 260–2, 269
  and mock-epic 193
  political dimension of 263–4
epistolary form, see letter
estate 59–63, 65, 123, 162–4
  and country house 61, 78, 98, 123
  see also property
executions, see theatre

farming, see agriculture
feelings, see natural feelings
Ferguson, Adam 130, 135, 175, 249
Fielding, Henry:
  views of, on executions 173–4
form, see genre
form and content 7, 8, 10–11, 64, 79, 89, 97, 212
France:
  prospect survey of 76–8
French Revolution 30–2, 42–3, 147–9, 290–4
  Burke's personal identification with 30–1, 52, 212–13, 285–6, 296–7
  causes of 43
  as comedy 168, 185–7

Directory (1795) 238–9, 242–4, 247–8, 253
Directory, proposals to negotiate with 251–2, 283
educational reform in 276–9
execution of Louis XVI 229
march on Versailles (October 1789) 168–70, 172–3, 176–7, 188–90, 202, 204–5, 226, 228
monied, commercial interest as fomenter of 214
parallels with English Civil War 91–2, 97, 168, 182, 184–5, 189–92
and Scriblerian satire, see Scriblerian satire
as theatre 165–6, 184, 200, 230
as tragedy 165, 168, 188–90, 192, 199, 205–6

gardens and gardening, see improvement
gender 161–2, 176, 206–7, 219, 288–9
  see also women
generalist, see comprehensiveness, gentleman, professional
genre(s):
  18th-c. theory of 12–14
  generic change 20–3, 27, 89–90, 93–4, 108, 110, 141, 168–9, 215–16, 295
  hierarchy of 168–9, 170, 266
  interrelations among 12–13, 23, 51, 168–9, 256
  mixtures and mixed forms 13–14, 23, 27, 51, 73 n., 74, 217, 219, 254, 269–71, 273, 292
  and modes 16
  see also comedy; elegaic mode; epic; form and content; georgic; jeremiad, 'letter to a noble lord' form; political theory; prophecy; Scriblerian satire; tragedy
gentleman 25, 58, 111–64
  and agriculture 62, 86–7, 98–103
  comprehensiveness of 116–17, 125–32, 147
  defined 114–15, 119–20, 158–60
  disinterestedness of 118–20, 127–9, 137–8, 149–50, 155–6
  education of 2–5, 116–17
  and gender 162–3
  as generalist 120–1, 129–30

gentleman (cont.)
  georgic ideal of 98–103, 139, 145–6, 158–9
  judgement and rationality of 121–2, 137–8, 155–6
  Lord Keppel as ideal type of 55–7
  Lord Munodi as ideal type of 87–8
  martial ideal of 101–3, 145
  nineteenth-century redefinition of 158–9
  and political party 152–5
  and political representation 155–6
  as problematic ideal 113, 124–32, 149, 153–4, 157–8, 160–3
  and property 34, 37, 57, 118–19, 129, 159–61
  and prospect view 113, 115–17, 119–20, 124, 136–40, 149–50
  sacerdotal role of 123–4
  and taste 122–3
  transformation in conception of 101–3, 113, 125–32
gentry, *see* gentleman
George III:
  as gentleman farmer 98–9, 105
georgic mode 3–4, 65–7
  defined 72–4
  and economic discourse 65, 72–4, 100, 106–10
  flood imagery of 91–2, 94–101, 106, 108
  ideal of gentleman in 98–103, 139, 145–6, 158–9
  in *Gulliver's Travels* 86–8
  heroic dimension of 134, 142–3
  happy husbandman in 107, 115
  and historical change 66, 74, 78–80, 108, 158
  imperialism as theme in 143–7
  labour as theme in 109, 142–3, 145–6
  and prospect view 74–8, 89–90, 124–7, 142–6, 162–4
  relation of, to Sciblerian satire 66, 82, 97
  see also improvement; prospect view; Virgil
Glorious Revolution 167, 178, 181–2
Godwin, William 81–2
Gordon Riots, *see* crowd
grotesque, *see* classic

Harrington, James 104, 280–1
Harte, Walter 100–1

Henry VIII 53, 98–100
heroic mode, *see* epic
Hervey, Lord John 31–2, 49–50
  Sporus 36–8
hierarchy 108–10, 113–14, 126, 161–3, 175–6, 186–7, 195, 207–8
  class mobility within 131–2, 158–9, 241, 259
  cultural (high vs. low) 254, 258, 267–72
  literary 168–9, 170, 249, 256–8
  middle-class challenge to 163–3
  symbolism and ritual of 175, 207–8, 237–9, 249
  see also inversion
history:
  didactic function of 182, 197–8
  as narrative 169–70, 182, 190, 197–8
  tragic conception of 198–9, 294
historical change 66, 74, 78–81, 88–90, 95–8, 101, 105–8, 158
  as cyclical 199, 218–22, 234, 287–9, 297
  and critical reception 211, 216
  as progress 198–9
  and prophecy 141, 293–5
  as revolution 199, 232–3, 280, 290
Home, Henry, *see* Kames
Homer:
  Ulysses 261–2
Horace:
  De Arte Poetica 235
  parodied 218
husbandry, *see* agriculture

impartiality, *see* disinterestedness
imperialism 143–7, 156
improvement 59–110
  agricultural 62, 67–71, 84, 87–8, 101–3
  defined 64, 67–70
  economic 65, 69–70, 72–4
  and industrial revolution 70, 74
  and innovation 67, 80–3, 89, 97–9, 105–7
  and landscape gardening 70, 85, 87
  as metaphor for constitutional change 63, 81
  see also georgic mode
independence 19, 23, 36–8, 45–6, 128, 154
  basis in ownership of property 34, 57

see also disinterestedness; gentleman; patronage
inheritance, *see* entailment, estate
innovation 67, 80–3, 97–9, 105–7, 289, 292
  see also historical change; improvement
intertexuality 218–20
inversion 174–5, 178–9, 181–7
  see also comedy; Scriblerian satire

jeremiad 141, 210, 285–9, 292, 294–6
  see also prophecy
Johnson, Samuel 43–4, 129, 141
  pension 44
judgement 116, 121–2, 156
  see also gentleman
Juvenal 51–2

Kames, Henry Home, Lord 101–3
Keppel, Augustus, Viscount 53–8
  court martial of 53–4, 57

labour 108–9, 129, 142–3, 145–6
land, *see* estate, property
language and meaning 249–51, 254, 265, 273–7
  and revolution 273–7
Leadbeater, Mary Shackleton 62
letter:
  personal or private 21, 24–5, 27–9
  public, *see* 'letter to a noble lord' form
Letter to a Member of the National Assembly 187, 199–201, 252, 258–9
'letter to an eminent person' form, *see* 'letter to a noble lord' form
Letter to a Noble Lord 20–3, 30–58, 89–90, 103–5, 157, 244–5, 272, 279–82
  genesis of 20–3
  prospect view of Windsor Castle in 89–99, 148
'letter to a noble lord' form 20–30, 49–51, 53
Letter to Sir Hercules Langrishe 88, 121
Letter to the Sheriffs of Bristol (1777) 153
Letter to William Elliot 253, 286, 288–90
Letters on a Regicide Peace 135, 147–9, 165–6, 209–85, 289–95
  carefully calculated rhetoric of 212–13, 282
  critical reception of 210–11
  genesis of 212, 252
  literary and rhetorical criticism in 236–7, 252–63
  rhetorical vehemence of 210–13, 282
  thesis or argument of 212
literary genre, *see* genre
literature:
  18th-c. definition of 5–6, 13, 215–17
  and philosophy 7–8
  and political discourse 215–18, 252–63
  see also canon, classic
Louis XVI 77, 82, 188, 190, 193, 198, 201, 202, 229

Macaulay, Catharine 154
madness, *see* Scriblerian satire
Marshall, William 64
masquerade, *see* Scriblerian satire
meaning, *see* language; Scriblerian satire
metamorphosis, *see* Scriblerian satire
millenarianism, *see* progress
Milton, John 260, 262, 285, 291–2
  as georgic poet 142–3
  Apology against a Pamphlet 285
  Lycidas 256–7
  Paradise Lost 40–1, 138–40, 142, 159, 170, 231–2, 234–5, 284, 291–2
  Paradise Regained 142–3, 145, 159
mob, *see* crowd
mock-epic, *see* epic
modes 16
  see also genre
Montagu, Lady Mary Wortley 31–2, 228
money and credit 118–19, 123, 129, 214–15
Montesquieu 139–40

natural aristocrat, *see* aristocrat
natural feelings 194, 201–7
nature and the natural:
  contrasted with the unnatural 232–8, 250–1, 270
  as norm 232–8
nobility, *see* aristocrat; gentleman

opera, *see* Scriblerian satire
order, *see* hierarchy, nature

Ovid:
  Metamorphoses 234–6

Paine, Thomas 165, 203
  Rights of Man 169–70, 193, 203–5, 253
parliamentary representation, see representation
parody, see county-theatre; inversion; political calendar; Scriblerian satire
party, see political party
patronage 19–20, 36–8, 42–5, 55, 156
  and clientage 2, 23, 28–9, 40
  and literary form 20
Peter, Hugh 189–91
Philosophical Enquiry into the Origin of Our Ideas of the Sublime and Beautiful 122, 201–3, 206–7
pilgrimage 194–5, 198
Pitt, William, the younger 18, 45, 261, 264
political calendar 177–82
  as parody of Hanoverian political calendar 178–9, 181–2
political party 54–5, 151–5, 157
political theory 8–10
  canon of 9
  genre of, defined 9, 16–17, 295–7
  as prophecy 296–7
politicians 147, 157
  as misguided rationalists 135–6
  see also professionalism; specialization
Pope, Alexander 216
  anti-selves of 37–8, 41
  authorial persona of 31–2, 36–8, 45–7, 58
  independence of 23, 36–8, 45–6, 128
  Dunciad 4, 39–40, 170, 182–4, 186, 211, 213, 217–21, 223–5, 227–30, 232, 234–7, 247–51, 253–4, 256, 264, 267–8, 272, 274, 277–9, 284, 286, 292
  Epistle to Bathurst 118, 139, 265
  Epistle to Burlington 75–6, 102, 139, 146
  Epistle to Dr. Arbuthnot 23, 31–4, 36–8, 45–7, 50, 53, 58, 272
  Essay on Criticism 244, 254–5, 276
  Essay on Man 137–8, 154, 236
  Letter to a Noble Lord 32–4, 45, 49–50
  Peri Bathous 243–4, 250
  Rape of the Lock 232–3, 238
  Three Hours after Marriage 235–6, 279
  Windsor-Forest 74–5, 77, 90
  see also Scriblerian satire
Preface to the Address of M. Brissot to His Constituents 275
Price, Dr. Richard 82, 159–60, 167, 181–2, 184–6, 188–90, 192–4, 198, 202, 229
print culture, see authorship
professionalism and professionals 116–18, 157, 268–72
  defined in terms of self-interest 116–18, 144–5
  in French legislature 117–18
  mechanical, as opposed to liberal, character of 120–1, 135, 144–5
  partiality of 116
  positive value of 161
  as specialists 117, 129–30
progress 87–8, 198–9, 276–7, 280
  and millenarianism 189–90, 292–3
  in sense of 'stately journey or parade', see Scriblerian satire
property 34, 37, 57, 78, 118–19, 129, 159–61, 162–3, 176
  gentleman defined by 114, 118–19, 123, 159–61
  and monied, commercial interest 214–15
  see also estate
prophecy 141, 273, 283–97
  see also jeremiad
prospect view 74–8, 89–90, 97, 111–64
  basis in Lockian empiricism 116, 121
  defined 111–12
  and gender 162–4
  ideal of gentleman expressed in 111–13, 115, 119–20, 124, 130–1, 136–9
  historical element in 112, 141, 197
  as metaphor for rationality 124, 137–8
  political uses of 112, 136–9, 147–8
  prophetic dimension of 141
  visual, spatial dimension of 111–12, 126–7
public and private, interrelation of 47–50, 52–3, 58, 116–17, 129, 137, 150–5, 158
public opinion 26, 29–30, 149–50
public sphere 268, 270

Reflections on the Revolution in France
  26–7, 42–3, 76–8, 110, 159,
  165–208, 246
  constitutional principles discussed in
    59–60, 78
  composition of French legislature
    analysed in 117–18, 226–7
  genesis of 167, 173, 180
  and Scriblerian satire 81–6, 88–9,
    135–6, 226–7
  theatrical metaphor in 167, 169–70,
    184, 194, 197, 202–4
  tragic in narrative shape 168, 170,
    188–94, 196, 198, 204, 208, 256,
    287
reform, political 81, 83–4
Reformer 220–1
Regency crisis 221
representation, political 149–50
  virtual representation 155–6
revolution, *see* historical change
Reynolds, Sir Joshua 53–4, 56
Rockingham, Lord 101–2
Rockingham Whigs 28–9, 41, 54–5,
  136–7, 150, 153, 156–7, 209
Rousseau, Jean-Jacques 199–201,
  258–9

Santerre, Antoine-Joseph 227–9, 231,
  243
Scriblerian satire 209–82
  apocalyptic strain in 182–4, 213,
    221, 227, 229, 283–4, 290–93
  binary oppositions in 233, 254,
    265–9
  carnivalesque in 183, 226–30, 237,
    245, 266–8
  critical reception of 211–12, 216–17
  cultural decline and debasement of
    learning in 182–4, 213–14, 217,
    219–22, 236, 238, 244, 273–9
  defined 41, 212–13
  dullness in 4, 220–1
  dunces 31–2, 39–40, 170, 176, 184,
    236, 253
  and French Revolution 31–2, 41,
    82–9, 97, 103–5, 170, 226–82,
    284, 291
  and gender 219, 266
  and Grand Tour 278–9
  and Grub Street 271–2
  and harlequin 264–5
  inversion in 182–4, 218, 227–8,
    237–40

  Lord Mayor's parade in 227–30
  madness in 221, 230, 233
  masquerade in 218, 237–49
  and meaning 249–51, 254, 265,
    272–5
  metamorphosis and transformation
    in 231–8, 250
  mob in 223–7, 230
  mock-heroic element of 227, 239,
    245, 248, 264
  and monsters 231, 234–5, 251
  and novelty 258
  and opera 265–6
  and parades or processions 227–30
  parody in 176, 218, 232, 264, 272
  and popular culture 217, 226–7,
    230, 264–6, 268–9
  and political corruption 214–15, 218
  and progress 227
  projectors and virtuosi 82–9, 103–5,
    253, 279–82
  Queen Dulness in 247, 250, 253–4
  relation to georgic of 66, 82, 97
  rhetoric of exclusion in 170–1,
    268–70
  as Tory political idiom 82, 213–15,
    283
  'world upside-down' motif in 183–4,
    227, 237
  see also Pope, Alexander; Swift,
    Jonathan
Shaftesbury, Anthony Ashley Cooper,
  third Earl of 195
Shakespeare, William 187, 260–2, 270
  Hamlet 265
  Henry V 261–2, 264
Sieyès, Emmanuel-Joseph, Abbé 280–1
Smith, Adam 72–4
specialization 129–30
  see also professionalism
*Speech at Bristol Previous to the
  Election* (1780) 149–50
Speech at the Conclusion of the Poll
  156
*Speech on Conciliation with the
  Colonies* 112–13, 132–4, 136,
  147, 156
Speech on Fox's India Bill 146
Speech on the Nabob of Arcot's Debts
  144–5
Sporus, *see* Hervey
Steele, Richard 124
sublime 133–4, 206
subordination, *see* hierarchy

Swift, Jonathan 214–15, 216
  Battle of the Books 259, 264
  Discourse Concerning the Mechanical Operation of the Spirit 24–5, 30
  Drapier's Letters 86, 87–8
  Gulliver's Travels 82–8, 104, 211, 217, 246, 279, 281
  Tale of a Tub 184, 244, 245–6, 256, 285

taste 122–2, 258, 273
theatre 165–208, 240
  French Revolution as 165–6, 184
  history as 197
  life as 194–5
  of official authority 166, 173–83, 200–1, 203, 204, 207–8, 265, 273
  politics as 165–6, 203, 239–40, 247–8
  trials and executions as 173–5, 191–2, 201–5, 273
  see also comedy, counter-theatre, tragedy
theory:
  enlightenment 135–6
Thomson, James 154–5
  use of prospect view 111–12, 115–16, 125–7, 130–1
  'The Happy Man' 115–16, 124
  Poem Sacred to the Memory of Sir Isaac Newton 125
  The Seasons 56, 73, 111–12, 125–7, 130–1, 133–4
Thoughts and Details on Scarcity 108–9
Thoughts on the Causes of the Present Discontents 151–4
Townshend, Charles, Viscount 71, 102
Tories, see Country party
tragedy:
  executions as 173–4, 191–2, 201–5
  French Revolution figured as 165, 168, 188–90, 192, 199, 205–6
  and generic change 193
  march on Versailles (October, 1789) as 170, 188, 202
  Marie Antoinette as tragic heroine 188, 193
  political theory of 194–7, 203, 207–8, 287, 296
  trial of Charles I as 189–92, 198
transformations, see Scriblerian satire

Varro 109
Virgil:
  Aeneid 134, 141, 260
  Georgics 65, 69, 90, 92–4, 143, 260–1
  georgic themes of 72, 109
  see also georgic mode
virtual representation, see representation

Walpole, Sir Robert 33, 125, 128, 139, 150, 213–14, 217, 266, 284
Whigs 58, 78, 79, 110, 150–4, 163, 178–9, 213–15
Wilkite disturbances, see crowd
Windham, William 20, 44–5, 51
Wollstonecraft, Mary 160–4, 203, 205–7
  Vindication of the Rights of Men 162–4, 205–7
  Vindication of the Rights of Woman 160–2
women 160–4, 207, 226
  and French Revolution 172, 176
  see also gender
world upside-down 183–4
writer, see authorship

Young, Arthur 62, 77, 87, 99, 101–2, 210

OHIO UNIVERSITY LIBRARY

Please return this book as soon as you have finished with it. In order to avoid a fine it must be returned by the latest date stamped below. All books are subject to recall after two weeks or immediately if needed for reserve.

DEC 0 7 2000

NOV. 2 2 2000

APR 0 2 2005

MAR 0 4 2005

CF